WITHDRAWN

HARVARD STUDIES IN BUSINESS HISTORY, 46

Published with the support of the Harvard Business School
Edited by Thomas K. McCraw
Isidor Straus Professor of Business History
Graduate School of Business Administration
George F. Baker Foundation
Harvard University

Alfred D. Chandler, Jr.

Shaping the Industrial Century

The Remarkable Story of the Evolution of the Modern Chemical and Pharmaceutical Industries

HARVARD UNIVERSITY PRESS

Cambridge, Massachusetts, and London, England 2005

Library of Congress Cataloging-in-Publication Data

Chandler, Alfred Dupont.
    Shaping the industrial century : the remarkable story of the modern chemical and
pharmaceutical industries / Alfred D. Chandler, Jr.
        p.   cm.—(Harvard studies in business history ; 46)
    Includes bibliographical references and index.
    ISBN 0-674-01720-X (alk. paper)
        1. Chemical industry—United States—History. 2. Chemical industry—Europe—History.
    3. Pharmaceutical industry—United States—History. 4. Pharmaceutical industry—Europe—
    History. 5. Biotechnology industries—United States. I. Title. II. Series.

HD9651.5.C457   2005
338.4′766′00973—dc22   2004054320

Contents

Preface *vii*
Acknowledgments *ix*

I Overview

1 Differences, Concepts, Themes, and Approach *3*

2 Evolving Paths of Learning *19*

II The Chemical Industry

3 The Major American Companies *41*

4 The Focused American Companies *83*

5 The European Competitors *114*

6 The American Competitors *144*

III The Pharmaceutical Industry

7 The American Companies: The Prescription Path *177*

8 The American Companies: The Over-the-Counter Path *213*

9 The American and European Competitors *230*

10 Commercializing Biotechnology *260*

IV Paths of Learning

11 The Three Revolutions: Industrial, Information, and
Biotechnology *283*

Notes *315*

Index *345*

Preface

My previous book, *Inventing the Electronic Century: The Epic Story of the Consumer Electronics and Computer Industries,* focused on the creation of the infrastructure of the Information Revolution between the 1950s and the 1990s, a revolution that will continue to transform life and work on this planet over the decades to come. The present volume concentrates on the evolution of two related high-technology industries of the Second Industrial Revolution after the completion of their infrastructure. Their infrastructure, as were those of nearly all modern industries, began in the 1880s when the railroad and steamship, the telegraph and cable, made possible mass production and distribution of goods and services to national and international markets.

By the 1920s the creation of the infrastructure had been completed. Of the fifty leading chemical companies and the thirty leading pharmaceutical companies in terms of revenues in the 1990s, only two chemical companies had entered successfully and they did so during World War II. Therefore, this volume, which reviews the creation of the chemical and pharmaceutical infrastructure, concentrates on the evolution of these eighty companies during the next seventy years.

As a result, the hazards of writing what becomes contemporary history are even greater than was true in my earlier book. I had planned to end the stories of the individual companies in 1993, the year I began research on these two high-tech industries. Writing, however, took more time than anticipated, as it always does. Hence, I wrote postscripts at the end of some chapters. For example, by the beginning of the new century, the attempts of the major U.S. companies to enter pharmaceuticals had failed.

Fortunately in meeting these hazards the business press had enhanced its coverage. The press was providing the statistical and information data base from which the limited success and failure of the individuals in terms of financial performance and innovative success could be appraised.

No source was more valuable than *Hoover's Handbooks,* produced annually since 1990 for both American and non-American companies. Each handbook includes a ten-year review of the companies' financial statistics and a portfolio of their major product lines, with percentage of sales and income from these lines as well as a brief resume of their history. *Hoover's Handbooks* certainly remain a reliable basic source for business and economic historians to carry out their central analytical tasks.

Acknowledgments

Of the several persons who made possible the writing of this book, the most important were the two to whom I have dedicated it—Anne O'Connell and my wife, Fay Chandler. For many years Anne has transcribed my garbled, dictated, handwritten copy into smooth, readable typescript, at the same time keeping the numerous revisions of the text and the endnotes in their proper order and place. Just as critical has been Fay's constant encouragement and support, as we reached our sixtieth wedding anniversary.

The initial research and writing was achieved with the assistance of Takashi Hikino and Andrew von Nordenflycht. Before Takashi had to return to his homeland, Japan, his assistance was essential in getting this writing under way, as well as in shaping the initial drafts of the chapters. Andrew played as critical a role in the completion of the book, particularly in those chapters concerning the chemical story. Max Hall copyedited the initial drafts of chapters. Lance Wickens did the same for the finished manuscript. I am indeed indebted to both. Eileen Hankins provided essential secretarial and library services. At the front desk of my apartment building in Cambridge, Theresa Hardy faxed messages and correspondence and assisted in other ways.

I am particularly indebted to Ralph Landau, who provided a valuable learning experience at a series of meetings at Stanford University in preparation for the publication (with Ashish Arora and Nathan Rosenberg) of *Chemicals and Long-Term Growth*, published by John Wiley in 1998.

I am most beholden to Davis Dyer, the founding director of the Winthrop Group, who made a careful review of the chemical story, as did Louis Galambos of the pharmaceutical story. In addition, Davis persuaded me to sharpen the focus of the book's major themes. I continue to benefit from Robert Wallace's advice and support.

Many have contributed to this book, but the final text is mine, and for it I take full responsibility.

SHAPING THE INDUSTRIAL CENTURY

PART I

Overview

CHAPTER 1

Differences, Concepts, Themes, and Approach

This volume reviews the evolution of the modern chemical and pharmaceutical industries from their beginnings in the last decades of the nineteenth century until the last decade of the twentieth. I define a high-technology industry as one in which new learning in science and engineering leads to opportunities to commercialize—to develop and bring into public use—new products based on that new learning. The evolving paths of learning in the chemical and pharmaceutical industries are similar to those in the high-tech industries reviewed in my earlier book, *Inventing the Electronic Century: The Epic Story of the Consumer Electronics and Computer Industries.* The process of defining these paths of learning in the high-tech industries under review can be explained using the same set of concepts and the same historical approach.

So I begin this introductory chapter by emphasizing some significant differences between the evolution of the consumer electronics and computer industries on the one hand, and the chemical and pharmaceutical industries on the other. Then I define the underlying concepts and review basic themes and my historical approach.

The Differences

Four major differences mark the two sets of high-technology industries. The first and most obvious is the historical timing of the creation of the initial infrastructures—that is, the building of the technological and institutional foundations of the respective industries. In consumer electronics and computers, the creation of the infrastructure began in the 1950s, thirty years after that in chemicals and pharmaceuticals was being completed. Thus, this book records primarily the evolution of a set of mature industries, whereas *Inventing the Electronic Century* deals with the creation of new ones.

The creation of the chemical and pharmaceutical industries began suddenly in the 1880s, simultaneously in the United States and in Europe. In the United States, the maturing of key technologies in transportation and communications—the steamship, telegraph, steam-powered railroad, and the transatlantic cable—made possible mass production and distribution for national and worldwide markets. Chemical and pharmaceutical producers were among the first to take advantage of these enabling technologies. At the same time, the unification of imperial Germany and the growth of its economy based on heavy industry in the Rhine Valley gave chemical and pharmaceutical manufacturers scale of operations from which they could dominate European markets.

The second difference involves the number of new technologies invented and the number and variety of products commercialized, and consequently in the number of competing enterprises involved. In the two electronic industries, only a very small number of companies were initially engaged in commercializing the products, based on four electronic devices—the vacuum tube, the transistor, the integrated circuit, and the microprocessor. In chemicals and pharmaceuticals, on the other hand, a much larger number of new technologies based on the new learnings in chemical and biological sciences brought forth a host of yet other new technologies, especially in inorganic and organic chemistry, biochemistry, and biology. Whereas the evolution of the two high-tech industries derived from electronics is reflected in the history of a small number of enterprises, that of chemicals and pharmaceuticals requires a review of at least fifty competing chemical enterprises and thirty producing pharmaceuticals.

The third difference is that the products commercialized by the two sets of industries were dramatically different and directed toward different markets. Consumer electronics and computers transformed the ways of communication through sound (audio), sight (video), and manipulation of information (computers). Their products required two sets of hardware devices, one for transmission and the other for reception, with software to process the information within both and that flowing between them. The mature chemical and pharmaceutical industries, on the other hand, utilized the new scientific knowledge to create a vast array of new materials and medicines that replaced natural ones—metal, wood, and other organic products—that so transformed the processes of agriculture and industry and the practice of medicine. Note that the products of the Information Age did not compete with those of the Industrial Age. Instead, by revolutionizing communications and information processing, they reshaped the nature of life and work in the existing industrial world.

The fourth difference between these two sets of industries is the relative success and failure of national industries. In consumer electronics, Japan's industry conquered their American and European rivals in American, European, and world markets. In computers they captured most of the European industry and offered serious challenges to their American competitors. In chemicals and pharmaceuticals, on the other hand, European enterprises at the end of the twentieth century—primarily those based in Germany and Switzerland—remained leaders in sales and revenues, while yielding substantially to American competitors in the capacity for innovation. During the 1920s and 1930s, the American companies became the Europeans' major challengers. The Japanese producers of chemicals and pharmaceuticals, by contrast, were unable to enter markets the long-established European and American companies dominated—markets that their compatriots in electronics had captured during the 1970s and 1980s.

These radically different performances cannot be explained in terms of national culture, national political processes and institutions, or national educational systems. Since the executives who commercialized the products of the new technologies in these industries possessed similar cultural and educational backgrounds and operated within the same political and financial nexus of institutions, a critical question thus emerges: why were the performances of these two sets of national industries in worldwide markets so different? The answer is barriers to entry.

Despite the major differences, both sets of industries evolved in much the same manner. In both, the pioneers in commercializing the products of a new technology did so by accumulating learning that in time created powerful barriers to entry into existing markets. In consumer electronics and computers, these barriers restricted entry to enterprises whose basic hardware and related software were narrowly confined to the four electronic devices mentioned above. In chemicals and pharmaceuticals, on the other hand, such learning prevented, with rare exceptions, the entry of new startup enterprises until the emergence of biotechnology in the last quarter of the twentieth century. Because of the historical timing, the Japanese producers in the new electronics industry did not have to face the barriers to entry that had been erected in the mature chemical and pharmaceutical industries. Indeed, they played a major role in creating the initial barriers to entry in these industries in which they became so powerful.

Basic Concepts: Organizational Capabilities

The concepts presented in Chapter 1 of *Inventing the Electronic Century* provide the conceptual framework for understanding the evolution of high-technology industries worldwide.

In market economies, the competitive strengths of industrial firms rest on learned organizational capabilities. This is my basic concept, one that derives from the findings of these two historical studies. The capabilities are product-related in terms of technologies used and markets served. These product-related capabilities, moreover, are learned and embodied in an organizational setting: individuals come and go, but the organization remains. Thus, in modern industrial economies, the large enterprise performs its critical role in the evolution of industries not merely as a unit carrying out transactions on the basis of flows of information, but, more important, as a creator and repository of product-related embedded organizational knowledge.

The process of organizational learning in industrial enterprises begins with the building of a viable profit-making enterprise, which is accomplished through the creation of organizational capabilities based on three types of knowledge—technical, functional, and managerial.

Technical capabilities are those learned by applying existing and new scientific and engineering knowledge to the creation of new technologies and from which new products and processes can be commercialized. Technical capabilities are knowledge-based. They are the capabilities required for the R in R&D (research and development).

Functional capabilities, on the other hand, are product-related. They involve organizational capabilities of the following kinds:

- *Development* capabilities. These are created by learning the product-related know-how required to commercialize a product or a new or existing technology to be sold in national and international markets. These capabilities represent the D in R&D.
- *Production* capabilities. These emerge from learning how to build and operate large-volume production facilities for the new product and how to recruit, train, and supervise the labor force essential to operating

these facilities efficiently. A somewhat similar but less important set of capabilities is that of purchasing in volume the necessary materials for production.

- *Marketing and distribution* capabilities. These are acquired in learning the nature of the product's customers and markets and building extensive advertising, sales, and distribution systems to reach them.

The evolving relationship between technical and functional capabilities is a basic theme of this study. In addition to these two major types, there is one more.

Managerial capabilities—a third set of organizational capabilities, based on management knowledge and experience—is essential to the creation and sustained viability of a profit-making enterprise. These capabilities are learned to administer the activities of the functional operating units, integrate their activities, and coordinate the flow of goods from the suppliers of raw materials through the processes of production and distribution to the retailers and final customers. Most essential to the successful maintenance of the long-term health and growth of the enterprise are the learned capabilities of *top management.* These managers monitor the performance of the operating units and make the critical decisions in allocating personnel and financial resources determining the fate of their enterprise, and often of the entire industry of the country in which it operates.

As vital as managerial capabilities are, they are not a central focus of either the present volume or my earlier one, on electronics. One reason is the difficulty in generalizing about managerial capabilities. They are affected by different kinds of operating structures, national educational systems, and broader cultural patterns in which they have been learned and in which their enterprises have evolved. So capabilities differ from nation to nation, industry to industry, and often from company to company in the same industry. For example, the broader environment in which Japanese managers learn and work is quite unlike those in the United States and Europe. But, to repeat, these differences cannot explain the success and failure of these national industries.

The first enterprises whose managers learn to develop, produce, and sell in national and often worldwide markets—that is, to commercialize new scientific and technical learning—become the initial builders of the high-tech industries. I term such enterprises *first movers.* They are not necessarily the first to produce and sell the new product. Instead, they are the first to develop an integrated set of functional capabilities essential to commercialize the new products in volume for national and usually worldwide markets.

Once the new enterprise's competitive power has been demonstrated, its sets of integrated organizational capabilities become *learning bases* for improving existing products and processes and for developing new ones in response to changes in technical knowledge and markets, and in reaction to macroeconomic developments, including wars and depressions.

These integrated learning bases, in turn, provide the first movers with retained earnings, one of the cheapest sources of long-term capital for investment in commercializing new products. In addition, the learning gained in commercializing the initial product typically is proprietary and gives the first mover a head start in commercializing the next round of new or related products.

Establishing such an integrated learning base in a technologically new industry, together with the resulting continuing flows of funds and enhanced knowledge, creates powerful barriers to entry. Startup firms must begin to develop their basic set of capabilities while competing with first movers that are refining their operations through continuous learning and deriving income from the sale of their initial products. Within each national economy, only a small number of challengers succeed in building comparable learning bases. The first movers and those that quickly follow them into the industry become what I term that industry's *core companies.*

Once these core companies establish a viable national industry, entrepreneurial startups are rarely capable of entering. Instead, competitors to the core companies remain either foreign core companies or domestic core companies in other industries—that is, industries with comparable technical capabilities of the technologies and markets involved with processes of product development, production, and distribution and marketing.

First movers, of course, cannot create an industry by themselves. They must develop close relationships with supporting enterprises—suppliers both of capital equipment and materials to be processed, research specialists, distributors, advertisers, and providers of financial, technical, and other services. Thus, the needs of the core firms lead to the emergence of a *supporting nexus* of interconnected and complementary—rather than competitive—enterprises. The nexus may contain small, medium, and even large firms in supporting lines of a wide variety of products and services. And it soon develops into a source for the creation of a wide variety of specialized firms. But only rarely do core companies emerge from the nexus.

In this way, the competitive strength of national industries depends on the abilities of the core firms to function effectively and to maintain and enhance their integrated learning bases. If these bases begin to deteriorate, so too does the industry's supporting nexus and its national industry's competitive strength versus that of other countries.

Once an industry is established, however, learning is sustained with powerful momentum. The integrated learning bases of the first movers become the primary engines for the continuing evolution of their industry through commercializing products of new technologies fostered by advances in science and engineering. The integrated learning base embodies within the enterprise the procedures to bring together and coordinate the enterprise's technical and functional capabilities. The development of such integrating and coordinating procedures must evolve into a basic function of top management if the enterprise is to benefit from the internal economies of scale and scope and continuing advances in proprietary knowledge. Such integrated learning bases thus initially define an industry's continuing path of organizational learning. They set the direction in which an industry evolves.

Three Basic Themes

The continuing evolution of the enterprises and the industries in which they operate as told in the following pages focus on three basic themes: creating barriers to entry, defining the strategic boundaries of the enterprise, and evaluating the limits to growth of an industry and the enterprises within it.

The integrated learning base not only sets the direction in which the industry evolves, but also, to reemphasize, creates powerful *barriers to entry*. The concentrated power of technical, often proprietary, and functional knowledge embedded in the first movers' integrated learning bases is such that a relatively small number of enterprises define the evolving paths of learning in which the products of new technical knowledge are commercialized for widespread public consumption. The barriers to entry thus prevent startups from creating effective integrated learning bases essential to compete in the industry. The barriers were so high that after the 1920s, of the fifty largest chemical companies and the thirty largest pharmaceutical companies, only two chemical companies and no pharmaceutical companies were able successfully to enter their respective industries.

The building of the barriers to entry, in turn, creates an arena or playing field in which the first movers and close followers define their *strategic boundaries* through competition with one another. These boundaries reflect the competitive success and failure of the individual enterprises in terms of technical achievements and financial returns. I use the term *boundaries* because these enterprises are nearly always diversified multiproduct producers. Within these boundaries the players are protected from enterprises in other industries that did not participate in the creation of the capabilities needed to compete successfully. By the same token, if they move beyond the barriers created by their learned organizational capabilities, they may be—and often are—at a competitive disadvantage.

A third basic theme is that of evaluating the *limits to growth* for enterprises in high-technology industry. One of the basic differences in the evolution of the chemical and the pharmaceuticals industries is that, by the 1970s, chemical science and engineering was no longer generating significant new learning, whereas at the same time biology and related disciplines, especially molecular genetics, witnessed an explosion of new research and insights. Based on this new learning, chemical and pharmaceutical companies built new integrated learning bases, erected new barriers to entry, and defined new strategic boundaries.

Paths of Learning: Strategy and Structure, Scale and Scope

The evolutionary sequence of the appearance of the three main themes was as follows: first came the erection of barriers to entry, then the defining of the strategic boundaries of the competing firms within the industry's competitive arena. Finally, the end of growth in chemicals brought a realignment of the strategic boundaries of the major core companies in chemicals, although the core companies in pharmaceuticals continued to grow rapidly due to the continuing stream of new learning in biology and related disciplines.

The critical question, then, is how these chemical and pharmaceutical companies created their initial barriers to entry. The answer is that they did so by adopting a corporate strategy and a supporting managerial structure that permitted them to lower unit costs by benefiting from the economies of scale and scope. Before considering this essential strategy and structure, I need to define these concepts.

Economies of scale reflect the speed and volume of a product being commercialized through its integrated learning base. As the speed and volume of what I term the *throughput* increases, unit costs fall. Of course there is a limit to the cost reduction. That is defined as the minimum efficient scale—the smallest size a processing plant can be to operate viably.

Economies of scope or joint costs refer to the use of the same materials, equipment, personnel, and knowledge for more than one product line, as the throughput moves from research and development to production and marketing and distribution. In addition, the economies of scope increase as the amount of throughput grows. In addition to these static economies of scope in production, *dynamic* economies of scale and scope in knowledge—based on new learning on the part of high-tech industries—have become increasingly significant.

The basic strategy required to obtain the cost advantages of scale and scope was one of related diversification—related in terms of market and/or technology. The management structure was that of the multidivisional enterprise. The divisions represented the integrated learning bases of the major related product lines. The division managers were responsible for the success of their unit, measured in terms of profit and technological achievement. Corporate headquarters included general executives with enlarged duties for the continuing success and health of their enterprise. Working with division managers, they defined and redefined the changing strategic boundaries of the enterprise in the face of the always shifting global economy. From the start the headquarters also included a large corporate staff, providing a multitude of services to both the division managers and the general executives. One of the major tasks was to ensure that the enterprise maximized the potential economies of scale and scope.

The alternative strategy of growth was, of course, unrelated diversification, that is, companies that moved beyond the industry's competitive arena that its barriers to entry protected. That strategy not only meant competing at a disadvantage in terms of organizational capabilities, even more significant is that the enterprises embarking on a strategy of unrelated diversification could not benefit from the interrelated economies of scale and scope. Nevertheless, a good number of the enterprises reviewed in the following chapters did leave their competitive arena and a few became conglomerates. Nearly all paid the price, in terms of a failure in technological achievement and in maintaining long-term financial performance.

The companies that adopted the strategies of related growth, and so benefited from the economies of scale and even more those of scope, successfully commercialized products that transformed life and work throughout the world. In a little more than a century, nearly all became and remained financially profitable enterprises.

The Approach

My basic purpose in this volume is, as it was in *Inventing the Electronic Century*, to undertake the fundamental task of the historian: to record when, where, and by whom scientific and technical knowledge were commercialized into new products that created a wide variety of manmade materials central to the shaping of a modern industrial economy and manmade pharmaceuticals that sustained modern medicine. I do this by focusing on the relative successes and failures of the first movers and their close followers in the national industries of Europe and the United States. (That of Japan competed successfully in chemicals or pharmaceuticals only in Asia.) I review these histories from their beginnings through the end of the twentieth century.

This book records the creation and continuing evolution of the high-technology chemical and pharmaceutical industries. It uses as a point of departure the histories of the fifty largest industrial chemical companies that accounted for 86 percent of the total U.S. sales in 1993, as listed in *Chemical Engineering News*, and the thirty largest pharmaceutical companies in much the same time period as taken from *Fortune Magazine* and *Hoover's Handbook of American Companies* for 1993 and 1996, and *Hoover's Global 250* for 1993 and 1997. (See Tables 1.1 and 1.2. These tables include some of oldest and best-known names in the industrial economy—Du Pont, Dow, Monsanto, Exxon, Shell, Merck, Pfizer, Bayer, Hoechst, ICI, GlaxoSmithKline, Ciba-Geigy, Roche Holding, Johnson & Johnson, and Procter & Gamble, to cite but a few.)

I use 1993 as the year for presenting the cast of characters in both chemicals and pharmaceuticals because that is when I began to concentrate research on these industries (as well as those covered in *Inventing the Electronic Century*). But note that 1993 is not the ending date of the study. Rather, the stories presented here continue up to the time of this writing (early 2003), through years of challenge and restructuring and even the disappearance of some companies listed in the tables. The stories also include the startup ventures that are contributing to the development of the contemporary biotechnology industry (Chapter 10).

Tables 1.1 and 1.2 provide a relatively complete and neutral sample of the

Table 1.1   The fifty largest industrial chemical producers in the United States, 1993 (in $ billions of chemical-product revenue)

Rank	Company	Revenue ($ billions)
Industrial chemical multisectored core companies (6)		
1	Du Pont	15.6
2	Dow	12.5
5	Monsanto	5.6
7	Union Carbide	4.6
20	Allied Signal	2.9
37	American Cyanamid	1.4
U.S. subsidiaries of foreign industrial chemical core companies (10)		
4	Hoechst Celanese	6.3
9	BASF	4.0
13	ICI America	3.5
17	Miles (Bayer)	3.1
23	Ciba-Geigy	2.5
26	Akzo	2.7
27	Rhône-Poulenc	2.2
33	Unilever	1.8
42	Solvay America	1.2
49	Henkel	1.0
Petroleum companies (12)		
3	Exxon	10.0
8	Occidental	4.1
11	Shell*	3.9
12	Amoco	3.7
14	Mobil	3.5
16	Arco	3.2
21	Chevron	2.7
22	Ashland	2.6
25	Phillips	2.3
35	Elf-Atochem*	1.7
47	Texaco	1.1
48	BP America*	1.0
Industrial chemical niche core companies (10)		
15	Rohm and Haas	3.2
18	Air Products and Chemicals (1940)	2.9
28	Dow Corning (1842)	2.0
31	Hercules	1.8

Table 1.1   *(continued)*

Rank	Company	Revenue ($ billions)
34	Great Lakes Chemical	1.7
36	Lubrizol	1.5
38	Nalco	1.4
41	Witco	1.2
43	Cabot	1.2
44	International Flavors and Fragrances	1.2
U.S. companies in other industries (3)		
6	General Electric	5.4
10	Eastman Kodak	3.9
45	PPG Industries	1.5
Conglomerates (5)		
19	W. R. Grace	2.3
29	Ethyl	1.9
32	FMC Corp.	1.8
40	Morton International	1.2
46	Olin	1.1
Spin-offs from core companies (4)		
24	Praxair (Union Carbide)	2.4
30	Huntsman (Texaco)	1.8
39	Lyondell (Arco)	1.3
50	Cytec (American Cyanamid)	1.0

Source: Compiled from William J. Storck, "Top 100 Chemical Producers Post Little Sales Growth," *Chemical and Engineering News,* May 9, 1994, p. 14.

Note: No Japanese subsidiaries in top fifty.

* Subsidiary of foreign petroleum company. Elf-Atochem was formed in 1983 by the French government.

major players in each industry. The companies reviewed are selected neither to test nor support specific theories or hypotheses. They provide the historical reality from which one can derive valid generalizations about the paths of learning followed in the respective industries. Any theory, hypothesis, or broad general statement concerning the evolution of these industries must take into account the histories of the enterprises presented in the following chapters.

Chapter 2 provides a chronological overview of the creation and evo-

Table 1.2 The world's thirty largest producers of pharmaceuticals, 1993 (in $ billions of pharmaceutical and medical devices revenues)

Rank	Company	Estimated revenue ($ billions)
U.S. core companies (10)		
1	Bristol-Myers Squibb	11.1
2	Merck	10.4
4	SmithKline Beecham[a]	9.2
5	Abbott Laboratories	8.4
6	American Home Products	8.3
10	Pfizer	7.4
14	Eli Lilly	6.4
16	Warner-Lambert	5.7
21	Schering-Plough	4.3
22	Upjohn	3.6
Non-U.S. core companies (12)		
3	Roche Holding (Switzerland)	9.6
8	Glaxo Holdings (U.K.)	8.0
12	Takeda Pharmaceutical (Japan)	6.7
19	Sankyo (Japan)	4.7
20	Pharmacia (Sweden)	4.5
23	Boeringer-Ingelheim (Germany)	3.4
24	Yamanouchi Pharmaceutical (Japan)	3.4
25	Schering (Germany)	3.2
26	E. Merck (Germany)	3.2
27	Shionogi (Japan)	3.1
28	Wellcome[b] (U.K.)	3.1
29	Astra (Sweden)	3.0
U.S. companies in related industries (2)		
18	Johnson & Johnson	5.2
30	Procter & Gamble	3.0
Non-U.S. chemical companies (6)		
7	Hoechst (Germany)	8.1 (1995)
9	Bayer (Germany)	7.7 (1995)
11	Ciba-Geigy (Switzerland)	7.0 (1991)
13	Rhône-Poulenc (France)	6.5 (1995)
15	Sandoz (Switzerland)	6.3 (1991)
17	ICI Zeneca (U.K.)	5.5 (1994)

Source: Compiled and calculated from "*Fortune* Global 500," *Fortune,* July 25, 1994, pp. 178, 180; *Hoover's Handbook of American Companies;* and other sources.

a. Formed as a merger of SmithKline Beckman and Beecham in 1989.

b. Acquired by Glaxo Holdings to form Glaxo Wellcome in 1995.

lution of the chemical and pharmaceutical industries and essential background for placing subsequent chapters in their broader context. The chapter answers the critical questions of when, where, and by whom the processes of industrial change were carried out. Subsequent chapters carefully review the historical record to answer the other critical questions of how and why industrial change occurred and what factors accounted for the success or failure of individual enterprises.

Chapter 3 reviews the competitive evolution of six American chemical enterprises formed at the end of the nineteenth century. By the close of the twentieth century, only two—Du Pont and Dow—remained chemical producers. The others had remade themselves as pharmaceutical companies or had been acquired.

Chapter 4 considers the focused American chemical producers that competed in specialized niches, making specialty chemicals for a variety of markets and purposes. These companies had the best record of technological and financial success during the industry's troubled years in the mid-1970s and early 1980s.

Chapter 5 considers the major European chemical producers since the 1880s. Nearly all of these enterprises were based along the Rhine River, from Belgium in the North to Switzerland in the South, although one British company also became an effective worldwide competitor.

Chapter 6 deals with the American competitors in petrochemicals. Nearly all were major petroleum companies that had been established before World War I. They played an important role in commercializing products originating in the polymer/petrochemical revolution. Several attempted unsuccessfully to compete with the major chemical companies in polymer-based products. By the 1980s, however, several netted 25–30 percent of their profits by producing basic feedstocks and polymers.

Chapters 7–10 cover the evolution of the pharmaceutical industry. In Chapter 7, the American producers began after World War I to challenge the German leaders for global leadership. With the coming of World War II and with it the antibiotic revolution, five American companies became worldwide leaders in prescription drugs. A comparison of their evolutionary paths provides insights into reasons for success and failure in terms of technological achievement and financial return.

Chapter 8 reviews the American companies that followed the over-the-counter (OTC) path. In the United States, unlike in Europe, most pharmaceutical enterprises began producing OTC, not prescription drugs, based on vegetables, minerals, and other natural sources. From the 1960s forward, these enterprises sought to remake themselves as producers of prescription drugs. Two companies succeeded, while two others failed.

Chapter 9 covers the U.S. companies that entered pharmaceuticals from another industry. Two succeeded and one, Eastman Kodak, failed spectacularly. The European competitors were all long-established enterprises. Three were German companies profiled in Chapter 5. Following a prolonged absence during and after World War II, two of the three returned to the United States in the 1970s and quickly moved into pharmaceuticals. Meanwhile, the Swiss chemical enterprises followed the Swiss pharmaceutical giant Roche Holding AG and moved quickly and successfully into the new biotechnology industry. In the late 1990s and early 2000s, a wave of mergers completely restructured the global pharmaceutical industry.

Chapter 10 provides another remarkable story, the commercialization of the new science of biotechnology, which required the building of a new basic industrial infrastructure. This process began in the 1970s and continues today.

Chapter 11 provides a summary and conclusion and compares the remarkable stories of the chemical and pharmaceutical industries with the epic stories covered in *Inventing the Electronic Century.*

It may be helpful, however, to point out several major lessons and conclusions of the study here.

First, more than any other variable, corporate strategy determined success and failure in relation to technological innovation and financial performance in the long run. The most successful strategy—what I term the *virtuous strategy*—involved reinvesting earnings and learning to strengthen existing integrated learning bases that in turn constitute the foundation for continuing growth. The least successful strategy involved unrelated diversification, which almost invariably failed because companies pursuing it could not capture economies of scale and scope to obtain lower unit costs. They also encountered high barriers to entry erected by the first movers in unrelated industries. Several leading chemical companies, for example, sought to diversify into pharmaceuticals. They either failed or were acquired by pharmaceutical companies. Several leading pharmaceutical companies attempted to enter electronic medical equipment. None of these companies succeeded.

Second, high-technology industries form over a period of decades in which they establish their infrastructures. The first movers and their close followers become core companies and a supporting nexus of specialized suppliers of products and services emerges. Once this infrastructure is completed—a process that in the past has taken fifty years or more—entry becomes nearly impossible and competition involves only the established rivals. In both chemicals and pharmaceuticals, infrastructures were built between the 1880s and the 1920s. In the information industries covered in *Inventing the Electronic Century,* the consumer electronics infrastructure formed between the 1920s and the 1970s, and the computer industry infrastructure between the 1940s and the 1990s. We are presently witnessing the ongoing formation of the biotechnology industry infrastructure that began in the 1980s. One might predict that this process will continue for another two decades or so and that, when the infrastructure is completed, new entrants will rarely succeed—unless another new source of learning should emerge to lead the industry in new directions.

Third, high-tech companies can encounter limits to learning as well as limits to growth. The chemical industry in the early twenty-first century is no longer truly a high-tech industry because chemical science no longer generates basic new learning to stimulate commercialization of fundamentally new products. Today's chemical leaders are still mining scientific learning that emerged as early as the late nineteenth century with subsequent bursts in the 1920s and then again in the 1940s and 1950s. They are succeeding by focusing on product and process development, and only rarely commercializing new learning from basic research. In pharmaceuticals, in contrast, new scientific disciplines continue to emerge and provide opportunities for commercialization and rapid growth. While the industry has roots in the nineteenth century and expanded greatly in the middle of the twentieth with the development of antibiotics, it benefited from such new disciplines as microbiology, enzymology, genetic engineering, and genomics that developed in the last third of the twentieth century. The new learning in genetic engineering and genomics is only beginning to be exploited at the present time.

Finally, the stories recounted here have implications for practitioners in today's high-technology industries. In fact, the stories of these companies—some more than a century old—are their stories, in which patterns of success and failure over the long term are revealed. Those managers in today's pharmaceutical and biotechnology industries may derive particular insights from observing the histories of the completion of infrastructures and the dynamics of competition in older high-tech industries.

CHAPTER 2

Evolving Paths of Learning

The purpose of this overview is to provide a broad picture of the commercializing of the products of the new chemical and biological technologies. It does so by relating enterprise-level developments—particularly expansion, diversification, and restructuring—as well as macroeconomic events and eras. In this way, the transformation of new scientific knowledge into products that have so revolutionized daily life and work over the past century can be properly explained.

The modern chemical and pharmaceutical industries were established in the 1880s, during what historians call the "Second Industrial Revolution." The First Industrial Revolution had begun at the end of the eighteenth century in Britain with the development of coal-powered machinery that made possible the factory, wage-earning workers, and modern capitalism. But it was the advent of the Second Industrial Revolution, based on the emergence of modern transportation and communication—coal-powered locomotives, steamships, the telegraph, and the telephone—that signaled that the production and transportation of goods were no longer dependent on the power and speed of animals and the vagaries of wind and water. Modern mass production and distribution for national and worldwide markets suddenly became a reality. The chemical and pharmaceutical industries represent the high-technology frontier of the Second Industrial Revolution— along with the electrical and telecommunications industries, the heirs of which, the consumer electronics and computer industries, are reviewed in my earlier book, *Inventing the Electronic Century*.

For the chemical industry, the key events and eras following the industry's launch in the 1880s during the Second Industrial Revolution began with the impact of World War I, during which the United States ceased importing German products and developed domestic industrial capabilities and capacity. Next came the polymer/petrochemical revolution and the advent of World War II. The postwar period witnessed a sustained boom that finally leveled off in the 1960s. Then came the turbulent decade of the 1970s, ending with the industry crisis between 1979 and 1982, resulting in the restructuring of the industry and further followed by the drive of the chemical companies into pharmaceuticals. In pharmaceuticals, events and eras were much the same until the 1970s; the difference was that World War II precipitated a revolution in prescription drugs. Of more significance is that, in the late 1970s and 1980s, the coming of new pharmaceutical technologies—those based on biochemistry and microbiology and then on a new science, molecular genetics—resulted in a dramatically different pattern of growth than the chemical companies experienced. For the pharmaceutical industry, the late twentieth and early twenty-first centuries were years of opportunity rather than restructuring.

The Creation and Evolution of the Chemical Industry

Table 1.1 lists the American and European companies whose evolution is reviewed in Part Two (Chapters 3–6). These core companies created the modern chemical industry at the turn into the twentieth century and continued to dominate it through the period covered by this study.

Of the multisectored core companies listed in Table 1.1, all except Allied Chemical were American first movers in products based on new chemical technologies. Du Pont, Dow, Monsanto, and American Cyanamid established their initial learning bases between 1896 and 1907. Du Pont was the first mover in nitrocellulose-based explosives, Dow in electrically produced inorganic chemicals, and Monsanto in the synthesis of foods and flavors. The several companies that in 1917 made up Union Carbide had also pioneered in a range of electrically based inorganic products. On the other hand, only one of the enterprises that merged into Allied commercialized a new technology.

Whereas the initial strength of the American chemical industry lay in inorganic chemicals, that of the European leaders—the German and Swiss—was based in organic chemistry. Their products, including manmade dyes, pharmaceuticals, and film, quickly captured worldwide markets. The three major German companies, BASF, Bayer, and Hoechst, and the two Swiss leaders, Ciba and Geigy, were established before the American enterprises. In the 1880s and 1890s they dominated international markets. Their giant production plants offered the economies of scale that lowered unit costs and, as they diversified into closely related industries, economies of scope that spread costs over multiple markets. Their marketing organizations maintained offices in four continents. They were the first to build research laboratories, set up development units, and establish close ties to universities and research institutes.

Two of the other German firms, Henkel and Vereinige Glanzstaff-Fabriken, the predecessor of Akzo, as well as the Belgium company Solvay, were also established before the turn of the century. All were located in the Rhine River valley, an area where excellent river and railroad communications soon created a strong supporting nexus. The three remaining European companies listed in Table 1.1—Imperial Chemical Industries (ICI), Rhône-Poulenc, and Unilever—became challengers only in the interwar years.

The American Chemical Industry during the Interwar Years

World War I, with Britain's naval blockade and the U.S. government's appropriation of German facilities and patents, permitted the American chemical industry to come into its own. The major core companies, again with the exception of Allied Chemical, diversified into the industry's different sectors and then created an integrated learning base to manage their product lines within each of these sectors. By 1930 all except Allied Chemical had entered anywhere from four to all eight of the U.S. government's three-digit Standard Industrial Classifications in industrial chemicals.[1] I view these multisectoral firms as core chemical companies. (My use of the term *sector* for these classifications parallels the use of that term in *Inventing the Electronic Century*.) To manage such a multisectored enterprise, the major chemical companies adopted multidivisional management structures. Pioneered by Du Pont in the 1920s (as reviewed in the next chapter), it enabled that company to operate in all eight of the industry's three-digit SIC classifications by the 1930s.

The rapid multisectoral diversification of the core companies was facilitated by the accompanying rapid growth of a supporting nexus, which included both specialty chemical producers, those supplying intermediate chemicals, and specialized engineering firms (SEFs), those helping to design and build chemical plants. The expanding number of smaller companies during the interwar years reflected the growing range of their customers' product lines. Because of these close relationships, I term the smaller entities *focused companies.*

The focused companies usually adopted one of two growth strategies.

They either focused on a single specialty such as bromides or lubricants, which they sold to a wide variety of customers, or they used their specialized skills, for example, those in water treatments, in several of the major sectors. Over the decades these specialty chemical firms remained among the industry's most profitable enterprises.

The European Chemical Industry during the Interwar Years

As the U.S. companies became multisectoral, the Europeans became less dominant in world markets. Nevertheless, during the years between the two world wars, three giant German and three smaller Swiss companies remained the leaders in these markets. German recovery had to wait until 1924, when an international agreement ended Germany's destructive inflation and military occupation. Within a year, its Big Three had merged into a single enterprise, I. G. Farben Industrie. The consolidated enterprise quickly returned to the United States by acquiring and building plants and marketing facilities. By 1929 it was again a leader in the U.S. production of dyes and pharmaceuticals. In addition, Bayer was posing the first challenge to Eastman Kodak in film. The three Swiss firms made their first postwar direct investments in 1920. The predecessor of Akzo, Vereinige Glanzztaff-Fabriken, soon became the third-largest U.S. producer of rayon, behind Du Pont and the British leader, Courtauld's Ltd.

During this same period the British and French chemical companies were still not serious challengers. Indeed, it was the formation of I. G. Farben that impelled British industrialists and government officials to form in 1926 Imperial Chemical Industries (ICI) as the industry's national champion. But ICI had little success in competing with the Germans and the Swiss; the capabilities simply were not there. Rhône-Poulenc added little to the evolution of the industry, relying as it did on foreign-based technologies whose products were protected by high tariffs.

The Polymer/Petrochemical Revolution and World War II

The emergence of petrochemical-based polymer technologies and products underlay the most significant upheaval in the twentieth-century chemical industry. The 1920s witnessed a growing interest in polymer-based synthetic materials such as Bakelite, celluloid, and cellulose acetate. In the 1930s concentrated efforts—particularly by Du Pont, Dow, and Union Carbide—

led to significant technological advances and introduced remarkable new synthetic materials. It was, however, the unanticipated demands of World War II that ushered in the polymer/petrochemical revolution.

In the United States, the government-sponsored crash programs for the production of synthetic rubber and high-octane gasoline provided the funding and research essential to increasing the volume production of petroleum-based chemical feedstocks and intermediates, but had less impact on the growth of the newly developed polymer-based end-products. The commercialization of the latter generated an outpouring of new innovative materials that rapidly replaced existing markets for fiber, fabrics, metals, metal-making machinery and devices, and indeed this created a new industry—petrochemicals—as illustrated in Table 2.1. In addition to precipitating the most significant wave of new products and processes since the formation of the modern chemical industry in the 1880s and 1890s, the wartime programs led first to the large-scale entrance of oil companies into the chemical industry, and then to a postwar boom still unsurpassed in the industry's history.

The Entry of the Petroleum Companies

The timing of the petroleum companies' entry into the chemical industry determined their long-term position in the industry. The four that commercialized petrochemicals before the Japanese attack on Pearl Harbor—Standard Oil of New Jersey (Exxon by 1993), Shell, Standard Oil of California (Chevron by 1993), and Phillips—were the first movers. By the 1950s they had become the leaders in the basic feedstocks and commodity polymers such as polystyrene, polyvinyl chloride, polyethylene, and polypropylene. Those companies that entered after 1941 achieved success by focusing on specific niche products in the manner of the smaller U.S. companies. As shown in Table 1.1, these include Arco (Atlantic Refining Company), Amoco (Standard Oil of Indiana), Ashland, and BP America (acquirer of Standard Oil of Ohio).

The full-scale entry of these oil companies into the chemical industry was hastened by the specialized engineering firms (SEFs). These firms became the critical unit in the industry's supporting nexus. Because the production of chemicals involved a very complex mixing of chemicals and other materials under a variety of temperatures and pressures with relatively few employees, its production technologies differed sharply from the mass-produc-

Table 2.1   Ubiquitous products of the petrochemical industry

Packaging	**Building**
Soap bottles	Shuttering and molds for concrete
Mineral and carbonated drink bottles	Damp course film
Caps for bottles and aerosols	Thermal insulation
Carboys for industrial chemicals	Window frames, guttering, and
Coatings for tinplate cans	drainage pipes
Bottle crates	Gas, sewage, and water pipes
Tote boxes	Electrical conduit
Flexible packaging for frozen food	Foaming agents for plasterboard
Yogurt and cream containers	Binders for particleboard and plywood
Stretch and shrink wrap for pallets	Solvents for paints
Industrial strapping	Insulation and sheathing for power,
Refuse sacks	telephone, and TV wire and cables
Sterile packs for medical use	Electrical plugs, sockets, and switches
	Vandal-proof and security glazing
Transport	Building film for site cover during
Dashboards	construction
Bumpers	
Radiator grilles	**Textiles—fibers for:**
Gasoline tanks	Coats
Tires and inner tubes	Suits
Laminate film for safety glass	Underwear
Battery cases	Shirts
Wire insulation	Skirts
Knobs	Socks
Seat foam	Stockings
Seat covers	Curtains
Interior linings	Upholstery fabrics
Anticorrosion treatment	Carpet-backing fabrics
Paints	Pillow fillings
Brake fluids	Quilt fillings
Degreasing solvents	Cassette housings and drives
Truck cabs	Tarpaulins
Train bodies	Soil-stabilization fabrics
Bus parts	Industrial clothing
Aircraft parts	Fireproof clothing
Yacht parts	
Space shuttle elements	

Table 2.1   (continued)

Other uses

In the home
Molded chairs
Mattresses
Decorative laminates
Vinyl wall coverings
Washbowls
Canisters for food
Buckets
Bristles for brushes
Floor tiles
Soles, heels, and shoes
Washing machine drums and agitators
Microchip toy casings

In the office
Telephone handsets
Pocket calculator casings
Carpet pile fibers
VDU housings

And all over the place
Printed circuit laminates
Audio and video tapes
Adhesives
Antifreeze
Telephone poles
Roadmarkers and paints
Fishing nets, ropes, and string
Fish and vegetable boxes
Horticultural film
Powder and liquid detergents
Dry cleaning fluids
Disposable syringes
Contact lenses
Artificial hips and other replacement surgical items
Antiskid road surfacing

Source: Peter H. Spitz, *Petrochemicals: The Rise of an Industry* (New York: Wiley, 1988), p. 267.

tion techniques used to make motor vehicles or electronic devices, or those employed in fashioning metals and even industrial machinery. The SEFs emerged in the 1920s but came into their own only during the war and the early postwar years. By 1960, SEFs designed and built nearly three-fourths of all petrochemical plants worldwide.

In the 1960s the petrochemical divisions of major oil and gasoline companies began to realize the limits to the potential of their recently created organizational capabilities. In the 1950s Exxon moved energetically beyond the production of the basic polymers into a wide variety of polymer-based end-products, including fabrics and film, engineered and laminated products, containers and other plastic goods, as well as agricultural chemicals. The other oil companies soon followed suit. By the mid-1970s, however, their challenges to the multisectored core industrial chemical companies failed precisely because they lacked the critical product development and marketing development capabilities.

Thus competitive boundaries within the industry were defined. The petrochemical companies would remain the producers of the basic feedstocks and commodity polymers. By the 1980s those products were providing a number of these companies with as much as a quarter of their revenue and a somewhat larger share of their income.

The Europeans Return to the American Market

During the same years that the petroleum companies were capturing the commodity polymer/petrochemical business from the American multisectored core companies, the European producers, primarily the Germans and the Swiss, were beginning to return to the American market. Because of the war, the Germans only entered the polymer/petrochemical revolution in the early 1950s. The victors divided I. G. Farben into its three major constituent companies—BASF, Bayer, and Hoechst. Of these, BASF concentrated on petrochemicals by forming a joint venture first with Dow and then Phillips and began to produce polyethylene. Although BASF made little attempt to move into polymer-based end-products, the U.S. subsidiaries of Bayer and Hoechst did so. Hoechst, working with the American company Hercules, entered into the production of polymer commodities. Then, again in a joint effort with Hercules, it entered the production of polymer-based film and fabrics. At the same time, it began to enlarge its traditional pharmaceutical business by acquisitions. Bayer, in collaboration with Monsanto ventured into engineered plastics, but the product line was not a success. Like Hoechst it returned to focusing on enlarging its pharmaceutical lines.

The three Swiss companies, Ciba, Geigy (which merged with Ciba in 1970), and Sandoz, had made no attempt to enter petrochemicals. Ciba's strength remained its prewar organic chemical lines, particularly dyes and pharmaceuticals, while Geigy pioneered in insecticides after the commercializing of DDT in 1940, and expanded its agricultural chemical business. Sandoz focused more on pharmaceuticals.

The Postwar Boom and Its Aftermath

During the 1950s and 1960s the major U.S. industrial chemical companies and their mid-sized competitors concentrated on exploiting the opportunities created by the polymer/petrochemical technology. In these two decades, the rate of growth of the industry was two-and-a-half times that of the gross national product (GNP). During the 1960s, value added by manufacturing in plastics and synthetic rubber grew twice as fast as that in metalworking. By the 1970s synthetic fiber accounted for 70 percent of U.S. fiber production. In building and expanding their capabilities in these new products, the existing companies continued to maintain and enhance the product lines they had commercialized during the prewar years in organic, inorganic, and other chemicals.

But, beginning in the mid-1960s and increasingly in the 1970s, the rate of commercializing new polymer/petrochemical products fell off. At the same time, the European competitors had returned to the U.S. market in strength and the oil companies were still challenging for higher-value synthetic fiber and plastic markets.

The Search for New Product Lines

In the 1960s, in responding to the increasing competition and decreasing rate of successful new product introductions, the core companies of the U.S. chemical industry began their search for new product lines to commercialize. Du Pont was the first to systematically explore the potential for developing new products outside its existing learning bases. As early as 1959 its executive committee established a new-venture program housed in its development department. That program tested several markets, of which housing was the most ambitious. But none proved to be commercially viable. By the end of the 1960s the senior management decided that the most reliable source of new products were the product development units of the different divisions, including both those created before and after World War II. Monsanto followed Du Pont's example in 1968 by establishing a new-enterprise division; its managers soon came to the same decision. The success of its agricultural chemical unit in commercializing new products provided an impressive example of relying on long-established capabilities. In the 1960s Union Carbide, unlike the others, actually embarked on a strategy of unrelated diversification—carried out, of course, through acquisitions. After attempting to rationalize this strategy of buying and selling companies, in the late 1970s it sold off nearly all of its unrelated lines. At the same time, it began to dispose of its commodity polymers and the less profitable of its older product lines. By the early 1980s Union Carbide was concentrating on its long-established successful end-products.

Others followed suit. Two of the smaller companies, Hercules and Rohm and Haas, realizing that they were no longer able to compete with the major players in polymer end-products, set up new-venture programs and met the same fate as the bigger core companies. Both Hercules and Rohm and Haas would continue to rely on their existing divisions as a source of new product lines. Of the other three major core companies, Dow, probably the most successful during the 1950s and 1960s in terms of revenue and profits, waited until 1978 to begin planning a large-scale redefinition of its strategic boundaries. American Cyanamid, which had entered pharmaceuticals during World War II, now turned to consider pharmaceuticals rather than chemicals as its path for future growth. Allied Chemical, on the other hand, had made no systematic analysis of its capabilities before the industry encountered a deep crisis beginning in 1979 that forced a massive restructuring of the U.S. chemical industry's major core companies.

The Crisis and Restructuring of the American Core Companies

The 1970s, the years during which the American chemical companies began to redefine their product lines firms, were a turbulent decade. In 1973, an embargo by the Organization of Petroleum Exporting Countries (OPEC), engineered a price rise of crude oil from less than $2 a barrel to close to $30 by the end of the decade. Moreover, these years were characterized by stagflation (recession and high unemployment combined with rising prices) and the breakdown of the postwar system of international monetary exchange.

Nevertheless, the major restructuring of the chemical industry developed only after the crisis precipitated by a second oil shock following the revolution in Iran in 1979, and extended through 1982 by a double-dip recession that created the worst economic times between the Great Depression and the end of the century.

The initial response of the core companies with polymer/petrochemical lines was to protect their crude oil supplies. Then they began the large-scale restructuring of their product portfolios. Broadly speaking, they concentrated on a strategy of moving out of the low value-added intermediate chemicals and commodity petrochemicals that they still produced, strengthening their learning bases in the paths where they had long been leaders, and focusing on transferring into closely related high-technology product lines, particularly pharmaceuticals.

The companies achieved these goals through a proliferation of buying and selling of their integrated divisions and other self-contained operating units. During the 1980s these transactions involved the reshaping of their product portfolios totaling billions of dollars. The new and growing market for corporate control—that is, the coming of the buying and selling of corporations as a special business activity—assisted this restructuring.

Nevertheless, the new "corporate raiders" succeeded in dismantling two of the six major U.S. core chemical companies, Allied Chemical and Union Carbide. After the raiders had finished, Allied Chemical became a specialty chemical unit in Allied Signal, accounting for roughly 25 percent of that company's revenues. In 1986, after a deadly accident at Union Carbide's plant in Bhopal, India, raider Samuel Heyman forced the company to sell off its major, long-established product divisions. It never fully recovered. Finally, in 2001, what remained of Union Carbide was acquired by Dow.

The remaining four core U.S. multisectored companies completed their restructuring by the mid-1980s. Their product lines included those they had commercialized before World War II and those generated by the polymer/petrochemical revolution during and after the war. These companies continued to readjust their product lines by buying and selling units from one another and their European competitors in specialty chemicals. The restructuring, in turn, solidified the position of the oil and gas companies in the production of commodity petrochemicals and polymers.

The crisis had less of an impact on the focused American companies and the multisectored European competitors. The Europeans had completed their reentry into the U.S. market during the 1970s and experienced little pressure to redefine the boundaries of their U.S. subsidiaries. The focused companies continued to provide both the chemical and petroleum companies with the wide variety of chemicals they required. They also began to make large-scale investments abroad. For most of the specialty chemical companies, the decade of the 1980s proved prosperous.

Upgrading to Pharmaceuticals

During the 1980s, the major growth strategy of the four multisectored core U.S. chemical companies focused on becoming strong competitors in pharmaceuticals—that is, in products based on the science of biology rather than chemistry. American Cyanamid and Monsanto succeeded to a point; Du Pont almost did; and Dow quickly failed. Their histories attest to the competitive strength acquired by the pharmaceutical industry's first movers. American Cyanamid prevailed because it had pioneered in the commercializing of antibiotics during World War II. Monsanto was a first mover in agricultural products based on the new molecular biology. The two companies became so successful that in the mid-1990s both spun off their chemical businesses. Not long afterward, however, American Cyanamid was acquired by a pharmaceutical giant, American Home Products (now Wyeth), while Monsanto merged with Sweden's Pharmacia.

Of the other two, Dow eventually abandoned its attempt to enter through acquisitions, including the major purchase in 1989 of Marion Laboratories. Within five years Dow's leaders realized they simply did not have the necessary capabilities to compete and sold the company's pharmaceutical businesses to the German giant Hoechst for $7.1 billion. Du Pont, on the other hand, took the one route that might have succeeded. After its research department commercialized two drugs, the company in 1993 formed a joint venture with Merck, the nation's leading pharmaceutical prescription drugmaker, in which Merck would teach Du Pont how to develop the necessary functional capabilities—product development, production, and most important of all, marketing and distribution. At first, the experiment seemed to be successful, and in 1997 Du Pont acquired Merck's 50 percent of the joint venture. In 2001, however, Du Pont sold its pharmaceutical business to Bristol-Myers Squibb for $7.5 billion. Despite its entry strategy, Du Pont was unable to compete with its century-old rivals in pharmaceuticals.

During this period the German and Swiss companies were also shifting their focus from chemicals to pharmaceuticals. Their evolution differed from those of the U.S. companies in that they had from their beginnings commercialized products in the biology-based pharmaceutical technologies, as Table 1.2 shows. In Europe, the Swiss made the transition more quickly than the Germans. In 1995 Ciba-Geigy and Sandoz merged to form Novartis and began quickly to sell off their chemical businesses. In the later 1990s Hoechst purchased Dow's pharmaceutical businesses and acquired full control of Roussel Uclaf, a French pharmaceutical company, and then merged with Rhône-Poulenc Rorer to form Aventis. This new entity also began to spin off its chemical businesses.

Thus by the end of the twentieth century, the American chemical industry consisted of two multisectored core companies, Du Pont and Dow, as well as a number of specialty chemicals manufacturers still focused on products commercialized in the 1920s or in the 1940s and 1950s. The oil and gas companies produced feedstocks, basic petrochemicals, and commodity chemicals. Except for the German and Swiss companies, which from the start had commercialized pharmaceuticals, the European multisectored chemical companies had also become producers of specialty chemicals. For example, Britain's ICI, after spinning off in 1993 its most profitable division (pharmaceuticals) as a separate enterprise (Zeneca), used the funds generated to acquire Unilever's specialty chemical division.

The Creation and Evolution of the Pharmaceutical Industry

The evolution of the chemical and pharmaceutical industries is remarkable for two reasons. First, the industry in Europe and in the United States evolved in very different ways. Second, after the 1920s, the science of chemistry was no longer providing new learning to be commercialized by the many operating companies, while at the same time biology was producing new learning in existing disciplines, creating new disciplines and even a new science.

Differing Origins in the United States and Europe

The companies whose remarkable evolutions are reviewed in Part Three (Chapters 7–10) are recorded in Table 1.2. The most important lesson to be gleaned from the table is the very different beginnings of the pharmaceutical industry in the United States and Europe. In Europe, the first movers were German and Swiss core chemical companies, which commercialized drugs based on organic chemistry. From their beginnings in the late nineteenth century, these giant enterprises quickly led the world in commercializing drugs and did the same in dyes and photographic film.

This was not the case in the United States. Of the major U.S. core firms listed in Table 1.2, eight of the ten (all but Merck and Pfizer) created their initial integrated learning bases in the 1880s and 1890s, after the completion of the railroad and telegraph networks. They were, in the jargon of the day, "wholesaler/producer enterprises." Operating in commercial cities, they processed, packaged, and marketed a variety of existing drugs based largely on natural sources—botanical, animal, and mineral—and distributed them to pharmacists, drugstores, and other retailers in the hinterland. Until World War I, the U.S. companies relied on the German and Swiss firms to supply the new drugs based on the revolutionary organic chemical technologies using coal tar. (Merck and Pfizer evolved into core companies during World War II by commercializing new antibiotic drugs.)

As a result, the core U.S. firms evolved along two paths of learning. One was the production and marketing of their existing and largely patented pharmaceutical remedies—"proprietary" drugs, as they were called—which were sold "over the counter" (OTC) without prescriptions and commercialized from natural sources, both vegetable and mineral. The other was the development and commercializing of prescription or "ethical" drugs, based on newer pharmaceutical technologies. Each path required its own set of technical and functional capabilities. The first path involved the volume production of branded, packaged products for mass markets. The second, those that required a physician's prescription, called for the commercializing of manmade, chemically based drugs sold to pharmacists and doctors. The first developed into an advertising-intensive path, similar to those in consumer chemicals SIC 284 ("soaps, cleaners and toilet goods") and SIC 20 ("food and kindred products"). The second evolved into a research-intensive path similar to those in chemicals.

In Europe, as Table 1.2 illustrates, the German and Swiss leaders were the Rhine Valley chemical companies, whose evolution has been sketched above. The British companies became significant competitors after World War II, but France's Rhône-Poulenc failed to become a factor in world markets. The most successful European pharmaceutical company of all in terms of revenues and profits was F. Hoffmann–La Roche (now Roche Holding), established in 1894 in Basel, Switzerland, the headquarters site of the three Swiss chemical companies listed in Table 1.1.

The Interwar Years: The American Firms Move into Prescription Drugs

The growing divergence between the American pharmaceutical industry's two paths of learning first appeared during and following World War I. In those years a small number of the largest wholesaler/producer enterprises, including Eli Lilly, Abbott, SmithKline, Upjohn, Squibb (acquired by Bristol-Myers in 1989), and Parke Davis (later merged with Warner-Lambert), pioneered in building the technical capabilities needed to produce and market prescription drugs for national and international markets. The American subsidiaries of the two German leaders, Merck and Schering, brought those capabilities with them. The others effectively incorporated European, largely German, learning and technologies in biology and immunology, built their research laboratories to enhance their development capabilities, and created the necessary production facilities and marketing organizations. Even before World War II, these prescription drug producers began to make inroads against the German/Swiss dominance in the United States by commercializing new prescription drugs on their own. At the same time, they maintained production of their earlier offerings and often introduced new products for the advertising-intensive path.

The majority of the U.S. producers, however, continued to focus on OTC drugs. They concentrated on strengthening their marketing capabilities, especially through advertising, and their distribution channels. They were, for example, among the first companies to use the new radio networks of the 1920s to reach mass markets. By World War II, leading core firms in the advertising-intensive branch of the industry included Bristol-Myers, Warner, Plough, and American Home Products.

World War II and a Revolution in Prescription Drugs

The World War II crash programs in penicillin and sulfa drugs transformed the pharmaceutical industry by providing financing that expanded research and facilities even more than did those in high-octane gasoline and synthetic rubber in chemicals. The resulting "cascade of discovery," first in penicillin and other antibiotic drugs—those miracle cures for infectious diseases—and then in other therapeutic areas, led to rapid growth along the prescription path. The result was a therapeutic revolution, underwritten in part by the simultaneous rapid growth of the healthcare insurance industry. In 1929 sales of prescription drugs accounted for 32 percent of all consumer expenses for medical drugs; by 1969 that figure had risen to 83 percent.

The wartime program in antibiotics brought more companies into the production of prescription drugs. In the 1950s, two major suppliers of fine chemicals in the industry's nexus, Merck and Pfizer, acquired functional capabilities including the marketing facilities needed to reach doctors and hospitals. Merck did so by acquisition, Pfizer by internal investment. Two other large firms, the multipathed American Home Products and the industrial chemical company American Cyanamid, both entered the prescription drug business by becoming major producers of antibiotics and then of other prescription drugs.

The impact of antibiotics differed in Europe because of the historical coincidence between the scientific discoveries and the outbreak of World War II. Before the war, American, German, and Swiss enterprises completely dominated Britain's prescription drug markets. The huge wartime demand for antibiotics permitted Glaxo, ICI, and Beecham (Britain's only major drug producer, and only an OTC producer at that time) to become first movers in commercializing the new technology. By contrast, on the continent, the French and German producers were preoccupied with wartime exigencies, and the Swiss were landlocked and unable to export.

As in chemicals, the war-engendered wave of new pharmaceutical products leveled off in the 1960s. Again, as in chemicals, the U.S. core companies diversified. Except for American Home Products, those in the advertising-intensive paths made only a feeble attempt to produce prescription drugs. They concentrated instead on moving into the related consumer chemical path (SIC 284) with soaps, cosmetics, cleaners, and other household goods, and even beyond chemicals into food and drink. The research-intensive core companies, in turn, expanded their OTC offerings and followed their low-technology brethren into consumer chemicals and other paths. Some also began to enter another related high-technology path, medical instruments and devices (SIC 383–385), which were related in terms of markets but not technology. The European producers, on the other hand, continued to focus on ethical (prescription) drugs.

During the 1970s the goals of the American core firms in both paths of learning began to converge. The managers of the advertising-intensive sector increasingly realized that moves into product lines beyond the boundaries of drugs and consumer chemicals (SIC 283 and 284) generated smaller revenues—and more important, lower net income—than products within the two classifications. As a result, by the end of the decade the primary goal of the leaders in the advertising-intensive branch had evolved into becoming producers of prescription drugs. By then, however, they were able to reach that goal only by merging with a strong core research-intensive company.

At the same time, the research-intensive firms were learning the same lessons. Income as percentage of revenue was substantially higher in their own core path than in most others, including less research-intensive health-care products. As in chemicals, the less the companies had diversified beyond core pharmaceuticals, the more quickly they returned and the better was their financial performance. More important, those firms that returned quickly to the core path were in a much stronger position to exploit the new learning in microbiology and molecular biology and so to participate in the third wave of new drug-product developments worldwide, which began in the late 1970s and early 1980s.

The 1970s and 1980s: Opportunities and Challenges of the New Technologies

The evolution of the pharmaceutical industry during the 1970s and 1980s differed dramatically from that of industrial chemicals. Whereas the chemical industry encountered limits to growth and began restructuring, the pharmaceutical industry enjoyed new opportunities as advances in scientific learning introduced new technologies to be commercialized for worldwide markets. This new scientific knowledge created two sets of opportunities and with them different challenges.

The first set of opportunities emerged from the new sciences of microbiology and enzymology and the new learning in biochemistry. These combined with a basic new approach in commercializing new drugs—namely, discovery by design instead of a process of trial and error. These advances, among others, were acquired and incorporated by the long-established core companies that continued to rely on the support of the existing nexus that had been so enlarged by the post–World War II therapeutic revolution.

The second set of opportunities was much more revolutionary. The advent of the new scientific discipline of molecular biology, which evolved from the discovery of the molecular structure of DNA in 1953, paved the way for genetic engineering. The new discipline and the new engineering technology required specially trained scientists and their supporting staffs, innovative approaches to drug discoveries, and a fresh set of ingredients and services—that is to say, a new supporting nexus.

These new needs, in turn, generated a wave of startup enterprises in the late 1970s and early 1980s. Together, the products commercialized from the new technology based on the new science created the infrastructure of a new industry—biotechnology. For the long-established core pharmaceutical companies, the resulting challenge has been to incorporate the new technical knowledge into already existing learning bases. For the startups it meant creating from scratch the functional capabilities, especially those of product development and marketing, if they were to profit from producing and selling the drugs they had invented. The newcomers' task was obviously far more challenging than those facing the century-old core companies.

Nevertheless, by the end of the 1980s, a small number of startups had succeeded in building their integrated learning bases. They were able to do so, however, primarily because a federal statute enacted in 1983 granted a seven-year monopoly to enterprises that commercialized drugs to treat relatively uncommon life-threatening conditions. These "orphan drugs," as they were called, thus allowed the startups the necessary time to create fully integrated learning bases. The result was that, by the 1990s, this initial infrastructure underpinning the new biotechnology industry had created a division of labor: the major core pharmaceutical companies focused on commercializing the new genetically engineered drugs for national and international markets, whereas the smaller startups concentrated on high-priced specialty drugs for much smaller markets.

The 1990s: A Decade of Mergers

The challenges of the 1980s—not only those in adapting to new technologies but also those in meeting the competitive entry of the leading chemical companies into pharmaceuticals (as they also were exiting from chemicals)—led to a wave of international mergers in the 1990s.

The first of these mergers, between the American company SmithKline French and the U.K. enterprise Beecham, occurred in 1989 for somewhat different reasons. SmithKline French was reeling from a failed strategy to diversify into medical instruments, while Beecham was the victim of another strategy, that of attempting to finance expensive research in high-technology pharmaceuticals with earnings from the sales of OTC drugs and consumer products.

The ensuing mergers, however, more directly reflected the technological and competitive challenges of the era. Most had three goals in mind: to combine strengths in different geographical markets, to expand the number and potential products in the pipeline, and to capture economies of scale and scope in the commercializing of new products. Such mergers included the aforementioned Novartis (a combination of the Swiss firms Ciba-Geigy and Sandoz) and Aventis (a mega combination of the French American enterprise Rhône-Poulenc Rorer and the German American French firm Hoechst Marion Roussel). Others were GlaxoSmithKline (Glaxo Wellcome and SmithKline Beecham), Pharmacia (the Swedish firm that after acquiring Upjohn merged with Monsanto, then spun off most of Monsanto's activities before merging with Pfizer), and Astra Zeneca (another Swedish firm that merged with the pharmaceutical subsidiary of ICI).

The purpose of this overview has been to introduce the cast of leading players in these two high-technology industries and to provide a chronological narrative of their evolution—their paths of learning—during the twentieth century. This overview reflects the historian's initial concern with the questions of who, when, and where in the story. But it does not consider the how and why questions, which are taken up in Chapters 3–10. Only the details of the competitive interaction, framed in the terms of the three themes central to this book—barriers to entry, strategic boundaries, and the limits to growth—can explain how and why particular companies succeeded or failed. Thus I close each of the following eight chapters by analyzing the paths of learning of the competing enterprises in the light of these three themes.

I begin by reviewing the history of six companies that created the modern chemical industry in the United States.

PART II

The Chemical Industry

CHAPTER 3

The Major
American Companies

This chapter treats what two historians of the chemical industry, Ashish Arora and Alfonso Gambardella, call "all-around" companies that compete in multiple sectors (SIC codes) of the industry.[1] A very small number of the American and European enterprises, six American "all-around" core companies and a somewhat larger number of European companies, were responsible for commercializing the initial wave of chemical products flowing from the new science-based technologies at the end of the nineteenth and the beginning of the twentieth century. These companies, along with most of the petroleum companies listed in Table 1.1, were also responsible for the polymer/petrochemical revolution in the middle decades of the past century.

I focus first on the six American core companies: Du Pont, Dow, Monsanto, American Cyanamid, Union Carbide, and Allied (listed as Allied Signal in Table 1.1). All but the last of these were first movers in commercializing the products of new technologies based on the new learning in chemical science and engineering during the Second Industrial Revolution. By the first decade of the twentieth century, Du Pont was a world leader in producing Alfred Nobel's new high-explosive technology based on nitroglycerin. Dow became the American first mover in employing new electrolytic techniques to produce sodium chloride and synthetic chloroform from brine. American Cyanamid was the first American company to use a German-licensed electrolytic process to make cyanide. And Monsanto created the initial American learning base in the more specialized organic path of synthetic food and flavors, beginning with saccharin and caffeine.

The other two major American core chemical companies—Union Carbide and Allied Chemical—were formed through mergers, the first in 1917 and the second in 1920. The components that evolved into Union Carbide employed the new electrolytic technology to commercialize a variety of basic products such as calcium carbide, acetylene, and liquid oxygen, as well as more complex related products such as welding and cutting apparatus and metal alloys. Of the five firms that merged into Allied Chemical, however, only one served as a first mover in a new technology, which it did by becoming the U.S. licensee of the revolutionary Solvay process for producing soda ash—the basic ingredient in glass, the bleaching of textiles, and the production of ammonia and other chemicals. Allied Chemical long remained the weakest of the six majors companies in terms of competitive success.

In the 1920s these firms became multisectored by commercializing products of related technologies, either through internal investment or acquisition. I begin to trace the evolving paths of learning at Du Pont, the nation's oldest major chemical company and, throughout the twentieth century, its largest.

E. I. du Pont de Nemours and Company:
The American Leader in Product Development

E. I. du Pont de Nemours established his gunpowder company on the banks of Brandywine Creek near Wilmington, Delaware in 1802. For the next hundred years it remained a typical family firm, with du Ponts serving as both managers and owners. The firm produced gunpowder for small arms and military armaments, and later manufactured explosives used for land-clearing, mining, canal and railroad building, and urban construction, which it produced in the traditional manner by mixing saltpeter, sulfur, and charcoal.

The modern explosives industry began when Alfred Nobel commercialized dynamite based on a nitroglycerine technology. In 1880, well after Nobel established British Dynamite (later renamed Nobel Explosives) in Scotland, Lammot du Pont belatedly entered the dynamite trade by forming the Repauno Chemical Company. Repauno was financed by E. I. du Pont de Nemours and its leading friendly competitor, Laflin & Rand Powder Company. As their dynamite production expanded, the two older firms founded the Eastern Dynamite Company to combine their capabilities (including those of Repauno). Then, on the death of Du Pont president Eugene du Pont in 1902, the remaining five partners, all du Ponts, decisively searched for his successor. Four of the five were too old and together they considered the youngest, Alfred, too inexperienced and erratic to take over their enterprise. They decided to sell out to Laflin & Rand. Alfred then phoned two cousins—Pierre and Coleman—both of whom were young yet experienced businessmen. They agreed to purchase Du Pont. A merger of Du Pont and Laflin & Rand followed.[2]

With Alfred in tow, Pierre and Coleman immediately reorganized the American explosives industry, much as John D. Rockefeller had been doing in oil and Andrew Carnegie in steel. They did so through an exchange of stock that brought 70 percent of the nation's production facilities into the Du Pont enterprise. They then concentrated production facilities into a small number of large plants strategically located with regard to suppliers and markets; created a national distributing and marketing organization; established a central purchasing department, a central engineering department, and one of the nation's first research and development units; and built a multistoried headquarters in Wilmington to house the executive committee of senior managers and their staffs. To ensure their plants a steady flow of supplies, the company built its own glycerin plants, and then acquired and operated nitrate beds in Chile. Its output grew as the market for explosives in mining, railroad, and urban construction boomed. This dominance, however, prompted an antitrust suit that led in 1912 to the spinning off of the former Laflin & Rand facilities and other properties into two new competitors, Hercules Powder Company and Atlas Powder Company.

World War I precipitated the transformation of Du Pont from a single to a multisectored enterprise. The company swiftly built new facilities for the production of propellants (smokeless powder) and military explosives, first for the Allies and then for the U.S. military forces. Production rose from 8.4 million pounds of propellants in 1914 to 455 million pounds in April 1917. The number of employees and salaried workers as well as capital expenditures and profits grew proportionately.

A New Strategy and New Structure

In 1917 the executive committee (all full-time managers) of the company's board of directors began planning for the postwar world. Their initial strategic decision was that no existing industry could fully use their huge new product-specific wartime physical facilities. On the other hand, several new product lines could be based on "our organization," that is, on the company's human technological, functional, and managerial capabilities. These were industries whose production was based on nitrocellulose technology, including paints and varnishes (SIC 2851), pyroxylin (celluloid), artificial leather (fabricoid), and artificial fibers (rayon) (SIC 2823). In addition, the company upgraded its capabilities in organic dyes (SIC 2865) and inorganic ammonia (SIC 2819), product lines whose commercializing it had embarked on to meet wartime shortages. (For an explanation of the SIC codes, see Chapter 2, note 1.)

To further enhance Du Pont's abilities to market and continue to develop new products, the senior executives set up a pioneering management structure with a separate integrated learning base for each major product line. The management of these autonomous departments was responsible for production, marketing, research, and profit and loss; that is, they were accountable for building and maintaining the company's capabilities in their related but different product paths. Corporate headquarters included the senior executives, who were now relieved of their day-to-day operating duties, and a corporate staff. That staff comprised the financial officers—treasurer and comptroller—and advisory offices including research and development, legal, traffic, personnel, and, in time, public relations. This was one of the earliest multidivisional structures, which enabled an enterprise to commercialize multiple products from major technologies and so to benefit from the economies of scope as well as from scale. By World War II all the major chemical companies with the exception of Allied had followed a strategy of related diversication and adopted comparable structures.[3]

During the 1920s Du Pont's growth rested on commercializing products from its inherited nitrocellulose-related technologies. The paint and finishes department (SIC 2851) developed fast-drying Duco enamel to meet the demands of the swiftly expanding automobile industry. In pigments (SIC 2816), Du Pont made the move from lithophone to titanium dioxide. In the rayon department (SIC 2823), the commercialization of rayon and closely related cellophane and film were advanced by collaborating with French pioneers. As these products came on-stream, Du Pont purchased the foreign companies' minority interest.

However, in the paths entered during wartime shortages—dyes and ammonia—Du Pont's success in commercializing new products was much slower. A joint venture with Lazote, Inc. permitted the company to use the Claude process for high-pressure production of synthetic nitrates and ammonia (SIC 2873). By 1929 Du Pont accounted for 40 percent of the synthetic ammonia and 30 percent of the synthetic nitrates used primarily in agricultural chemicals (287) produced in the United States. Nevertheless, the ammonia department became profitable only in the early 1930s. In dyes (SIC 2865), Du Pont experienced even greater difficulty than in ammonia because of competition from a revived German industry.

Acquisitions rounded out Du Pont's multisectored enterprises. In 1928 it purchased the Grasselli Chemical Company, which provided heavy chemicals used in the manufacture of Du Pont's inorganic products, thus ensuring a reliable and steady source of supply, and also enhanced its strength in pigments, particularly titanium dioxide. Finally, in 1930, the acquisition of Roessler & Haaslacher, the U.S. subsidiary of the German leader in inorganic chemicals, DEGUSSA, gained Du Pont entry into electrochemicals (SIC 281) and a potential base for the production of agricultural herbicides and fungicides (SIC 2879). By the coming of the Great Depression, Du Pont had commercialized profitable products in all seven of the SIC codes allocated to the chemical industry.[4]

The Polymer/Petrochemical Revolution Begins: A Shift from D to R

During the 1920s the new Du Pont products were developed from existing technologies initially commercialized in the Rhine valley industrial complex. Those of the 1930s, on the other hand, came from new technologies created by the company's central research establishment. In 1935 Charles M. A. Stine, head of central research, working with the product-development units of the operating divisions, decided to concentrate on the search for new products in three principal areas—physical chemistry, colloid resins, and polymerization (primarily for manmade fibers and rubber products—SIC 2821 and 2822). The initial products of the new polymer technology were nylon and neoprene. Nylon—a manmade silk—was introduced in 1938 and quickly discovered a profitable market, with clothing manufacturers producing nylon stockings in 1940. On the other hand, neoprene, a high-strength synthetic rubber, was only barely profitable by 1939. After Pearl Harbor, however, nylon found only limited uses, for example, in parachutes. But the demand for neoprene soared.

Thus, even before the war, Du Pont had created first-mover advantages based on new technology and commercializing products from it. Du Pont, however, did not participate in the massive wartime projects to develop high-octane aviation fuel and synthetic rubber—projects that spawned commercialization of many petrochemical and polymer/petrochemical products. Instead, its principal government program was the Manhattan Project— the building of new nuclear bomb plants at Hanford, Washington and Oak Ridge, Tennessee—projects that did not foster large-scale chemical capabilities. By 1945, nonetheless, Du Pont had begun to produce basic polymers, particularly polyethylene; but as the historians at Du Pont research and development note, "R&D efforts were directed at adapting and improving existing Du Pont products for wartime applications."[5]

Understandably, Crawford Greenewalt, who became Du Pont's president in 1948, defined the company's postwar strategy as one that "would marshal its resources to do what most other companies could not. From these efforts, 'new nylons' would emerge." Such products would evolve from the work of the central research laboratory and the product-development units of the divisions. As a result, Du Pont invested little effort in commercializing intermediate chemicals and plastics on which polymer technologies rested. In implementing this product-development strategy, the company sustained its long-held policy of not competing with its customers, thus concentrating on industrial rather than consumer products. Moreover, it dropped its prewar policy of relying on acquisitions to assist in moving into new product lines; it would now depend on its own technical and development capabilities. This strategy reflected, in part, the strong antitrust thrust by the government in the immediate postwar years, a legacy of the New Deal.

The Postwar Polymer/Petrochemical Boom

During the same years that witnessed the explosive expansion of polymer products, the "engine" of Du Pont's growth was first synthetic fibers and then plastics. Its prewar introduction of nylon ensured it powerful first-mover advantages in fibers. The production of nylon had reached 2.5 billion pounds by 1960. In the 1950s, the fiber department applied its capabilities learned from the commercializing of nylon to bring forth Dacron and Orlon. Dacron, a polyester fiber, was initially considered a substitute for wool. Blending well with cotton, it gave Du Pont comparable first-mover advantages in the new wash-and-wear market. Orlon, originally developed for awnings and window shades, quickly discovered a larger and more profitable market in socks and sweaters. By 1960 the company produced 1.9 billion pounds of each product. At the same time, Du Pont began to phase out its cellulose-based rayon products. The practice of replacing old products with new ones commercialized from the learning and profits of the previous one was comparable to the successful strategies in consumer electronics and computer industries I previously described in *Inventing the Electronic Century*. That virtuous strategy became the keystone of Du Pont's postwar competitive strength.[6]

In plastics, after the consolidation of the prewar plastic and ammonia departments, Du Pont introduced a broad line of polymer-based plastics and materials (SIC 2821), produced in somewhat lower volume than in fabrics. These included nylon-based, high-performance engineered plastics that replaced metals in machinery, motor vehicles, and appliances. Among the most successful were Deralin, also called "synthetic stone," and Teflon, which was initially used for insulating the wiring of jet engines, space missiles, computer cables, and other electrical/electronic devices, as well as in the chemical industry itself, and then later in cookware and clothing. Another plastic Du Pont produced was Mylar, a polyester film (discovered in the development of Orlon), whose resistance, insulating properties, and strength rendered it a base for photographic film, magnetic tapes, capacitor dialectics, and packaging products. Although Du Pont's other prewar polymer product, neoprene, was suitable for tire production, its high cost led the elastomer chemical department to develop a number of specialty rubber products rather than a high-volume tire material. In these two divisions, Du Pont became a leader in all of the four-digit industries in SIC 282 (plastic materials and synthetics).[7]

In addition to exploiting the potential of polymer chemistry, Du Pont continued to commercialize new products in the divisions that had created their integrated learning bases before World War II. It did so in chemicals, including ammonia and methyl, and also in paints, finishes, and nonporous fabrics. After World War II, Du Pont began to build on its earlier potential in the production of insecticides and other agricultural chemicals (SIC 2879). Its innovative selective-weed-control products enabled it to capture 20 percent of the U.S. herbicide market by 1960.[8]

Redefining the Strategic Boundaries of the Firm: The Shift from R to D

In 1956 the Du Pont executive committee decided not to expand its output of basic petrochemicals, olefins, aromatics, and basic polymers, even though it produced these chemicals during the war and had pioneered in the commercializing of polyethylene. The reason for the committee's decision was that the rapidly increasing competition from Dow, Union Carbide, and major oil companies was driving down prices and profits. Nevertheless, the committee decided that it should remain in basic polymers because "it provided an entré for Du Pont into all kinds of many lucrative markets for polyethylene (PP) and other plastics." Therefore, it continued to work on commercializing new high-performance linear high-density polyethylene (HDPE) and polypropylene (PP).[9]

Until the mid-1960s Du Pont's profit margin was twice that of the other chemical companies. Nevertheless, by the late 1950s, the swift growth of the polymer-based products was leveling off. With the rapid expansion of production capacity, competition increasingly intensified, not only from long-established U.S. competitors but also from revived European ones and, most of all, from the large-scale move of oil companies into petrochemicals (Chapters 5 and 6). At the same time, the number of new products commercialized by Du Pont began to decline.

In 1959 the executive committee responded to the changing situation by undertaking two strategic moves. One was to concentrate more on overseas markets by reorganizing and enlarging the foreign relations department. By 1963 foreign sales accounted for 18 percent of total sales as compared with 5 percent in 1939. The other tactic was to search for product lines beyond those in the broad SIC 28 classification that could utilize the individual or combined capabilities of the company's several different learning bases.[10]

To implement the second move, the committee created a new-ventures program to reside within the reorganized development department and to work closely with the executive committee. Such fresh opportunities proved difficult to identify. One of the initiatives was to commercialize analytical and process instruments that the company could produce for its own use. Another was to develop an office copier. The products the program commercialized were unable to compete with those of existing manufacturers— the office copier in the short run and the scientific instruments in the long run.

The most ambitious project of the new-ventures program was to enter the home-construction market with mass-produced, low-maintenance housing exteriors, roofing, sidings, trims, windows, and doors, supplemented by a line of interior furnishings. The products developed were of high quality, but they could not be produced on a scale that warranted major investment. Housing equipment was not yet a mass-market industry. The company's existing functional capabilities in production, distribution, and marketing proved insufficient to provide the competitive strengths required to enter the home-construction business. By 1969 all agreed that the continuation of the new-ventures program into what appeared to be related products resulted in a failure. In this way, Du Pont was one of the first American industrials to recognize that its strategic options were limited by the potential of its existing organizational capabilities. In particular, leadership understood that the company could not succeed in areas outside the strategic boundaries defined by its existing integrated learning bases. Moreover, its managers learned the lesson at relatively little cost.[11]

During the same period of the 1960s, the learning bases of the autonomous operating departments continued to develop a stream of new profitable products within their respective paths of learning. In fabrics, Lycra spandex fiber, an extremely strong and elastic fiber, met its initial goal of $30 million annual revenues by 1969. By 1972 it enjoyed a return on investment of over 30 percent. Lycra was followed by Kevlar fabric, which had four times the strength of steel, and then by new paper-like fabrics including Tyvek and Typar. In engineering plastics, Zytel ST replaced Mylar. In photographic products, a new coloring process produced Cronar, a polyester film, which became the market leader in its niche. Other departments enjoyed comparable success.[12]

By 1970 Du Pont's senior managers, having appreciated the limits of their corporate capabilities for new-product development, redefined the role of corporate R&D in their industry, as they had lost their "strong faith" that "research, particularly fundamental research, would be the salvation of the company." They now understood that the postwar product-specific technical, functional, and managerial capabilities developed in the several operating departments clearly served as a more reliable source for the improvement and commercializing of new products and processes than did basic research or even centrally planned, related-product diversification into new markets.

With this lesson in mind, the company reduced its expenditures for basic research. Its overall R&D outlays as a percentage of sales dropped from 7.1 percent in 1970 to 4.7 percent in 1975 and 3.6 percent in 1980. The larger proportion of these funds devolved onto departments, such as photographic film and biochemicals, that were utilizing their particular technological and marketing skills to commercialize products for new markets. Strategically, Du Pont's managers were correct, for in chemicals no new transforming technology of the 1970s and 1980s appeared comparable to those in organic and inorganic chemicals during the 1880s and 1890s, and in petrochemicals in the mid-twentieth century.[13]

Redefining the Boundaries of the Enterprise during the Crisis Years

Instead of continued growth, then, the 1970s signaled years of crisis for Du Pont. Difficult times began in 1973 with the OPEC embargo but culminated after 1979 with the advent of the Iranian revolution. At Du Pont, the apex of the crisis prompted a short and then more sustained response. The first was to acquire a relatively stable source of raw materials. The second involved a long-term restructuring of product portfolio in order to concentrate on the company's distinctive capabilities.

The company's first response led in 1981 to the acquisition of Conoco. As the oil crisis deepened, Du Pont had collaborated with Conoco in joint exploration for gas and oil. When the oil company faced an unfriendly takeover by the Bronfmans of the Canadian distilled liquor company Seagram, Du Pont acquired control. As the oil crisis eased, Conoco proved to be a profitable enterprise whose revenues helped to stabilize the earning fluctuations in the two very different industries of chemicals and petroleum. Du Pont successfully maintained profitability in both by adhering to distinctly separate sets of learning bases in each of the broad paths of learning[14]

In 1982, Du Pont made its second response, initiating its strategy of moving out of basic polymers, expanding existing and commercializing new higher value-added, polymer-based end-products, and, at the same time, maintaining lines commercialized in the 1920s where it still enjoyed first-mover advantages. In 1982 and 1983 a number of the older, less profitable, more specialized lines were sold. In 1984, large-scale divestitures began.

As Conoco's petrochemical output specialized in polyvinyl chloride, vinyl chloride monomers, and related products that were not intermediates used by Du Pont, the company decided to spin these off. It did so in a $600 million leveraged buyout transaction with the Vista Chemical Company, which was headed by Gordon M. Cain, the manager of Conoco's petrochemical division. It then disposed of its relatively small vinyl acetate and ethylene resin business and its 50 percent share of a polymer venture with Mitsubishi Chemicals. Over the next year Du Pont sold off or shut down a number of individual plants, including the sale of three HDPE plants and one ethylene plant in Texas to the newly formed Cain Chemical. It addition to shifting out of commodity polymers, Du Pont disposed of its less profitable end-products, including its plastic packaging to Amelen, its urethane rubber business to

Uniroyal, its consumer paint to Clorox, some of its pigments to Switzerland's Ciba-Geigy, and some of its industrial finishes to Whitaker.[15]

Next came acquisitions, funded in part by the divestitures, that reinforced the learning base in the paths that the firm had long followed. In films and fibers it purchased Exxon's carbon fiber business in 1984, Exxon's film composites activities in 1985, and Hercules's olefin fiber carpets in 1989. Later, in 1992, it traded its acrylic assets to ICI for the latter's nylon business, plus $41 million. In paints and finishes Du Pont obtained Ford's North American automotive paint division in 1986, followed by a joint venture with ICI to expand the same market in Europe, and one with Kami Paint to do so in Japan and East Asia. In agricultural chemicals it acquired Shell's agricultural chemicals division in 1986, and later in 1992 collaborated with Shell to develop specialized insecticides. For Du Pont, sustaining its technical and functional capabilities in long-established paths in which it was a competitive leader remained a basic strategy.[16]

The Entry into Pharmaceuticals

Du Pont also entertained a third response to the crisis of the late 1970s and early 1980s—diversification into pharmaceuticals, the one classification in SIC 28 where new transforming technologies were still emerging. The company had dabbled in pharmaceuticals from the 1950s on, first developing Symmetrel, an antiviral drug, but lacking marketing capabilities or experience with FDA procedures, the venture was hardly a success. Next, it acquired a small drug company, Endo, which produced an anticoagulant with annual sales of only $20 million. Again earnings were minimal, even though biology and biochemistry were becoming central research's largest single activity. In 1979, pharmaceuticals represented only 2 percent of Du Pont's total earnings.

In the early 1980s, Edward Jefferson, a leading researcher who became CEO in 1981, made a determined effort to enter the prescription drug path of SIC 284. He introduced plans to triple the number of life science researchers and build major new laboratories. The undertaking was to be roughly divided between plant-related and human-related health sciences. These investments were followed in 1986 by a move into the production of analytical and surgical equipment through the acquisition of two smaller companies and the medical divisions of two major companies.[17]

Profits from these new businesses emerged slowly. The Du Pont executives quickly realized once again the need for radically different development, production, and, especially, marketing capabilities in the commercial-izing of pharmaceuticals. To enhance these capabilities, Du Pont in 1989 signed a marketing agreement with the highly successful pharmaceutical leader, Merck, to employ Merck's development skills to commercialize Du Pont's successful research into new components of high blood pressure and heart disease drugs, and to have Du Pont learn by doing by taking over the marketing of two of Merck's most successful drugs. By 1992 all of Du Pont's pharmaceutical activities were folded into a Du Pont–Merck joint venture, as told briefly in Chapter 7.

Du Pont's Product Lines in the 1990s: Building on Great Traditional Strengths

In the fall of 1992 Du Pont's research chief emphasized the importance of maintaining the businesses in which "we have great strengths." Slightly more than 80 percent of the R&D budget of $1.3 billion was directed toward supporting existing business, with a renewed emphasis on improving pro-duction processes as well as the development of innovative products. The re-maining 20 percent went to seeking new closely related technologies or fresh business opportunities. Of this last, about half was allocated to central research, the rest to the operating divisions.[18]

In this way, Du Pont in the early 1990s continued to focus on its long-es-tablished lines, those commercialized in the years before World War II and those it commercialized during the polymer/petrochemical revolution. By 1994 Du Pont still operated as an oil as well as a chemical enterprise, pre-serving the management of the two different sectors' products as separate, autonomous entities. Its sales that year were just under $40 billion and its operating income was $4.4 billion. Conoco accounted for 43 percent of sales but only for 24 percent of income. Of Du Pont's chemical business, fibers represented 17 percent of total sales and 24 percent of income; other poly-mer products 16 percent and 24 percent, respectively; chemicals (intermedi-ates, fluorochemicals, specialty chemicals, and pigments) 10 percent and 14 percent; and other businesses 14 percent and 12 percent. The latter included agricultural chemicals as well as electronics, imaging, and medical products.

Thus, Du Pont's profits and its primary competitive strength resided in the product lines whose organizational capabilities had been shaped during the dramatic years of new product development as the polymer/petrochemical technology unfolded. The second major source of income and competitive strength derived from the capabilities developed in the 1920s and 1930s. In fibers, they rested on the nylon and polyester of the 1950s and the next generation of specialties, including Lycra, Nome, and Kelvin. In plastics, they came primarily from engineering plastics, including elastomers (such as neoprene) and other resins, fluoropolymers (including Teflon), and specialty ethylene polymers and performance film, including Mylar and Cronar for color film.

Nevertheless, products commercialized before World War II also remained profit makers. This was especially true of automotive finishes and other automotive products. In chemicals, the leading revenue producer remained titanium dioxide, in which Du Pont in 1992—after seventy years of production—still held 53 percent of the North American market and 21 percent of the world market. So too, agricultural chemicals, the most profitable business listed under "diversified products," originated in the 1920s and stayed profitable in the 1970s and 1980s. On the other hand, electronics and imaging systems often reported losses and were being spun off, while medical products, and particularly the Du Pont–Merck venture, had yet to prove themselves.

Du Pont's experience helps to define the path-dependency of long-term corporate financial success. Long-established learned organizational capabilities function as the most durable base for maintaining competitive advantage in existing product lines. At the same time, they provide the soundest base for commercializing new ones.[19]

Postscript

The initial plan of this book was to concentrate on the histories of the individual companies until 1993, the date of the listings of the top fifty chemical companies as in Table 1.1. Nevertheless, the events of the past few years require an update to the story just told, for Du Pont quietly cast off its major remaining nonchemical activities—namely, oil and pharmaceuticals. So it entered the twenty-first century still as a multisectored enterprise, with the product lines it had commercialized while shaping the Industrial (twentieth) Century before the chemical crisis of the late 1970s and early 1980s.

In 1998 Du Pont's top managers disposed of Conoco by first selling 30 percent of its stock for $4.4 billion, in what was the largest public stock offering in history. The firm had already acquired in 1995 the shares still held by Seagrams. The remaining 70 percent was then offered to the Du Pont stockholders.

The year before DuPont continued to expand its long-established product lines by acquiring ICI's polyester and titanium dioxide businesses for $3 billion as part of a major three-company deal, in which ICI acquired Unilever's specialty chemicals businesses (described in Chapter 5). Additionally in the late 1990s, Du Pont purchased several operations to bolster its existing lines in pigments and coatings, polyester resin intermediates, and agricultural chemicals. The biggest of these deals by far was the $9.4 billion acquisition of Pioneer Hy-Bred International, the world's largest producer of commercial seeds, which used genetic research to boost crop yields.

Meanwhile, with an eye still on pharmaceuticals, in 1997 Du Pont purchased Merck's 50 percent of their joint venture. But despite its carefully planned entry into pharmaceuticals, Du Pont's relatively new learned capabilities proved insufficient to ensure its long-term competitiveness. In 2001 Du Pont sold its pharmaceutical activities to Bristol-Myers Squibb for $7.8 billion in cash.[20]

In this manner, Du Pont, once a world leader in new-product development, entered the electronic-based twenty-first century (and the third century of its existence) by returning to its strong foundation in specialty chemicals. That is, its new chemicals were commercialized by the product-development units in its several integrated learning bases, working closely with its corporate R&D organization. The company's great strength remained in commercializing the products based on scientific learning, particularly from the middle decades of the twentieth century. The acquisition of Pioneer Hy-Bred International, however, signals its intention to explore the commercial potential of the new science of genetic engineering in the production of agricultural chemicals.

By the opening of the new century, Du Pont's only remaining multi-sectored U.S. chemical competitor was Dow Chemical Company. Du Pont played a critical role in creating the barriers to entry to the chemical industry through product innovation. Dow did so primarily through process innovation.

Dow Chemical Company: The U.S. Leader in Process Development

From their beginnings, the product lines of Dow and Du Pont evolved along entirely different paths of learning. After it moved beyond the nitrocellulose path in the 1920s, Du Pont became a multisectored core chemical company primarily through acquisition and then commercializing of high-end products—paints, pigments, agricultural chemicals, rayon, and solvents—from different technologies for different sets of markets. In contrast, Dow became a multisectored core company primarily through commercializing of basic chemicals—bromides, chlorides, magnesiums, silicon, and the like. During the boom years of the polymer/petrochemical revolution, Du Pont pioneered in commercializing polymer technology; Dow gained dominance in commercializing petrochemicals.

Pioneering in Bromide and Chlorine Chemistry

Dow became the first mover in the United States in the electrolytic techniques pioneered by the Belgian producer Solvay of producing chemicals, which became possible only with the advent of the modern electric dynamo in the 1880s. In 1897, after five years of perfecting an electrolytic process for extracting bromine and chlorine from brine, Herbert Dow formed the Dow Chemical Company in Midland, Michigan. Its initial products were chlorine-based bleaching powder and caustic soda. In 1900 the company expanded this path of learning by producing sodium chloride, which in turn was the base for commercializing a synthetic chloroform (SIC 2812), which had a wide variety of uses. That commercializing process generated carbon tetrachloride, a base for insecticides and agricultural chemicals. The production of sodium chloride was next used to make magnesium chloride and then calcium chloride.[21]

During the shortage of German-made chemicals created by World War I, Dow turned to the production of phenol (SIC 2865) and other organic chemicals for military explosives. Although these plants were shut down at the war's end, the experience provided an initial learning base in organic chemistry and thus resulted in the development of chlorabenzyl-phenol used for biocides and agricultural chemicals. During the war, Dow also experimented in fashioning magnesium from brine through an electrolytic process of production comparable to that used in making chlorine. By 1920 Dow was producing and selling magnesium.[22]

Becoming a Multisectored Enterprise

Throughout the 1920s Dow continued to expand into products that derived from their process technology learning bases. By 1930 it was the nation's leading producer of calcium chloride, magnesium chloride, and then magnesium compounds (all SIC 2819). By then, too, it had acquired a near monopoly in the production of basic magnesium. During the later 1930s process development in magnesium products led to comparable commercializing of silicon, which, in turn, prompted in 1942 the formation of Dow Corning, a joint venture with Corning Glass Works, to produce silicones and related products (see Chapter 4).

During the 1930s Dow had become the most prolific first mover in commercializing manmade nonferrous metals. That achievement, in turn, relied on new processes that required innovation in the design and building of processing plants. These processing and plant-building capabilities were essential to Dow's accomplishments in commercializing petrochemicals.

Entering Petrochemicals

Dow's initial entry in the 1930s into petrochemicals occurred in the commercializing of chemicals used to increase the yields of gas and oil fields. Success in this market provided a rationale for creating in 1932 a new division—Dowell—to produce and sell these products. Of more enduring importance was the formation in 1933 of a 50–50 joint venture with the Ethyl Corporation, a joint venture of General Motors and Standard Oil of New Jersey (Exxon), the producer of the recently developed "no knock" gasoline, to extract bromide from sea water in a plant on the North Carolina coast in enough volume to meet Ethyl's high-volume requirements. That venture, in turn, became the learning platform for the construction of a much larger facility at Freeport, Texas, which would use the same technology to produce a range of feedstocks, intermediates, and polymerized plastics.[23]

During the 1930s, such process development encouraged the commercializing of chemical products efficiently produced from oil and natural gas. In 1932, the upshot of experimentation to improve benzene was the commercializing of liquid styrene, a monomer. Then, in 1937, work "in controlling the styrene production process with precise accuracy" resulted in the commercializing of a new versatile product, Styron, of which Styrofoam is one of its many end-products. In the meantime, investigations in chloride chemistry brought forth vinylidene chloride, which paved the way for another versatile product, Saran. It could be extruded into pipes and tubing, injected into molded parts, made into sheets of varying thickness (the household Saran Wrap, for example), or woven into fabric. In the same way, work on ethyl cellulose yielded Etocal, a cellulose product with foil and coating uses. It was followed by Methocel, which found thousands of uses as a thick-ener, binder, film-former, and suspending agent. These innovations ex-panded Dow's output in industrial plastics (SIC 2821) and provided an entry into the more advertising-intensive consumer goods path that included new plastic wraps and bags, as well as household cleaners, detergents, and stain removers (SIC 284). This path in consumer products became and remained for the company a major revenue source for the rest of the century.[24]

The differences in Du Pont's and Dow's contributions to the demands of World War II offer dramatic testimony to their different ways of commer-cializing new technologies. At Du Pont the technology commercialized in polymer science resulted from its own research laboratories and was little affected by the new wartime demands. Dow, on the other hand, pioneered technologies that served a completely different market in commercializ-ing the new polymer/petrochemical technology (reviewed in Chapter 6). Dow's giant plants on the Gulf Coast at Freeport and Velasco produced—from brine, petroleum, and natural gas—vast amounts of feedstocks and intermediates for petrochemicals including styrene, polystyrene, ethylene, ethylene dibromide, ethylene glycol, vinylidene chloride, magnesium chlo-ride, and finally, commodity polymers such as high- and low-density poly-propylene. In addition, Dow provided styrene for a synthetic rubber plant that it built and operated at the request of the Canadian government in Sarnia, Canada; this plant marked the beginning of Dow's Canadian subsid-iary. No other chemical company benefited more from the polymer/petro-chemical revolution than did Dow.[25]

Riding the Postwar Polymer/Petrochemical Boom

In the 1950s Dow concentrated on maintaining its momentum in the high-volume production of olefins, aromatics, and other basic petrochemicals and polymer plastics. It expanded the Freeport and Velasco plants. Then, in 1958, a still larger plant near Baton Rouge, Louisiana came on-stream, using the new "single train technology," which had a far greater minimum ef-ficient scale and much lower per unit costs than the existing plants. To en-sure a stable flow of oil and natural gas into these works, Dow integrated backward, purchasing 265,000 square miles of oil and gas holdings, primar-ily in Texas and Louisiana, and completing a five-hundred-mile pipeline. This commitment to vertical integration so critical in these scale-dependent process technologies long remained a Dow heritage.[26]

As Joseph Bower has pointed out, Dow's postwar strategy of expansion based on commercializing these new basic technologies was well defined and very successful. The company's goal was "to be the world's largest and most profitable producer of commodity chemicals and plastics based on low-cost leadership and aggressive marketing in the businesses in which it competed. Low cost, in turn, was achieved by vertical integration, technical excellence, near or maximum scale, and leveraged financing, all on a world-wide basis." Particularly innovative was the use of debt in financing the swift expansion at home and overseas.[27]

In the early postwar years, according to historian E. N. Brandt, Dow was "totally absorbed in its domestic expansion" and "barely aware of a world beyond North America. Its sales abroad amounted to only 5 percent." The company showed more interest in foreign markets after the mid-1950s. Its overseas growth was carried out both by direct investment and by joint ventures with foreign firms, but rarely by acquisition.

Dow, which had successfully pioneered joint technology-sharing instruments in the 1930s, undertook joint ventures overseas, beginning in 1954 with the founding of Asahi-Dow in Japan. In 1954 another joint venture was formed with Britain's Distillers (Dow purchased Distillers' 50 percent in 1968), followed by one with Germany's BASF in 1957—an unsuccessful effort to enter polymer-based fibers—and with France's Pechiney in 1959. Yet another between France's Schlumberger and Dowell furnished oil and gas field services outside of the United States. At the same time, Dow made large direct investments in plants and in distribution, marketing, and development facilities in the Netherlands, Greece, Italy, Yugoslavia, Brazil, and South Korea. To provide a European financial clearinghouse for its transactions, Dow obtained a 40 percent interest in a Dutch bank. Then, in 1965, it created the Dow Banking Corporation in Zurich, Switzerland, where it had established its overseas headquarters.[28]

During the 1960s and 1970s Dow continued to concentrate on its basic strategy of growth through internal development. As Brandt stresses, "The great bulk of Dow's postwar expansion was built on the company's own products. In an era where many of the nation's largest firms were growing by merger, Dow did little of this." It maintained and enhanced its much smaller learning paths in downstream end-products and consumer goods. It did make, however, an initial move into pharmaceuticals with the acquisition of Allied Laboratories in December 1960, and then acquired two small companies that produced the Salk polio vaccine and other vaccines; Dow thereby had an international presence in pharmaceuticals. In the 1970s Dow expanded its oil and gas properties in the U.S. Southwest and the Middle East. It made some effort to improve its end-products, and to cut back on its high-density polyethylene and its government business. Nevertheless, in 1979, 85 percent of Dow's businesses remained in basic petrochemicals and commodity plastics. By then Dow's managers had decided to make a sudden shift in basic strategy.[29]

Reorientation: Redefining the Strategic Boundaries of the Firm during the Crisis

In 1978—after the first energy crisis but before the second—thirty of Dow's senior managers met for a three-day retreat to define a new strategy and a new organizational structure to support it. After quickly agreeing that the market for basic petrochemicals had become overcrowded and that the future lay in moving to higher value-added products, they set a goal of having 50 percent of Dow's revenues generated by the latter by 1987. The leading prospects for such products were pharmaceuticals, consumer products, and agricultural chemicals. The transformation would be carried out primarily by acquisition, representing another fundamental change in strategy, and was to be financed in part by the sale of the lower value-added commodity polymers and basic petrochemical lines. To implement this global strategy, Dow management reshaped its operating structure and created worldwide product divisions for the higher value-added lines. At the same time, management increased corporate control, particularly over the allocation of resources, in the other lines.[30]

In a major shift, Dow—like Du Pont, Monsanto, and American Cyanamid—targeted the pharmaceutical industry as a major growth area. Dow's leaders believed that the company's twenty years of experience at Allied Laboratories provided a modicum of capabilities in that path. In 1981, in order to obtain the functional capabilities that it lacked, Dow acquired, for $260 million worth of common stock, the Merrell Drug Division of Richardson-Vicks, a pioneer in the commercializing of nonsedative antihistamines. That same year Dow formed a joint venture with Otsuka Pharmaceutical of Japan to market jointly in Japan and the United States, thus acquiring a marketing organization in Asia to supplement the small one already existing in Europe. In 1986 ensued the acquisition of an 84 percent interest in Funai Pharmaceuticals, another Japanese firm. As the Merrell-Dow pharmaceutical division expanded worldwide, it began to acquire a reputation for strong marketing capabilities.[31]

Dow's primary shift, however, was a retreat from its massive commitment to basic petrochemicals. It began in 1982 with the sale of portions of its oil and gas properties to Apache Petroleum for $402 million and in the following year to Dome Petroleum of Canada for $88 million. Next came the divestiture of its overseas joint ventures in commodities: its 50 percent holdings of Asahi-Dow Chemical for $231 million in 1982 and its share of the Korean venture for $60 million in 1983, followed by comparable sales of joint ventures in Saudi Arabia and Yugoslavia. In 1984 it sold its 50 percent share of the Dowell Schlumberger joint venture to the French company. Then, in 1986, it divested itself of its foreign banking and financial services. At the same time, it disposed of its original bromide business. In commodity plastics, however, Dow decided to shut down its plants rather than sell them off, as Du Pont did. Indeed, in 1985, the company wrote off $600 million in plants and related assets, and continued to reduce personnel.

Starting in 1985 Dow undertook the acquisitions, funded in part by these divestitures, to expand its consumer and its specialty industrial chemicals businesses. In that year, Dow acquired two enterprises: the Terize Division of Morton Thiokol and the Italian firm Dompak. The first, a manufacturer and marketer of home cleaners and other household products, complemented Dow's existing line of Saran Wrap and other household packaging films, cleaners, and detergents. The second afforded Dow a presence in that market in Europe. In the same year, it made purchases in specialty engineered plastics with the acquisition of three polymer-based businesses, that of the Upjohn Company, Film Tec, and United Agriseeds. The first delivered a product that was essential to obtaining a worldwide presence in polyurethane foams; the second gained access for the company to a new technology for spiral-bound membranes for water and fluid purification and separation; and the third provided initial entry into crop genetics and agricultural biotechnology. Next, in 1986, Dow purchased for $50 million Bromide Products, a leader in super-hard ceramics technology, and Haeger and Kaesner, a German manufacturer of specialty chemicals. In nearly all these acquisitions, Dow's existing learning bases that had been created in the 1920s and 1930s provided essential technological and functional capabilities for further new-product development.

By the end of 1986 the strategy envisioned at the 1978 meeting had been fully implemented. By 1987 basic chemicals and commodity plastics still accounted for 48 percent of revenues (35 percent from chemicals and 17 percent from plastics), and 52 percent of revenues came from higher value-added end-products (29 percent from industrial and 19 percent from consumer specialties). In undertaking this strategy, the company focused on worldwide markets. By 1991, 48 percent of its sales were in the United States, and 52 percent of sales and 39 percent of operating income came from foreign countries.[32]

Three years earlier, in 1988, Dow's managers had defined its new strategy more explicitly. The company would reduce its commitment to basic polymer hydrocarbons (ethylene, propylene, butadiene), thus redefining the boundaries between its capabilities and those of the petroleum companies. It would then focus on three sectors: basic chemicals, industrial specialties (largely plastics), and consumer chemicals. Dow began to carry out this strategy in 1989 by acquiring Essex Chemical, a premier supplier of adhesives and sealants, thus gaining for Dow its first entry into the automobile market. At the same time, it undertook joint ventures with Exxon Chemical, Britain Oxygen, and Japan's Sumitomo to expand its specialty plastics overseas.[33]

In 1989 Dow strengthened its specialty lines by collaborating with Eli Lilly, the pharmaceutical giant, in a joint venture, DowElanco, of which Dow held 60 percent and Lilly 40 percent. Its expressed goal was to produce agricultural products based on the revolutionary new biochemistry and genetic engineering technologies. Lilly provided capabilities both in research and development, while Dow contributed those in production and especially marketing.

Large-Scale Entry and Prompt Failure in Pharmaceuticals

During the early 1990s, Dow successfully maintained the paths of learning in which its integrated learning bases had been established. It had managed to enhance its competitive capabilities in industrial inorganic chemicals, including chlorine, chlorinated solvents, caustic soda, vinyl chloride, and a number of more specialized performance products, all of which had been developed in the pre–World War II years. In plastics (SIC 282), it produced a number of thermoplastics and thermo sets, as well as fabricated products based on them. In consumer chemicals (SIC 284), it built on the lines that had come into fruition in the 1950s, including Ziploc bags, Saran and Handiwrap film, bathroom cleaners, haircare products, and the like. By

1994, 37 percent of Dow's sales and 42 percent of its profits were derived from plastic products, 29 percent and 30 percent from specialty consumer products, 23 percent and 23 percent from specialty industrial chemicals and performance products, and 10 percent and 3 percent from hydrocarbons and energy. Fifty percent of sales and 55 percent of profit came from the United States, 26 percent of sales and 12 percent of profit from Europe, and 24 percent of sales and 33 percent of profit from other regions.

At the same time, Dow moved to bolster its position in pharmaceuticals by acquiring a leading mid-sized firm, Marion Laboratories. Dow consolidated its new property with Merrell-Dow Pharmaceutical and its Allied Laboratories to form Marion Merrell Dow, the ninth-largest pharmaceutical company in the United States. To finance this move, it took the company public while retaining 67 percent of its equity.[34]

Dow's attempt to become a pharmaceutical enterprise failed because the barriers to entry erected by the major pharmaceutical companies proved too high. By 1989 Merrell-Dow had had little success in product development. The two major products developed by Dow's original unit, Cardizan and Seldane, were nearing the end of patent protection and there was little in the pipeline. Meanwhile, Marion's two major drugs, a heart remedy and an anti-ulcer product, had been licensed from Japanese firms. Indeed, Dow had acquired first Merrell and then Marion for their strong marketing, not their development capabilities. Both had failed to build ties with university and research institutes so imperative for creating a learning base in new pharmaceutical technologies. Nor before 1989 had they developed ties with startups in genetic engineering.

Consequently, during the early 1990s Marion Merrell Dow's performance began to deteriorate rapidly. By 1994 the company's equity had fallen one-third of its value since Dow had taken it public five years earlier, and its senior executives were searching for buyers. In 1995, Dow sold its controlling interest in Marion Merrell Dow for $7.1 billion to Hoechst, Germany's leader in pharmaceuticals throughout the twentieth century. In the end, Dow received a good price for a business in which it could not compete.[35]

Postscript

In the late 1990s, after the sale of its pharmaceutical business, Dow continued to enjoy success in DowElanco, its joint venture with Eli Lilly in agricultural biotechnology. Dow had a well-established manufacturing and marketing learning base in agricultural chemicals. In 1997 it bought out its partner and renamed the unit Dow AgroSciences LLC. Subsequently Dow and Dow AgroSciences augmented their holdings with additional acquisitions, including Mycogen and Rohm and Haas's agricultural chemicals business.

Meanwhile, Dow refocused on specialty chemicals in two major moves. In 1998 it sold off most of its consumer products businesses. Three years later, signaling its sustained commitment to its core chemical business, Dow bought a crippled Union Carbide for $9.3 billion (see pages 76–77). At the dawn of the twenty-first century, Dow, like Du Pont, had returned to its roots as a specialty chemicals company, albeit operating on a vast global scale.[36]

Monsanto: Success in Defining Strategic Boundaries

An entrepreneurial startup like Dow, Monsanto became the American first mover in a new synthetic organic chemical path—namely, flavors and foods. It bore more of a resemblance to Du Pont immediately after World War I and during the 1920s in that its growth depended more on acquisitions than on internal investment.

Monsanto's founder, John F. Queeney, established his company in St. Louis in 1901 to produce saccharine. In order to broaden his line into caffeine, vanilla, and similar fine chemicals, he recruited three scientists with doctoral degrees from the University of Zurich. Until World War I Queeney continued to rely on German producers for his intermediate chemicals and his equipment. During that war, however, Monsanto was forced to develop its own intermediates and did so in part through the purchase of a neighboring producer of phenol, chloride, and caustic soda. This acquisition also delivered chemicals for explosives. In 1917 Monsanto also entered the pharmaceutical sector by producing an antiseptic and bulk aspirin, based on Bayer's expropriated patents.[37]

In the 1920s Monsanto continued its strategy of vertical integration, producing basic and intermediate chemicals to expand its product lines in flavors and foods and in closely related fine chemicals. This extension came primarily through acquisitions. That growth was capped in 1929 with the acquisitions of three companies: one in Akron, Ohio, producing rubber chemicals; one in Newark, New Jersey, making intermediates for food and perfume products; and one in Woburn, Massachusetts, making products similar to Monsanto's and thus providing a production base in the East. During the 1930s Monsanto sustained its growth via acquisitions, entering plastics through the purchase of Faberloid in 1938 and two smaller units that produced cellulose acetates and nitrates, vinyls, styrene, and polystrene. Other purchases included firms producing phosphates, fertilizers, and related agricultural products, resulting in Monsanto's operating in five three-digit SIC categories.

These acquisitions and the expansion of its rubber chemicals operation in Akron served as a base for the company's participation in the synthetic rubber programs during World War II, for which it became a major provider of styrene and polystyrene and thus a major player in the polymer/petrochemical revolution. By the time the industry returned to peacetime production, Monsanto had become the nation's fifth-largest diversified multisectored chemical company.

In the early boom years of the polymer/petrochemical revolution, Monsanto followed Dow's strategy of concentrating on basic polymer commodities. It enlarged its production of polystyrene, invested in polyvinyl chloride plants, and started the large-scale production of polypropylene. To ensure a steady stream of supplies, it integrated backward into oil and gas through the acquisition of the Lion Oil Company. Although it expanded abroad less aggressively than did Dow, Monsanto entered into joint ventures with European firms to build styrene and polystyrene plants in France, Belgium, and Spain.[38]

Monsanto, however, soon moved into the production of higher value-added polymer products. Its initial entry surfaced with the formation of Chemstrand in 1949, a 50–50 joint venture with American Viscose (a leading rayon producer) to make acrylic fibers. The partnership was unsuccessful until 1951, when Du Pont, under antitrust pressures, not only licensed its techniques to produce nylon but arranged for its engineers to assist in the design, building, and startup of a million-pound-per-year plant. By providing this assistance, it could thereby assure the government that it had a strong nylon competitor in Chemstrand. In 1961 Monsanto acquired its partner's 50 percent of this activity. At the same time, Monsanto enlarged its agricultural business by moving into herbicides and phosphates. In the early 1950s it made its first foray into consumer products by commercializing All, a low-sudsing detergent. Lacking the necessary functional capabilities to support it, the product was a disappointment and Monsanto sold it to Lever Brothers in 1957.[39]

In 1967, as competition intensified, particularly in commodity plastics, Monsanto, like Du Pont, set up a new-enterprise division for the purpose of "searching for and creating new business ideas inside and outside the company, for testing and evaluating them, bringing them to predetermined profitability levels." That division made exploratory investments in other higher value-added products, including graphic systems, protein foods, educational toys, engineered composite systems, and electronic chemicals. Only one of these projects proved successful—that involving the production of instruments used in chemical operations. Unlike Du Pont, Monsanto diversified by making a major acquisition. In 1969 it purchased the Fisher Governor Company, a producer of valves, regulators, and control systems. As Fisher International, Monsanto expanded its facilities based on its years of experience in chemical processing.[40]

Defining and Redefining the Boundaries of the Firm

By the early 1970s top managers at Monsanto had learned the same lessons as their counterparts at Du Pont. The most profitable new-product lines derived from Monsanto's integrated learning bases on established paths. After a major reorganization in 1972, the company regrouped its activities and did so in both petrochemicals and polymers. It maintained its basic and commodity products, and actually expanded its drilling activities by moving into the North Sea oil fields. It enhanced capabilities in basic petrochemicals and commodity polymers, including acrylonitrile, butadiene, and styrene and nylon. In high-end polymers it brought on-stream new and improved products in engineering plastics, with a focus on thermoplastics used in appliances and automobile production. In fibers, it sold off its European nylon business and concentrated development on its acrylic-based line. Then with the purchase in 1977 of Rohm and Haas's acrylic fiber business, the firm became the country's leading producer of carpet fibers, including the new product Astro Turf.

Monsanto's major effort, however, was in agricultural chemicals. Its original herbicides, Lasso and Roundup, quickly made the company the world's largest producer of herbicides and the leader in plant-growth regulators. This move, in turn, led Monsanto to become a pioneer in the new learning in biology. In 1979 Monsanto expanded its R&D efforts in plant biology by bringing in Howard A. Schneiderman, former dean of the School of Biological Sciences at the University of California at Berkeley, to head its research activities. In 1980 the company acquired a $20 million stake in Biogen, one of the nation's first biotech startups, and also partnered a research alliance with Genentech, another biotech startup. In the following year, Monsanto formed its own biotechnology R&D subsidiary (see Chapter 10). These moves made Monsanto in the 1980s a first mover in genetically engineered agricultural chemicals.[41]

Monsanto's Response to the Industry Crisis

As with Du Pont and Dow, the crisis years of the late 1970s and early 1980s prompted a major shift in Monsanto's strategic boundaries. The second oil crisis occasioned the formation in 1982 of Monsanto Oil to consolidate its existing oil and gas activities. Then, in 1983, it began selling off its less profitable fertilizer and high-explosive blasting powder businesses that it had entered during World War I.

But only in 1984, with the appointment of Richard J. Mahoney as CEO, did Monsanto begin to systematically implement a policy of reshaping its product portfolio, as the new executive's commitment to biology replaced chemistry as the most promising path for long-term growth. The summer of 1985 saw the only major acquisition, which like Dow's, involved a large pharmaceutical company—the purchase for $2.5 billion of G. D. Searle. Besides producing prescription drugs, Searle made aspartame-based sweeteners.

Even before Searle's acquisition, divestitures were under way. I here list these divestitures and their acquirers, many of which figure in the following chapters, in order to indicate the broad extent of reshaping product lines by the chemical companies during the 1980s.[42] Mahoney began by selling Monsanto's basic chemical plants and polyester latex operations (to Morton Thiokol), its phenolic resins business (to Borden), and its plastizer activities (to Witco). The company then sold its North Sea oil holdings and its gas interests to Amerada Hess. Next came the sale of Monsanto's investments in both petrochemical and polymer-based products. These included the sale of Monsanto Oil Company to Broken Hill Properties of Australia; several specialized polymer units to BSM; much of its polystyrene business, including three plants, to Polymers (a Canadian firm); a single acrylonitrile plant for $160 million to a leveraged buyout (LBO); its nonwoven fiber business to James River; and its paper chemicals to Akzo, the leading Dutch chemical producer. Divestitures of higher value-added units whose profits were waning followed, including the sale of Astro Turf and the electrical chemicals business to two German companies; its global analgesics (bulk aspirin and related products) business to Rhône-Poulenc for $500 million; its polyethylene nonfood bottle business to Innopack; and its hot-plastic-bottle technology to Johnson Controls. Monsanto even went so far as to arrange the sale of its original vanilla business to Rhône-Poulenc. These divestitures far outnumbered the acquisitions of a small number of units from such companies as British Petroleum and Rhône-Poulenc to support its major lines.

By the end of 1988 Monsanto had reached its goal: it had become a world leader in acrylic fibers and in rubber and other thermal plastics. In agricultural chemicals, it was directing its profits from Roundup and Lasso toward expanding its research in biotechnology. By 1991, two-thirds of its operating income derived from high-value chemicals and agricultural products. During that decade the company continued to focus on its strengths. It sold off its animal feed business and then its process control business, Fisher Controls (to Emerson Electric), and acquired in 1993 Chevron's Ortho lawn and garden division for $416 million, as well as Merck's specialty chemical division, Kelco, for $1 billion. Most important, Monsanto was concentrating on its growing capabilities in biochemistry and biotechnology, including those units acquired with the Searle purchase. It did so by commercializing new chemically based and genetically engineered agricultural products. In 1994 its first genetically engineered drug, Prosalic, arrived on the market.

By 1994 agricultural biological and chemical products accounted for 27 percent of Monsanto's revenues and 48 percent of its operating income. Its fabrics and plastics and other industrial chemicals represented 25 percent of revenues and 27 percent of income; NutraSweet, 8 percent and 14 percent; and Searle, 20 percent and 7 percent, respectively. At the same time, Monsanto, which, unlike Dow and Du Pont, had not gone extensively overseas, concentrated on increasing its foreign sales, which grew from less than 10 percent of total sales in 1989 to 49 percent in 1994.

Then, in 1996, came a major strategic shift. Monsanto sold its plastics business to Bayer for $5.8 billion and the rest of its chemical businesses were spun off as a new company, Solutia, with total equity of $3 billion. As a result its revenues in 1997 from bio-engineered agricultural products amounted to $3.1 billion, pharmaceuticals $2.4 billion, and food products (thickeners as well as sweeteners) $1.5 billion. By the end of that year it had put its lawn products up for sale.

Postscript

Ironically, Monsanto's transition was not a success, even though the company was becoming a successful pharmaceutical producer. In 1999, for example, it introduced Celebrex, a drug used to treat arthritis, that set a record for sales of new drugs. Yet the transition failed for two reasons. One was a growing worldwide protest against genetically modified foods. In 1999 both the United Kingdom and Brazil banned the use of genetically modified foods, and other countries quickly followed. In 1999 Monsanto halted producing seeds with a terminator gene that rendered them sterile. All the while, the public protest intensified. Class-action legal suits multiplied.

The second reason Monsanto's transition fell short is that the company's leaders began to realize the scale and significance of existing barriers to entry. A recent study concludes that "Monsanto lacked the marketing and distribution infrastructure it would need to capitalize on the drugs it was preparing to bring to market." The company explored merger talks with Novartis AG, a recently formed combination of the Swiss pharmaceutical giants Ciba-Geigy and Sandoz, but could not reach a satisfactory deal. Monsanto then turned to Pharmacia & Upjohn Inc., the result of a 1995 merger between Swedish and American pharmaceutical companies. In 2000 Pharmacia & Upjohn acquired Monsanto, creating a new entity called simply "Pharmacia."[43]

Monsanto did not fare well under new ownership, however. Having exploited Celebrex, Pharmacia restructured many of Monsanto's businesses. Late in 2001 Pharmacia sold off the agricultural biotechnology business, which reemerged under Monsanto's name. (Pharmacia was subsequently acquired by Pfizer.) Early in the new century, Monsanto, which had been one of the most innovative and successful multisectored chemical companies, may be devolving into a small, focused agricultural biotechnology enterprise.

This summary of Monsanto's performance during the twentieth century provides an impressive example of successful shifting of strategic boundaries as wars, depressions, and energy shortages brought about massive changes. During the 1950s and 1960s, the growth years of the polymer/petrochemical revolution, Monsanto commercialized both petrochemical and polymer-based products. As their markets became crowded it became a leader in agricultural chemicals, and a first mover in the commercializing of such products through genetic engineering. Then, following the industry's crisis, it began to move from commercializing chemically based to biologically based products. Monsanto completed the shift by 1996, only to be struck by the unexpected outcry against its products in Europe. At the same time, it had learned, as had several of its leading competitors, that existing barriers to entry in pharmaceuticals remained too high for outsiders to surmount.

American Cyanamid Company: From Chemicals to Pharmaceuticals—and Being Bought

By the 1990s American Cyanamid had also successfully completed its strategic shift from chemicals to pharmaceuticals. But its task was much easier than that of Monsanto, for in the 1940s the company had the good fortune to become a first mover in both the polymer/petrochemical revolution in chemicals and the therapeutic revolution in pharmaceuticals. So, through the postwar decades, its managers had a choice of when and how to move from one basic path of learning to the other. Because the transactions involved in the shifting of strategic boundaries were quite straightforward in the case of American Cyanamid, I omit the details regarding the buying and selling of divisions and companies of the sort provided in the accounts of Du Pont, Dow, and Monsanto.

Beginnings in Electrolytically Based Chemicals

In 1907 Frank Washburn formed American Cyanamid to produce a basic ingredient for fertilizer, calcium cyanamide, through new electrolytic technology, for which he had an exclusive U.S. license from the German innovators, A. Frank and N. Caro. Washburn's plant for making calcium cyanamide on the Canadian side of Niagara Falls went into production in 1909. In 1919 this first mover acquired two producers of phosphate, the other basic ingredient in fertilizer. The firm's primary growth as an "all-around," multisectored company was accomplished through acquisition rather than internal investment. Its purchases during the 1920s culminated in 1929 with the buying of Calco Chemicals, another multisectored enterprise. By then, American Cyanamid was producing dyestuffs, phosphates, pigments, intermediate chemicals, textile resins, household products, and rubber chemicals, and had acquired marketing rights for urea-formaldehyde molding materials (the raw material for Formica products). Finally, in 1930, American Cyanamid completed its initial diversification strategy by purchasing a pharmaceutical firm, Lederle Antitoxin Laboratories, as well as a surgical supply company.

During the 1930s it expanded its urea-based products into thermoset plastics, including the successful Formica brand of molded products. Its Lederle Laboratories extended into the production of diphtheria, tetanus, and typhoid vaccines. During World War II this subsidiary was more involved in producing vaccines, blood plasmas, and surgical sutures for the military than in the new antibiotics, although it was soon meeting the wartime demands for penicillin and sulfa drugs.[44]

American Cyanamid's first-mover position in prescription drugs came in 1948 when its Lederle Laboratories discovered and commercialized aureomycin, one of the most successful of the new antibiotics. Owing to American Cyanamid's integrated learning base that was built during the 1930s through the development, production, and marketing of prescription drugs, aureomycin would become the company's most profitable product, at times accounting for almost half its income.[45]

The Shift from Chemicals to Pharmaceuticals

American Cyanamid, nonetheless, still considered itself a chemical enterprise and entered polymer/petrochemicals on the basis of its capabilities developed in plastics before World War II. It became competitive in the production of acrylonitrile and then acrylic fiber. For the production of its intermediates, it formed in 1944 a joint venture with Texaco, the Jefferson Chemical Company.[46]

But as the postwar wave of innovations in both chemicals and pharmaceuticals leveled off in the 1960s, American Cyanamid responded more like a pharmaceutical competitor than a chemical one. It began as early as 1956 to acquire brand-name over-the-counter consumer chemical products, including in 1963 Breck shampoo and Pine-Sol cleaner, and in 1971 Pierre Cardin and Old Spice fragrances.[47]

Redefining the Boundaries of the Firm

The crisis years of the late 1970s and early 1980s forced American Cyanamid to decide between chemical and pharmaceuticals. Given the need to restructure in chemicals and the potential for commercializing new products in pharmaceuticals, the choice seemed an easy one. First came the sale of the its acrylic fiber and intermediates business, including its share of Jefferson Chemical, followed by that of the Formica and Titanium divisions. Then ensued the divestitures of its calcium phosphate business, phosphate rock processing plants, lead chemical products, and, in 1989, the dye business. Finally, in 1989, the company disposed of its consumer products for a total of $850 million, with Pine-Sol going to Clorox, Old Spice to Procter & Gamble, and Breck to Dial. At the same time, through internal investment and joint ventures and acquisitions, it expanded its pharmaceutical line beyond antibiotics by acquiring producers of veterinary products and medical equipment, and by exploring new biotechnology techniques for commercializing vaccines, herbicides, and growth hormones.

By 1991, 63 percent of the company's operating income derived from medical products, 32 percent from agricultural ones (increasingly based on genetic engineering), and only 5 percent in chemicals. Two years later it spun off its chemical business to its shareholders in a new corporate entity, Cytec, thus completing the transformation from chemicals to pharmaceuticals. The following year American Home Products (AHP; now Wyeth) acquired American Cyanamid for $9.7 billion in cash, forming the fourth-largest pharmaceutical company in the world, with estimated sales of $13 billion (as reviewed in Chapter 7). Clearly, AHP paid an impressive price to acquire American Cyanamid's pharmaceutical organizational capabilities.[48]

The two remaining major multisectored core companies whose evolution I now describe, Union Carbide and Allied Chemical, differed from the others in that they were formed as mergers. Both were decimated by Wall Street corporate raiders in the 1980s. But more significant for my comparative competitive analyses, both had moved out of the industry created by Du Pont and Dow into markets where their capabilities provided little competitive advantage. By the mid-1990s Union Carbide was no longer an effective core competitor, and Allied Chemical had become part of Allied Signal, an automotive aerospace enterprise in which related chemicals accounted for 25 percent of its total revenues.

Union Carbide and Carbon Corporation:
Multisectored from the Start

The initial learning base of the merger that formed Union Carbide was very different from that of the four first movers just described. The company, unlike Dow, Monsanto, and American Cyanamid, was not a startup that expanded capabilities developed from a single product and process. Nor was it, like Du Pont, a horizontal merger that began by consolidating and integrating a number of established enterprises in a single industry. Instead, it was a merger in 1917 of U.S. leaders in different but complementary product lines both using electrochemical processes (using chemicals in the production of electrical products), including electrolytically produced calcium carbide and acetylene (Union Carbide); carbon electrodes for lighting systems and Ever

Ready batteries (National Carbon); bicycle and auto headlights and welding and cutting equipment (Prest-O-Lite); liquid oxygen used in the production of acetylene (Linde Air Products); and electrolytically produced metal alloys (Electro-Metallurgical Company). Thus, the merged enterprise operated across a wide range of SIC codes, including respectively 2819 (calcium carbide), 2813 (acetylene), 3623 (electrodes and electric welding), 3647 (batteries, headlights), 3549 (welding and cutting apparatus), 2813 (liquid oxygen), and 3313 (electrometallurgical products). Most of these products and processes were based on European, particularly German, technologies.[49]

All of these enterprises were the U.S. first movers in somewhat different paths of learning within the new electrolytic chemical technology that came into being with the invention of the dynamo. The operating units in the merged enterprise thus included integrated learning bases in materials and the end-products made from them. Each required a somewhat different set of product-specific functional capabilities, but their competitive success rested on much the same related technical capabilities.

As at Du Pont, these integrated operating entities remained autonomous, in this case as subsidiaries rather than departments. In 1920 Union Carbide's senior managers formed a new subsidiary, Carbide and Carbon Chemical Company, that initially pioneered in producing propane from natural gas. In the late 1920s, by setting up plants next to Standard Oil of Indiana's largest refinery at Whiting, Texas and another at Texas City, Texas, that unit became the first enterprise in the United States to focus solely on the commercializing of petrochemicals.

In the 1930s the Carbide and Carbon Chemical subsidiary paved the way for the development of such basic petrochemicals as butadiene, ethylene (from grain alcohol), and polymers including polyvinyl chloride (PVC), vinyl chloride monomers, and ethyl vinyl chloride, as well as polystyrene. By 1936 Carbide and Carbon started to commercialize high-value end-products—Vinylite for flooring, phonograph records, and fabric coatings—and then in 1939 a synthetic fabric, Vinyon. That same year Carbide and Carbon purchased the Bakelite Company, which was founded in 1910 to produce phenol-formaldehyde-based molded plastic products for electrical applications. In these same years the products of the other major subsidiaries became and remained major players in their markets.[50]

Only in meeting the demands of World War II, however, did Union Carbide begin to produce basic petrochemicals and polymers in vast amounts. As the nation's pioneer in petrochemicals, it became a leader in the production of butadiene, styrene, ethylene, and then most successfully, polyethyl-

ene. In the immediate postwar years, Union Carbide became for a brief period the nation's largest producer of petrochemicals, and it remained a major
player in the product lines in which it had operated since the 1917 merger.

Partly because of its broad portfolio of products, Union Carbide initially
fell behind Du Pont and Dow during the postwar years of the most dramatic
growth of the polymer/petrochemical paths. It commercialized more high-
end products including Dynal, a new acrylic fiber, and developed a packaging film (Glad Wrap) and a car polish (Simonize) as it enlarged its activities
in engineering plastics, pesticides, and agricultural chemicals. But its senior
managers soon realized that they were having increasing difficulty competing with Du Pont in fibers and high-performance plastics. More serious was
the continuing loss of market share in basic petrochemicals and polymers to
Dow's aggressive strategies of effectively focusing on large-scale investments
in plant and facilities, and expanding on a global scale, for which it relied on
unprecedented use of debt. Like Dow, Union Carbide integrated backward
into purchasing oil and gas leases, but did so to a lesser extent. Also during
this time international competition increased rapidly in its alloys and industrial gases businesses.[51]

A New Strategy: Unrelated Diversification

In 1949 the company was incorporated into a single operating enterprise
with the name of Union Carbide Corporation and its subsidiaries became operating divisions. Then in 1957 it changed its name to Union Carbide, and
Carbon Corporation, and (reflecting its evolution from the 1930s) placed its
eighteen autonomous divisions into four domestic groups: chemicals and
petrochemicals, plastics, carbides, and air products. But the corporate office
remained relatively small, with few general executives and a small staff, a
contrast to Dow and Du Pont.

In the mid-1960s Union Carbide's management, following the growing
trend in American business, decided on a new strategy, that of unrelated diversification. It would grow through the acquisition of enterprises outside
the chemical industry's competitive arena that Du Pont and Dow had created—that is, it would enter markets in which its learned organizational capabilities gave it little or no competitive advantage.

In 1964 Union Carbide purchased a Canadian mattress bedding company.
Two years later, it obtained a maker of lasers and laser systems. By investing
in uranium mining and processing equipment, it expanded the nuclear division it had created to operate the U.S. government's facilities at Oak Ridge.

In this stream of acquisitions, only one, the 1965 purchase of the pharma-ceutical enterprise Neisler Laboratories, held a possible potential to comple-ment Union Carbide's traditional capabilities.[52]

In 1970 a new set of top managers established a department dedicated to the development of new business. Its task was to rationalize the strategy of unrelated diversification by making the decisions concerning what to ac-quire and then overseeing their continued performance. The new areas of acquisition included at first medical systems and electronic products, and even consumer products such as deodorants and disposable diapers. Then ensued the purchasing of municipal waste systems, chemical production from coal and synthetic gas, and specialty chemicals such as motor additives and others for increasing oil-well output.

Union Carbide then attempted to rationalize its acquisition process by em-ploying new portfolio planning techniques popularized by the Boston Con-sulting Group (BCG), which classified businesses according to catchy terms: "Cash Cows" generated cash flow to fund growth of "Stars" and "Question Marks," while companies were encouraged to fix or divest their "Dogs." Union Carbide bought most of its new properties believing that it could uti-lize its technical and functional capabilities to create successful growth busi-nesses. However, most of its new acquisitions—including medical systems, electronic products, municipal waste systems, and consumer products—proved to be "Dogs." The lone significant success from all this activity was the reconstituted agricultural division.[53]

The differences between Union Carbide, on the one hand, and Du Pont and Monsanto, on the other, were that Union Carbide's managers discov-ered the strategic boundaries of their enterprise through this expensive strategy of buying companies, whereas the other two companies carefully tested the waters through their respective new-venture programs. As a re-sult, by the mid-1970s Union Carbide owned a diverse portfolio of busi-nesses that were mostly unrelated and that also proved difficult to manage through purely financial measurements. Over the following decade, its managers started to reexamine the wisdom of this strategy of growth and the mode of executing it.

Returning to the Chemical Industry's Competitive Arena

In the mid-1970s Union Carbide began to define its strategic boundaries in terms of its competition within the industry's competitive arena. Unable to compete with Du Pont, it withdrew in 1974 from fibers and continued its shift away from packaging film, which it had begun in the 1960s. More dramatic was the exiting from basic petrochemicals and plastics that Dow had come to dominate. Under William Sneath, who became Union Carbide's CEO in 1977, the company sold off its operations in PVC, styrene, and polystyrene. At the same time, it withdrew from the European market by selling its petrochemical assets to British Petroleum Chemicals for close to $400 million. These divestitures also included some traditional products such as calcium carbide, one of the companies original businesses. Most important of all, Sneath cast out most of the unrelated businesses acquired in the late 1960s and early 1970s, which included not only the product lines already listed, but also aluminum, automobile radiators, brain scanners, and shrimp fishing. "We are in too many things," he explained, "most of them growing very rapidly and demanding a lot of cash, and therefore you begin to limit each business."[54]

By the late 1970s Union Carbide had returned to relying on its long-established integrated bases to enhance existing product lines and commercialize new ones. These products included polyethylene (both HDPE and the older LDPE), ethylene oxide end-products, industrial gases, calcium carbide, agricultural chemicals, and alloys, as well as the company's decades-old consumer products—batteries, flashlights, headlights, and the like.

Moreover, at the same time, Carbide's long-term development work in polyethylene brought on-stream a revolutionary new process, Unipol, to produce linear low-density polyethylene (LLDPE), which sharply reduced the cost and greatly improved the quality of that product. Using the same Unipol technology, Union Carbide (working this time with Shell Chemical to meet the high development costs) commercialized a comparable process for linear polypropylene (LPP) that promised to represent another high-income producer through licensing. With Unipol, Union Carbide hoped to use licensing as a means to set the standard for that product, as the demand for the new technology was significant. Licenses would be sold worldwide.

By the late 1970s Union Carbide had redefined its strategic boundaries to be within the industry's competitive playing field. But in the early 1980s the industry was in crisis, so revenues from licensing were slow in coming. The company's financial performance in 1982 and 1983 was lackluster. In 1982 it sold off a portion of its ferro alloy and metals (tungsten, vanadium, and uranium) businesses for $240 million. As the income stream from licensing began to flow, the senior executives at Carbide initiated planning that continued to define their product portfolio along the paths it returned to and reinforced in the late 1970s.[55]

Disaster

Then disaster struck. In December 1984 a gas leak in its pesticide plant in Bhopal, India killed and injured thousands. But for Carbide the disaster was not just the gas leak, tragic as that was. It was the response to that tragedy in the emerging market for corporate control in the United States. Within days of the news of Bhopal, the vultures began to circle, believing that Union Carbide's breakup value far exceeded its current market value. Of the several Wall Street raiders that had an eye on this financial opportunity, Samuel Heyman—fresh from a successful takeover of General Aniline and Film (GAF), the former U.S. subsidiary of I. G. Farben—was the most aggressive. After buying Union Carbide stock during the summer and fall of 1985, he made a $4.3 billion tender offer at $68 a share, which he raised to $72. (It had been selling at below $30 before the raids began.) Carbide's management responded on January 6, 1986 by offering to buy back 55 percent of its shares at $85. The buyback netted Heyman's GAF $268 million, doubling its net worth.[56]

The financing of the buyback forced a fire sale of Union Carbide's assets, including many of its "crown jewels" in terms of long-term revenue producers and as learning bases for upgrading its product portfolio. In January its managers announced the sale of its engineered (high-performance) polymers and composites division for $210 million. Then came the sale of its carbon business to Amoco. Next, the remainder of its packaging film business went to Envirodyne for $230 million. During the spring the Ever Ready battery operations (the nation's largest producer) were sold to Ralston Purina for $1.42 billion, making the purchaser the world's largest producer of batteries. Carbide's home and automotive products, including Prestone antifreeze (also the nation's largest brand in the category) went to an investment group headed by First Boston for $100 million, and its worldwide chromium interests to General Mining Union for $83 million. In the autumn the company sold off its global agricultural chemical business to Rhône-Poulenc. At the same time, it disposed of its headquarters building for $345 million (though remained the building's major tenant). In addition, it wrote off $650 million worth of assets, shutting down most of its older commodity works, concentrating production in its new Unipol LLDPE and LPP plants. Even these sales proved insufficient. The company's increase in debt was so large that for a brief time it enjoyed the dubious distinction of being the largest American corporate issuer of junk bonds. The basic strategy was to sell off the consumer products and specialty chemicals units that the company's leaders had expected to sustain the profit stream.[57]

After 1986 Carbide concentrated on its underlying strengths: ethylene-based basic polymers, industrial gases (in which it remained the third-largest producer in the world), and carbon and graphite electrodes (in which it was the world's largest manufacturer). But when the recession in 1990 sharply reduced sales and prices and when the revenues from licensing fell off, Union Carbide initiated once again the cycle of divestments. In 1991 it sold its propylene glycol and urethane polyols business to Arco Chemical and the 50 percent of its joint venture in electrodes to its partner Mitsubishi for $235 million. Then, in 1992, it sold its coated resins business to Georgia Pacific, placed its silicon operations on the block, and spun off its industrial gases unit, Praxair, to its stockholders.[58]

Union Carbide never recovered from Heyman's raid. In the early 1990s its debt ratio was higher than any of its competitors. By 1991 its revenues were half of what they had been before the sell-off began. By 1994 sales and income derived entirely from basic chemicals and petrochemicals, including olefins, polyolefins, and intermediates. Carbide no longer had the capabilities or the funds essential to implementing growth and competitive strategies comparable to those of Du Pont, Dow, or Monsanto, or even of its own managers before December 1984. It had lost its long-established learning bases in higher value-added paths of learning with the revenues and the broader technical and functional capabilities essential to maintain the competition and the potential for improving both product and process. Whatever the outcome, Heyman's raid ensured the dispersal of Union Carbide's strength. Even had its managers permitted Heyman to acquire the company, a comparable sell-off would have been necessary to reduce Heyman's debt of more than $5 billion in high-interest junk bonds, and surely Heyman did not plan to take over the management of Union Carbide.[59]

The epilogue to Union Carbide's story can be expressed in a single sentence. In 2001 Dow Chemical acquired Union Carbide for $9.3 billion.[60] The situation was similar to that of Fujitsu's acquisition of Siemens Nixdorf, Europe's leading computer company in 1999, as described in my earlier book *Inventing the Electronic Century.* Where else could the remaining weaker multisectored core company have gone?

Whereas the evolution of Union Carbide's path of learning provides a striking example of the failure of the strategy of unrelated diversification, Allied Chemical's history offers a dramatic example of the failure to perform the basic activity of a high-technology industry, that of a strong commitment to research and development.

Allied Chemical: A Failed Strategy and Structure

Allied Chemical, formed in 1920, was modeled after Union Carbide. It was a merger of five chemical companies, but their initial learning bases were very different from those of Union Carbide. Only one, the Solvay Process Company, established in 1880 in Syracuse, New York, was a first mover in a new technology, after it received a license from Belgium's Solvay brothers to produce soda ash using their revolutionary new technology (see Chapter 5). Solvay Process Company, in turn, founded Semet Solvay (the second of the five merged companies) to produce in volume supplies of ammonia and also coke, and in time, coke ovens. The third company was General Chemicals, a somewhat speculative merger of producers of several different acids. The fourth, National Aniline and Chemical, was a small, specialized dye producer that had expanded rapidly during World War I in an attempt to meet the shortages of German dyes. In that effort, it had relied on Barrett, the fifth merged company, a producer of coal-tar roofing and asphalt material to supply its essential coal-tar chemicals. Thus overall there was no basic related technology or raw materials, as there was in the case of Union Carbide, to tie these companies together.[61]

Whereas both Union Carbide and Allied began as holding companies, Union Carbide in time categorized its subsidiaries under separate groups: chemicals, gases, plastics, and air products. Its corporate office and board remained in close touch with the operating subsidiaries. On the other hand, at Allied Chemical, control of the subsidiaries rested in the hands of a single executive, Eugene Weber, from the company's beginning until 1935. During those years executives in one subsidiary could communicate with those in another only through Weber. As a result the subsidiaries remained completely autonomous, with no communication among them. From the outset, Weber prohibited operating units from employing research necessary to commercialize new products. His motto was "Let other companies invent specialized products for end-users." His companies would supply their basic chemicals. Weber, too, remained in complete control of the allocation of funds, an understandable move during the depressed years of the 1930s. In a short time, Allied Chemical became known as a bank with a chemical company on the side.

Things did not change much after Weber's retirement. As chairman he had ensured that the three presidents to follow him, from 1936 to 1959, would be professional accountants. Nevertheless, these executives did begin to create a corporate office including a central research unit to encourage new-product development in the operating divisions. But this move came too late for Allied Chemical to participate in commercializing the new products of the polymer/petrochemical revolution. As the *International Directory* emphasizes, the resulting gap in expertise was to plague Allied Chemicals for the next thirty years. Moreover, its analysis adds "the company continued to drift without any coherent policy or long-term strategy."[62]

In 1962 a new set of top executives began to diversify into petroleum. Its initial move was the purchase of Union Texas Natural Gas Company, a petroleum producer with large holdings in North and South America. The arrangement was not a financial success. By 1968 Allied Chemical was reporting serious losses. A new president, John T. O'Connor, a former secretary of commerce, was brought in and started to turn the company around. As its oil and gas business became profitable and O'Connor shifted the company away from concentrating on producing basic petrochemicals and polymers, the company began commercializing specialty products, including engineered plastics, nylon fibers for tires and carpets, and fluorides for refrigeration and air conditioning. Nevertheless, at the end of the 1970s, 80 percent of Allied's income derived from petroleum products and supplying raw materials for the petrochemical industry.

Dismemberment by Corporate Raiders

In 1979, Edward L. Hennessey, a senior executive at United Technologies and former colleague of conglomerators Royal Little and Harold Geneen, pioneers in that new corporate form, succeeded O'Connor as CEO. Hennessey's immediate goal was to transform Allied Chemical into a conglomerate. After changing its name to Allied Corporation he sold off its petroleum and basic chemical businesses, while retaining the chemical product lines that his predecessor had sponsored. He then went on an acquisition spree, purchasing electronics companies, instrument makers, and defense contractors.[63]

In 1983, Hennessey acquired Bendix, a long-established producer of automotive and aircraft equipment, but did so in a completely unplanned manner. The details of his move are complex, but do provide an example of the bizarre world of the creation of conglomerates in the 1980s. The CEO of Bendix, William Agee, was attempting to take over Martin Marietta, a major

U.S. defense contractor, when Marietta fought back by launching a take-over of Bendix. When United Technologies joined Marietta's countermove, Agee turned to Hennessey as a "white knight" and sold Bendix to Allied Corporation.

Two years later Hennessey purchased the Signal Company, itself a con-glomerate of oil producing, automotive (Mack Truck) and aerospace compa-nies, to form Allied Signal. In the next year Hennessey sold thirty-five of Allied Signal's operating units to Michael Dingman, a Wall Street specialist in the new game of buying and selling companies. The raider Dingman then formed the Henley Group and made a record initial public offering of $1.3 billion. The only part of Allied Chemical that remained in Allied Signal was defined as "engineered materials," products relating to Allied Signal's auto-motive and aircraft divisions. In 1986 and 1987, such products accounted for 25 percent of Allied Signal's total sales.[64]

The evolution of Allied Chemical provides a striking parable of the route to failure in the high-technology chemical industry. From the beginning, Weber failed to incorporate the essential element for success: it was his strategy explicitly *not* to fund research and development. In addition he for-bade direct communication among the heads of his operating companies, thus depriving the managers of potential ways to enhance the economies of scope that exist in a large, multiproduct enterprise. His successors were unable to create the strategy and structure needed to revive the enterprise. As a result the new set of managers that took over in 1962 essentially had to start almost from scratch just as the potential opportunities in polymer/pet-rochemicals were disappearing. That late start almost ensured that Allied Chemical would be taken up by the exploiters of the market for corporate control in the 1980s.

Conclusion

I conclude this chapter by considering how the three basic themes of this book—barriers to entry, strategic boundaries, and limits to growth—relate to the evolution of the six multisectored core chemical companies that created the U.S. chemical industry in the first decades of the twentieth century.

The modern chemical industry began in the United States at the end of the nineteenth century as its first movers and close followers established their integrated learning bases. Until the coming of World War I, however, the pioneering German chemical companies had established their barriers to entry to international markets.

World War I removed these barriers. During the decade after 1914 the American companies had the chance to exploit the full potential of modern chemical science and engineering. Throughout the 1920s five of the six U.S. leaders (Allied Chemical was the exception) were operating in four to all seven of the SIC three-digit chemical industries. They did so by using European technologies to build their initial learning bases through the development of new products and by acquisitions in related product lines. Du Pont's strategy was based on nitrocellulose technologies, Dow's on chloride technologies, Monsanto's on saccharine, American Cyanamid's (as the name indicates) on cyanamides, and Union Carbide's on electrochemically based products and processes. Allied Chemical produced only basic chemicals used by the others to commercialize new products.

During the 1930s, the years of the Great Depression, Du Pont and Dow were building the foundations of a second period of unprecedented growth, that of the polymer/petrochemical revolution. Du Pont did so through research and development in commercializing polymers; Dow through evolutionary process technologies in commercializing petrochemical technologies. Force-fed by the demands of World War II, the U.S. industry created new barriers to entry during the 1940s and 1950s. It was within this new competitive arena that the five leaders defined their strategic boundaries during the postwar years.

Each of the multisectored core chemical companies redefined their strategic boundaries differently. Du Pont concentrated on the commercializing of polymers; Dow on those of petrochemicals. By 1960 Du Pont's profit margin was twice that of its nearest competitor. Dow had become the world's largest and most profitable producer of commodity chemicals and plastics. Monsanto and American Cyanamid concentrated on their specialized capabilities within both polymers and petrochemicals.

As Du Pont and especially Dow overtook Union Carbide, the first company to commercialize petrochemicals turned to a strategy of unrelated diversification and soon paid the price. After an attempt to rationalize its new strategy of unrelated diversification proved to be technologically barren and financially unsuccessful, the company refocused on its chemical businesses, only to be destroyed by a corporate raider. In these years, Allied Chemical had all but departed from the chemical competitive arena, in part because its initial CEO, Eugene Weber, had scorned R&D decades earlier. It devolved into a division producing specialty chemicals for Allied Signal's automotive and aircraft units.

By the 1970s, the industry's major players realized that the chemical science and engineering were no longer promising continued growth by providing new learning. Du Pont was the first to appreciate the change, redefining its strategic boundaries in the 1960s. Product development of its operating divisions, not central research, now became the source of new and improved products that were based on science and technology first mastered in the 1920s and later in the 1940s and 1950s. Dow only came to the same conclusion in 1978 and then drastically redefined its strategic boundaries. American Cyanamid, a first mover in antibiotics as well as in chemistry, began its move to pharmaceuticals from chemicals, while Monsanto became a first mover in molecular genetics, a new source of biological learning especially in markets for agricultural chemicals.

The 1990s witnessed the culmination of the attempt by the four remaining chemical companies to shift strategic focus from low-tech chemistry to high-tech biology. American Cyanamid moved early, spinning off its chemicals in 1993, and Monsanto, though less successful, did the same by 1996. Neither Du Pont nor Dow, the shapers of the American chemical competitive arena since the 1930s, planned to leave the chemical industry. But their attempts to enter pharmaceuticals failed. Dow's effort to enter through acquisition failed in a very short time. Du Pont's attempt to overcome the barriers to entry was carefully defined, based on learning its necessary functional capabilities from Merck, the leading American pharmaceutical company. But in the end, it too failed and sold its business. The barriers to entry created by the American and European prescription drug companies in national and international markets were simply too high to overcome.

By the end of the century, Du Pont (the industry's leader in product development) and Dow (its leader in process development) were the only two major American chemical companies still operating. Monsanto had moved successfully into pharmaceuticals, only to be acquired by the Swedish firm Pharmacia at the end of the century. American Cyanamid after a successful shift into pharmaceuticals was purchased by a leading company, American Home Products. Union Carbide and Allied Chemical, weakened by failed strategies, were acquired by Dow and Allied Signal.

CHAPTER 4

The Focused
American Companies

During the 1920s, the first six multisectored chemical companies created the modern U.S. chemical industry. In the 1940s and 1950s, these enterprises with the leading petroleum companies fashioned the polymer/petrochemical revolution worldwide. They were helped in this, however, by the activities of the smaller, more specialized chemical companies listed in Table 4.1 (as well as Table 1.1). These focused enterprises provided a wide variety of chemicals used by the majors in commercializing products based on the new learning in chemical science and engineering. Moreover, they constituted a foundation on which the larger core companies defined and redefined their strategic boundaries.

While this chapter concentrates primarily on the ten focused chemical companies, it also considers the evolution of a comparable set of specialty enterprises, the specialized engineering firms (SEFs). After World War II, the SEFs designed and built a substantial number of chemical processing plants around the world. These firms had the potential to become focused core companies, but in the United States, at least, only one such firm, Scientific Design, made the attempt, which proved unsuccessful.

The focused companies fall into four groups. The largest of these groups in terms of size and product lines features members with ambitions to become multisector core companies. Hercules's attempt to attain this goal led to long-term failure in terms of technical achievement and financial success. Rohm and Haas, on the other hand, expanded into petrochemicals and then returned to focusing on its long-term strength in acrylic chemistry. Air Products and Chemicals entered the industry in response to the needs of World War II and became a world leader in industrial gases.

Table 4.1 Ten U.S. core niche chemical companies

Company	Year founded	Chemical revenues, 1993 ($ billions)	Original product lines	Product lines, 1993	Strategy
Hercules	1912	1.8	Explosives, including nitrocellulose	Water-soluble polymers and specialty chemicals	To become a multisectored core firm by diversifying into basic polymers in 1950s, and to higher value-added products after 1975; forced retreat to cellulose-based products and other specialties in late 1980s
Rohm and Haas	1909	3.2	Resins and then acrylic-based products	Acrylic-based and specialties for agriculture and electronics	In 1950s, to diversify broadly; retreat after 1975 to core business; in 1990s, measured diversification into new specialties such as chemicals for electronic industry
Air Products and Chemicals	1940	2.9	Industrial gases, beginning with oxygen, followed by hydrogen, nitrogen, etc.	Industrial gases and polyurethane	From the outset, successful in industrial gases; in 1960s, diversification into chemicals and beyond; retreats in late 1970s to specialty niches in chemicals
Great Lakes Chemical	1933	1.7	Bromide-based products	Bromide-based products	Dominate the sector and diversify within it
Lubrizol	1928	1.5	Petroleum additives	Petroleum additives	Focused with no significant diversification

International Flavors and Fragrances	1909	1.2	Food flavorings and cosmetic fragrances	Food flavorings and cosmetic fragrances	Focused with no significant diversification
Nalco	1928	1.4	Water treatment chemicals for industrial and locomotive boilers	Water treatment chemicals	Focused and pursuing new markets for specialty chemicals
Dow Corning	1943	2.0	Silicone-based products	Silicone-based products	Focused with no significant diversification
Cabot	1882	1.2	Carbon black/natural gas	Carbon black, fused silica, specialized high-performance materials	Related diversification in 1950s; unrelated diversification in 1960s; retreat to core business in 1980s with selective, highly specialized remnants of diversification era
Witco	1920	1.2	Marketing of carbon black	Broadly diversified in chemical and petroleum specialties	Becomes a highly diversified manufacturer in 1950s; after late 1970s, focuses on chemical and petroleum specialties; fails to find a secure niche

Note: Eight of the companies expanded overseas in the 1950s, and two (Lubrizol and Nalco) followed in the 1960s. Overseas markets provided significant opportunities for growth in these years.

The second group consists of three smaller companies—Great Lakes Chemical, Nalco, and Dow Corning. All three pursued a strategy of developing different product markets within their specialties: Great Lakes in bromides, Nalco in water treatment, and Dow Corning in silicones.

The third group includes two companies, Lubrizol and International Flavors and Fragrances, which sought to dominate a sector and diversify within it. Lubrizol did this in petroleum additives and International Flavors and Fragrances within specialties.

The final group consists of the remaining two idiosyncratic companies, Cabot and Witco, which evolved in their own individual manner over the decades.

Group 1: The Largest Focused Companies

I begin by reviewing three of the largest companies in terms of revenues—Hercules, Rohm and Haas, and Air Products. Of the three, Hercules, although a technical achiever, was the least successful in terms of financial returns because it left its niche to compete—for a time successfully—with the major core companies in commercializing products of the polymer/petrochemical revolution. In contrast, the other two companies continued to focus successfully on their initial niches.

Hercules Incorporated: Learning the Strategic Boundaries of the Firm

The Hercules Powder Company was one of the two companies cut out of Du Pont by the antitrust ruling in 1912. (The other, Atlas Powder Company, was acquired by Britain's Imperial Chemical Industries in 1971.) The capabilities of its inherited learning base in nitrocellulose-based explosives and propellants (the latter for military and sporting weapons) were almost immediately expanded and enhanced by the huge increase in volume during World War I. Like Du Pont, Hercules recognized that it would have to find alternative businesses after the war to sustain employment. Unlike Du Pont, which decided to move away from explosives and propellants, Hercules remained focused on these products, which in the late 1920s accounted for 60 percent of its revenue. Hercules also moved into the related business of nitrocellulose intermediates used in the production of paints, pigments, film, rayon, and other coated textiles. It also ventured into an unrelated area of specialty chemicals, using steam-solvent distilling technology to produce naval stores—turpentine, rosin, and pine oil. The key raw material for this product line was pine stumps, which were blasted from farms in the South using Hercules's dynamite. That was the extent of the technological relationship, however, and although Hercules became the world's leading producer in this set of specialties, it took more than a decade to make the business securely profitable.[1]

In 1926 Hercules integrated backward by acquiring the Virginia Cellulose Company, the leading producer of cotton pulp, a major ingredient in nitrocellulose and related products. By the early 1930s, its lines had been expanded to include cellulose acetate, ethyl acetate, gum rosin, chlorinated rubber, and, with the acquisition of the Paper Makers Chemical Corporation in 1931, a line of products for paper production, which complemented the naval stores business. By then, in addition to the 60 percent of sales in explosives and propellants, 25 percent were in cellulose products and 15 percent in naval stores.

During the Great Depression of the 1930s Hercules continued to add to its existing lines of specialty intermediates, but made no attempt to enter the production of petrochemical polymers or polymer intermediates. During World War II it played a minor part in the crash program for synthetic rubber and no role in the high-octane gasoline program that transformed the industry. Instead, it became a major producer of military propellants including those for bazookas and the first rockets, producing as a defense contractor more than did the major multisectored companies reviewed in Chapter 3.[2]

After the war Hercules returned to the production of commercial explosives as well as military propellants and continued to build on its cellulose and naval stores capabilities. In 1958 its explosives department created a chemical propulsion division to develop propellants for missiles and space vehicles. In 1959 it received contracts from the U.S. Air Force to develop new solid-fuel rocket motors and subsequently produced the motor for the third stage of the nation's first solid-fuel intercontinental ballistic missile (ICBM), the Minuteman. Hercules played an even larger role in the development of the Navy's submarine-launched Polaris ICBM. With cellulose came new specialties, including synthetic resins and paper chemicals, as well as carboxymethylcellulose (CMC), an intermediate used in the production of foods, pharmaceuticals, and cosmetics. From naval stores came other new specialty chemicals and an effective insecticide, toxaphene, and other agricultural chemicals.[3]

THE ENTRY INTO PETROCHEMICALS   Because the early 1950s were a period of rapid innovation in polymer/petrochemical technology, Hercules was able to build a new learning base in that industry and become a first mover in one of the most versatile of the new commodities, polypropylene (PP). Its strategy was excellent. The company worked closely with European inventors and companies that, like Hercules, had not been involved in the new technology's wartime development. After pioneering the invention of a new process for phenol resins, it joined with Britain's Distillers Company to commercialize and license the process. Its first plant came on-stream in 1952.[4]

The most dramatic move was a joint effort to commercialize a basic new product—low-density polyethylene (LDPE). Here it worked with its inventor, Karl Ziegler, and a leading German firm, Hoechst, which was also looking for an entry into polymer production. In 1955 Hercules acquired Hoechst's pilot plant for LDPE. Although Hercules was the first company in the United States to produce polymers using the Ziegler process, the market was already crowded. Four firms were producing LDPE using a process developed by Philips, and others soon followed. Nevertheless, because of this learning experience, Hercules became the first producer in the world to market crystalline polypropylene and continued as a major polypropylene producer. From there, it then moved downstream to commercialize polypropylene fiber and film.

In the meantime, Hercules's alliance with Hoechst began to pay off in another area. In 1966 the two firms formed a 50–50 joint venture, Hystron Fibers, for the production of dimethylterephthalate (DMT), a critical intermediate for polyester fibers that was sold to Du Pont and Imperial Chemical Industries (ICI). The joint venture's South Carolina plant came on-stream in 1968 and was highly successful. Hoechst pressed for expansion but Hercules's management decided it could not make the investment on the scale Hoechst desired and so sold its 50 percent share to Hoechst in 1970. This was a critical component in the failure of Hercules to become a major core chemical company: the investments simply were deemed too risky for a company of its size. As the company's historians note, the Hystron episode illustrates its "unwillingness and inability to commit the resources necessary to break into a major new field."[5]

During the 1960s Hercules, like Dow, expanded its new business aggressively overseas, relying increasingly on debt to finance this growth. By the early 1970s approximately 40 percent of Hercules's revenue came from overseas, a higher portion than that of all the major core companies except for Dow. Hercules's overseas direct investment earned a higher return than its domestic operations between 1962 and 1973. On the other hand, unlike Du Pont and Dow, Hercules could not afford to integrate backward into oil and gas production. It continued to expand its production of polypropylene resins but fared better in downstream applications such as fiber and film. During the 1960s Hercules's profits still came largely from its long-established pine and paper chemicals, synthetic resins, and cellulose-based products, all based on its pre–World War II learning base. Steady but smaller profits came from its solid-fuel propulsion capabilities that evolved from its initial propellant base.[6]

As competition intensified, Hercules in 1968 set up a new-enterprise department comparable to the new-venture programs Du Pont and Monsanto had instituted earlier. The ventures included investments in modular housing, furniture frames, magnetic detection devices, photocomposition printing, credit card reading terminals, polyethylene netting, conversion of solid waste into fuels, and intermediate chemicals for flavors and fragrances in both food and cosmetics. All except the last venture failed, and that one success was an extension of its earlier 1950s entry into starch (with a similar molecular configuration as cellulose) and food additives via a small acquisition. Its attempt at modular housing was a debacle comparable to Du Pont's in the same market. Meanwhile, as at Du Pont and Monsanto, new and improved products came out of the Hercules operating division: cellulose intermediates, propellants, and other specialty chemicals. Indeed, the success of these products made 1974 Hercules's fifteenth consecutive year of record sales and the fifth straight year of improved profits. The virtuous strategy of commercializing new products based on past learning of the 1920s and 1950s appeared to be paying off.[7]

FAILURE IN REDEFINING THE STRATEGIC BOUNDARIES In 1975 began what the company's historians call a "time of trial" for Hercules. The reality of the end of growth hit hard as the first energy crisis and the ensuing recession lowered demand. The lifting of price controls on oil proved nearly catastrophic, resulting in a "disaster in DMT," which had been one of the first and most profitable of Hercules's ventures into polymers. Du Pont, with the continuing expansion of its polyester business and the threat of price rises in feedstocks and intermediates, decided to build its own DMT facilities, depriving Hercules of one of its two major customers and greatly expanding overall U.S. production capacity. That left Hercules management with only one real option: to sell its DMT business at a loss. In 1975, after being turned down by Exxon, Texaco, and other oil companies, Hercules formed a joint venture, Hercofina, with the U.S. subsidiary of Belgium's national oil company, Petrofina. Initially, Hercules held a 75 percent share of the equity, but over time it gradually liquidated its stake. Meanwhile, Hercules continued to produce polypropylene and other polymer/petrochemical products.[8]

In the fall of 1977, new CEO Alexander F. Giacco met with the heads of the operating departments (divisions) at a retreat in Hershey, Pennsylvania to determine a new strategy and structure. The result was similar to that Dow would reach in the following year. For Giacco, the preferred strategy was the increasingly standard one for American chemical companies: forward integration to "mov[e] the company towards higher value-added products and services," accomplished by spinning off low value-added products while concentrating on enhancing its capabilities in aerospace and the polymer end-products, film and fiber. A new matrix structure realigned power and responsibility, ending the hold of the highly autonomous divisions.

The company then sold off the two methanol plants owned by Hercofina, one to Ashland Oil the other to Bombay Dye and Manufacturing Company of India; its toxaphene, used in agricultural chemicals, to a joint venture with Boots, the British Drug Company (with Hercules holding a minority stake in the venture); its intermediates for pigments to the Swiss giant Ciba-Geigy; and a substantial share of its holdings in Hercofina to Petrofina. By 1982 the company's gross assets in commodity chemicals had dropped from 43 percent to 28 percent. (By 1985 they would drop to 19 percent.) By that same year, more than 20 percent of Hercules's product lines had been sold, representing $650 million in assets, including the remaining facilities in explosives and insecticides. Its long-term public debt had been reduced so that its debt/equity ratio fell from 55 percent in 1977 to 40 percent in 1983.

Meanwhile, its major polypropylene business continued to produce growth but not significant earnings. By 1983 all senior executives, except Giacco, agreed that the polypropylene market was overcrowded and urged that the business be sold. Instead, Giacco persisted and formed Himont, a 50–50 joint venture with Montedison, the giant Italian chemical company. The aim was to give Hercules the use of Montedison's new polypropylene process while providing Montedison an entry into the U.S. market.[9]

Shortly after new CEO David Hollingsworth took command in 1987, Hercules sold off its 50 percent share of Himont to Montedison. "Once and for all," the new CEO proclaimed, "we have declared [ourselves] out of the game of petrochemical and chemical commodities."

At the same time, Hercules was forced to cut back on another of its major product lines, those of its aerospace products group. During the 1980s it had been a principal contractor for the Defense Department's rocket motor systems. The group's products came to include those for the Trident II and SCAM missiles, and the Trident IV and Delta II Space Launch Programs. In 1989 Hercules had to post a $96 million loss for taking $327 million overcharges on these products. Then the explosion of the Trident IV in 1991 led to further losses. Finally, in 1995, Hercules sold off its aerospace business.[10]

In this way Hercules fell back to commercializing new products from the learning bases it had established in the years between World War I and the 1950s. In 1988, for example, on the basis of its cellulose technologies, it formed Aqualon, a joint venture with Henkel, Germany's largest producer of soap, cleanser, and related chemicals (see Chapter 5). Aqualon became the unquestioned global leader in cellulose derivatives and water-soluble polymers. Subsequently Hercules bought out its partner and later acquired BetzDearborn, a leading American maker of water treatment chemicals, which it later sold to General Electric.

By the early 1990s the company was concentrating its resources on improving and commercializing existing specialty chemicals based largely on its pre–World War II technologies, including paper chemicals, absorbents, resins (including wood-, gum-, and oil-based resins, and peroxide chemicals), flavor and fragrance intermediates, advanced materials, molding systems, and fibers. As a result Hercules had to rely for continued profits and growth on a narrower set of product lines than did the other two of the three largest focused firms, Rohm and Haas and Air Products and Chemicals. Hercules's ranking in terms of sales dropped from 22 to 32 between 1986 and 1993, while the rank of the other two rose slightly, the first from eighteenth to fifteenth and the second twentieth to eighteenth (see Table 1.1).

As a smaller, focused specialty chemical company, Hercules struggled in the late 1990s and was forced to respond to a hostile takeover threat from Samuel Heyman, who had mounted a previous raid against Union Carbide, leading to that company's restructuring and eventual acquisition by Dow. Hercules successfully fended off Heyman but nonetheless put itself up for sale. To manage the process, the board recruited William Joyce, the former Union Carbide CEO, who had led that company into the deal with Dow. The significance of the Hercules story is that the company failed in redefining its strategic boundaries once the chemical industry had reached its limits to growth.[11]

Rohm and Haas Company: A Successful Focused Strategy

In the 1990s Rohm and Haas was still achieving its revenues on the basis of a solid learning base in acrylic chemistry that had been created before World War I. Whereas Hercules's initial capabilities evolved out of Du Pont's learning base, those of Rohm and Haas came from its German parent. The German company was established in 1907 by Otto Röhm, an innovative young entrepreneur who had recently received his Ph.D. in acrylic chemistry from the University of Tübingen, and a young associate, Otto Haas. The company produced a synthetic intermediate for the production of leather. In 1909 Haas set up the company's U.S. subsidiary with a major plant near Philadelphia to produce chemicals for the tanning of leather. During World War I that subsidiary began to produce intermediates for the making of dyes and other textile intermediates. By 1920, after extended legal negotiations with the U.S. government, it had become an American company. During the 1920s it began production of a fast-drying synthetic resin for the varnish trade that Otto Röhm, who continued to head the German company, had commercialized. From that resin technology evolved a new plasticizer for nitrocellulose lacquers, a new insecticide, and most important of all for the company's future, a new plastic material.[12]

Based on Röhm's pioneering work in acrylic chemistry, the U.S. company's researchers, working with their German colleagues, in the 1920s developed methyl acrylate monomers, then polymers, and then in 1936 an end-product: a crystal-clear, shatter-proof methyl acrylate sheet called "Plexiglas." Introduced in 1936, Plexiglas subsequently found a huge market in military aircraft with the coming of World War II. Sales of Plexiglas surged from $431,577 in 1938 to $4.5 million in 1941. The vast expansion of aircraft production permitted Rohm and Haas to mass-produce Plexiglas and its intermediates. By 1945 its output of methyl acrylate was twice that of Du Pont, its only U.S. competitor.[13]

At the end of the war, Rohm and Haas moved quickly to strengthen its hold on the methyl acrylate business. It expanded its wartime capacity in both acrylic monomer and polymer production, then built a large plant to produce the basic feedstock. At the same time, to protect its supply, it acquired oil and gas properties. With the much lower costs resulting from the scale of its operations, Rohm and Haas continued to dominate the U.S. production of both acrylic intermediates and end-products.

In the 1950s, Rohm and Haas moved into higher value-added end-products based on acrylic polymers. These included multiviscosity oils (for automobiles and oil well drilling), and fluid process chemicals. It expanded its older lines in plasticizers and entered, enlarged, and improved its insecticides, fungicides, and herbicides for weed control. In 1960 it moved further into end-products, producing such acrylic-based fibers as Nylon 6 and acrylic elastomeric thread in large plants it built in Fayette, North Carolina and Scranton, Pennsylvania. In the meantime, it moved further afield by acquiring small producers of vaccines and serums for both human and animal use, makers of medical diagnostic equipment, and even a producer of video tape. In 1973, to lower the cost of intermediates, it integrated backward, building a plant to oxidize propylene into acrylate monomers.[14]

Hit hard like Hercules by the rise in costs and drop in demand in the mid-1970s, Rohm and Haas in 1976 reported the first loss in its history. Its management responded quickly to the new situation. Initially, the company decided against competing with Du Pont. In 1977 it sold its acrylic fiber plants to Monsanto and then closed down all fiber-related activities. In the next year came the sale of its medical and pharmaceutical operations (much of these going to the British company Boots). At the same time, following the examples of Hercules, Monsanto, and Du Pont, the managers formed a corporate new-venture group. After viewing the field for potential new products, that group in 1979 reinforced their decision to focus on products where its learned and tested capabilities provided the competitive strength. Because of this disinvestment, Rohm and Haas, unlike Hercules, was less affected by the industry's crisis of 1978–1983. Indeed, the value of its securities rose over this period, while those of nearly all other major chemical companies sharply fell, providing an exemplary demonstration of the financial rewards that result from an early understanding of the limits of the enterprise's capabilities.[15]

After selling off all its oil and gas properties in the early 1980s, Rohm and Haas concentrated almost wholly on developing products that rested on well-developed learning bases. In 1982, it acquired a minority stake in Shipley Co. Inc., which made coatings for electronic components using technology related to Rohm and Haas's expertise in resins. This opened up important new opportunities for the company.

By 1987, 52 percent of its operating profits came from intermediate acrylic polymers, monomers, and resins whose competitive strength was based on capabilities learned during the 1920s and 1930s. Thirty-three percent of operating profits came from acrylic plastic sheet, molding powders, and other acrylic products for which the capabilities had been developed in the 1940s and 1950s; 16 percent were from acrylic lubricants, oil drilling chemicals, and other related intermediates for industrial chemicals. However, its agricultural chemicals, whose production had begun in the 1920s, recorded small losses in 1985 and 1986. In these same years came a determined effort to expand global business, both by direct investment and joint ventures. Between 1983 and 1987, Rohm and Haas's income from foreign sales rose from 32 percent to 58 percent of total revenue.[16]

In the 1990s the company continued to build on existing and closely related product lines, acquiring a unit that produced acrylic vinyl, a minority stake in a maker of precision-surface polishing technology, and Lea Ronal, a maker of specialty chemicals for the electronics industry. In 1998 Rohm and Haas reorganized its operations into three sectors: performance polymers, chemical specialties, and electronic materials. The following year, it completed a major acquisition, paying $4.9 billion for Morton International, including its salt and specialty chemicals businesses (see Chapter 6). This was not an attempt by Rohm and Haas to transform itself into a multisectored core chemical enterprise, but rather to follow its established path in specialty chemicals by adding more specialties. In 2001, Rohm and Haas divested its agricultural chemicals businesses in a $1 billion transaction with Dow.[17]

The evolution of Rohm and Haas's product lines provides an impressive example of how a company used a technology that it was first to commercialize to remain a dominant force during the succeeding decades. Although it had difficulties in competing with the major companies in fiber and agricultural chemicals, it eventually redefined its strategic boundaries within the limits of its technical and functional capabilities. Having learned this lesson, the company chose to grow instead by focusing on new specialties, such as chemicals for the electronic industry.

Air Products and Chemicals, Inc.: Successfully Defining Strategic Boundaries

Air Products and Chemicals was only one of two among the fifty companies listed on Table 1.1 to establish its initial learning base after the 1920s. (The other was Dow Corning (see below), a joint venture created during World

War II.) In 1940 Leonard Pool patented a revolutionary mobile oxygen generator that allowed the gas to be distilled at a customer's plant, thus eliminating the high cost of shipping. Moreover, the timing of his invention proved critical to the creation of the firm's initial learning base. As Pool emphasizes, even in 1940 there was little demand for mobile oxygen generators produced by his company, Air Products. Then came Pearl Harbor and the soaring demand for mobile oxygen generators from the Armed Services and heavy industry.[18]

After the war Air Products concentrated at first on producing generators, which it leased. But soon it was building multibillion dollar operations close to customers like Ford and U.S. Steel. It continued by expanding its lines into liquid hydrogen, and then nitrogen, argon, and synthetic gases. It did so by investing its retained earnings in improved processes and products, and through acquisitions. By the 1970s this expansion made it the second-largest producer of industrial gases in the United States behind Union Carbide. The same vigorous expansion was also pursued in Europe, and by 1970 Air Products ranked fourth worldwide behind France's L'Air Liquide, Germany's Griesheim-Elektron, and Britain's BOC.

In the 1960s Air Products began to diversify through acquisitions, purchasing Catalytic Construction Company, a specialized engineering firm focused on gas processing. It moved into chemicals in 1962 with the purchase of Houdry Chemicals and two other small specialty chemicals companies. Then in 1971 it purchased the chemicals and plastics business unit of Air Reduction Company (Airco), a smaller rival. At the same time it acquired a small medical equipment enterprise.

In the mid-1970s Air Products endured a time of trial comparable to those of Hercules and Rohm and Haas when they confronted the industry's end of growth. However, by selling off its medical equipment and plastic products businesses, as well as undergoing a major internal reorganization of its U.S. and overseas operations, it soon recovered. As the company's historian has written, "By 1978, Air Products had overcome many of its troubles. On balance, moreover, there were more triumphs than troubles."[19] The Air Products story during this period further illustrates the complexities of defining the boundaries of a chemical company in the mid-1970s.

One business that was adversely affected by the 1979–1980 recession was Air Products's engineering services division. Management first attempted to strengthen its less-than-successful engineering business by purchasing in 1982 a Denver-based engineering and construction firm, which was merged into the catalytic construction division. But in 1986, when the merger failed to enhance its engineering activities, Air Products sold off its engineering equipment, service, and construction businesses.

As *Chemical Week* reported in 1988, according to "Air Products's game plan, 70 percent of growth in coming years [was] expected to emanate from the company's core businesses including that of nitrogen and hydrogen, and from chemicals including emulsion and urethane additives." The plan also called for global expansion, for in 1987, 76 percent of its profits still came from the United States.[20]

In the late 1980s and early 1990s Air Products maintained its strength in industrial gases that by then accounted for 80 percent of its operating income. It maintained its smaller chemical business that came with the Air Reduction acquisition. In the United States it increased its market share in part because of Carbide's financial difficulties, although in 1993 it was still second to Praxair, the division spun off by Union Carbide (see Chapter 6). In Europe by 1990 it was tied for second place with a German company, Griesheim, each having 13 percent of the business while L'Air Liquide had 27 percent.[21]

At the same time, Air Products managers reorganized its chemicals business, selling off its commodity polyvinyl chloride (PVC) business to specialize in polyurethane chemicals, and becoming a world leader in that specialty by developing epoxy and polymer emulsions. As the manager of the chemical division noted in 1991, "The key to our chemical business is a strong niche position backed up with good technology and low cost of manufacturing. With the problems of commodities behind us, close to 90 percent of our business is in a niche position, which gives great stability and solid platform for growth."[22]

Air Products and Chemicals, like Rohm and Haas, remained within the boundaries of its learned organizational capabilities. More than Rohm and Haas and Hercules, it became a successful international competitor. Most noteworthy was its ability to focus its small chemical business to become a leader in a much more focused specialty chemical niche.

Group 2: Focused Companies Applying Technology for Different Markets

I now turn to reviewing the evolution of three smaller niche companies—Great Lakes Chemical, Nalco Chemical, and Dow Corning—that remained focused on their original specialties but applied them across a range of markets. I begin with Great Lakes Chemical (GLCC), which had its beginnings in the 1920s, but did not establish its integrated learning base in bromides until the 1950s. It then quickly became a dominant producer of bromide chemicals.

Great Lakes Chemical Corporation: Defining a Basic Niche Strategy

Since the 1950s, GLCC's niche has been bromides and brominated chemical products. By 1970 it had become the largest producer in the United States and during the 1980s grew to be a major player in Europe. Its strategy and structure rendered it one of the most successful of the smaller focused chemical companies. In addition, its story provides an example of a successful latecomer and the reasons for its success.

A small producer of bromides from brine in the 1920s, Great Lakes Chemical was incorporated in Michigan in 1933. In 1948 the McLanahan Oil Company, an oil and gas exploration enterprise in Michigan, purchased Great Lakes Chemical and recast itself as Great Lakes Oil & Chemicals. Through the 1950s, the merged enterprise remained primarily an oil company with bromide wells on the side.[23]

In 1960, on the advice of Earl T. McBee, a professor of industrial chemistry at Purdue University, Great Lakes resolved to withdraw from the oil business and expand in bromine. Besides changing its name to Great Lakes Chemical Corporation, the company acquired several bromine-rich wells in Arkansas. Its next step was to obtain a contract from Du Pont to supply bromide for a plant it was building in Canada. To fulfill that contract, the company's president Charles Hale apparently convinced Dow's managers, who were then conquering the world in petrochemicals, to turn over much of its bromide business to its small neighbor.

Under the guidance of McBee, who succeeded Hale as president in the late 1960s, GLCC then began moving downstream, commercializing bromine-based specialty chemicals, including those for agricultural chemicals (biodegradable soil fumigants and herbicides), and those used in the making of dyes, cleansing powders, synthetic rubber, refrigerants, photographic papers, and flame-retardant additives for plastics. In 1969 the company turned multinational by acquiring three bromine-based manufacturers in Britain. It then formed a joint venture with the French chemical company Pechiney Ugine Kuhlmann to develop biodegradable agricultural chemicals, and formed yet another with a smaller French company to do likewise in flame retardants.

This strategy of growth through focusing on the bromine niche proved so successful that GLCC was less affected by the industry crisis than were the major companies in the United States and Europe. Indeed, senior managers implemented a systematic strategy of commercializing new brominated products for other niche markets. In 1982 the firm entered the bromide-based water treatment business by acquiring control of the Enzyme Technology Corporation, specialists in that new biological discipline. In 1985, its managers decided to concentrate on recreational water treatment by purchasing Pyrex Pool Products. Back in 1982, the company had bought a small enterprise in oil field chemicals, as fluids containing bromide salts were effective agents in flushing oil out of the ground.

In 1989 GLCC entered the European specialty chemicals market by acquisition. It employed these acquisitions to attain dominant positions in other niches. In 1989 it obtained control of the British company Octal Associates and of its operating subsidiary Associated Octal Ltd. Octal was the world's largest supplier of motor fuel additives and Europe's leading producer of key chemical raw materials for those additives. GLCC's commitment was raised to 88 percent when it purchased Shell U.K. Ltd.'s minority stake. This pattern was replicated after the company moved into polymer stabilizers by acquiring two German and one French manufacturers, thus becoming the leader producer in that market.

These acquisitions reflected GLCC's underlying strategy, which in the words of Emerson Kampen, McBee's successor, amounted to "a specialty chemical orientation, leveraging a strong raw materials position, being a low-cost manufacturer, and developing high-performance products." This strategy accounted for gaining a "disproportionate share of the growth markets for bromine-based chemicals, both domestically and internationally." The almost hundred-fold increase in annual revenues over the twenty years of Kampen's tenure resulted from "having operations in one dominant industry segment, but being diversified in that segment." The structure employed to carry out this strategy featured six autonomous business units by product type: flame retardants, intermediates, fine chemicals, petroleum additives, polymer stabilizers, and water treatment. Each group included "its own manufacturing, research and development, and marketing functions."[24]

The history of GLCC demonstrates one strategy for the success of niche chemical companies. Nalco Chemical provides a comparable illustration of this strategy that evolved over a longer period of time.

Nalco Chemical Company: A Single Niche for Many Markets

Since 1920 Nalco Chemical's niche has been chemicals for treating water. The first mover in that industry, it still dominated in the 1990s, controlling one-fifth of the $3 billion worldwide market. On the basis of its initial product, a water softener for steam and diesel locomotives, it commercialized specialized water treatment chemicals for an increasingly broad set of markets. By the 1990s its products were used in pollution control, oil production and refining, steel manufacturing, food processing, energy conservation, papermaking, food products, and mining. This wide-ranging application of its specific learned capabilities has made Nalco a pioneer in the shaping of a new kind of company, the chemical service enterprise.

Nalco originated as National Aluminate Company, the result of a merger in 1928 between two water treatment pioneers, Chicago Chemical Company and Aluminate Sales Corporation. The first of these firms was established in 1920 and manufactured products for industrial plants. The other, formed in 1922, did so for steam locomotives. In 1935 National Aluminate built a giant plant in Naperville, Illinois (its headquarters site near Chicago) that produced zeolite—a water-softening, gel-like chemical—which required several blocks of streets for drying. The demands of World War II greatly enlarged the company's facilities, and enhanced its technical capabilities. After the war, the firm commercialized combinations of specialty chemicals to preserve cooling systems in diesel engines.[25]

During the 1950s the company concentrated on expanding its overseas operations in Italy and acquiring others in Germany, Spain, and Venezuela. In the same decade it upgraded its technical capabilities by commercializing water treatment chemicals for other forms of transportation. For example, it started consulting in the use of its products in the development of the new nuclear submarines and aircraft carriers. Changing its name to Nalco Chemical Company in 1958, it began in the years following to commercialize specialty products based on the new polymer technology, which set new standards in waste management and pollution control. Then, employing a new electrolytic technology, the company developed antiknock additives for gasoline. In these forays, the firm worked with Britain's ICI, creating joint ventures based in the Britain and Australia to make products used in the manufacture of synthetic and natural gas, ammonia, and hydrogen.

Nalco's pattern of new-product development continued in the 1970s with commodities for the pulp and paper industries. During the 1980s the company performed similarly to commercialize products for automobile manufacturers and then for auto dealers, auto-servicing companies, and automobile owners. By then, the company had received 700 patents.

Nalco's strategy proved so successful that the company was little affected by the industry crisis at the end of the 1970s. In 1984, *Fortune* named Nalco one of the thirteen "corporate stars of the decade," with a 22 percent shareholder return to equity during the previous ten years. In 1989 Nalco reported sales of over $1 billion and still held virtually no debt.

Early in the 1990s, the company operated as both a chemical producer and a chemical service company. It did so by directing its global force of 2,200 sales people not only to sell products but also to focus on assisting customers in their many markets to meet increasingly stringent regulations, improve efficiency, and solve technical problems. In 1994 Nalco formed a worldwide collaborative effort with Exxon Chemical to combine their respective specialty petrochemical businesses, a move that further boosted Nalco's international position. Also in the mid-1990s, Nalco concentrated further on international expansion, acquiring small water treatment operations and companies in the Netherlands, Finland, Italy, Sweden, Brazil, and Malaysia, as well as in the United States and Great Britain.

As a postscript: in 1999, the French utility firm, Suez Lyonnaise des Eaux, acquired Nalco for $4.1 billion *in cash* and changed its name to ONDEO Nalco, making it the centerpiece of a worldwide water treatment group.

Dow Corning: A Specialty Chemical Joint Venture

Dow Corning differs from the other smaller niche companies in that it was formed as a joint venture in 1943 between a major core chemical company (Dow Chemical) and the dominant first mover in the American glass industry (Corning Glass Works).

As a joint venture of the two first movers created to meet unexpected wartime needs in the new silicones technology, Dow Corning simply brought together the existing integrated learning bases of its parents. Dow Corning grew steadily and profitably by discovering and exploiting new applications for silicones. Unfortunately, one of these was human implants, a small market that eventually triggered one of the most costly product liability suits in industrial history and the company's bankruptcy in 1995.

In the mid-1930s, Corning scientist J. Franklin Hyde discovered a new way to make silicones, a material that combines the chemical- and temperature-resistant properties of glass with the versatility of plastic. Corning lacked the functional capabilities and scale to commercialize silicones and so joined with Dow in a gentleman's agreement to manufacture the product for use in lubrication and insulation. Because of the sudden huge wartime demands for silicones in aircraft motors, Dow and Corning agreed in April 1942 to build a plant to produce silicone resins adjacent to Dow's complex in Midland, Michigan. Early in 1943 the two companies formed a 50–50 joint venture and incorporated the enterprise as Dow Corning.

The new plant came on-stream in January 1945, with management facing the challenge of finding civilian markets for Dow Corning's products. Meeting that challenge took time as the company slowly built an integrated learning base, which was completed by the late 1950s. The company made some consumer products such as Silly Putty and SightSavers (for cleaning eyeglasses) but discovered much bigger markets in a variety of industrial applications for lubricants, insulators, adhesives, and sealants. By 1992 Dow Corning was the world's largest producer of silicones, with sales of $1.9 billion out of total worldwide silicones sales of $5.5 billion.[26]

In 1964 Dow Corning began making human implants, including female breast implants for cosmetic surgery. Although this business never accounted for more than 1 percent of sales, it almost caused the company's demise. In the 1980s the health effects of breast implants became controversial, with allegations that they could cause cancer. Although the evidence was ambiguous, in 1992 the Food and Drug Administration (FDA) declared a moratorium on the use of silicones breast implants. This ruling opened the door to thousands of lawsuits against manufacturers, including Dow Corning. In 1995, the threat of staggering financial liability forced the company into bankruptcy. Dow Corning remained focused on its initial learning base in silicones and continued to produce thousands of silicone-based specialty products while awaiting an eventual court settlement.

Group 3: Focused Companies Commercializing Related Products in a Single Major Market

Whereas GLCC, Nalco, and Dow Corning illustrate a strategy of dominating a major product and diversifying within many markets, another group of focused companies—Lubrizol and International Flavors and Fragrances—illustrate an alternative strategy: concentrating on a single and increasingly international market.

Lubrizol: Concentrating on Petroleum Additives

The *International Directory*'s sketch of Lubrizol in 1988 begins thus: "When scrutinizing Lubrizol, the world's largest manufacturer of petroleum additives, industry analysts have to pinch themselves to make sure they aren't dreaming. Until recently, the company had no long-term debt."

This story begins in 1928 when two sets of brothers—three Smiths and two Nelsons—founded the company. All had worked at Dow, where the father of the Smiths, a chemistry professor, had long served as principal adviser. Their company, Graphite Oil Products Company, produced chemical additives to enhance the performance of motor vehicle engines. Its initial success resulted from adding chlorine to lubricants used to alleviate overheating in diesel and motor vehicle engines. The most successful product, Lubrizol, became the company's name as well as the source of their integrated learning base, with production plants and marketing networks residing primarily in the United States.[27]

In 1942, with the advent of the spiraling demand for petroleum products, the company concentrated on manufacturing a variety of specialized petroleum additives, including oxidation inhibitors, detergents, and chemicals to reduce breakdowns at high temperatures. These additives were then sold to major oil refineries. This new strategy held risks, as became apparent in the mid-1950s when Texaco decided to integrate backward and produce its own additives. But the risks were clearly worth taking.

By the 1960s Lubrizol was already the world's leading producer of chemically based petroleum additives used in the production of lubricants for heavy machinery and transportation vehicles. During this period, the company enlarged its U.S. operations and moved overseas by creating a marketing organization and then building production plants. This pattern of international expansion through direct investment rather than acquisition continued into the 1980s. By the early 1990s, Lubrizol maintained plants in England, France, Spain, Canada, Australia, South Africa, Venezuela, and Japan. In implementing this strategy, Lubrizol appeared "extremely combative in guarding its patent rights," an indication of its technical and development capabilities that were the result of following the virtuous strategy of bringing to market new products on the basis of learning and profits from earlier innovations.

During the 1980s Lubrizol's sales were not in the top hundred of the *Fortune 500*, yet it ranked as one of *Fortune*'s top forty companies in terms of stock performance. This success signals that the chemical industry's crisis had little impact on Lubrizol's competitive and financial performance. Indeed, the company profited further when the government placed a prohibition on the use of leaded gasoline, thereby creating fresh demand for new lubricants to replace the lubricating action of leaded fuel. As a result, Lubrizol's managers clearly saw no reason to stray beyond the boundaries defined by the integrated learning base built to meet the expansion of its product line during World War II.

In the mid-1980s Lubrizol completed a set of acquisitions to exploit the potential of the new genetic engineering technology (see Chapter 10). In 1983 it purchased a small biotechnology seed company, which was followed by a major acquisition of Agrigenetics, the leading producer in this field. Although that firm reported a $40 million annual loss, Agrigenetics was a first mover in plant genetics, employing recombinant DNA (rDNA) technology to develop hybrid seeds. Oil from these seeds held potential for Lubrizol to incorporate in improved additives. Although the company made additional investments and participated in several small joint ventures in biotechnology and bioengineering, it retreated from these and other noncore business investments in the mid-1990s. By the end of the century, Lubrizol remained fully focused on its core business in chemical additives.

Lubrizol thus provides an example of an enterprise that dominated a single niche successfully for more than four decades. International Flavors and Fragrances accomplished much the same in very different markets.

*International Flavors and Fragrances: Comparable Success
in a Very Different Market*

Like Lubrizol, International Flavors and Fragrances (IFF) was a business-to-business enterprise. But whereas Lubrizol's customers were primarily large, often giant, petroleum companies, IFF's represented a multitude of companies—large, mid-sized, and small—in consumer chemicals (soaps, cosmetics, and the like), food of all kinds, and pharmaceuticals. In such markets, scale was less of a factor in creating barriers to entry.

Although the company's current name came into being only with a major merger in 1958, IFF originated in 1909 as Morana, Inc., a producer of perfumes. In 1917 Arnold Lewis Van Ameringen, a Dutch perfumer, moved to New York City to start his own company and then merged it with Morana. As its employees were highly skilled, highly paid, and sworn to secrecy, the company became during the 1920s a leader in its unique small specialized niche. In 1958 it was still a small perfume-producing enterprise with sales of $28.4 million, only 10 percent of which derived from food flavoring.[28]

In 1958 Van Ameringen merged with a leading Dutch company by whom he had been employed before setting up his own company in New York. The new company, named International Flavor and Fragrances, became an immediate success in Europe, where it focused on food flavors. Facilities were quickly established in Holland, Switzerland, France, and Brazil. Within two years, makers of food products in these countries were employing IFF flavors to produce cake mixes, gelatin deserts, candies, and even over-the-counter pharmaceutical products. By 1960 the new flavors division accounted for 35 percent of the $34.2 million total sales of the new company.

The next year Van Ameringen retired, turning the presidency over to Henry Walter, a trusted adviser for years. Walter continued to focus on the overseas market, which by 1965 represented 51 percent of sales. During the 1960s, however, the fragrance market grew faster than food in the United States, with such firms as Revlon, Procter & Gamble, and Colgate-Palmolive becoming major customers. By early 1970, flavors (food) had retreated to 25 percent of net income.

The chemical industry's oil crisis of the 1970s did affect IFF, especially after the second oil shock, as the price of oil-based ingredients quadrupled and those derived from chemicals soon followed suit. At the same time, the fragrance market leveled off with sales at $450 million. Walter then refocused on expanding the food division through increases in research budget and in meeting the new demands for health foods, so that by 1984 the food division once again accounted for 38 percent of total sales. In the 1980s and 1990s the company continued to enhance its learning in all its functional capabilities. By 1993 sales had risen to over a billion dollars.

From the start, Van Ameringen had created a highly focused company, a leader in U.S. markets. Moreover, after 1958 the firm became a highly successful competitor in international markets. But, unlike the other enterprises described in this chapter, its barriers to entry lay not in scale but in the quality of its products, protected by secrecy, by a stream of improved products, and by patents.

Group 4: The Idiosyncratic Companies

The paths of learning of the two remaining focused companies evolved in a very different manner than those of the other eight. Cabot was a 125-year-old company that passed through several distinct stages of business. Witco remained a marketing company until after World War II and then paid the price as a latecomer. It searched for and ultimately failed to find a satisfactory niche.

Cabot Corporation: Exploring the Strategic Boundaries of the Firm over Eight Decades

The Cabot Corporation started operations in 1882 when Godfrey Cabot, following graduation from Harvard, built a plant in eastern Pennsylvania to produce carbon black, an essential additive used in his brother Samuel's paint and stain business. Seven years later, Godfrey acquired Samuel's factory. Simultaneously, he was integrating backward into buying and drilling natural gas sites that provided the basic raw materials for making carbon black. As the Pennsylvania fields began to dry up, Cabot made further acquisitions in West Virginia. By 1897 his company was one of the nation's largest carbon black producers.[29]

The coming of the automobile at the beginning of the new century transformed Cabot's markets, for carbon black became a stabilizing and reinforcing agent in tires. Cabot's growth echoed that of the motor vehicle industry, a source of demand that lasted until 1930, the first year of the Great Depression. By then, Cabot had built eight carbon black plants in Texas and one in Oklahoma. At the same time, the company transferred its headquarters to Texas, where its investments in natural gas drilling and production evolved into its principal business, with the residual from these operations used for its carbon black manufacturing. Indeed, by 1939, over 50 percent of its sales derived from its natural gas business, 35 percent from carbon black, and the rest from related products. The onset of World War II precipitated the government-sponsored synthetic rubber program, in which Cabot played a significant role. By 1950 Cabot had become the largest producer of carbon black in the United States and a major producer of natural gas.

In the 1950s, like Dow and the other major core companies, Cabot looked to opportunities abroad. It built its first carbon black plant in 1950 near Liverpool in England, followed by one in Canada (1953), France (1958), and Italy (1966), as well as investing in partially owned plants in Australia in 1959 and the Netherlands in 1960.

At the end of the 1950s Cabot's top managers turned to process-related diversification. Employing a technology closely related to that used in producing carbon black, they began in 1957 to make fumed silica, which was processed from sand and provided reinforcement, viscosity, control, and free-flow properties in the production of a variety of products, including silicones, adhesives and sealants, and reinforced plastics and coatings. At the same time, Cabot pioneered in commercializing liquefied natural gas, again using a closely related process that was fed by natural gas shipped from abroad to depots in Everett, Massachusetts and New York City.

Then, in 1963, Cabot moved beyond the existing boundaries of its capabilities into "two completely new arenas": the production of titanium, a high-performance metal, and experimental plastic polymers and compounds. In time, it became a world leader in the production of thermoplastics used in film. The year 1970 witnessed another move by Cabot into high-performance materials with the acquisition of Union Carbide's Stellite division, a producer of nickel- and cobalt-based alloys designed to withstand extreme heat, corrosion, and wear. In 1978, the company expanded this line by purchasing a producer of several high-performance metals including tantalum, used extensively by computer and electronics manufacturers. Then, prompted by the continuing energy crisis, Cabot stepped up its gas exploration, upgraded its pipeline and distribution systems, and acquired further pipelines and processing plants.

In implementing this diversification strategy, Cabot, like Union Carbide, heeded the advice of the Boston Consulting Group, which advised the company to treat its chemical business, particularly carbon black, as a "Cash Cow" to fund the costs of entering the high-performance metals and plastic materials businesses in which Cabot possessed no technical capabilities. Consequently, chemical plants were allowed to deteriorate. When natural gas prices collapsed in the mid-1980s, Cabot was left without profits with which to reduce its increased debt resulting from the acquisitions and construction of facilities during the 1970s.

In 1987 the Cabot family, still the major stockholder, brought in new CEO Samuel Bodman, a former MIT chemistry professor who at that time was a senior executive at Fidelity Investments, Boston's leading investment house. Bodman succeeded in turning the company around. First, he allocated half a billion dollars to upgrade the existing chemical plants and facilities, particularly those in carbon black and fumed silica. To cover these costs and to enhance the company's competitive strength, he adopted a strategy that Jack Welch, CEO at General Electric, had made famous: "Fix it, close it, or sell it." Welch's aim was to position his major operating units to be the largest or second-largest in revenues in their industry. Bodman began by selling off

Cabot's high-performance metals business, retaining only its specialized operation in capacitor tantalum and a smaller one in niobium metals and alloys. He then disposed of Cabot's almost century-old natural gas business, but retained the newer liquefied natural gas unit.

By the 1990s Cabot was the largest producer of carbon black in each of the world's four industrial regions—North America, Latin America, the Pacific area, and Europe. It also achieved status as number one in North America and number two worldwide in the highly specialized market for fumed silica. The Cabot performance division had become smaller and more focused. It was the world's dominant producer in another small niche, that of tantalum products. In plastics, it had become a major producer of monoplastic concentrates, with plants in Belgium, Italy, Great Britain, and Hong Kong. It also established growing businesses in pigment-based inks and in drilling fluids.

Under Bodman, Cabot transformed itself into a successful enterprise by focusing on economies of scale not only in major markets but also in highly specialized ones. Its managers successfully defined strategic boundaries around the existing technical and functional capabilities of its long-established learning base and a few carefully selected products from its earlier broad diversification moves.

Witco Corporation: Failing to Find a Niche

Witco, like Cabot, began with carbon black but, from its start, it evolved along a very different path. Its story is essentially the antithesis of Cabot's and ends in strategic failure. The company's evolution reflects its origins, for unlike the other niche companies reviewed here, Witco started up and remained until after World War II a distributing rather than a processing enterprise. Lacking the learning and profits generated by an integrated learning base, its postwar growth depended on acquisitions, a strategy ultimately doomed to failure.

In 1920 Robert Wishnik, whose family had migrated from Russia at the beginning of the century, established a company to market carbon black and various other colorings to Chicago's printing industry. He soon added asphalt to his line. In 1924 his firm purchased its first factory, an asphalt plant in Louisiana.[30]

With the increasing demands for his products following the advent of World War II, Wishnik and his partners quickly resolved to shift to being a manufacturing enterprise, selling only the products that their company produced. Its initial growth therefore, had to arise largely from acquisitions, primarily in stearates, a fatty acid processed in much the same way as carbon black and asphalt.

For Witco, the 1960s was a decade of diversification, inevitably by acquisition. The first new deal was the purchase of Sonneborn Chemical and Refining Company, whose specialty was additives for motor oils and lubricants, including petroleum sulfates. Then Witco bought a tar distilling company that produced detergents, as well as tar and comparable products. Next came a move overseas with the purchase of companies in Belgium, Great Britain, and France, as well as Canada, producing the same lines. Witco invested in another new area in 1966 by acquiring a plastics manufacturer, which also produced petroleum specialties that complemented Witco's existing line. Still another purchase extended its detergent line, and yet another expanded its plastics line by adding plasticizers and stabilizers. Acquisitions continued into the 1970s, but they were fewer in number and some were even less related to Witco's existing lines. By 1979 the company had eighteen operating divisions producing a variety of chemical and petroleum products, some related and some not. It had, in fact, developed a strategy of unrelated diversification within the chemical industry's competitive arena.

With the onset of the second oil crisis in 1979, Witco repositioned with an about-turn, selling off over the next seven years a sizable number of product lines, including detergents and urethane, and slowly began to upgrade its aging facilities in its existing operations for chemical and petroleum markets. By 1985, 53 percent of its sales came from petroleum specialties and 41 percent from chemicals.

In the early 1990s a new president made the first serious attempt to restructure the headquarters by building an effective corporate advisory staff. Witco's many divisions were consolidated into a smaller number of chemical groups. He then acquired the industrial chemicals and natural substance divisions of Germany's Schering AG for $440 million. As a result, Witco's chemical sector accounted for 58 percent of its sales and its global presence increased.

Witco's search for a substantial niche was an unprofitable one. Its income as percentage of sales ranked lower than any of the other focused companies described in this chapter. In the early 1990s its income averaged $60 million on revenues of $1.4 billion. Because Witco grew through acquisitions, its patent record was as weak as its financial one. In 1999 it was absorbed by

Crompton & Knowles in a $2 billion exchange of stock. The new company, Crompton Corporation, manufactured specialty chemicals and equipment used in products such as tires, paper, auto parts, and other specialty markets.

The Specialized Engineering Firms

During the 1980s the chemical industry had become an industry of producers of specialty products based on the science of chemistry. I close this chapter by reviewing the evolution of a similar branch of the industry based on chemical engineering—namely, the specialized engineering firms (SEFs). These institutional arrangements further emphasized the differences between manufacturing processes in chemicals and in other high-volume, capital-intensive industries such as metals, machinery, motor vehicles, and others. And, above all, production processes in chemicals diverged markedly from those in electrical and electronic equipment, as I described in my earlier book, *Inventing the Electronic Century.*

For these reasons, the technical capabilities in the chemical industry are based not only on the potential of chemical sciences but also on the practice of chemical engineering. This discipline involves controlling the flows within the high-volume plant in very precise quantities and to very specific qualities, so as to ensure the maximum advantage of economies of scale in reducing unit costs and economies of scope in producing distinct products from closely related mixtures. Thus the emergence of modern chemical engineering proved central to the process of commercializing the fruits of chemical science. The crucial institution in the nexus became, in turn, the SEFs that built the processing plants.

Critical to the discipline of chemical engineering was the concept of unit operations. In the words of Arthur D. Little, an MIT professor who pioneered this concept: "Any chemical process, on whatever scale conducted, may be resolved into a coordinating series of what may be termed 'unit actions,' as pulverizing, mixing, heating, roasting, absorbing, condensing, lixiviating, precipitating, crystallizing, filtering, dissolving, electrolyzing, and so on. The number of these basic unit operations is not very large and relatively few of them are involved in any particular process." This approach enabled chemical engineering to develop into a quantitative discipline with a set of methodological tools and a standardized educational curriculum. Here, MIT played the pioneering role.[31]

The unit approach made it possible to build large plants that guaranteed the critical commercial advantages of scale and scope. In scaling up, chemical engineers used the "sixth-tenths rule," with capital costs increasing only 66 percent of the increase in a chemical processing plant's rated capacity. Hence, the "scaling up" process from the bench-scale design, to pilot plants, to those of commercial plants, or from small-scale to large-scale plants, became critical for long-term competitive success.

The SEFs had appeared well before World War II. In the United States, they included Stone & Webster, a long-established Boston-based industrial consulting firm, M. W. Kellogg (which along with Stone & Webster maintained close ties with MIT), Badger, Foster-Wheeler, Universal Oil Corporation, and the Lummus Company. They served at that time primarily as suppliers of specialized equipment and provided specialized technology. Then, with the advent of the polymer/petrochemical revolution and the resulting soaring of output and explosion of new chemical products, the SEFs assumed their central place in the industry. By 1960 a pioneering study reported that "[nearly] three-fourths of the new major plants were engineered, procured, and constructed by specialized plant contractors." In so doing, the SEFs also evolved into a major source of new process technologies. According to the same study, from 1960 to 1966, they were responsible as a group for almost 30 percent of all licenses issued for chemical processes. A later study demonstrates that, from 1980 to 1990, three-fourths of the world's plants were designed by SEFs.[32]

Although the SEFs first became central nexus institutions in the United States, once the nexuses of other national industries expanded, they spread abroad. In 1966 the U.S. firms accounted for close to 60 percent of the plants built worldwide. Between 1980 and 1992, their share of the world market had fallen to 26 percent while the German competitors had risen to 11.7 percent, those in Great Britain to 8.1 percent, with those in Italy, France, and Japan accounting for 5.1, 3.2, and 4.0 percent, respectively.

The most successful American SEF in these years was Universal Oil Corporation (UOC), founded in 1914. It licensed out the first continuous catalytic process for refining petroleum (see Chapter 6). During the 1930s, as the industry's leading research enterprise, the firm transitioned from catalyst innovation to developing "more elegant techniques to shape the molecules of petroleum feedstock." By the early 1950s, according to Peter Spitz, the historian of the petrochemical industry, UOC was "in a position to serve as the primary licenser of aromatic technology to the petroleum and chemical industries." Of the major postwar SEFs, Ralph Landau's Scientific Design quickly became a leader in the industry. By the early 1980s Scientific Design and its successor, Halcon, had sold over one hundred licenses or corresponding patent rights.[33]

During the postwar polymer/petrochemical boom the SEFs had the potential to become significant focused enterprises. They possessed the essential specialized processing and engineering capabilities and had pioneered in the development of many specific technologies. But none of the SEFs nurtured the product development, manufacturing, and marketing capabilities necessary to create an integrated learning base with which to compete with existing core producers.

Only one tried, and it failed—the postwar newcomer, Landau's Scientific Design. His story helps to understand why, with the exception of the wartime babies, Air Products and Dow Corning, the fifty largest chemical producers in the United States had established their learning bases by the 1930s.

As Landau has written, he planned from the beginning to become a successful entrant into chemical manufacturing. "Our goal was to enter the chemical manufacturing industry using our own technology. The reason was simple: in the words of bank robber Willie Sutton, 'That is where the money is.'" This conviction was "formed as we saw our licensees increasingly willing to pay for our successes but not for our failures."[34]

Landau's approach involved "corporate partnerships," and he pursued two. The first was a proposal to Amoco (Standard Oil of Indiana) in 1955 to make a key ingredient of polyester fiber, using a process developed by Scientific Design. Amoco scoffed at the proposal, however, and its vice president of research told Landau that such a deal "would be like the mating of an elephant and a mouse." The proposal failed and Scientific Design ended up selling its technology to Amoco.

The other move, this time consummated, was partnering with Atlantic Richfield (Arco) in 1966. Based on Scientific Design technology to make propylene oxide, the two companies formed a 50–50 joint venture, the Oxirane Corporation, "primarily concerned with R&D, and engineering design." Arco provided 90 percent of the project's initial capital. After the first plant was completed at Bayport, Texas, two more were built, one of them in Rotterdam. Construction of these new larger plants was required to ensure the benefits of the essential economies of scale and scope. Next came the construction of a fourth plant, which "cost many hundreds of millions of dollars." Then, in October 1979, Paul Volcker, chairman of the Federal Reserve Board, boosted the prime interest rate to 21 percent and, wrote Landau, "suddenly, all our cash-flow was going to the banks." So Landau sold out to Arco. Thereafter, no other nexus firm attempted to build an integrated learning base comparable to the niche firms. And no nexus enterprise had grown large enough to become listed in Table 1.1.

Conclusion: The Focused Specialty Companies Become the Industry

As the twenty-first century opened, only two of the nation's six multi-sectored companies that had created the U.S. chemical industry still existed—Du Pont and Dow. On the other hand, all but two of the smaller focused companies—Hercules and Witco—were now the leaders in a healthy American specialty chemical industry.

Before reviewing their achievements, a word is needed on the troubled Hercules and failed Witco. Hercules's misfortunes resulted from its delay in redefining its strategic boundaries after it encountered limits to growth. In 1977, around the same time that Dow had massively redefined its strategic boundaries, Hercules's management reached similar conclusions. But unlike Dow, Hercules remained committed to petrochemical and chemical commodities. By the time a new CEO took the company out of petrochemicals in 1987, it was too late.

Witco failed because it was unable to surmount the barriers to entry created by the chemical industry's major competitors and first movers. (Allied Chemical's initial strategy, which restricted investment in R&D, meant that even a much bigger company had been unable to establish such barriers.) As a latecomer, Witco was unable to find a profitable niche. By the 1950s the barriers to entry created by the focused specialty chemical companies through the economies of scale and scope were already too high.

The evolution of the two idiosyncratic companies, Witco and Cabot, well illustrates the themes of this book. Witco proved unable to overcome the barriers to entry created by the focused companies and failed to find a secure niche. Cabot, on the other hand, prospered through the decades as a producer of carbon black before turning in the 1950s to the strategy of closely related diversification. Then, as its historian notes, it entered into "two completely new arenas." In 1987, however, a new CEO sold the new businesses and returned the company to profitability by concentrating on the base business and closely related businesses.

From their beginnings, the other smaller focused companies played critical roles in the evolution of the U.S. chemical industry. Established in the 1920s, they provided the major American chemical companies with a variety of specialty chemicals needed to support the U.S. industry. At the same time, these specialty chemicals found a multitude of uses in many other industries. As a result, the focused companies became and remained central players in the competitive arena in which the strategic boundaries of the chemical companies were defined.

The focused companies played an even greater role with the coming of the polymer/petrochemical revolution, which, because it took place during World War II, was commercialized primarily by American companies. Once postwar Europe was on its way to recovery, eight of these companies, including Cabot and Witco, quickly entered the European market in the 1950s, followed by Lubrizol and Nalco in the 1960s. Thus, they provided a range of specialty chemicals not yet fully commercialized in Europe. The specialized engineering firms played a comparable role in the building of chemical plants abroad, primarily in Europe.

The end of chemicals as a growth industry in the 1970s had much less impact on most of these specialty chemical and engineering companies than it had on the major core chemical companies. Most of the focused companies continued to prosper in the 1990s and beyond. In the 1980s and 1990s Great Lakes Chemical, Lubrizol, and Nalco were listed among the nation's most prosperous industrial enterprises. Obviously, these companies made no attempt to enter pharmaceuticals. Nor did they search for merger partners, although Nalco was eventually acquired. Because new learning in chemical sciences and engineering was no longer creating major new technologies, the American industry had become one of producers of specialty chemicals based on technologies introduced in the 1920s and again in the 1940s and 1950s. As we saw in Chapter 3, this was true not only of the focused companies, but also of Du Pont and Dow, the lone remaining multisectored companies.

CHAPTER 5

The European Competitors

Table 1.1, which lists the largest chemical companies in the United States by sales in 1993, includes ten subsidiaries of European chemical producers. The Europeans, in fact, created the modern chemical industry in the late nineteenth century, when German and Swiss producers in the Rhine Valley took advantage of local sources of raw materials and energy and of relationships with local universities and research institutes to establish formidable enterprises that dominated world markets until World War I.

The evolution of the European chemical industry differs in significant ways from that of the American chemical industry. First, the world wars disrupted production and closed off markets for the powerful German companies, leaving them in the wars' aftermaths to face much stronger competitors abroad. Second, because of World War II, the European companies, including the Germans, were latecomers to the polymer/petrochemical revolution, although by the 1960s they had become significant players. Third, the European competitors were geographically more concentrated. For example, of the European companies listed on Table 1.1, seven are (or were) located on or close to the Rhine. Fourth, the major German and Swiss companies were from the start first movers not only in chemicals but also in pharmaceuticals, and remained so throughout the twentieth century. Finally, smaller focused companies, so central to the building of the American industry, appear to have played much less of a role in Europe.

The story begins with the Big Three German producers: Bayer, Hoechst, and BASF. I turn then to reviewing the evolution of the principal Swiss challengers, Ciba, Geigy, and Sandoz, followed by that of the British Imperial Chemical Industries (ICI), a less successful competitor. Then I examine the evolving paths of learning of the remaining Rhine River companies that did not compete directly with the German Big Three, the Swiss, or ICI. These were Henkel, Solvay, and Akzo. The chapter then ends with the failure of the leading French company, Rhône-Poulenc, to challenge the Rhine Valley companies, and indeed to compete successfully in international markets.

Bayer, Hoechst, and BASF: The First European Path-Definers

The creation of the modern chemical industry by Bayer, Hoechst, and BASF is one of the most impressive achievements in the annals of industrial history. The three began in the 1880s to commercialize the first manmade dyes. They were not the inventors of this new technology; they acquired them from British and French pioneers.[1]

Then, in the 1880s and 1890s, these firms built their integrated learning bases and established the new industrial organic chemical industry. They constructed large plants covering hundreds of acres on the banks of the Rhine River that provided economies of both scale and scope. Vast supplies of coal—both the source of energy and the raw material for the production processes—entered from river docks and adjoining train yards and were transformed first into large-scale quantities of aromatics and other intermediates and then into a number of end-products. At the same time, the firms formed marketing organizations in Europe, and then in the United States and Asia, since every customer of the new synthetic dyes had to be taught the techniques of their use and application, as these differed substantially from those of the existing natural dyes.

During this same period the firms created the world's first large-scale industrial laboratories, where highly organized research concentrated on improving existing processes and products as well as discovering new ones. All three quickly developed close ties with the leading research-oriented university faculties and played a significant role in setting up independent research organizations, all critical to the commercializing of existing and potential knowledge. At the same time, they recruited managerial staffs for each of the functions of development, production, marketing, and distribution, and established a general staff, headed by doctoral-level chemists, to assist the senior executives to oversee and monitor the enterprise's overall activities. In this way, they were the pioneers not only in the chemical and pharmaceutical industries but also in shaping the management organization of modern high-technology enterprises.

In the 1880s the three firms were the first to use the same coal-tar feed-stocks, intermediates, and technical knowledge acquired in dye production to develop a variety of coal-tar-based pharmaceuticals, thereby becoming world leaders in commercializing such new synthetic drugs as sedatives, pain killers, serums, vaccines, and fever depressants. Somewhat later, employing the same technical knowledge, they began to lead the way in commercializing photochemicals.

The evergrowing needs of Bayer, Hoechst, and BASF greatly expanded their supporting infrastructures. The operating requirements of these three firms and their relatively few smaller competitors vastly increased the demand for basic acids and other chemicals, especially ammonia, produced by the recently invented Solvay process. Their capital equipment needs, especially for complex processing and process-control equipment, like their demands for technical knowledge, sustained their expanding ties to universities and independent research institutions. In this way, by 1913, the requirements of these core firms and their smaller dye-producing satellites, Accumulatatoren Fabri (AGFA), Cassella, Kalle, and Weiler-ter-Mer (as well as Griesheim-Elektron, a producer of needed organic chemicals by the new electrolytic process), created a national infrastructure in organic chemicals that by then dominated the world in the production of synthetic dyes and then pharmaceuticals, and led the way in photographic chemicals.

In 1913, of the worldwide dye production of 160,000 tons, the German companies accounted for 140,000, and another 10,000 was produced by their Swiss neighbors. Britain, the industry's innovator, produced only 4,000 tons that year, while France, the United States, and other nations produced even less. And of the total German sales of £13.5 million, the Big Three accounted for £10.5 million, with the other German firms just listed producing most of the rest.[2] These three largest producers of chemicals worldwide in the early 1880s would remain the largest producers of chemicals worldwide more than a century later, despite Germany's turbulent history during that century, during which four different "Reichs" were built. (As will be discussed below and in Chapter 9, however, Hoechst transformed itself in the 1990s into a pharmaceutical company, joining with partners to form Aventis.)

By 1913 the individual paths of learning of these multisectored first movers had begun to diverge. Bayer, the largest, which had paved the way in dye production, had already developed a strong base in pharmaceuticals by commercializing in the 1890s aspirin and several sedatives. A little later, Bayer moved into photochemicals and then started to make paints, pigments, and lithopone (used in rubber and linoleum products). Bayer was also the first to invest directly in the United States, building a plant in Rensselaer, New York before the turn into the twentieth century to produce specialized dyes for the leather market. By 1905 that plant was turning out aspirin and other pharmaceuticals as well.

Hoechst entered pharmaceuticals in the 1880s, even earlier than Bayer, when the company financed the Robert Koch Institute in Berlin, which was advancing the new technology with a staff of pioneers, including Emil von Behring and Paul Ehrlich, who were developing new pharmaceutical knowledge. Under their guidance, Hoechst commercialized serums for diphtheria and other contagious diseases, vaccines, pain killers (Novocain), and the new therapeutic drug Salvarsan, a cure for syphilis.

BASF, on the other hand, concentrated more on the manufacture of standard dyes, and produced much more of the basic intermediates, both organic and inorganic. Of the Big Three, BASF was the leader in chemical engineering and process innovation. Between 1903 and 1913, two of its chemists—Fritz Haber as the discoverer and Carl Bosch as the co-developer—pioneered a way to produce nitrates from air that became the basic ingredients for fertilizers and military explosives.

As these different learning bases continued to evolve, the three companies and their smaller allies increasingly came to rely on interfirm cooperation. By 1904, Bayer, BASF, and the smaller AGFA formed Interessengemeinschaft, or "I. G."—that is, a community of interest. The Driebund, as it was called, pooled profits—43 percent apiece to BASF and to Bayer and 14 percent to AGFA—and coordinated policies on technical activities, sales, and patents. In 1907 Hoechst and Cassella acquired 88 percent of the stock of Kalle with the goal of comparable cooperation. In 1916, under the challenge of World War I pressures, the two groups joined together with Greisheim Elektron, the electrochemical producer, in a single I. G.

The basic structure of the German chemical industry remained much the same throughout World War I and then through the postwar years of superinflation and the French and Dutch military occupation of the Ruhr region in 1923. After the Dawes Plan introduced stability to the German economy by reconstructing the nation's banking system and its debt structure, the eight members of the 1916 I. G. began extended negotiations in April

1924 to merge into a single enterprise. They finally agreed to exchange their corporate shares for those of a new enterprise, I. G. Farbenindustries AG, and so in October 1925, the giant I. G. Farben came into being.[3]

The Interwar Years: The Role of the Big Three in I. G. Farben

Although much of the industry was merged into a single enterprise, the long-established integrated learning bases remained largely independent. The newly created enterprise was to be managed through "operating communities." In the words of Carl Duisberg, Bayer's CEO and major planner of the merger's management structure, each operating community "*shall manage its own work* as far as possible under the supervision of a central office, [and] shall *control* its own and compete with other operating communities in ideal competition [*idealem Wettbewerb*]." The three major operating communities were the Upper Rhine Community (basically BASF), the Middle Rhine Community (Hoechst), and the Lower Rhine Community (Bayer). After the consolidation, the number of dyes produced was sharply reduced.[4]

Each of the operating communities remained multisectored around a broad set of comparable technologies. The Upper Rhine Community (BASF) continued to produce dyes, intermediates, and other chemicals, but its primary activity centered on the manufacture of synthetic ammonia and nitrogenous fertilizers. The Middle Rhine (Hoechst) remained the hub of the production of pharmaceuticals, and also manufactured vat dyes, acetylene, and acetates, as well as developed synthetic rubber. The Lower Rhine (Bayer) sustained making fine dyes, pharmaceuticals, and photochemicals and paper. In addition, a fourth and smaller operating community in central Germany, with headquarters in Berlin, handled AGFA's photographic film and camera activities. Somewhat later, the Griesheim Works of Liepzig became a fifth operating community, responsible for chemically produced light metals, magnesium, and aluminum.

Essential for maintaining the existing learning bases in each operating community was top management's decision to direct the laboratories to continue the work they had been doing. At the central laboratory of the Lower Rhine unit at Leverkusen there was, in addition to the established color laboratory, a moth laboratory (for developing mothproof clothing as well as for insecticides) and a rubber laboratory that retained earlier work on synthetic rubber. The central laboratory of the Middle Rhine operating community sustained its focus on vat dyes. And another laboratory conducted research on acetylene, whose production had been concentrated in that community. Of the major laboratories of the Upper Rhine, one devoted its attention to the development of synthetic intermediates, including resins, styrene, and ethylene, while another concentrated on high-pressure synthesis technology.

Thus, I. G. Farben had no corporate central laboratory comparable to that of Du Pont. As a Du Pont executive was told in 1936, "There is no standardization of practice in the operations of these different laboratories, as it is felt very desirable to maintain as far as possible the old tradition and independence of the functioning of each laboratory. Many of these laboratories have had administrative practices in operation for many years, and no attempt has been made to standardize a particular procedure." Although "some overlapping existed," Farben's senior research executive felt "that is relatively unimportant and above all he wishes to preserve, as far as feasible, the traditions of each research laboratory." For the I. G. Farben managers, learning remained a continual self-reinforcing process for maintaining its capabilities in each of its major existing as well as commercializing new product lines.[5]

After its formation, I. G. Farben quickly returned to its foreign markets. During World War I the German firms not only were driven out of overseas markets by the British blockade but also their direct investment in foreign plants and offices, as well as patents, was expropriated by the victorious powers. In 1928 I. G. Farben founded a U.S. subsidiary, General Aniline and Film (GAF), to operate two dye works and a pharmaceutical factory Farben had recently acquired, as well as to market its German-made products, particularly dyes. By 1929 GAF had become not only the market leader in dyes in the United States, but also a strong competitor in pharmaceuticals. In addition, after purchasing a small photographic equipment firm, I. G. Farben incorporated AGFA-Anesco to position that firm as the first successful challenger in the United States to Eastman Kodak. Farben's recovery was comparable in the markets of the British Empire and continental Europe. As noted by William Reader, the historian of Britain's ICI, the Swiss I. G. in the 1920s was "the only effective competitor in world markets of I. G. Farbenindustrie."[6]

There then ensued a decade of economic, political, and social turbulence beginning with the Great Depression and followed by the Nazi takeover in 1933, the shift to national autarky, and industrial mobilization for war and conquest—all of which directed I. G. Farben's focus toward the new governmental and military demands. The enterprise maintained a profit from its major commercial lines—dyes, pharmaceuticals, and films—but its principal research efforts were in the production of synthetic gasoline and rubber, both from coal-based intermediates, as well as of silicon and magnesium. The research laboratories continued to concentrate on developing new product lines, including those based on polymer chemistry, but they were not commercialized in the manner of comparable developments in the United States during the 1930s. Moreover, since the developments in synthetic gasoline and rubber were based on coal, not petroleum, their production did not result in the same learning of high-volume petrochemical production that occurred in the United States. Also, postwar recovery was further retarded because the Rhine-based facilities of the original Big Three had been seriously damaged.

Postwar Recovery of Germany's Big Three

Between 1945 and 1951, each of the major operating units were under the control of different Allied governments. Bayer's facilities were in the British zone, Hoechst's in the American, and BASF's in the French. With the termination of Allied occupation and the formal breakup of I. G. Farben in 1952, recovery began in earnest. BASF returned to operating its pre-1925 facilities, and Bayer now included AGFA. Hoechst, in addition to its pharmaceutical and fine chemical businesses, retained the Behring Werke (its longtime pharmaceutical subsidiary) and Kalle, which had become a producer of cellophane and cellulose derivatives and intermediates during the I. G. Farben period. Hoechst also acquired in 1954 Bobengen, a producer of rayon that became a springboard for the development of synthetic fibers. But it did not regain Cassella, a maker of dyes and fibers, until 1969.[7]

All three big companies faced major postwar challenges. They remained far behind their American rivals in commercializing products from the new polymer/petrochemical technologies. They possessed none of the basic petroleum raw materials, nor had they developed and begun to commercialize on any scale the new polymer commodities and end-products.

Entering the Polymer/Petrochemical Revolution in the 1950s

Each of the Big Three proceeded in somewhat different directions in confronting these challenges. In 1952 BASF formed Rheinische Olefin Werks, a joint venture with British-based Royal Dutch Shell whose plant capacity was almost doubled while it was still under construction. After obtaining licenses from ICI for both low- and high-density polyethylene, that petrochemical complex became one of the largest in Europe. Then, to enhance its technological catch-up, it formed a joint venture with Dow Chemical to enter the production of polymer-based textile fibers. The plan went on-stream in July 1958. A few years later, BASF acquired Dow's share. Shortly afterward a comparable joint venture was initiated with Phillips Petroleum.[8]

Bayer gained its entry into petrochemicals by moving into higher value-added product technology. It did so by undertaking a joint venture with Monsanto, called "Mobay," to produce dyes and the new engineered plastics. However, the latter product line was not a success. So in 1958, after lengthy but failed negotiations with Standard Oil (New Jersey), Bayer turned to British Petroleum to create a joint venture to produce synthetic fibers, which would be supplied by a new refinery that BP was building. Overall, Bayer's foray into polymers remained limited.

Hoechst's entry strategy into polymer/petrochemicals was more successful. Its managers decided to rely on outside suppliers for its petroleum and polymer feedstocks, olefins, aromatics, and other intermediates and to concentrate initially on employing the new technologies to enhance its dyes, pharmaceuticals, and its more recently developed insecticide products. It then turned to producing polymer end-products directly by concentrating on the high-end polyester fiber, Trevira, based on an exclusive license acquired from ICI in 1953. In 1955 it launched into commodity polymers, where its success, as noted in Chapter 4, was based on working closely with the Hercules Powder Company to commercialize Karl Ziegler's crystalline high-density polyethylene (HDPE), and then polypropylene (PP). Thus it became a first mover in PP, one of the most versatile of the basic polymer commodities. These products that came on-stream in 1956 ensured for Hoechst the strongest position among the Big Three in both commodity and high-end polymer products.[9]

Evolution of the Big Three before the Second Oil Shock

By the early 1960s Hoechst maintained the most balanced line of Germany's Big Three. The five operating divisions in its multidivisional structure—organic chemicals, agricultural chemicals, pharmaceuticals, polymers and plastics, and fiber and film—were defined, as at Du Pont and Dow, along both old and new paths of learning. In the early 1960s Hoechst undertook expansion abroad by setting up plants in Europe and then Asia. Then, on a smaller scale, it gained initial entry into the U.S. market in 1966 by forming Hystron Fibers, a 50–50 joint venture with Hercules to produce Trevira polyester fiber, as the ICI patents expired. Given its earlier close working relationship with Hercules in polymers, Hoechst chose Hercules because the latter company had become the major producer of the critical intermediate for that fiber—DMT—which it supplied to both Du Pont and ICI. The collaboration, whose South Carolina factory came on-stream in 1968, proved highly profitable. Hoechst pressed for expansion, but Hercules's management, also as noted in Chapter 4, decided it could not afford the investment on the scale Hoechst desired, and sold its 50 percent share to Hoechst in 1970. At the same time, Hoechst initiated a comparable move with Stauffer Chemical to produce an upgraded cellophane line of film, building a factory in Delaware. Hoechst's postwar American subsidiary, through which these joint ventures were operated, then changed its name from International Chemical Corporation, by which it had been known since 1952, to American Hoechst, and established new headquarters in Bridgewater, New Jersey. In addition to these U.S. activities, in the early 1970s the parent German Hoechst company acquired Britain's largest paint producer and a controlling interest in Roussel Uclaf, a leading French pharmaceutical company.[10]

BASF and Bayer rounded out their U.S. holdings a few years after Hoechst and just as the second oil shock precipitated the chemical industry's major crisis. In 1978 BASF acquired Dow's 50 percent and Phillips's 50 percent in these two respective joint ventures. At the same time, its U.S. subsidiary began to move into specialty chemicals, acquiring in 1979 Allegheny Ludlum's paint, pigments, and varnish division, and in the following year Knoll, an American manufacturer of flavors and fragrances, although the latter was soon sold to the Swiss pharmaceutical giant F. Hoffmann–La Roche.[11] Subsequently, BASF remained committed to chemicals but less so to pharmaceuticals.

Bayer consolidated its American holdings at about the same time as BASF. But, given its history, it focused on a somewhat different set of product lines, especially pharmaceuticals. In 1977, partly from antitrust pressure, Bayer acquired Monsanto's 50 percent in Mobay, the joint venture that had expanded its line to polyurethane and agricultural chemicals. Bayer's primary drive, however, continued to be in pharmaceuticals. In the same year, it also purchased Cutter Laboratories, makers of nutrients and ethical drugs. Soon thereafter, Cutter recorded its first profit. Bayer's success in turning around the financially weak company encouraged it to buy a much larger drug enterprise, Miles Laboratories (established in 1885), a major producer of proprietary over-the-counter drugs, including Alka-Seltzer, "the world's #1 cure for the hang-over," and Flintstones and other children's vitamins. Also, at the same time, Bayer reinforced its finishes business by acquiring Allied Chemical's pigments division.[12]

Expansion in the 1980s

The Germans' U.S. subsidiaries suffered less from the industry's crisis at the end of the 1970s and early 1980s than did their American competitors. Only recently having completed their initial reentry into the American market after World War II, they had not diversified in the manner of many American companies and so did not need to redefine the boundaries of their capabilities. Instead, they concentrated on reinforcing their strong product lines.

In the 1980s Bayer concentrated on reinforcing its existing strong pharmaceuticals and photography divisions. For Bayer, pharmaceuticals remained, as they had been since the 1890s, a major product line. The company focused on transforming an advertising-intensive, over-the-counter drug business into an increasingly research-intensive, prescription pharmaceutical and diagnostic equipment enterprise, and started to enter into the new biotechnology field (reviewed in Chapter 10).

In the 1980s Bayer also enlarged its photographic business, assuming full control of AGFA, once a major European competitor in which Bayer had long held 60 percent. Bayer's U.S. subsidiary in 1989 bolstered its position in imaging technology by acquiring a pioneering U.S. competitor in electronic imagery. Thus, Bayer, through its AGFA operations, continued to compete successfully with Eastman Kodak.

In the next year Bayer enlarged its synthetic rubber commitment by purchasing a Canadian firm, making Bayer a world leader in that product. Finally, in 1994, it was in a position to obtain quite unexpectedly the over-the-counter business of Sterling-Winthrop. This move permitted the company to use the trade name Bayer in the United States, a privilege it had lost when the U.S. Alien Custodian Office expropriated Bayer's U.S. property during World War I. Moreover, the acquisition resulted in Bayer's becoming one of the world's five largest over-the-counter producers.[13]

Turning now to Hoescht, over the twenty-five years from 1970 to 1995, it made only two major acquisitions in the United States. In 1987 it acquired Celanese, the second-largest producer of polyester fibers in the United States after Du Pont. Its purchase, for $2.8 billion, was intended to replace Hystron Fibers after Du Pont began to produce its own DMT. After the deal, American Hoechst changed its name to Hoechst Celanese. Polyester accounted for 50 percent of the U.S. subsidiary's revenues; the other 50 percent came from industrial chemicals, 9 percent of which were engineering plastics.

Shortly after the Celanese acquisition, which made Hoechst overall the world's biggest chemical company, Hoechst's managers executed a remarkable change in strategy, recognizing that chemistry was no longer generating new opportunities for commercialization and shifting to biology as the source of new products. The first indication of this extraordinary switch came in the early 1990s, when senior management became concerned about slowing growth in the core chemical businesses. At the same time, the company's pharmaceutical businesses, including the majority-owned Roussel Uclaf, were delivering strong growth and earnings.

In the mid-1990s Hoechst Celanese made two moves to support its new focus on pharmaceuticals. In 1995 it bought Marion Merrell Dow from Dow Chemical. At the end of the next year, Hoechst Celanese acquired the remaining interest in its French subsidiary Roussel Uclaf on the open market for $7.1 billion. It then combined these units into a new entity, Hoechst Marion Roussel (HMR). Then, in 1999, as further discussed in Chapter 9, HMR joined with Rhône-Poulenc Rorer in still another megamerger to produce Aventis. Following this deal, Aventis continued to spin off the chemical properties of its constituent companies, a story well beyond the scope of this book.

At the beginning of the twenty-first century, two of the leading German companies that had created the modern chemical industry, Bayer and BASF, remained giant multisectored chemical enterprises, while Hoechst, transformed into Aventis, had become a major pharmaceutical company. In chemicals, the Germans' primary competition on the world stage consisted of Du Pont and Dow. In pharmaceuticals, they faced strong competition from the Swiss in commercializing the products of molecular biology and genetic engineering. This competition with the Swiss had originated much earlier, however, in the products of the Second Industrial Revolution in Europe.

The Successful Swiss Challengers

The paths of learning pursued by the Swiss multinational companies followed the pattern of the Germans. One dissimilarity, however, reflects the very different impacts the two world wars had on the German chemical industries compared with the Swiss. Another is that the Swiss moved more energetically and swiftly into commercializing the products of the new pharmaceutical technologies. In 1995 the original three Swiss chemical companies—Ciba and Geigy, which had combined in 1970, and the smaller Sandoz—all merged into a single company, Novartis, which quickly withdrew from the chemicals business altogether.

During the twentieth century, of the European chemical producers, Switzerland's three companies were the most successful in responding to the three German giants' powerful first-mover advantages. All three Swiss companies entered the synthetic dye business in the 1880s. At that point, Ciba (the abbreviated title of Gesellschaft fur Chemische Industrie in Basle) and Geigy operated as already established enterprises, whereas Sandoz was a startup. During the 1890s, as the German competitors grew into powerhouses, the strategy of the three smaller Swiss rivals embraced was to withdraw from bulk dyes and concentrate on high-end, high-priced specialized dyes. After 1900, 80 percent of their raw materials and intermediates came from Germany. Each of the three firms focused on a specialized line of dyes, in which they functioned as the technical leaders. In addition, before 1900 Ciba had begun to diversify into pharmaceuticals, concentrating on antiseptics for internal bodily use, and soon had a major operating unit devoted to specialized drugs. By 1914 the three had built factories in France, Britain, Russia, and Poland.[14]

World War I presented the three Swiss chemical makers their opportunity. They formed a joint venture that permitted them to produce necessary intermediates, arranged to obtain their coal-tar material from Britain, and moved quickly into the European, American, and even Asian markets that had until 1914 belonged to the Germans. In 1919, to meet the potential return of the Germans and their powerful capabilities, the Swiss formed the Basel AG (all three were headquartered in Basel), with Ciba getting 52 percent of the group's profits, and Geigy and Sandoz 24 percent apiece. In 1920 the Basle AG established two U.S. subsidiaries, the Cincinnati Chemical Company to manufacture its dyes, and the Ciba Company to market them. They quickly set up branches in the principal U.S. textile centers. Following 1929 and the advent of the Great Depression, Basel AG joined I. G. Farben in a cartel agreement. It was soon enlarged to include France's Les Etablissements Kuhlmann and then, in 1932, Britain's recently established ICI.[15]

During World War II the Swiss companies maintained their markets abroad and their properties and patents were not expropriated. Nevertheless, and even more than their German rivals, the Swiss missed out on the polymer/petrochemical revolution. Unlike the Germans, they had undertaken little research during the initial developments in polymers. However, the formulating of DDT in 1940 provided an opportunity for entering pesticides and then agricultural chemicals.

The post–World War II breakup of I. G. Farben and the Japanese *zaibatsu* meant that cartels were clearly out of fashion. So, in 1951, the Basel AG dissolved itself. In the following years, Geigy's output, revenues, and profits grew much faster than Ciba's and Sandoz's. These gains were based in part on the rapid expansion of its agricultural chemical business, and also on the continuing growth of its long-established pharmaceutical lines. CIBA's strength lay in its older dyes, resins, and chemical sectors. Then, in response to "the powerful wave of competition, principally from petrochemicals, that was besieging the citadel of specialty chemicals," the two companies merged in 1970 to form Ciba-Geigy Ltd., with integrated learning bases extending out to U.S., British, and Brazilian subsidiaries, the American subsidiary being the largest of the three. The still smaller Sandoz remained independent.[16]

After the merger, Ciba-Geigy grew much more steadily from internal investment than from acquisitions. By 1978 the sales of its U.S. subsidiaries had reached $1 billion and six years later, in 1984, the company purchased two U.S. agrichemicals companies, Airwick Industries and Funk Seeds. In 1990 it acquired the agricultural chemical business of its Swiss neighbor, F. Hoffmann–La Roche.

The most important of its U.S. direct investments, however, was in biotechnology. In 1986 it formed a joint venture with Chiron, the U.S. biogenetic pioneer in the production and marketing of genetically engineered vaccines; in 1990 it acquired full control of Chiron (as reviewed in Chapter 10). Indeed, by the late 1980s, Ciba-Geigy and the remaining Swiss chemical company, Sandoz, were concentrating on pharmaceuticals, so much so that, finally, in 1995, they merged to form Novartis AG and began to phase out their chemical activities.[17]

Meanwhile, the one successful British chemical producer, ICI, shifted in the opposite direction, spinning off its most successful operating division in pharmaceuticals as Zeneca, a newly independent company. ICI took this step to reinforce its balance sheet and refocus on its core business in chemicals (see pages 253–254).

Imperial Chemical Industries: The British Response to I. G. Farben

October 1926 saw the announcement of a merger of four British companies that bore the imposing title of Imperial Chemical Industries. The stated goal of ICI was "to extend the development and importance of the chemical industry throughout the Empire."[18] The merger united Britain's two largest and strongest chemical companies (Nobel Industries and Brunner, Mond) with two companies (United Alkali and British Dyestuffs) that were among Britain's weakest. Neither of the first two possessed the technical, functional, or managerial capabilities required to commercialize the products of the new learning in organic and inorganic chemistry and to compete in the development, production, and marketing of dyes and other synthetic organic chemicals. Nobel Industries, founded in 1887 by Alfred Nobel and a group of Scottish industrialists, commercialized the inventor's new high-explosive technology, dynamite. Brunner, Mond, the British licensee of the Solvay patents for production of alkali, as well as soda ash and bleaching powder, became the British first mover in the path that Solvay had created. It did so by constructing a major production facility at Winnington in 1882.

Of the two smaller companies, United Alkali was formed in 1891 essentially as a cartel of existing British alkali producers, employing the older small-scale LeBlanc technology that the Solvay process was displacing. The company had continued to exist only due to the sufferance of the much larger Brunner, Mond. The other smaller, weaker firm, British Dyestuffs Corporation, resulted from a 1919 government merger of British Dyes (the government-owned enterprise established during World War I to fill the void for dyestuffs no longer available from Germany) and Levinsteins (one of the very few surviving specialized dye producers in Britain). That merger had combined two deeply antagonistic managements into an uneasy confederation, British Dyestuffs Ltd. By 1926 British Dyestuffs had not managed to develop the facilities and capabilities necessary to compete with the German and Swiss leaders. Considering the limited technical and functional capabilities of these four companies, the merged enterprise faced a difficult challenge in competing with I. G. Farben.

From the end of World War I until the 1926 formation of ICI, Nobel Industries had continued to produce primarily explosives and propellants. Unlike Du Pont following World War I, Nobel did not attempt to diversify into nitrocellulose-based products such as paints, pigments, finishes, rayon, and plastic products. Between 1919 and 1926, of its £12.3 million profits, £9.4

million were derived from explosives, £2.8 million from metals (chiefly used within the enterprise), and a tiny £100,000 from coated textiles.[19]

By 1926, Brunner, Mond had become even more committed to the production of basic ingredients of fertilizers and bleaches than it had been before the war, because of the huge plant the firm began to build at Billingham in 1920 with the encouragement of the British government and financial support from Nobel Industries. The plant was designed to make synthetic ammonia and nitrates, using the Haber Bosch process expropriated from BASF.

Shortly after construction started, however, Nobel Industries withdrew. As William Reader, ICI's historian, points out, "Brunner, Mond was thus left the sole owners of an enterprise which looked like it was becoming much the biggest thing that it had ever taken on. It was certainly much the biggest project in the British chemical industry of the day. . . . Once Brunner, Mond had set out along this road, there could be no turning back, and by bringing Billingham with them into ICI, they dictated where a large part of the new concern's expansion must inevitably lie, for with so much capital, by that time, committed there, it was impossible not to commit more." But, again lacking the technical and developmental capabilities, ICI proved unable to build a competitive learning base in the new high-pressure technology for producing synthetic ammonia and nitrates, to say nothing of its efforts to create competitive capabilities essential to challenging I. G. Farben. In the early 1930s, because of ICI's continuing losses and the growing concern of the British military regarding gasoline and other fuels, the Billingham project was reoriented toward the production of synthetic fuels. Only the British government's commitment in 1934 to guarantee a market for the fuel produced at Billingham permitted ICI to retrieve a portion of its investment.[20]

After the formation of ICI, the enterprise continued to operate as a major producer of basic chemicals, including soda ash and bleaching powder, synthetic ammonia, and explosives. Hobbled by the Billingham investment, however, senior managers were only partially successful in creating a learning base for the production of dyestuffs before World War II and for the new polymer/petrochemicals during the war. ICI did, however, develop into the largest dye producer in Britain. Under the cartel agreements of 1932, ICI received 8.3 percent of the European market, still much lower than its continental competitors. By 1938, dyes still accounted for just under 10 percent of ICI's total sales.

Nevertheless, the attempt to compete with the German dyemakers did allow for new technical capabilities and research. As one senior executive noted, "The only way BDC [ICI's dyestuffs group] could get into the dyestuffs business on anything approaching a substantial scale . . . was to invent its way in. The IG [Farben] never took much notice of BDC until they found that BDC could invent."[21]

Close ties began to be established for the first time among scientists at Oxford and Cambridge and in London. Between 1933 and 1935, the Dyestuffs laboratory developed eighty-seven potential commercial products, including synthetic rubber, synthetic resins and lacquers, detergents, pesticides, and pharmaceuticals, as well as new dyestuffs intermediates and high-quality dyes. In 1935 a chemist in the Alkali Group laboratory invented the basic polymer, polyethylene.

Belatedly Entering the Polymer/Petrochemical Revolution

However, ICI still lacked the functional capabilities to make products for new and different markets, and particularly those in the new polymer path. By the outbreak of war in 1939 only one polymer product, a glazing material for aircraft, had appeared from ICI's development efforts. War needs brought transformation, although not on the scale that occurred in the United States. Polyethylene came on-stream in 1940, followed by polyvinyl chloride, based on the Union Carbide technology, and then nylon through an agreement with Du Pont. These moves created a learning base that permitted the company to enter the polymer/petrochemical path. In the early 1950s ICI had developed a competitive fabric with its own polyester, Terylene (which became the source of Hoechst's and Hercules's Trevira). In this way, ICI entered into the commercializing of the products of the polymer/petrochemical revolution before their continental European competitors.[22]

Yet again the difficulty rested in the limited ability of the senior managers to build the necessary integrated learning bases essential for ICI to compete with the Americans and Germans. Again, to quote Reader, "The size of ICI and the weight of established interests in the larger divisions, directly represented as they were on the Board, made rapid decision impossible on the creation of new Divisions, the amalgamation of old and proud ones, and the transfer away from some Divisions of activities over which they had presided from the start, in which they took pride, and which they had run as profitable enterprises."[23] Because of the slowness in developing its new marketing organizations and integrating them with the product development and production units during the 1950s, ICI licensed its major new product lines to German and U.S. firms, lines that in the 1960s and 1970s would evolve into strong competitors.

During these decades ICI moved along the postwar paths created in the late 1940s and 1950s. In polymer/petrochemicals, it expanded its commodity polymers, concentrating on low-density polyethylene (LDPE), polyvinyl chloride (PVC), and then polypropylene (PP). In fibers, it maintained its strength in polyester fabrics and added polyester film, but because of its tardy and slow start, it did not succeed in developing new fibers and film in the manner of Du Pont or Hoechst. In the 1960s it began integrating backward, forming a joint venture with Burma Oil to explore for North Sea oil, and it began to acquire oil and gas properties in the United States and elsewhere. In its prewar lines, it continued to produce dyestuffs and other heavy organic products. Alkalis, chlorides, soda ash, lime, and salt continued to be large revenue producers, but with small profit margins. At the same time ICI made its initial investments in the United States, by constructing a major facility at Bayonne, New Jersey; then came the acquisition in 1971 of Atlas Powder Company (one of the two spin-offs from Du Pont in the 1912 antitrust decision).

On the other hand, by the 1970s, its high-pressure ammonia group developed an innovative process that, in turn, made ICI a world leader in the production of ammonia and methanol and a major competitor in bulk fertilizers, as well as fungicides, insecticides, and plant growth control chemicals. Most significant for the long term was the wartime commercializing of antibiotics, which quickly made ICI one of Britain's three leading drug companies. Nevertheless, in 1979, commodity petrochemicals, polyester fiber and film, general chemicals, and products for agriculture accounted for 60 percent of ICI's revenues and 72 percent of its profits.[24]

Redefining the Strategic Boundaries of the Firm

Then ensued the industry crisis following the second oil shock (the one created by the Iranian Revolution) that forced ICI to transform itself even more dramatically than Dow, the leading creator of the polymer/petrochemical revolution, had attempted in the late 1970s. According to Andrew Pettigrew, who carried on Reader's history of ICI, "By 1982, the percentage contribution of ICI's Petrochemicals and Plastics, General Chemicals, and

Agricultural business classes to Group sales had declined to 56 percent, and Group trading profits to 45 percent. By 1982 three of ICI's business classes—Petrochemicals and Plastics, Organics, and Fibers—were making losses. Petrochemicals and Plastics alone lost £39 million. . . . The company thus became highly dependent on its agricultural, pharmaceutical, and oil business which between them contributed 76.2 percent [of profits]."[25]

The response of the ICI board to the oil crisis was to appoint a new CEO, John Harvey-Jones, who then implemented a large-scale restructuring of the company's portfolio by focusing on its strengths. In 1984 negotiations that had begun earlier culminated in a swap of ICI's LPDE for British Petroleum's PVC, permitting both to benefit from economies of scale. In 1991 ICI would make a comparable swap by trading ICI's nylon for Du Pont's acrylic fibers. After 1984 a two-pronged strategy was followed: selling off low-end lines balanced by acquiring high-end ones, and expanding into the U.S. market.[26]

The company expanded its U.S. holdings in 1988 by acquiring Glidden, a major, established paint company, which resulted in ICI's becoming the largest paint manufacturer in the world. In 1987 it expanded its agricultural chemicals by buying Stauffer Chemical, a California enterprise, and then selling off all but Stauffer's agriculture business. Then, in 1990, ICI purchased Edward J. Funk, a leader in the U.S. hybrid corn market, from Ciba-Geigy.

The Success of ICI's Pharmaceutical Division

The most significant development during the postcrisis years was ICI's success in pharmaceuticals. In that sector, it succeeded precisely because it was able to accomplish what it had failed to do in dyes and polymer chemicals. The company created an integrated learning base in the early years of the introduction of the revolutionary antibiotic technology. Its first pharmaceutical products emerged from research on dyes. But the initial large-scale commercialization ensued only with meeting the unprecedented demands of World War II. During the war ICI pioneered in commercializing penicillin and was especially successful in doing likewise with the antimalarial drug Pauldrine. In 1954 the pharmaceutical division was split off from the dyestuffs division. The new unit quickly set up its own research laboratories, then built its own production facilities and global marketing organization.

By the 1970s that division was turning into a truly international enterprise with research laboratories and processing plants in the United States, Europe, Latin America, Asia, and Africa.[27]

ICI's pharmaceutical business prospered because of the postwar therapeutic revolution (described in Chapter 9) that brought forth a plethora of new prescription drugs. It also benefited from the large British home market created by the National Health Service. In addition, its two major British competitors—Beecham and Glaxo—were just beginning to establish their production and marketing organizations for prescription drugs. Throughout the 1970s ICI's pharmaceuticals remained the most profitable of its operating units, even though its percentage of total ICI sales fell off from the heights of the late 1960s.

During the corporate restructuring of the early 1980s the pharmaceutical division at ICI adopted a strategy of concentration on the capabilities that had developed since the 1950s, in "areas where proven expertise exists." This was particularly true in cardiovascular agents and cancer treatments, which by 1988 accounted for 74 percent of ICI's pharmaceutical sales. In the second half of the 1980s, the pharmaceutical division's trading profits averaged just under 30 percent of sales, far greater than its other product lines.[28]

The success of ICI's pharmaceutical unit in building powerful capabilities and its resulting profit performance during the 1980s paved the way for a dramatic restructuring of the company in 1992. Spurred on by the threat of an unfriendly takeover the year before by the British conglomerate Hanson, ICI spun off its pharmaceuticals business and its agricultural and smaller, related specialties into a separate corporation, Zeneca. ICI retained the remaining product lines. Not only was this a sensible strategic maneuver, but it was also a brilliant financial one, because Zeneca also assumed ICI's long-term debt of $3.5 billion. The enthusiastically received public offering of Zeneca's stock sharply reduced this debt.[29]

Following the separation of Zeneca from ICI, the almost debt-free chemical firm continued to diversify away from the less profitable heavy chemical products, while simultaneously pursuing expansion into North America and Asia. It concentrated more intensively on its long-established paths of learning, including paints and pigments as well as a variety of agricultural chemicals. ICI's primary goal during this period was the expansion of its specialty chemicals business. In 1997 the opportunity arose: Unilever, the British soap, cosmetic, and packaged food giant, decided to sell its specialty chemicals activities. Its executives perceived ICI to be one of several potential purchasers. The story of this transaction provides a fitting epilogue to ICI's twentieth-century evolution.

Postscript: The Acquisition of Unilever's Specialty Chemicals

In February 1997, Unilever resolved to sell subsidiaries it had acquired over the years to provide materials used in the production of its end-products. The package comprised four units: Crosfields, a competitor purchased in 1919 that became a specialist in silicon- and aluminum-based compounds; National Starch, a turn-of-the-century U.S. merger, which, when bought in 1978, was the world's largest producer of industrial adhesives; and two Dutch acquisitions, Unichema, the world's leader in oleo chemicals, and Quest, a leading fragrance and food-ingredient supplier. (These businesses accounted for Unilever's revenue of $1.8 billion in 1993 as listed in Table 1.1).

The ICI and Unilever negotiations were consummated by early May. ICI paid Unilever $8.1 billion for the properties. Then ICI sold its "polyester chain,"—including polymer commodities, intermediates, and film—and its titanium dioxide division to Du Pont for $3 billion (see Chapter 3). Another $1.7 billion resulted from the sale of other businesses, primarily its Australian subsidiary, which was spun off as a leveraged buyout (LBO).[30]

ICI's strategic moves in the 1990s indicate that the company's leaders had recognized they were faced with making a choice: whether to become a specialty chemicals company commercializing products based on older technology mastered in the 1920s and the 1940s and 1950s, or to become a full-fledged pharmaceutical enterprise. Given the existing barriers to entry in pharmaceuticals, their choice of the former was clearly the right one.

The Other Rhine Valley First Movers

Three of the remaining four subsidiaries of European companies listed in Table 1.1 were Rhine Valle first movers. Henkel, based in Düsseldorf, and Solvay, headquartered in Brussels, fifty miles from the Rhine, became the first movers during the 1880s in their respective industries. Both maintained their competitive capabilities for more than a hundred years. A third Rhine Valley pioneer was the forerunner of Akzo, Vereinigt Glanzstaff-Fabriken, a first mover in rayon and related artificial fabrics. Owing partly to World War II, the company did not participate in the polymer revolution in fibers and so lost its basic market. As a consequence, it attempted to enter new paths of learning, but with little success. This was also true of Rhône-Poulenc, France's leading producer of both chemicals and pharmaceuticals. Its evolution provides an impressive example of strategic failure.

Henkel KGaA: Continental Europe's First Mover in Soap and Cleaners

By the beginning of the twentieth century, Henkel, the fourth-largest German chemical company, had created a learning base in soap (SIC 284) that permitted it to compete successfully with the two world leaders, the American Procter & Gamble, whose Ivory Soap was introduced in 1879, and Britain's Unilever, whose Sunshine brand was being marketed in the 1880s. Yet Henkel's beginnings differed from the other two. It had started as would be expected as an industrial chemical company focusing on industrial cleaning and allied products rather than on a basic consumer product like soap.

Fritz Henkel, who formed Henkel & Cie in 1876, built its large plant in Düsseldorf in 1878, expanded its continental sales force, and in 1899 constructed a larger plant to fully exploit the economies of scale. The initial products were detergents used in commercial laundries and industrial activities. Backward integration into the production of their basic ingredient, sodium acetate, soon made Henkel one of the major producers of that product.[31]

Like the other Rhine River chemical firms, Henkel soon became a multiproduct enterprise. In 1907, working with DEGUSSA, one of Germany's few producers of inorganic chemicals, Henkel commercialized Persil, a packaged, branded chemical soap powder primarily for household use. Rather than entering that British market, Henkel licensed Persil to Crosfields, which continued to dominate the British market until it was acquired by Unilever. Relying on heavy advertising, Henkel, the leading detergent producer on the continent, became Lever Brothers's major competitor in soap. Because Henkel had concentrated on the European rather than overseas markets, it suffered less from World War I than did other large German industrial enterprises. Indeed, it benefited, as Lever pulled out of Europe with the outbreak of the war.[32]

In the 1920s Henkel blanketed Europe with fifteen plants and massive advertising campaigns, producing explicitly for individual national markets. At the same time, it expanded its consumer lines in soap, soap powder, and other cleaning agents. As a result it increased its production of basic ingredients while volume packaging enabled it to become a leader in adhesives and adhesive materials.

During World War II, Henkel, like the other German multinational enterprises, lost its foreign holdings. Nevertheless, after the war, Henkel was able to fight off the powerful invasion of the European detergent market by Unilever, Procter & Gamble, and, this time, Colgate-Peet. By 1968 it enjoyed almost 50 percent of the European market. It then initiated a move into cosmetics and toiletries, but its primary postwar entry into the U.S. market was to concentrate on cleaners and chemicals.

With Henkel's reentry into the United States, it focused on industrial chemicals, starting with the purchase of Standard Chemicals in 1960, followed in 1974 by a large minority stake in Clorox, and in 1977 by the acquisition of General Mills's chemical division. In 1985 ensued a further set of acquisitions—of Nobo (specialty chemicals), Ford Parker Chemicals (metal surface pretreatment), Emory (the largest producer of oleochemicals)—followed in the late 1980s and 1990s by further additions as well as sell-offs. By 1995, 29 percent of Henkel's total revenues worldwide derived from detergents and household cleaners—28 percent, chemical products; 10 percent, "industrial adhesive and technical consumer products"; 15 percent, cosmetics/toiletries; 10 percent, institutional and hygiene products; 7 percent, metal chemicals; and 1 percent, others. However, Henkel's sales remained concentrated in Europe, which accounted for 77 percent of its sales.[33]

Henkel's 1995 product lines all evolved from its initial learning base and did so primarily from direct investment rather than acquisitions. The latter were intended largely as a means to reenter the American market, in which it, unlike Unilever, did not gain entry in strength until well after World War II. Subsequently Henkel narrowed its focus on its major consumer product lines in branded laundry, home care, cosmetics, toiletries, and adhesive products. In 1999 Henkel grouped its chemical-producing units except for adhesives into a new subsidiary called "Cognis." This was the prelude to divestiture two years later, when Henkel sold Cognis to a consortium of private equity firms.[34]

Solvay & Cie: Building an Initial Learning Base

Solvay's learning experience was comparable, although carried out in a different manner, to that of Henkel's. It built continually on its initial learning base. The Solvay brothers, Ernest and Alfred, invented and then commercialized the ammonium soda process to produce synthetic soda ash used for bleaches, particularly in the textile industry, and for the production of fertilizers. Its production quickly outperformed the existing Leblanc process. The two brothers, who established their enterprise in Brussels in 1863, had perfected their process by 1869. In the 1870s and 1880s Solvay constructed plants in nearby Belgium and France. As described earlier, it also set up associated companies in Britain (Mond) in 1882, in the United States (Solvay Process in Syracuse, New York, later part of Allied Chemical) in 1884 (see Chapter 3), as well as in Germany, Austria, and Russia. For the associated firms, Solvay licensed its patents and provided technological knowledge and some financing in return for substantial, but not necessarily controlling, shares of stock. From the Brussels office, the company carefully monitored the activities of the associated firms. In the case of the two listed in Table 1.1, it retained their holdings when Solvay Process became part of Allied Chemical in 1921 and Brunner, Mond became one of the two cores of ICI in 1925.[35]

Before the outbreak of World War I, Solvay expanded its European production facilities, and after 1885, just as electric power emerged, it perfected the new electrolytic process for producing not only soda ash but also chlorine and related products, much in the manner of Dow in the United States.

Following the war, Solvay expanded its output in its European factories and built new ones in Italy, Greece, and other countries. It maintained ties with all its earlier allies except, of course, with Russia, where its properties had been confiscated. Before World War I, however, it had done little to commercialize new chemicals through process technologies, as Dow had done in the United States. But it did move into polymer/petrochemicals quickly after World War II. In 1949 Solvay initiated the production of polyvinyl chloride, becoming a European leader in that basic polymer commodity. The company then entered into the production of HDPE in 1959 and PP in 1966. Shortly thereafter, it began to produce a variety of end-products in the manner of the American companies for use in both consumer and industrial chemical lines. In 1974 Solvay returned to the U.S. markets, setting up headquarters in Deer Park, Texas. By that time its soda ash and caustic soda processes had become obsolete.[36]

The technical obsolescence of the basic product that by then accounted for only 20 percent of its income, in tandem with the industry crisis following the second oil shock, prompted Solvay to redefine its product lines and strategic boundaries. Its restructuring was implemented in much the same fashion as that of the American core companies described in Chapter 3: buying units closely related to the lines in which its organizational capabilities ensured it competitive strength, and selling off those less related to its successful products.

With the fall of the Berlin Wall in 1989, Solvay regained access to facilities it had lost during World War II and the Cold War. It renovated them while continuing to prune noncore operations through divestitures and joint ventures. Although it suffered heavy losses in 1993, Solvay returned to profitability the next year, following more restructuring. By the end of the decade, the company organized its business in four major segments: chemicals, plastics, pharmaceuticals, and processing (manufacturing finished products such as pipes and fittings).[37]

I make no attempt here to evaluate the success or failure of its moves into these different specialty chemicals, but clearly the company prospered. Solvay enjoyed the option of moving into these new sectors because it employed the capabilities learned from the initial commercializing of the Solvay process to commercialize products early in the century in electrolytically based inorganic chemicals. It then succeeded in entering polymer/petrochemicals in the same manner as did the German Big Three, particularly Hoechst.

Finally, the two remaining European competitors in Table 1.1, Akzo and Rhône-Poulenc, possessed no comparable learning bases; they had to obtain critical technologies through acquisitions.

Akzo: The Heir of Vereinigte Glanzstoff-Fabriken Fails

Akzo was a direct descendent of the German firm Vereinigte Glanzstoff Fabriken (VGF), the first mover in the production of rayon on the European continent. Established before the turn of the century, after it acquired control of J. P. Bemberg in 1911, it became the second largest European producer of rayon, behind the British pioneer Courtaulds Ltd. After German producers returned to international markets in the mid-1920s, VGF began to focus on the American market, building plants in Tennessee and North Carolina during the years 1927–1929. At the same time, VGF's organizational capabilities and integrated learning base were so strong that I. G. Farben failed to develop a profitable rayon business even with VGF providing technical assistance. In 1929 VGF merged with Nederlandse Kunstzijdefabriek, a smaller Dutch firm, to form Algemene Kunstzijde-Unie

(AKU). By 1939 AKU was the third-largest producer of rayon in the United States behind Du Pont and American Viscose (a Courtaulds subsidiary).[38]

After World War II, AKU was unable to regain its interwar competitive strengths. Without the technical capabilities in the new polymer fiber technologies, its attempt to commercialize new synthetic fibers made little headway, although its production and marketing skills counted sufficiently for a time to make it an effective competitor. Then, in 1969, it merged with another Dutch firm, Koninklijke Zout Organon (KZO), which produced coatings, drugs, and detergents. During the 1970s the newly merged company, known as Akzo, continued to reduce the percentage of revenues from fibers from over 50 to 30 percent. Even so, profits almost disappeared.

In the 1980s Akzo altered its strategy to purchase more than thirty small companies, largely in U.S. specialty chemicals, coatings, and pharmaceuticals, at a total cost of $1.8 billion. Part of the cost was covered through the sales of its U.S. fiber business to BASF in 1985. The acquisitions in pharmaceuticals and paints and coatings were successful; the others proved less so. But the strategy of acquisition in these businesses did not yield the expected increases in income.

In 1994 Akzo shifted in another direction, announcing plans to acquire Sweden's Nobel Industries, a part of Alfred Nobel's nineteenth-century empire that primarily produced heavy chemicals. The transaction was finally approved two years later with the formation of Akzo Nobel. This was a rocky period for the company that resulted in a major restructuring, including divestitures, plant closings, and layoffs. The merger precipitated a vast reorganization creating four new groups: chemicals, fibers, coatings, and pharmaceuticals.

In 1998 Akzo Nobel purchased Courtaulds, the England-based producer of high-tech industrial coatings and fibers. It then combined its own fibers business with that of Courtaulds to create Accordis, a new company that it subsequently spun off. Meanwhile, Akzo Nobel continued to churn its portfolio, buying and selling businesses in its three main lines: coatings, chemicals, and pharmaceuticals. The company remained profitable throughout this continuing restructuring, but much less so than other European producers.

Rhône-Poulenc: A Study in Failure

The history of France's largest chemical firm, Rhône-Poulenc, provides another narrative of a major player not developing its own learning and thus contributing little to the evolution of the industry as a whole. It and other French firms were unable to create their own learning bases not only in polymer/petrochemical technologies but even in most of the new basic chemical technologies of the past century. They fell behind in dyes, pharmaceuticals, photochemicals and other related inorganic products, rayon and other cellulose-based technologies, and electrolytic and high-pressure inorganic technologies. The failure to develop strong initial learning bases meant that corporate growth and changes in product lines resulted more from external mergers and acquisitions than from internal investment and new product and process development.

Rhône-Poulenc, a 1928 merger, was France's response to the formation of I. G. Farben; but its beginnings and continuing evolution were very different from that of Britain's ICI. It began as a merger of France's leading chemical and pharmaceutical enterprises, the Société Chimique des Usines du Rhône and Etablissements Poulenc Frères. The first of these, established in 1895 in Lyon, originated with the production of synthetic dyes and fragrances. By 1905 it had abandoned its dye production but sustained its perfume lines and entered photographic acetate and film businesses. The latter led it to the production of rayon.[39]

The second participant in the 1928 merger, Etablissement Poulenc Frères, began as a pharmaceutical company. It was formed in 1900 by three Poulenc brothers, one of whom had operated a Parisian pharmacy since 1858 that had expanded to sell photographic supplies as well as drugs. Poulenc Frères soon began to commercialize photographic film and then rayon, as well as pharmaceuticals. The 1928 merger made Rhône-Poulenc the largest producer of organic chemicals (except for dyes) in France.[40]

Because of the Nazi occupation of France during World War II, Rhône-Poulenc played a minimal role in the polymer/petrochemical revolution, but did obtain a position in pharmaceuticals by pioneering in penicillin and sulfa. In the 1950s and 1960s the firm enhanced and enlarged its prewar synthetic fragrances, fibers, and film. During the 1960s, 60 percent of its sales derived from fibers, based on Du Pont and ICI licenses. In 1969 it became a conglomerate by acquiring full control of an earlier joint venture involving the aluminum producer Pechiney and the glassmaker St. Gobain. Other acquisitions followed, making the company the largest in France, according to one account.

Nevertheless, by the 1970s it had yet to develop a strong integrated learning base in any of these chemical lines. As a historian of French industry, Patrick Fridenson, notes, "But Rhône-Poulenc's strength in chemicals was more apparent than real. Moreover, although it had successfully made the postwar move into antibiotics, antihistamines and silicones, it had to rely on licenses from American patents for the most strategic products and on continued products dating from the beginning of the century. . . . Heavy losses came between 1979 and 1982."[41]

These losses, reflecting the impact of the second oil shock and then the nationalizing of the chemical industry in 1982, prompted the French government to undertake a grand restructuring of the chemical industry. (The French considered pharmaceuticals to be a part of that industry.) Under the guidance of a thirty-nine-year-old civil servant, Löik Le Floch-Prigent, who had no experience in managing an industrial enterprise, a new team of senior managers was placed in charge. In 1983 the company recorded a profit, but that included government aid of $229.4 million (as compared with government support in that same year of $204 million to Thomson in consumer electronics, and $191.2 million to Bull CII-Honeywell in computers). Billions more francs were spent in modernizing the industry and in fulfilling Le Flock's plans of making Rhône-Poulenc into the world's fifth-largest chemical company.[42]

The reshaping of Rhône-Poulenc's product portfolio led to the buying and selling of operating divisions and companies on an even grander scale than was carried out in the 1980s by many American companies. In the United States, Rhône-Poulenc acquired Union Carbide's agricultural business in 1986, and the following year it acquired Stauffer Chemicals via ICI. The major drive, however, was in pharmaceuticals (as described in Chapter 9). In 1990, Rhône-Poulenc merged its drug business with that of the U.S. company, Rorer, paying $2 billion. That same year, the French government granted to Rhône-Poulenc Rorer its 35 percent interest in Roussel Uclaf, the French pharmaceutical company controlled by Hoechst Celanese. Rhône-Poulenc Rorer subsequently sold this stake on the open market. In 1999, however, it agreed to merge with Hoechst Marion Roussel to form Aventis, one of the largest pharmaceutical companies in the world. (See Figure 9.1.) As Rhône-Poulenc's performance in pharmaceuticals has been even worse than in chemicals, its premerger history remains an unparalleled example of strategic failure.

Conclusion

I conclude this chapter by relating the evolution of the European enterprises to the three basic themes of this book: the barriers to entry, the defining of strategic boundaries, and the impact of the chemical industry's limits of growth during the 1970s.

The Rhine Valley companies created powerful barriers to entry by being the first to commercialize the potential of modern chemical science and engineering. From the 1880s and continuing for the following quarter of a century they dominated international markets. The Big Three—Bayer, Hoechst, and BASF—led the way in the production of dyes, drugs, and related products. In 1904 Bayer, BASF, and a smaller chemical company, AGFA, formed their I. G. as did Hoechst and the smaller Cassella in 1907. Finally, in 1916, the two I. G.s, plus Griesheim merged into a single I. G., the forerunner of I. G. Farben.

During these same years, before World War I, the Swiss companies—Ciba, Geigy, and Sandoz—sidestepped these barriers by focusing on specialized dyes and drugs. At the same time, the other Rhine Valley companies effectively defined their initial strategic focus. Solvay did so by commercializing products of a new technology that produced synthetic soda ash, used for bleaches and fertilizers. This remained the basis of its strategic boundaries until after World War II. Henkel, a first mover in commercial cleaning materials, entered the soap and other consumer cleaning products as early as 1907. A fourth Rhine Valley firm, VGF, became the continent's first mover in commercializing rayon, a manmade fabric.

Then, during the decade 1914 to 1924, World War I and its aftermath removed these German companies' barriers to entry, thus permitting American chemical companies to build the U.S. industry based on many of the technologies commercialized by the Germans before World War I. Nevertheless, with the establishment of I. G. Farben in 1925, the German industry quickly restored its pre–World War I barriers to entry in international markets. To compete, the Swiss firms had already formed their Basel AG in 1919.

During the interwar years, I. G. Farben dominated much of the German chemical industry. By 1929, its assets were listed at over 2 million Reich marks. Those of its German competitors averaged under 1,000 Reich marks.[43] I. G. Farben thus provides a useful way to define the strategic boundaries in the European competitive arena that it so dominated in the 1920s. Its operating communities can be considered as different subarenas in the broader competitive chemical arena in which each focused its strategic boundaries. When the Allied Command in 1952 disassembled I. G. Farben back into the original Big Three, they were defined roughly along these lines.

In the 1920s Britain and France both responded to the return of the

German competitors and the formation of I. G. Farben. Imperial Chemical Industries appeared in 1925, and the merger of Rhône and Poulenc came in 1928. Neither became effective challengers before the coming of World War II.

The second world war had an even more far-reaching impact on the chemical industries' barriers to entry worldwide than did World War I. Not only were the Rhine Valley companies isolated from the world markets again for over a decade but, even more significant, the coming of World War II had launched the polymer/petrochemical industry, the second major period of the commercializing of new technologies based on new learning in chemical sciences and engineering. The American chemical and petroleum companies became world leaders.

After the war, the German Big Three returned to their earlier strategic boundaries, with Hoechst and Bayer (but not BASF) continuing their activities in both chemicals and pharmaceuticals. Hoechst, for example, focused on commercializing a basic new polymer technology, polypropylene, then worked with Hercules to enter higher-end polymer products, so that by the late 1980s it was the second-largest producer of polyester fibers. Both turned to the new biological learning and were less involved in commercializing technologies based on them. Because of these focused strategies, the German Big Three were less affected than their American counterparts by the failure of chemical science and engineering in the 1970s to generate new opportunities for growth.

The Swiss companies, having missed out on the polymer/petrochemical revolution, increasingly sharpened their strategic focus on commercializing the new learning in biology and began to make their way out of chemicals. By the mid-1990s Ciba-Geigy and Sandoz had merged with Roche Holding to form Novartis, a world leader in the new biotechnology, and then spun off their remaining chemical businesses (as reviewed in Chapter 9).

Unlike the Swiss Rhine Valley companies, Solvay and Henkel maintained their focus in chemistry successfully over more than a century of their existence. Solvay increasingly became, after the 1970s, a specialty chemical company along the lines of the American focused companies; while Henkel remained one of the three worldwide competitors in both consumer and industrial cleaning products.

The British challenge to Germany's I. G. Farben, ICI, was able to benefit from World War II's polymer and antibiotic revolutions to become a major multisectored chemical company and at the same time Britain's number two pharmaceutical enterprise. When the time came to make the choice whether to be a chemical or a pharmaceutical company in 1993, however, it sold off its pharmaceutical division and used the funds to remain a major European multisectored chemical company.

The three remaining European companies were failures both in terms of technical innovation and financial returns. They really did not have a chance. When VGF's product line, rayon, became obsolete, its eventual successor, Akzo, had to acquire companies in which it had very few strong competitive capabilities. Like Witco, it paid the price of being a latecomer. Rhône-Poulenc had even fewer opportunities. By quickly diversifying into unrelated product lines, it could not benefit from the economies of scale and scope. Its chances of becoming a stable chemical and pharmaceutical company were threatened still further when it was taken over by the French government.

At the onset of the twenty-first century, Europe's multisectored chemical enterprises still dominated world markets, just as they had done for more than a century, but they were fewer in number. As in the United States, where only Du Pont and Dow remained of the six multisectored companies that had created the American chemical industry, the ten European producers listed in Table 1.1 in 1993 had dwindled to five: Bayer, BASF, ICI, Solvay, and Akzo. Four companies had merged and abandoned chemicals for pharmaceuticals, including Ciba-Geigy and Sandoz, constituents of Novartis, and Hoechst and Rhône-Poulenc, partners (among others) in Aventis. Henkel, meanwhile, sold off its chemical operations to concentrate on its core business in branded consumer products.

I now turn again to the American competitors listed in Table 1.1. Chapters 3–5 have covered twenty-six of the fifty companies listed in the table. Chapter 6 considers the evolution of the remaining twenty-four chemical companies.

The American Competitors

The twenty-four chemical companies listed in Table 1.1 not yet reviewed can be grouped in four categories: (1) twelve oil and gas companies (including three subsidiaries of European owners), (2) three industrial firms that used chemicals in their production processes, (3) five conglomerates that acquired chemical businesses as part of unrelated diversification strategies, and (4) four spin-offs that resulted from the redefinition of the strategic boundaries of the core chemical companies during the restructuring of the industry in the 1980s.

The oil and gas companies had entered the chemical industry in strength during and after World War II, when oil and gas began to replace coal in providing raw materials used in the production of basic petroleum products, and so played a critical role in the polymer/petrochemical revolution. By 1970 the companies that had succeeded in building a new integrated learning base—and some failed to do so—were receiving a quarter of their income from petrochemicals. The remainder still came from traditional oil and gas products.

In the second category, General Electric (GE) and Pittsburgh Plate Glass (PPG) had used chemicals in their initial products produced in the 1890s, whereas Eastman Kodak began making chemicals for film after its supplies from Germany were cut off during World War I. The products of their integrated learning bases differed from those of the oil and gas companies in that the industrial companies initially commercialized high-end specialties for their own use rather than as independent businesses in their own right.

The third category, the conglomerates, emerged in the 1960s and 1970s. These included chemical companies that acquired other unrelated businesses as well as companies in other businesses that purchased chemical producers. Finally, the fourth category consists of spin-offs from the existing companies, manifestations of the large-scale restructuring of bigger companies during the 1980s. The spin-offs, of course, took their integrated learning bases with them.

I begin by reviewing the largest and most significant of the American chemical industry's domestic competitors, the oil and gas companies.

The Petrochemical Companies

Of the dozen oil and gas companies listed in Table 1.1, six were descendants of John D. Rockefeller's Standard Oil Company: Exxon (Standard of New Jersey), Amoco (Standard of Indiana), Mobil (Standard of New York), Chevron (Standard of California), Arco (Atlantic Refining), and BP America (Standard of Ohio). Shell was the American subsidiary of Royal Dutch Shell, Rockefeller's strongest international rival in the late nineteenth century. The others included Texaco, established in 1901 with the opening of the Texas oil fields; Phillips Petroleum, formed in 1917 and which grew with the opening of the midcontinent oil fields; and Ashland, with roots going back to 1911 in Kentucky. The remaining companies—Occidental and Elf-Atochem—were latecomers and thus struggled. Occidental, a small local company, had only begun to challenge the first movers in the 1960s before it failed. Elf-Atochem was founded in 1983 to operate the petrochemical enterprises of France's state-owned gas enterprise, Elf-Aquitaine, and had little impact on the evolution of the petrochemical industry.

Four of these dozen companies—the forerunners of Exxon (Jersey Standard) and Chevron (Standard of California or Socal) and Shell and Phillips—began to lay the foundation of the petrochemical industry before the outbreak of World War II. These long-established petrochemical companies were very much pioneers among their competitors. As Williams Haynes, the chemical industry's historian, observed in the early 1940s, "Production of chemicals by the petroleum industry appeared to be economically and technically sound, but most petroleum executives could not see what appeared to them to be a tiny market for a multitude of chemicals produced by a complexity of operations and sold to a long and diversified list of customers, tasks for which they had neither the technical nor the sales staff."[1]

Entering the Chemical Industry: The First Movers and Followers

During the 1920s and 1930s, the four established petrochemical companies had commenced building their integrated learning bases either by producing for specialty chemical markets or by improving their basic product, gasoline.

Shell and Standard Oil of California made intermediates and agricultural chemicals, using the feedstocks from their West Coast refineries. (Royal Dutch Shell was a friendly minority owner of its American affiliate until 1985, when it acquired control. From the outset, the two companies shared technology and cooperated completely in technical matters.) Indeed, armed with its parent's advanced technology, in 1927 Shell became the first American oil company to set up an autonomous chemical subsidiary. The subsidiary first produced synthetic ammonia and subsequently added fertilizers and products for commercial refrigeration. But Shell's major achievement came in the mid-1930s when it pioneered the commercializing of high-octane gasoline.[2]

Meanwhile, Standard Oil of California, lacking Shell's technological capability, developed agricultural and horticultural insecticides through the acquisition in 1931 of the California Spray Chemical Corporation. In the 1930s Standard Oil of California began producing by-products, primarily naphthalic acids and derivatives.[3]

Jersey Standard and Phillips, on the other hand, focused on commercializing high-octane, primarily aviation, gasoline, initiating systematic research in the late 1920s, in part because of a threatened oil shortage in the mid-1920s. In 1927, a research group at Jersey Standard undertook work with Germany's I. G. Farben to develop synthetic gasoline based on the hydrogenation of brown coal. That project was cancelled when the opening of the vast East Texas oilfield created a glut in oil during the 1930s. The Jersey Standard development department then turned, again collaborating with I. G. Farben, to commercializing new catalysts based on butadiene. That proved successful, except that cost was too high. In the years before 1935, Phillips, the youngest of the four first movers, began to experiment in producing high-octane gasoline. Then in 1935 Phillips, with Shell and Jersey Standard, became the first movers in commercializing this product.[4]

The Entry into Polymer/Petrochemicals

The entry of the petroleum companies into the polymer/petrochemical revolution proved a critically important development and required significant upgrading of their technological capabilities. The entry can be dated by the delivery of experimental high-octane gasoline in 1934 by Shell to the Army Air Force at Wright Field. Within a year, Shell, Jersey Standard, and Phillips had begun to commercialize the process to polymerize gasoline by combining two unsaturated molecules, usually by catalytic action, to form a third large molecule.

In 1935 Shell began to produce high-octane gasoline at three of its refineries in California, Texas, and Illinois. It developed a cold-acid polymerization process that treated butanes, butylenes, and isobutylenes to produce di-isobutylene, a polymer product that was then hydrogenated to make iso-octane, a key ingredient in 100-octane gasoline. The next year, the process was improved through a hot acid technique. Then in 1939 came an even more efficient process called alkylation, in which isobutylene and butylenes were polymerized.[5]

During this same period, Jersey Standard took the lead over Shell in terms of output. After 1935 its learning was concentrated at the major refinery of an affiliate, Humble Oil and Refining Company, at its Baytown refinery in Texas. Its initial product, based on butane and propane came on-stream in 1937. That same year saw the construction of a thermal polymerization plant (whose construction rested on technology licensed from Phillips). When it came into operation in 1938 it was the world's largest polymerizing plant. Meanwhile, Phillips too was moving ahead in the same manner in commercializing polymer/petrochemicals.[6]

The new polymerization technologies forced continuing major improvements in cracking facilities. Here Jersey Standard led the way with a fluid process that ensured a continuous flow in catalyst regeneration. Coming on-stream in 1942, it became the model for the giant plants that the petroleum companies entering the industry after Pearl Harbor (Standard Oil of Indiana, Standard Oil of Ohio, Socony Vacuum, Atlantic Richfield, and Gulf) used to meet the enormous demands for high-octane gasoline during World War II. By 1944 Jersey Standard accounted for 19.5 percent and Shell 11 percent of total 100-octane aviation gasoline. Phillips was lower with 5.1 percent in good part because it concentrated more than the others on the production of synthetic rubber.[7]

Finally, the intermediate chemicals essential for the polymerizing cracking process were valuable in their own right. As Joseph Bower explains, ethylene and its derivatives accounted for roughly one-third of the shipments used in the cracking process. Other basic intermediates included propylene, chloride, and styrene. These, along with ethylene, were then polymerized into basic commodity petrochemicals, including high- and low-density polyethylene (HDPE and LDPE) and polypropylene, polyvinyl chloride, and polystyrene.[8] As the major supplier of these intermediates, Dow reshaped its strategic boundaries.

In this way, the crash programs in gasoline and rubber transformed the major oil and gas companies into significant producers of chemicals. By the war's end, most, but not all, of the principal American petroleum companies were producing basic feedstocks, intermediate petrochemicals, as well as commodity polymers. Some companies failed, for different reasons, including Mobil, Texaco, Gulf (later part of Chevron), Ashland, Occidental, and Elf-Atochem.

Expanding the Boundaries of the Petrochemical Companies

In the early postwar years, the oil companies realized, in the words of Peter H. Spitz, the historian of the petrochemical industry, that "petrochemicals, made from the raw materials in the gas fields and the refineries, were growing at 10 to 15 percent annually, or faster. Surely this would be a great area for business diversification. The only question was—how far to go downstream? That would have to be decided but, in the meantime, there was plenty to do."[9]

By the 1970s the question of how far downstream to go had been answered: not very far. The 1950s, the period of the incipient industry's growth and innovation, introduced the commercializing of a stream of new or specialized olefins, aromatics, and other intermediaries, and new basic polymers, such as polyethylene (PE) and polypropylene (PP). From these emerged a cornucopia of innovative plastics, fibers, films, and other end-products. The petroleum companies followed somewhat different paths as they learned the limits of their specific sets of organizational capabilities, which had been shaped by the enormous wartime demand. In the 1950s the four first movers that had entered the industry before 1941 paved the way in defining and redefining the strategic boundaries of the petrochemical companies' participation in the chemical industry.

Jersey Standard's Ambitions

I begin with the evolution of Exxon's chemical product lines during the postwar years, for they clarify how existing organizational capabilities define the limits of the company's potential for commercializing new products and processes. After reviewing the Exxon chemical story, the paths of learning in petrochemicals embraced by the other oil companies listed in Table 1.1 are very briefly described.

From 1943 on, senior Jersey managers, particularly Frank Howard, who had established and then managed Jersey's development department, and Monroe "Jack" Rathbone, who would become CEO in 1960, urged the company to define and implement an explicit strategy of diversification into petrochemicals and to create an autonomous operating division that would integrate the development, production, and marketing of these petroleum-based chemicals. In 1950, both leaders again issued the same strong recommendations to the senior managers on the executive committee. The two emphasized that Jersey's current 15.8 percent return on investment in petrochemicals was already much greater than that in gasoline and other petroleum products. Indeed, it was greater than the average return of fourteen chemical companies that they had studied. In basic olefins and aromatics, Rathbone pointed out, Jersey possessed the longest experience and the best research and production talent in the industry. These talents, they argued, could easily be transferred to large-scale production of basic polymers and then end-products. To do so, Rathbone stressed, required allowing the executives in charge of chemicals greater freedom of action and more responsibility for results.[10]

The members of the executive committee agreed, but they dragged their feet in implementing the proposal. Most still continued to view petrochemicals as essentially by-products of the company's primary lines. Growth in petrochemicals continued but in an ad hoc and somewhat uncoordinated manner. The move into the promising new PP technology was slowing down; improvement and innovation in synthetic rubber products was disappointing. Little effort was made to expand chemical production abroad. Meanwhile, Dow and other chemical companies were rapidly expanding their output of commodity and intermediate petrochemicals. The three other prewar pioneers were pulling ahead of Jersey. In 1960 Jersey's chemicals accounted for 4 percent of gross revenues as compared with 15.4 percent for Phillips, 8.2 percent for California, and 6.5 percent for Shell. At the same time, the huge expansion of oil-refining capacity worldwide had been driving down revenues and income for Jersey's primary oil and gas products, rendering the production of higher-value petroleum chemicals more attractive.[11]

In 1960, at the height of the polymer/petrochemical boom, Rathbone became Jersey Standard's CEO and chairman of the executive committee. Determined to change the direction of the company's growth so that it be part of the new expanding path, he and the executive committee encouraged the operating managers not only to expand production in basic polymers, particularly polypropylene, but also to seize opportunities in the markets for end-products before other firms, chemical as well as petroleum, grasped them. The executive committee was soon approving expenditures in all parts of the world for new plant construction and acquisitions of producers of agricultural chemicals, containers and other plastic goods, fibers, packaging film, and laminated products.

Large-scale direct foreign investments in agricultural chemicals, particularly fertilizers, were directed toward less developed countries, where Jersey's products were intended to assist in the "green revolution." Agricultural chemical plants were built in Colombia, Aruba, Costa Rica, El Salvador, and Argentina, and then in more developed countries—Spain, Greece, Lebanon, Holland, and Canada. In Europe and the United States factories came onstream to produce nylon and polypropylene fibers, plastics, and film, and often the basic and intermediate chemicals and polymers required for their production. The geographically defined operating subsidiaries that constructed these factories then created the necessary marketing and distribution organizations. By 1965, 30 percent of the company's chemical revenues and almost 50 percent of its capital expenditures for chemicals derived from the new polymer/petrochemical product lines. Fibers, plastics, film, and "especially fertilizers" grew faster than basic chemicals, solvents, additives, and synthetic rubber.[12]

In their enthusiasm for growth through diversification into chemicals, particularly end-products, the company's managers had paid little attention to defining an explicit strategy or providing the structure for its implementation. As Bennett Wall, Exxon's historian, emphasizes, the operating managers neglected to carry out their normal procedures for a "thorough analysis of markets, technologies and labor supply." Although Rathbone's administrative assistant had in 1960 outlined a consolidated blueprint structure for the company's chemical business, the executive committee failed to approve its formation as the Esso Chemical Company until March 1963. The committee then appointed two senior executives with a small staff to be responsible for Esso's activities. Even then, the new subsidiary did not include the chemical unit of Humble Oil (the Enjay Company), the creator of Jersey's petrochemical technology.[13]

Only in 1965, when Jersey's top managers reviewed the 1964 performance of the Esso Chemical Company, did they begin to realize that their move into petrochemicals was seriously flawed. The profits for 1964 of $24 million fell far short of the forecast $40 million and way below the realized $33 million for 1963. Capital expenditures for 1964 had soared to $273 million from an average of $53 million in the two previous years. In reaction, the executive committee immediately folded Enjay's operations into Esso Chemical, replaced the chemical company's two senior managers, cut capital appropriations to $150 million, and defined a new strategy of investing primarily in proven businesses where sound returns had been demonstrated. Despite this response, profits continued to drop. In 1968, Esso Chemical reported losses of $15.8 million.[14]

Top management then instituted a program of divestiture and consolidation. Divestitures occurred primarily in such end-products as fertilizers, plastics, and fibers, in which Esso Chemical had not developed the functional capabilities to compete effectively with core chemical companies. It did, however, retain a few specialty chemicals that were showing profits. The consolidation of personnel and facilities came more in the basic chemicals and intermediates. In these areas, technological improvements had increased minimum efficient scale, reducing the cost-efficiency of smaller plants Exxon had already built. In 1971 a senior executive reported that "a total of $500 million gross plant was divested."[15] The sturdy barriers to entry created by the long-established core chemical companies were becoming apparent.

During the 1970s Jersey Standard's chemical product portfolio had been reduced to resemble that in 1960. Its primary chemical business remained the production of ethylene, basic polymers (including LDPE, linear low-density polyethylene (LLDPE) using the Unipol process, licensed from Union Carbide, PP, and polyvinyl chloride (PVC), plasticizers (particularly for vinyl production), elastomers, and synthetic rubbers. Profits returned. The 1974 balance sheet listed earnings of $456 million on revenue of $3.3 billion, making Exxon Chemical one of the five most profitable chemical companies worldwide.[16]

During the industry's restructuring in the early 1980s, Exxon Chemical sold off most of its specialty petrochemical units to Du Pont and other chemical companies, and concentrated its R&D on intermediates and polymers. In the early 1990s product development was accomplished through joint ventures, such as one begun in 1990 with Monsanto to improve thermoplastic elastomers, another in 1992 with Mitsui Petrochemicals for the next generation of ethylene polymer resins, and a third in 1994 with Hoechst to refine and market metallocene catalysts and polymers. By focusing on these basic product lines, Exxon grew from the fourteenth-largest American chemical company in 1960 to the third-largest in 1986. During the late 1980s and early 1990s Exxon Chemicals contributed an average of 10 percent of Exxon's revenues and 20 percent of its profits.[17]

Prewar First Movers Follow Jersey Standard's Lead

The corporate paths of learning of two other prewar first movers—Shell and Phillips—were similar to that of Jersey Standard and defined the boundaries of these enterprises in a comparable manner. A third prewar first mover, Standard Oil of California, followed a somewhat different path by expanding its earlier move into agricultural chemicals. In the following brief reviews, I make no attempt to list the end-products these companies delivered to the market.

Shell moved downstream into end-products less enthusiastically than did Jersey Standard. However, as Joseph Bower notes in *When Markets Quake,* "On the basis of [a] sound position in olefins, Shell has constructed essentially a commodity business with a portfolio of higher-value businesses. Within commodities, they are more balanced toward propylene and its derivatives than other competitors, especially the other oil companies." However, Bower continues, "By the late 1970s, the disappearance of the basic factors that drove the expansion of chemicals was finally noticed and Shell began to put its house in order." It did so by selling off its high-end products, reducing its worldwide ethylene output—the product in which it was the world's largest producer—and its output of styrene and other intermediates. After its original parent, Royal Dutch Shell, acquired full control in 1986, the Shell group maintained its commitment to basic and commodity polymers and petrochemicals, which in 1995 accounted for 10 percent of sales but 24 percent of income (with oil and gas providing the rest).[18]

Phillips built its postwar capabilities on its early development work in high-octane gasoline, carbon black, and butadiene. With Standard of Indiana, the company developed a new catalyst resulting in linear high-density polyethylenes (HDPE), which came on-stream in 1957. Phillips eventually emerged as having the priority on the discovery of polyolefins (PE and PP) in resulting legal battles with Karl Zeigler and others. Then came unbridled growth in the manner of Jersey Standard. Thus Phillips, in the words of the *International Directory of Company Histories,* "suffered from over-expansion and ailing chemical ventures. Some of the petrochemical projects failed badly because of falling propane and fertilizer prices." It soon found it could not compete in higher value-added plastics. It reverted to its strength in HDPE and built a successful elastomer business based on what it had learned from its participation in the World War II rubber synthetic program.

These strengths enabled Phillips to survive a series of attacks during 1984 and 1985 from several of the most notorious Wall Street raiders, first by T. Boone Pickens, then by Ivan Boesky, and finally Carl Icahn. In order to pay off Icahn for the stake he had acquired, Phillips had to sell off many of chemical businesses. Even so, as reported in the *International Directory,* "unexpectedly strong earnings from its petrochemical business more than the effect of lower oil prices raised hopes for Philip's long-term recovery." In 1994 chemicals still provided 23 percent of Phillips' sales and 26 percent of its income.[19]

Standard Oil of California defined its postwar strategic boundaries by concentrating on expanding its prewar agricultural chemicals, including fertilizers—its initial product of the 1930s—and insecticides. It focused on expanding its Ortho brand of lawn and garden chemicals. Nevertheless, it ultimately pulled out of both, selling in 1993 its Ortho division to Monsanto for $400 million. In 1994 Standard of California purchased Gulf Oil for $13.3 billion, to save it from dismemberment by the corporate raider T. Boone Pickens. By 1989 chemicals accounted for 10 percent of sales and 29 percent of operating revenues. Five years later sales remained a close 9 percent but operating income had dropped to 12 percent. In 2000, Chevron merged with Texaco to form Chevron-Texaco, the second-largest U.S.-based energy company after ExxonMobil.[20]

The Successful Followers: Amoco, Arco, Sohio, and Ashland Rely on the SEFs

Whereas the prewar first movers in chemicals expanded their strategic boundaries by focusing on higher value-added end-products, three of the four successful followers concentrated on becoming a major producer of a highly specialized product. The fourth began in the same manner and then made a major shift in its basic strategy. The four consisted of Standard Oil of Indiana, renamed Amoco, Atlantic Richfield's Arco Chemical subsidiary, and two smaller companies—Standard Oil of Ohio (Sohio, controlled by British Petroleum after 1971, and later renamed BP America), and Ashland Oil. Ashland began the postwar years by commercializing a specialty chemical product but then redefined its strategic boundaries to become the leading distributor of chemical products.

AMOCO Of these four, Amoco built one of the most profitable niche specialties. A major producer, Amoco joined the polymer/petrochemical revolution during the war by beginning to produce high-octane gasoline in 1943. It entered the polymer business in 1955 by acquiring from Ralph Landau's Scientific Design a "process for the bromine-assisted oxidation of paraxylene to terephthalic acid, the main ingredient in polyester fiber." As described in Chapter 4, this move led in turn in 1957 to consolidation of the company's activities into two separate subsidiaries, Amoco Production and Amoco Chemicals. Over the course of the following decade, Amoco Chemicals expanded its chemical operation, starting with the purchase of Sun Oil's polypropylene business, and subsequently acquiring a license from another specialized engineering firm (SEF), Universal Oil Products (UOP), to commercialize the parex process to make paraxylene. On the basis of its new paraxylene capabilities, the company advanced into end-products by purchasing a carpet-fiber producer and became a serious competitor in polyester fiber. During the 1980s, it divided its chemical operations into four subsidiaries.

Nevertheless, Amoco's growth strategy proved to be unsuccessful. So it finally spun off all but its initial chemical learning base in paraxylene intermediates. As a result, "the profits from Amoco's chemical sector increased from $68 million in 1981 to $574 million in 1994, thanks in large part to its 40 percent share of the world's market for paraxylene and purified terephthalic acid, both used to make polyester, the demand for which grew dramatically, especially in Asia." By 1997, 16 percent of Amoco's sales and the same percent of its income derived from chemicals.[21]

ARCO (ATLANTIC RICHFIELD) Landau's entrepreneurial inventiveness further yielded Arco Chemical, Atlantic Richfield's chemical subsidiary, another highly profitable new process. In this case, however, the innovation was developed not through licensing, but through a joint venture to commercialize Landau's process for the production of propylene oxide, the principal ingredient in urethane foams and other polyurethane polymers (as reviewed in Chapter 4).

During these same years Arco had developed its own polyethylene and polypropylene businesses and had also acquired the chemical division of Sinclair in a 1969 merger with that oil company, which had been a major producer of high-octane gasoline during the war. As part of the redefining of its strategic boundaries after the second oil shock, Arco Chemical sold off both its PE and PP business as well as several other polymer operations. Then, in 1985, Atlantic Richfield spun off the commodity olefin part of Arco Chemical into a separate operating subsidiary, Lyondell Petrochemical. Two years later, it incorporated its chemical division into a separate company, Arco Chemical Company, and sold 17 percent of its shares to the public. Then, as Lyondell expanded dramatically, Atlantic Richfield exploited its success as a means of providing needed funds, and in January 1989 sold 50 percent of Lyondell's shares to the public, which netted Atlantic Richfield $1.5 billion. In this way, Atlantic Richfield was one of the first chemical companies to employ this financing technique of selling shares of subsidiaries to the public.[22]

SOHIO (BP AMERICA AFTER 1970)   The specialty that Standard Oil of Ohio commercialized was developed by another SEF, the Badger Company, which, in Spitz's words, was "the most experienced U.S. contractor in the application of fluid bed technology." Mastering that technology, Sohio so lowered the cost of acrylonitrile that it became the dominant American producer and world licenser, "but made no attempt to go into acrylic fiber manufacturing." In the United States, its strength continued to rest on the intermediate acrylonitrile.[23]

ASHLAND OIL   The evolution of Ashland Oil, which also entered the postwar chemical industry through an SEF, differed sharply from that of the three companies just reviewed. It became a successful enterprise only by making a complete reversal in defining its strategic boundaries.

Ashland participated in a minor way in the World War II gasoline programs through a government-funded 100-octane gasoline refinery that increased the company's revenues from $8 million in 1940 to $35 million in 1945. During the 1950s, collaborating with Universal Oil Products, Ashland developed a new process for producing naphthalene. It did not make a concerted move into petrochemicals, however, until the mid-1960s. After purchasing two small petrochemical companies in 1958 and 1963, it acquired seven more between 1965 and 1967, including the chemical unit of Archer-Daniels-Midland, the giant corn and grain processor and shipper. With this acquisition, whose primary activity was not production but distribution, Ashland had become by the 1990s "the nation's leading distributor of chemicals."[24]

By 1989, 23 percent of Ashland's sales and 39 percent of its income came from chemicals. By 1994 the continuing move toward distribution had resulted in a ratio of 42 percent of sales and 31 percent of income. The rest accrued from retailing (15 and 13 percent, respectively, of sales and profits), lubricants, its one consumer product, (9 and 12 percent), and construction, primarily a distribution cost, (9 and 16 percent). Ashland's transition into distribution distinguishes its evolution from that of the other chemical companies described in this book and certainly calls for detailed study.

The Unsuccessful Entrants

Four of the major oil and gas companies proved unable to enter the petrochemical industry profitably: Mobil, Texaco, Occidental, and Elf-Atochem. Of these, the Mobil story illustrates the essential need for an integrated learning base if the products devised by the enterprise's technical capabilities are to be commercialized, thus reaching national markets.

MOBIL   Socony Vacuum (later Mobil and now ExxonMobil) was one of the companies that joined in a 1941 agreement to build new synthetic gasoline plants using the Houdray process. By 1943 it had passed Standard Oil of California to become the third-largest U.S. producer. In the 1950s, on the basis of its wartime learning, it "built a position in shape-selected catalysts used for processes such as exylemeisomerization, and then ethyl benzene, lube oil treating, and for the conversion of methanol to gasoline." The patents alone on one such catalyst, "by some estimates, generated several hundred million dollars of profit for Mobil." But it made almost no effort to commercialize chemical products.

Instead of commercializing new products on the basis of these formidable technical capabilities, Mobil chose in 1974 to become a conglomerate through unrelated diversification with the purchase of two major U.S. companies, Montgomery Ward, for decades Sears Roebuck's primary rival, and the Container Corporation of America. Inevitably the strategy failed, and Mobil sold off the first in 1986 and the second two years later. In 1989, 7 percent of its operating income came from petrochemicals. By 1992 it was 2 percent.[25]

TEXACO   During World War II Texaco became the fifth-largest producer of 100-octane gasoline. It entered high-end polymers as early as 1944 by forming with American Cyanamid a joint venture, the Jefferson Chemical Company, to produce acrylonitrile and acrylic fibers (as reviewed in Chapter 3). By the early 1960s, Texaco had also moved into commodity petrochemicals concentrating on benzene, constructing one of the world's largest benzene plants. Its chemical business prospered until the 1970s, during which Texaco's chemical and oil business suffered more than most of its competitors from the destabilizing events of that decade. In 1980 its managers implemented a major reshaping of its operating structure that combined its worldwide activities in chemicals into a single unit, Texaco Chemical Company.[26]

The unit prospered until the settlement in 1987 of a court case that forced Texaco to seek protection from bankruptcy under Chapter 11. The origin of that case goes back to 1983, when Texaco purchased the Getty Oil Company with 1.9 billion barrels of reserves. But Getty had already agreed to sell a significant share of its equity to Pennzoil, who filed suit. In 1987 a Texas court ordered Texaco to pay Pennzoil $10.5 billion in damages. Ultimately, Texaco agreed to settle for $3 billion. Meanwhile, the raider Carl Icahn had quickly acquired a major block of stock, which the company then bought back at his price. In this parallel to the Union Carbide story, the resulting divestitures required to pay off these obligations included much of Texaco's chemical business.

By 1989 revenues of the chemical businesses it had retained accounted for only 5 percent of the company sales and 12 percent of its operating income. By 1994 the figures were 3 percent and 4 percent. The following year Texaco turned the remaining chemicals, primarily lubricating oils, over to a joint venture with Huntsman (see pages 171–172).

OCCIDENTAL AND ELF-ATOCHEM   Of the other two failures in petrochemicals, Occidental and Elf-Atochem, the former engaged primarily in buying and selling companies. Armand Hammer, a flamboyant Russian-born entrepreneur, in 1958 became president of Occidental, a small California oil and gas company. During the 1960s Occidental developed into a major producer, as Hammer acquired oil fields in Libya and then Russia, and built acid, ammonia, and urea plants in Britain and Saudi Arabia. With the purchase in 1982 of Cities Service Company, a major domestic oil company, Occidental ranked as the eighth-largest oil company in the United States. The year before Hammer had acquired Iowa Beef Processors, and the year after sold Citgo's refining and marketing units as well as Mid-Con's pipelines. In the mid-1980s Hammer turned to petrochemicals to balance his holdings in oil and gas. He did so by buying up cast-off divisions, including Diamond Shamrock's chemical units in 1986 and Shell's vinyl chloride monomers and Du Pont's chlor-alkali facilities in 1987; the next year he bought Cain Chemical, the spin-off created by Gordon Cain from Du Pont's ethylene and HDPE plants.[27]

By 1989 chemicals accounted for 26 percent of Occidental's sales and 76 percent of its income. Two years later, as recorded in *Hoover's Handbook,* chemicals made up 41 percent of sales and only 2 percent of income. By 1994 chemical sales had risen to 50 percent and jumped to 47 percent of operating income. Oil and gas activities represented the remainder. Nevertheless, Occidental reported that year an overall loss of $36 million. In the five years between 1989 and 1993 Occidental suffered an average loss of $5 million. As a result, in 1995, it sold its HDPE to Lyondell for $400 million and its PVC facilities to Borden Chemical & Plastics. I make no attempt to review Occidental's strategic moves, especially after Hammer's death in 1990. Hammer's strategy was one of a financial manipulator. He was not concerned with defining the strategic boundaries of the enterprise in relation to established organizational capabilities; rather he and his successors had become speculators in the buying and selling of chemical companies.

The youngest petrochemical company listed in Table 1.1 is Elf-Atochem, which is owned and operated by the French government. Like Occidental, it grew primarily through acquisitions. The company originated during the nationalizing and reshuffling of the French chemical industry in 1981, when the petrochemical activities of Rhône-Poulenc and Kuhlmann were consolidated into Elf-Atochem, a subsidiary of France's nationalized oil enterprise, Elf-Aquitaine (see Chapter 5). In the spring of 1984, its CEO reported that the chemical operations had been "heavy loss makers." Between 1983 and 1989, however, the company's performance went from FFr 1.1 billion in losses to FFr 2.4 billion profit after tax. This growth reflected acquisitions, including a U.S. specialty chemical company named Pennwalt. By 1995 Elf-Atochem accounted for 26 percent of its parent Elf-Aquitaine's revenues and 32 percent of its income. Nevertheless, Elf-Atochem appears to have followed in the steps of its two major predecessors, described by Patrick Friedenson as relying on licenses from the United States for most strategic products, and for tariff protection of its products (see Chapter 5). While more successful than Occidental, Elf-Atochem played almost no role in the technological development of the petrochemical industry.[28]

The Petroleum Companies: Diversification beyond Chemicals

During these same years petroleum companies also learned the limits of growth in other directions. Nearly all remained committed to the strategy of growth through diversification that so dominated the thinking of American businessmen and industrialists during the 1960s and 1970s. These petroleum companies moved into the mining of coal and then other metals, including uranium, and later into manufacturing, insurance, and other totally unrelated businesses in processing technologies. They did so, of course, by acquisition, not by direct investment. In early 1970 Exxon and Phillips, as well as Conoco, Gulf, and Standard Oil of Ohio, acquired coal-mining enterprises.

Coal mining was indeed a related industry, as coal had long been the industry's basic raw material and continued to be a feedstock for gas products, as well as a potential source even for gasoline. But, of course, they were unrelated in the technologies. It was the steep rise in oil prices during the OPEC embargo that caused the major transition of oil companies into the acquisition of coal-mining enterprises. These companies continued to stay in the business, although they received little income from it. In the early 1990s Arco appeared to be doing the best, obtaining in 1991 3 percent of its revenues and 1 percent of its income from coal. Exxon, Amoco, and Mobil, and probably some of the others recorded small losses in coal.[29]

Exxon, Arco, Amoco, Mobil, and Ashland also entered the mining of copper and other industrial minerals. For Mobil and Exxon, the latter included uranium. By 1993, however, these units had been spun off. A few firms strayed even further afield. Exxon and Arco undertook the production of computer products and provided computer services. Exxon even went so far as to acquire an innovative electric-motor enterprise, Reliance Electric. As mentioned above, Mobil purchased Montgomery Ward and the Container Corporation of America, while Occidental bought Iowa Beef, the nation's most successful meat packer. By the mid-1990s, however, the petroleum companies had sold off nearly all these acquisitions. By then, nearly all American industrial corporations had learned that such unrelated diversification could rarely remain profitable for more than a decade and defined their strategic boundaries accordingly.

The impact of the oil and gas companies on the American chemical industry was indeed profound. Under the pressure of the crash programs for high-octane gasoline and, to a lesser extent, synthetic rubber, these firms created new learning bases in the developing polymer/petrochemical technology. Employing the feedstocks produced in refining petroleum and processing natural gas, they commercialized the existing aromatic, olefin, and inorganic intermediates, which in turn served as building blocks for a wide variety of polymers and petrochemicals. Those companies that began to produce polymer/petrochemicals during the war relied more on SEFs to construct their initial plants in specialized niche products. The oil and gas companies that built successful learning bases had by the 1980s driven the older multisectored chemical companies out of the markets for commodity polymer/petrochemical products.

I close this review of the entry of the oil and gas companies into chemicals by merely noting the major mergers among these companies that occurred at the turn into the twenty-first century, the details of which are beyond the scope of this book. Here the strongest of the U.S. companies acquired two of their century-old rivals that failed to enter petrochemicals. In 1999 Exxon acquired Mobil. In the next year Chevron took over Texaco. Two years earlier, Chevron and Phillips merged their petrochemical units. Next, in 2002, Phillips and Conoco, the company Du Pont had acquired after its response to the oil crises of the 1970s, announced their merger and the formation of ConocoPhillips.

The other significant consolidation was British Petroleum's acquisition of the two most successful U.S. companies that entered petrochemicals during World War II: Amoco in 1998, and Arco shortly thereafter. By early 2003 there were five major players in international petroleum markets—in order of their revenues, ExxonMobil, BP Amoco, Royal Dutch Shell, ChevronTexaco, and ConocoPhillips—all still producing petrochemicals.

The Vertically Integrated Industrial Corporations

The evolution of the profitable chemical businesses in three of the oldest and largest American industrial companies provides quite a different perspective on interindustry competition than the evolution of the petrochemical businesses of the petroleum companies. General Electric, Pittsburgh Plate Glass, and Eastman Kodak each created their learning base in chemicals to provide essential ingredients for the production of their primary product lines. They then improved the initial products they had commercialized and developed new related specialty products primarily through internal investment.

General Electric

General Electric, an 1892 merger of the U.S. electrical equipment industry's first movers, Edison Electric and Thomson Houston, from its inception had to develop and produce chemically made insulation for its electrical equipment. From the formation of its research laboratory in 1900, it maintained a unit that concentrated on developing improved insulating substances. In its first years GE produced a new set of materials based on alkyd resins (organically based), commercialized under the trade name of Glyptal. These, in turn, served in the 1920s as a base for a line of Glyptal paints and lacquers, and then a line of plastics whose properties were close to Bakelite, the first synthetic plastic. Another line of research created an improved ceramic (inorganic-based) insulator. In the late 1930s, development work in organic material, particularly polyvinyl chloride, led to a new wire, Formex, and a new molding varnish, Permafils. At the same time the GE laboratory was beginning to base product development on a new field of "polymeric silicones," paving the way for new silicone oils and rubbers.[30]

After World War II the insulating unit of the laboratory reoriented its research for new polymer/petrochemical materials around polyphenoline, which when blended with polystyrene produced a thermoplastic resin named Noryl. As manager of polymer products manufacturing, Jack Welch took charge of building the plant that successfully commercialized the new product. He then expanded its use beyond insulation into such specialty products as car-body parts and computer cases. The next new product was Lexan, which had roots going back to Noryl. Among other of its qualities was that Lexan-glazed windows were 250 times stronger than existing products. Welch's success in expanding the market and research in GE's chemical products led to his promotion as head of the chemicals and metallurgic division, then to group executive of the components and materials group, and finally in 1981 to becoming GE's CEO. During the 1980s the Noryl and Lexan lines continued to be improved and the market for them expanded. In 1993 they were still the mainstay of GE's more than $5 billion annual revenues from chemicals—a total that climbed to nearly $8 billion by the end of the decade.[31]

Pittsburg Plate Glass

The evolution of the learning route in chemicals at Pittsburg Plate Glass (PPG) differed from that at General Electric only because it began as a second learning base. John Pitcarn established his firm in 1883 and in the 1890s built his enterprise in the classic manner of Du Pont and other first movers of the Second Industrial Revolution—by merging many small family firms into a single enterprise, concentrating production in a small number of large plants to ensure full exploitation of the economies of scale, and then creating a national and then international marketing and distribution organization. In 1899 Pitcarn set up a subsidiary to produce a basic raw material, soda ash. The next year he purchased a producer of paints. To help cover the costs of his expensive distribution network—given the fragile nature of glass—he decided to sell paint and glass to the same contractors and hardware stores. The learning from the first base propelled the company into the related production of cement, and the second, particularly in the 1920s, into auto lacquers, and then titanium oxide pigments and fast-drying flat paint.

World War II shortages pushed PPG into synthetic resins, then into plastics. At the same time, continuing improvements were being achieved in performance paints and industrial coatings. The company's commercializing of a new electrodeposition coating process is a good example of this continuing product and process development. By the early 1990s PPG had evolved into the world's largest supplier of automotive and industrial finishes and the third-largest producer of chlorine and caustic soda. By then, chemicals accounted for 19 percent of PPG's revenues but 34 percent of its income, and coatings and resins 39 percent and 45 percent, respectively; glass, long its primary line, accounted for 39 percent of revenues but only 23 percent of income. In this way PPG, by carefully tending its related initial learning bases, commercialized related products that became more profitable than its original flat glass, although it still remained the world's third-largest maker of flat glass.[32]

Eastman Kodak

If GE's and PPG's chemical businesses provide illuminating examples of the creation and maintenance of a highly specific path of learning, the Eastman Chemical story yields still another. That learning path, however, was not established in 1884 when George Eastman formed Eastman Kodak to mass produce and market its low-price camera. The learning path was not created until the coming of World War I, which created shortages in the chemicals—menthol, acetate acid, and acetone—needed to volume produce his films, and all but shut down his works in Rochester, New York. In 1920 Eastman formed a new subsidiary, Eastman Chemical, which constructed a plant in Kingsport, Tennessee to produce these chemicals.

Sustained learning at the Tennessee company resulted in the late 1920s in a bouquet of new products. In 1930 a new nonflammable acetate film that became the industry's standard went on-stream. In 1932, its new acetate yarn works, whose power plant had been built in 1928, came into full production and would become a market leader and profitmaker during the Depression years. That same year, Eastman Chemical began to produce the Tenite cellulose plastics used for radio parts, toys, telephones, and automobile steering wheels. Thus, by 1932, the Depression's low point, its sales were greater than those of its parent. In the 1950s the company developed a cellulose acetate filter for cigarettes, "which drove the sales upward for the next half-century and supplanted acetate yarn as its mainstay."[33]

In the mid-1980s Eastman Kodak, responding to lagging sales and intensifying competition, particularly from Japan, turned to becoming a conglomerate through unrelated diversification. It started in 1985 to acquire electronic publishing, batteries, and floppy-disk businesses. In 1988 ensued the major move into pharmaceuticals with the purchase of Sterling Drug for $5.1 billion. (This disastrous story is reviewed in Chapter 9.) It soon sold off its electronic businesses and then Sterling Drug, but its debts remained high and its income low. So, in 1994, following ICI's recent example with Zeneca (reviewed in Chapter 5), Eastman Kodak spun off its "crown jewel" and saddled the newly independent Eastman Chemical with $8.5 billion of its debt. Whereas Eastman Kodak all but destroyed itself by departing from its basic photographic competitive arena, Eastman Chemical, by staying in the chemical competitive arena, was able to cover its parent's financial losses.

As an independent company, Eastman Chemical has continued to prosper on the strength of its integrated learning bases in specialty chemicals and plastics. In the late 1990s the company announced plans to split into two separate entities, with each devoted to a major product line. The depressed stock market thwarted the plans, however, and Eastman Chemical continued to operate the respective businesses as independent divisions.[34]

The Conglomerates

The postwar chemical conglomerates listed in Table 1.1 all made early investments in the unrelated chemicals. Of the five, Grace and Olin stand as classic examples of the rise and fall of this post–World War II phenomenon.

The first became a conglomerate by entering chemicals, the second by leaving the industry. From the 1950s on, they expanded rapidly by acquiring a number of unrelated enterprises and then fell back on their most stable learning base—chemicals. Ethyl, a producer of fuel additives and a classic American focused company, was acquired by a conglomerate in 1962 and thirty years later had returned to its original product line. The FMC Corporation, unable to locate such a base, continued to flounder as a failing conglomerate; Morton International had a little more success in carrying out a strategy of ad hoc acquisitions and divestitures until it was acquired by Rohm and Haas in 1999.

W. R. Grace Becomes a Classic Conglomerate

In the early 1950s a young J. Peter Grace—who had taken over his family's enterprise, W. R. Grace & Company, the largest U.S. shipping and trading company in Latin America—embarked on a career involving the purchase and sale of companies. He established himself first in the chemical industry and then turned to the strategy of related diversification. In 1970 the company became a conglomerate of unrelated businesses only to retreat in 1991 into specialty chemicals.[35]

Convinced that future growth in shipping was limited, Grace embarked on the strategy of diversification in 1954 with the purchase of two long-established chemical companies with strong track records—Davison Chemicals and Dewey & Almy. Davison, established in Baltimore in 1832, had a large phosphate plant and several fertilizer works. In the 1930s it developed a "super gel," which it used as a fluid catalyst for high-octane gasoline in World War II and, following the war, as a dehydrating agent for a wide variety of industrial uses. Dewey & Almy, formed in 1929, initially commercialized a water sealant based on natural rubber. Continued learning led to the development of synthetic rubber and plastics and the building of a full-scale manufacturing plant in 1942. During the war Bradley Dure, a founder and CEO, was appointed director of the U.S. Synthetic Rubber Program on the strength of his experience. Grace rounded out its chemical division by acquiring Hatco Chemicals in 1959, which produced specialty polymer chemicals used in its products.[36]

Three years earlier, in 1956, Grace had entered the petroleum business through a joint venture with Texas Gulf in Libya, then in 1960 came the purchase of 63 percent of Cosden (which was sold in 1963 to Petrofina). In the 1960s Grace continued to expand its chemical business (evolving into

one of the nation's largest oetrikeyn producers) and enlarge its oil investments. It also began to provide specialized petroleum and other energy services. Then, in 1969, it completed its exit from its original path with the sale
of Grace Lines and Grace Air.

During the 1970s Grace became a full-fledged conglomerate. The company made a steady stream of unrelated acquisitions of consumer products
and marketing companies that, by the early 1980s, included the purchase
of several chains of different kinds of restaurants and fast-food purveyors;
home improvement stores; sporting goods stores; stores for leisure fashion
wear, specialty products, and leather goods; and a leading distributor of
books, video cassettes, and educational software. In these years, too, it acquired a cocoa and chocolate maker, and producers of automobile parts.
Throughout the period, however, Grace's specialty chemicals division remained the most profitable of its businesses. For example, Crovac, a plastic
vacuum pack for vegetables and meat, generated a billion dollars a year in
revenues.

The sustained profitability of specialty chemicals and the poor performance of the many acquisitions in different industries prompted a dramatic
change in corporate strategy beginning in 1986. That year, the sell-offs included first the several restaurants and then the retailing chains, other consumer goods, and the fertilizer business. At the same time, following the
pattern of its chemical competitors, Grace started to move seriously into
healthcare with the acquisition of kidney dialysis and respiratory services
and a collaborative venture in biotechnology. In 1985 specialty chemicals
accounted for 71 percent of the company's profits, but only 28 percent of its
assets. By 1987 the figures were 84 percent and 44 percent. By 1991 the
company reported that 58 percent of its sales and 65 percent of its operating
income derived from its specialty chemicals and that 17 percent of its revenues, 21 percent of its income, from healthcare. By that same year, the company sold off interests in agricultural chemicals, automotive chemicals, live-
stock feeds, and pharmaceuticals.

In November 1991 Peter Grace, then seventy-nine years of age, announced that the company would "divest $1.5 billion by the end of 1992
[with a] focus on six core closely related businesses where it is already a
market leader: flexible packaging, container sealants, construction products,
water treatment, catalysts, and other silica-based products." In healthcare,
Grace would divest itself of all its products except its highly specialized kidney dialysis service centers.[37]

Following Peter Grace's retirement in 1993, the refocusing continued. By the early 2000s, the company operated two major units: Davison Chemical, which manufactured silica-based products, chemical catalysts, and refining catalysts, and Performance Chemicals, which produced concrete and cement additives, packaging sealants, and fireproofing chemicals. The company's prospects had earlier dimmed, however, owing to an upsurge of asbestos-related litigation in the late 1990s, and it was forced to seek bankruptcy protection in 2001. Whatever the outcome of its spell in bankruptcy, Grace's postwar diversification had come close to full circle. It had begun with chemicals in 1954 and ended more than four decades later as a focused specialty chemical producer.[38]

Olin Corporation: From Chemicals to Chemicals

Olin Corporation's product portfolio also went full circle, but it differed from Grace in that Olin transitioned out of chemicals only to later reenter. Olin was one of the very few explosive companies that did not join Du Pont in 1903–1904 to form the E. I. du Pont de Nemours Powder Company (see Chapter 3). Unlike Du Pont, it remained a producer of explosives and ammunition, buying in the 1930s Winchester Firearms Company (at much the same time that Du Pont obtained Remington Arms). Olin did not participate in the polymer revolution. But in 1947 Du Pont, to satisfy the government's antitrust division, granted Olin the licenses and technologies to produce cellophane.[39]

In 1954 Olin merged with Mathieson, another medium-sized chemical company, which two years earlier had turned to a strategy of growth through acquisition with the purchase of Squibb, a major pharmaceutical firm, and Beechnut Chewing Gum. Olin Mathieson continued Mathieson's strategy by acquiring a major paper company in 1955, a wire and cable producer in 1957, and later a large brass company. In the 1960s Olin Mathieson continued to expand its existing businesses, particularly its paper-making activities and, through its long-established Winchester division, its defense business.

In the late 1960s Olin's managers decided to spin off Squibb (and with it, Beechnut, as described in Chapter 7), which was quickly transformed into a major pharmaceutical enterprise. With the proceeds from that move, Olin acquired in 1969 an aluminum extrusion company and two large residential construction companies. By 1971 chemicals accounted for only 25 percent of sales, metals 28 percent, fine paper 7 percent, crafts and other paperboard packaging materials 16 percent, firearms and defense 18 percent, and housing 6 percent. After 1971, as divestitures continued, they funded the acquisitions of the Ski Company, a maker of sleeping bags and down jackets, and a producer of carpet underlaying.

During the 1970s the strategy changed, beginning with the sales of its aluminum and fertilizer units. Then, in the 1980s, came a deluge, including the sales of consumer products, housing construction, carpets, cellophane, and most of the paper and metal operations. As at W. R. Grace, these sales funded the acquisitions in specialty chemicals, particularly those used in coatings for cars and appliances and foams used in cushions, carpet pads, and car seats. Thus, by 1987, 54 percent of the company's operating revenues derived from chemicals, 22 percent from metals and materials, and 24 percent from defense and ammunition. Two years later, after further sell-offs, the figures were 77 percent, 2 percent, and 21 percent. Olin was once again primarily a chemical company.

The refocusing continued during the 1990s as Olin concentrated on three specialty businesses: metal products (copper and copper alloy sheets, strips, and foil, clad metal, and stainless-steel strips); chlor-alkali chemicals for bleach, water purification, swimming pools, pulp and paper processing, and PVC; and the Winchester brand of ammunition.[40]

Ethyl Corporation: From Fuel Additives to Fuel Additives

Ethyl Corporation's history provides yet another classic example of a U.S. conglomerate during the 1970s and 1980s. A most successful specialized niche company, Ethyl was acquired by a conglomerator, the Albemarle Paper Company, which acquired a wide variety of unrelated companies only to later sell them off, so that by the mid-1990s Ethyl had returned to its original niche.

The Ethyl Gasoline Corporation was formed in 1924 as a 50–50 joint venture with General Motors and Standard Oil of New Jersey to commercialize an antiknock additive for gasoline-powered engines. During the 1950s, as the leader of its niche, the company continued to prosper. After its acquisition in 1962 by Albermarle Paper Company of Richmond, Virginia, the combined entity took the Ethyl name. The next year, the new Ethyl acquired Union Carbide's polyethylene film and its polyvinyl chloride businesses. In 1966 it purchased a major producer of shaped aluminum and in 1967 another paper company.[41]

During these same years the protest against leaded "no-knock" gasoline led to passage of the federal Clean Air Act, which mandated stricter emission controls and thus phased out Ethyl's initial product. Although its additives division continued to develop new legal additives, Ethyl's managers decided to take on more acquisitions. By 1982, when it purchased the First Colony Insurance Company, Ethyl had acquired two coal companies, a pharmaceutical enterprise, a timber business, and a tool and mold company. During the 1980s acquisitions continued, including the purchase of another coal company, Dow's bromide business, and a semiconductor enterprise.

Then, in 1989, the sell offs ensued. That year Ethyl disposed of its semiconductor, plastics, aluminum, and coal businesses to its stockholders under the name of Tredeghar Industries. In 1993 it spun off its insurance business to its stockholders as the First Colony Company. The next year, the managers did the same for its chemicals—olefins and their derivatives, bromides, and other specialty chemicals. This was accomplished by creating a new *Fortune 500* enterprise named Albemarle.

Meanwhile, Ethyl acquired petroleum-additives operations from Amoco, Texaco, and Nippon Copper. By 1996 the company had become as it had began—"a developer, manufacturer, and blender of petroleum additives"— both lubricant additives and fuel additives.[42] So it was once again a focused leader in the industry niche in which it had become the first mover seventy years earlier.

FMC Corporation: A Failed Conglomerate

The FMC Corporation was formed as a merger of two operating companies in related paths of learning. In 1928, John Beam, the inventor of the hand-held spray gun, merged his company, which had been established in 1884, with a California canning enterprise to form the Food Machinery Corporation (FMC). During World War II it expanded its spraying mechanisms to apply to military use and acquired a contract to build amphibious tanks for the Army. Then, in 1943, as part of its postwar plans, it acquired the Niagara Spray and Chemical Company, producer of insecticides and fungicides that FMC's machines sprayed. In 1948 it bought Westvaco Chemical Corporation, a major producer of phosphates and nitrates, and changed its name to Food & Machinery Company.[43]

Then, in the 1960s, its management caught the conglomerate bug, purchasing in 1963 American Viscose, a U.S. first mover in rayon, and in 1968 the Link Belt Corporation, a first mover in the belting material on which assembly lines were based. More unrelated diversification followed. In 1974 and 1975 the firm spent $400 million on relatively related "growth" products, including petroleum equipment and specialty chemicals. The enterprise grew but its income did not increase.

Buying and selling continued in the 1970s. In 1976 the pump division was sold along with 50 percent interest in an Alaskan pulp enterprise (which had been part of the American Viscose acquisition), followed by the sale of Link Belt and other recent purchases. Then came investment in businesses at home and abroad in mining and manufacturing, including even semiconductors. During these years the only division that developed new products was agricultural chemicals, and it did so on the basis of its 1948 chemical acquisition. The pattern continued through the 1980s, including a large investment in gold mining on which FMC lost $225 million.

In 1995 an analyst referred to FMC as "a hangover from the 1960s—competing with little strategic focus, betting on losing businesses." By 1994, 49 percent of revenues and 52 percent of income came from a scattering of not too closely related industrial and performance chemicals—25 percent of its revenues and 42 percent of its income from defense systems growing out of its tank production in World War II, and 23 percent of its revenues but only 7 percent of its operating income from the remaining machinery and equipment business.

In the late 1990s the company finally conceded defeat and disposed of many of its unrelated businesses. It sold its defense business in 1997 and sold off or formed joint ventures in a number of specialty chemicals operations in the following years. In 2001 came the big step: the spin off of the company's food and equipment businesses into a new company, FMC Technologies. FMC Corporation itself remained a focused producer of specialty, industrial, and agricultural chemicals—about half its size in the early 1990s, but more profitable.[44]

Morton International: An Unsuccessful Search for New Businesses

The evolution of Morton International differs from that of the other conglomerates just described. It did not buy and sell numerous companies in several different industries; instead, it entered unrelated industries in an ad hoc manner. Until the post–World War II years, it had remained the largest and indeed the only nationwide distributor of salt. Established in 1848 in Chicago, Morton Salt experienced its major growth from supplying the meat-packing industry in that city after the Civil War. In addition to meat packing, it processed and distributed salt for human and animal consumption, for use in chemical processing, and, after the coming of motor vehicles, for melting highway ice.[45]

In the 1950s Morton began to move beyond salt into related chemical niche lines, including bromides, adhesives, and dye stuffs. In 1965 it advanced further afield by acquiring Simonize, a maker of auto wax and cleaners. Then, in 1969, it progressed into pharmaceuticals by merging with Norwich Pharmaceuticals. The venture did not prosper, however, and Morton sold it off to Procter & Gamble in 1982.

Searching for a new product line, Morton next merged with Thiokol, a specialty chemical company and producer of solid-stage rocket motors, which also manufactured a line of household cleaners. The tragic explosion in January 1986 of the Challenger, the NASA space shuttle that used Thiokol's' motors in the booster rockets, ended the partnership. In the resulting division of their product lines, Thiokol continued to produce rocket fuel. Morton kept its specialty chemicals, and concentrated on the unrelated commercializing of air bags for cars, becoming the second-largest producer after TRW.

In the early 1990s Morton International continued to modify its portfolio. It acquired Whitaker Corporation, a maker of coatings and adhesives. Morton then sold off its food and cosmetics properties and concentrated on its fledgling air bag business. In 1994, 48 percent of its sales and 41 percent of its operating income came from specialty chemicals, 33 percent of sales and 25 percent of operating income from air bags, and 19 percent of revenues and 24 percent of income.

In 1999, as reviewed in Chapter 4, Rohm and Haas acquired Morton International for $4.9 billion and assimilated its operations into its own specialty chemicals business.

The Spin-Offs: A New Phenomenon

As this review of the evolution of the fifty largest chemical companies at the close of the twentieth century documents, there have been only two successful entrants since the 1920s, and both appeared to meet the extraordinary demands of World War II. Nevertheless, new companies did appear. These companies were spin-offs in the 1980s of existing enterprises that took with them parts of long-established learning bases. These spin-offs came about for different reasons, but primarily they reflected the restructuring of portfolios during the 1980s as the chemical industry readjusted to the limits of learning generated by chemical science and assisted by the increasing sophistication of financial techniques developed in the capital markets during that decade. As pointed out in Chapter 3, the formation in December 1993 of Cytec marked the culmination of American Cyanamid's move out of chemicals into pharmaceuticals. Similarly, the Union Carbide spin off of its industrial gases business into Praxair in 1992 ensured more freedom to a division loosely related to other product lines.

In the early 1980s Arco Chemical, a wholly owned subsidiary of Arco, began divesting its petrochemical commodities businesses. In 1985 Arco reorganized Arco Chemical into two parts. The first, still bearing Arco Chemical's name, included the traditional chemical operations; the other, Lyondell Petrochemical Corporation (subsequently Chemical Company), included the olefins businesses. In 1987 financial motives led Arco to spin off 20 percent of Arco Chemical. Two years later it sold off 50 percent of Lyondell Petrochemical, fetching $1.4 billion, the largest initial public offering of its day. In 1997 Lyondell and Millennium Chemicals (a recent offshoot of Hanson Plc.), joined forces to create Equistar Chemicals, one of the world's biggest producers of ethylene, propylene, and polyethylene and a major source of polypropylene and other polymer/petrochemical products.[46]

Finally, Jon M. Huntsman, an energetic manager who got his start developing plastic egg cartons, built a major specialty chemical company by purchasing the cast-off operations and divisions of companies in related businesses. Huntsman had built a successful packaging business based on polystyrene when he set his sights on bigger things. His major deals began in 1983 with the purchase of Shell's polystyrene plant for $42 million. Then in 1986 he purchased Hoechst's three polystyrene plants for $45 million, and later moved into polypropylene by buying Shell's plant, selling 40 percent of his own stock to Great Lakes Chemicals to provide his own funding. In this way, Huntsman became the largest American producer of styrene and olefins, as well as a significant producer of polypropylene.

Huntsman's acquisitions continued throughout the 1990s. In 1994 he completed two major deals, acquiring most of Texaco's petrochemical operations for $1 billion, as well as Eastman Chemical's polypropylene business. Five years later Huntsman nearly doubled in size again after purchasing ICI's polyurethanes, titanium dioxide, aromatics, and petrochemical global businesses. In 2000, with acquisitions and some divestitures continuing, Huntsman announced a major reorganization of the company into four distinct businesses: specialty chemicals, "tioxide" (titanium dioxide), petrochemicals, and "surface sciences" (surface effect chemicals and their intermediates). With $4.5 billion in sales in 2002, Huntsman Corporation, by collecting parts of existing enterprises, had become the largest privately held chemical company in the world.[47]

Conclusion

The final chapter in this history of the evolving paths of learning in the chemical industry provides an example of each of the three basic themes of this book. The entry of the petroleum companies into the chemical industry highlights the role of barriers to entry. For it was a new technology use of oil instead of coal as a basic raw material that permitted the oil companies to enter chemicals. During World War II they became dominant in the production of feed stocks, intermediates, and basic petrochemicals and polymers. Then in the 1950s and 1960s they began to compete with the long-established end products of the major chemical companies. By the late 1960s, however, they had learned that the existing barriers to entry were too high. Consequently, in the 1970s, a division of labor was fully established within the industry. Those oil companies that succeeded were receiving roughly a quarter of their revenues from petrochemicals.

The relative success of the chemical businesses of the three large manufacturing companies reflects the end of growth in terms of commercializing new technologies from new learning in chemical sciences and engineering, as well as the resulting evolution of the industry into one of specialty chemicals. Finally, the short-term existence of the conglomerates demonstrates the failure of the strategy of unrelated diversification.

The initial entry of the oil and gas companies came in the 1920s when four competitors—Socal, Shell, Jersey Standard, and Phillips—began to produce chemicals. The first two commercialized agricultural chemicals. The other two, Jersey Standard and Phillips, concentrated on commercializing petroleum-based gasoline. However, it was the totally unpredictable and extraordinary demand of World War II that created the petroleum side of the polymer/petrochemical revolution. The four companies that had created their learning bases in the 1930s became the first movers in this new industry.

The followers—Standard Oil of Indiana (Amoco), Atlantic Refining (Arco), Mobil, Texaco, and British Petroleum—entered the industry during the war. Of these, Mobil and Texaco proved unsuccessful in commercializing products from the new technology, as were Ashland, Occidental, and France's Elf-Atochem, which entered after the war.

During the late 1940s and 1950s these competitors defined and redefined their strategic boundaries. It was the goal of the first movers to not only provide basic feedstocks and petrochemicals, but also to compete with a wide range of products already commercialized by the leading chemical companies. Jersey Standard led the way into fabrics, plastics, fibers, and fertilizers. By 1966, however, the managers realized that the barriers to entry created by established chemical companies were too high to overcome. After spinning off these products, they redefined the boundaries of basic feed stocks, other petrochemical intermediates, and basic polymers.

The followers—Amoco, Arco, and BP America—succeeded by focusing on a single chemical specialty, commercialized with the assistance of an SEF. A fourth, Ashland Oil, remained profitable by dramatically reshaping its strategic boundaries to become the nation's largest marketer of petroleum products. On the other hand, Occidental and Elf-Atochem suffered the fate of latecomers and contributed little in the way of technological achievement and their own long-term financial success. Of the other two unsuccessful entrants, Texaco was the victim of a law suit and Mobil failed in its strategy of unrelated diversification.

The success of the chemical businesses of the three major U.S. manufacturing enterprises—General Electric, Pittsburgh Plate Glass, and Eastman Kodak—is part of the transformation of the industry into specialty chemicals after it had reached the limits of growth in the 1970s. Thus the stories are similar to those of the focused companies described in Chapter 4. Each of the three commercialized a small number of related products. Like the focused companies, they continued to prosper in the 1980s as the U.S. multiproduct companies restructured their product lines.

Far more dramatic is the failure of the strategy of unrelated diversification by chemical companies moving out and other companies moving into chemicals. Thus Grace in 1956 decided to replace its shipping business by entering the chemical and petroleum businesses. By 1970 it had become a true conglomerate by buying and selling a wide variety of companies in different businesses. But in the mid-1980s Grace began to sell off its existing portfolio so that by 1991 it had become a specialty chemical company. Olin

Mathieson, a chemical company, on the other hand, diversified by moving into comparable spread of businesses, only to return, like Grace, on a small set of specialty chemicals. While the Ethyl Corporation, acquired in the 1960s by a paper company, stayed close to chemicals, it nevertheless became a full-fledged conglomerate in the 1980s. Then in 1989 it began the sell-offs and a refocus on petroleum additives in which it had been a first mover in the 1920s. FMC Corporation was never a classic conglomerate in the sense that Grace was. And when its search for comparable unrelated acquisitions failed, it too retreated to its original base in specialty chemicals. Morton Salt was relatively unsuccessful in its search for new business before it was acquired by Rhom and Haas as an addition to its portfolio of specialty chemicals units.

By the end of the twentieth century, the American chemical industry consisted of a relatively large number of producers of specialty chemicals. These included Du Pont and Dow, the two major American chemical companies. The lack of new learning in chemical science and engineering after the 1960s was a primary cause of this outcome. The companies, of course, continued to commercialize new products, but they did so primarily on the basis of technologies first mastered in the 1920s and again in the 1940s and 1950s.

I turn now to the evolution of the chemical industry's companion, the pharmaceutical industry. The evolutionary paths of these two industries differ remarkably despite similar historical timing and geographical origins, as well as the involvement of some of the same enterprises.

PART III

The Pharmaceutical Industry

CHAPTER 7

The American Companies:
The Prescription Path

The evolution of the American pharmaceutical industry obviously differed from that of its sister, the American chemical industry, in that its technology increasingly drew on a different science—biology and related disciplines—its manufacturing on a different process, and its market for an entirely different use—healthcare. Therefore, its core companies required remarkably different technical and functional capabilities.

Moreover, the industry evolved in a very different manner in the United States than in Europe. In Europe it quickly emerged from the chemical industry—that is, the first producers of modern pharmaceuticals in Europe were chemical companies with expertise in organic chemistry. In the United States the industry evolved in response to the advent of modern transportation and communication—the railroads and the telegraph—from which the Second Industrial Revolution derived.

The Pharmaceutical Industry Begins in the United States and Europe

The major American core companies were, as industry historian Jonathan Libeneau describes them, "large wholesaler/producers who offer a full range of standard preparations," that is, proprietary drugs to pharmacists, druggists, and other retailers. "In 1885," Liebenau writes, "a buyer could choose between Merck, SmithKline, Parke Davis, Eli Lilly, Sterns, Schieffelen, John Wyeth, Upjohn, Mulford, Sharp & Dohme and many others for a complete line of basic medicines in convenient forms."[1]

These medicines included age-old preparations as well as those developed early in the nineteenth century by the isolation of drugs from natural sources, particularly plant-based alkaloids. The isolation of morphine quickly paved the way for that of quinine, cincohonine, caffeine, nicotine, atropine, and codeine from natural sources. In addition, the American wholesaler/producers pioneered pills to ensure precise specifications and dosages of mixed-drug preparations, as well as pill-making machinery to produce in volume. These makers also sold patent medicine and other "proprietary" drugs (using the manufacturer's copyrighted name) that competed with such remedies as Lydia Pinkham's "vegetable compound." These drugs could be purchased without a physician's prescription.

As with chemicals, the modern European pharmaceutical industry began in Germany. It arose in response at about the same time to the advent of two new revolutionary and complementary approaches to therapy that resulted in the commercializing of "ethical" drugs (patented drugs used for specific purposes as labeled). (As time passed these required a physician's prescription. Subsequently I refer to such drugs as "prescription" drugs to distinguish them from over-the counter (OTC) drugs, which were available without a prescription.) The first new therapeutical approach involved the use of serum antitoxins and vaccines, relying on the discoveries of Louis Pasteur and Robert Koch in microbiology and immunology. These new ways to treat and prevent disease were introduced largely in the government-sponsored Pasteur Institute in Paris and the Koch Institute in Berlin, funded by Hoechst, one of the Germany's first movers in modern chemicals.

The other approach consisted of the commercialization of synthetic coal-tar-based drugs, as well as chemicals discovered and commercialized by Hoechst and other German and Swiss chemical first movers in dyes. Both the Hoechst Company on the Rhine and its institute in Berlin funded the research of Koch, Emil von Behring, Paul Ehrlich, and others, which permitted the world's first movers in synthetic organic chemistry to become leaders in synthetic organic drugs. In addition to Hoechst, the German and Swiss leaders (including Bayer, Ciba, Geigy, and Sandoz), the smaller specialized German drug companies (encompassing E. Merck, Schering, and von Hyden), and Switzerland's F. Hoffmann–La Roche emerged as the first producers for global markets of aspirin, phenacetin, vernal and other barbiturates, serums for diphtheria, cholera, tetanus, and other deadly diseases, Novocain and other pain killers, and finally Salvarsan, the earliest chemotherapeutic drug and the first cure for syphilis.[2]

As happened in the chemical industry, the embargo of German products during World War I encouraged American drug companies to develop their technical and functional capabilities and to concentrate on improving existing products while developing new ones. During the 1920s and 1930s these companies began to set up their own research laboratories and foster larger, more integrated organizations. Several of them commercialized new drugs such as insulin, vaccines, vitamins, sedatives, tranquilizers, those for heart disease, and others, marketing them primarily as prescription drugs. As their technical, functional, and managerial capabilities unfolded in one therapeutic area, the companies applied the same capabilities to introduce new prescription drugs in other areas. Even so, most continued to develop, produce, and sell "proprietary" over-the-counter products.

During these interwar years, most of the long-established wholesaler/producers sustained a concentration on building their learning bases in the proprietary OTC path. They focused on enhancing their marketing and advertising capabilities rather than investing in R&D personnel and facilities. In the prosperous 1920s these companies expanded by marketing a broad range of such proprietary drugs, as well as by entering into the related consumer chemicals such as soaps, toothpastes, shampoos, cosmetics, and household products. As they did, they evolved into some of the nation's largest advertisers and pioneered in radio advertising, particularly with nationwide programs on the new NBC and CBS radio networks.

The Therapeutic Revolution

What Peter Temin has properly termed the "therapeutic revolution" that began in the United States in the 1940s was accelerated by the World War II crash programs in the production of the new antibiotics, especially penicillin based on fermentation and sulfanilamide derivatives. This fundamental breakthrough in medical science resulted in what Heinz Redwood terms "a cascade of discoveries. . . . By the end of the 1950s the traditional pre-war pharmaceutical industry had changed beyond recognition, and so had the practice of medicine."[3] As noted in Chapter 2, the major impact was the rapid growth of prescription drugs. In 1929 they accounted for 32 percent of all consumer expenditures on medical drugs. By 1949 they represented 57 percent, and by 1969 were up to 83 percent.

In addition to antibiotics, steroids, antihistamines, and tranquilizers, new prescription drugs for heart and lung diseases and for ulcers, cancers, diabetes, pain control, and other ills soon followed, as did new vaccines and vitamins. So, in the postwar years, the size of "detail" prescription-drug salesforces selling to doctors and hospitals as well as to pharmacies grew substantially. So too did the producers' commitment of time and money to R&D. In the late 1940s and 1950s, as the opportunities created by the opening up of new paths and the enhancement of new technologies expanded, the number of new drugs introduced rose from an annual average of roughly twenty in the 1940s to fifty in the 1950s, and then fell back to an annual average of fewer than twenty between 1963 and 1969, and even fewer in the 1970s. New regulations governing pharmaceuticals exerted a significant impact on these figures, but the pattern was similar to that in chemicals.[4]

Growth Falters

As in chemicals, the leveling-off of new products resulted in managers' turning to a strategy of related diversification executed primarily through acquisitions. During the 1960s and 1970s the leaders on the research-intensive path expanded their OTC drugs and in some cases moved into consumer chemicals (SIC 284), including toiletries, cosmetics, and other personal-care goods, as well as into chemically based household products such as cleaners. Some undertook the high-tech electronic medical equipment paths of SIC 383 and 384. The leaders in the low-tech path were beginning to take steps to enter the high-tech one, but for a while continued to concentrate on their OTC products, expanded their offerings in the SIC 284 path, and in some cases moved further a field into branded, packaged foods in addition to household products and nonhealth goods.

By the mid-1960s these new markets had grown crowded. Revenues and profit margins fell off. The competitors on the research-intensive paths returned to their core prescription drugs. By 1969 the goal of the leaders on the low-tech path was full-scale entry into the prescription drug business.

New Learning Transforms the Industry

The 1970s saw two fresh waves of drug innovation that created new opportunities calling for the restructuring of existing learning bases and the building of new ones. The sources of new learning for the first wave rested on scientific breakthroughs in biochemistry and in the new disciplines of microbiology and enzymology. The sources of the second issued from a relatively rare historical event: the coming of a radically new science—molecular biology—that emerged with the discovery of recombinant DNA (rDNA) and the techniques of genetic engineering.

The new discovery rested on the disciplines of microbiology and enzymology, and on the new science of molecular engineering. In most instances, however, the new learning was applied learning the pharmaceutical companies developed as they created new drug technologies. In so doing, their challenges were to commercialize new drugs marrying the new disciplines with each other and with biochemistry. The commercializing of the revolutionary biotechnology based on molecular biology required a great deal more, particularly the creation of a new supporting nexus. As one 1993 report noted, "Whereas the synthetic chemist and pharmacologist once ranged supreme in the research laboratory, they share this role today with the range of those who would class themselves as primarily biologists— the molecular geneticists and molecular modifiers, the biochemists, the biophysicists, the microbiologists, and the enzymologists."[5]

The applied learning in microbiology and enzymology was propelled by an innovation from the Information Revolution: "discovery by design." Previously, the discovery of new drugs had depended on a hit-or-miss, trial-and-error technique of screening chemical entities to find the molecules active against disease entities. In the mid-1970s researchers introduced their new knowledge "to conceptualize the structure of an 'ideal' molecule that is expected to restore the altered [pathological] equilibrium. The ideal molecule is then given to the laboratory chemists, who search for substances whose molecular structures match as closely as possible the theoretical model."[6] This approach involved for the first time an understanding of disease at the molecular level and focused attention on the enzymes that control vital biochemical sequences in all life forms. The new pattern of drug discovery was reinforced by two new spectroscopic techniques—x-ray crystallography and nuclear magnetic resonance—and by powerful advances in mathematical computation and computer analysis.

The new approach expanded, rather than displaced, existing functional and technical capabilities. Screening—sometimes random, sometimes targeted—continued to be used and in many cases was less costly than discovery by design. In the continuing research for new antibiotics, screening remained the most effective approach to discovery, though both approaches were often employed.

The products of the second wave, based on the new discipline of molecular biology, were the result of applied learning by leading long-established pharmaceutical companies. This new discipline evolved during the 1960s and 1970s following the discovery of the double helix structure of DNA by James Watson and Francis Crick in 1953. The first course in molecular biology was taught at Harvard in 1965, and the first department was created there two years later with Watson as chair. During the 1970s came the training of scientists and specialists in genetic engineering, necessary to a specialized supporting staff, as well as innovative approaches to drug discovery. Most important was the building of a supporting nexus to provide the necessary ingredients and services. This basic learning was concentrated largely in Massachusetts and California—at Harvard and MIT, and at the University of California campuses in San Francisco and Los Angeles.[7]

What might be termed the birthplace of the commercial application of the new learning in molecular biology and genetic engineering was the department at the University of California, San Francisco, headed by William Rutter. In the late 1970s conferences between Merck's staff and Rutter's department resulted in the development of the protein essential to commercialize the first genetically engineered vaccine for humans that was approved by the Food and Drug Administration (FDA) in 1986. During the same years Eli Lilly's researchers had joined with Herbert Boyer, a member of Rutter's department, to commercialize human insulin, which received FDA approval in 1982. Both Rutter and Boyer had set up their own companies—Boyer's Genentech operations in 1978, and soon after Rutter established Chiron in nearby Emeryville, California. Several years earlier, in 1975, a third old-line pharmaceutical company, Abbott, entered the new industry, developing a monoclonal antibody that was a critical ingredient in the commercialization of genetic engineering.

In this and the following chapters, I describe the entries of established enterprises into commercializing the revolutionary new molecular biology. In this chapter, I review the entry of Merck, Eli Lilly, and Abbott, that of Schering-Plough in Chapter 8, and that of Ciba-Geigy and F. Hoffmann–La Roche and Johnson & Johnson in Chapter 9. Chapter 10 focuses on the successes and failures of the startups in creating the integrated learning bases essential to competing with the long-established national and international pharmaceutical companies.

In this chapter each of the following histories of individual companies begins by referring to the product lines they had developed before 1940. This is done as a way of indicating the technical, product development, production, and marketing capabilities they had acquired by then. These paths evolved from three different starting groups. Before the war, two competitive firms, Merck and Pfizer, operated in the supporting nexus, producing fine chemicals for pharmaceutical companies. Five others, Eli Lilly, Abbott, Upjohn, SmithKline, and Squibb, were by then "old-line" producers of research-based prescription drugs. Together they are the subject of this chapter.

Merck and Pfizer: Emerging from the Industry's Nexus

Before World War II, Merck and Pfizer ranked as America's leading producers of fine chemicals in the nexus that supported the pharmaceutical industry. The extraordinary historical coincidence of the discoveries of penicillin and new antibiotics between 1940 and 1945 and the huge wartime demand for these products enabled the two companies to become immediate first movers in commercializing the new technology—Pfizer in penicillin and Merck in antibiotics. Both grew rapidly but, at war's end, came to face the challenge of creating marketing organizations almost from scratch.

From that point on their strategies and paths diverged. Merck acquired a long-established pharmaceutical house. Pfizer built its own marketing organization. Both continued to discover and commercialize new prescription drugs. Then, as the development of new products leveled off, Pfizer turned to growth through acquisition and diversified more enthusiastically than Merck. Merck concentrated far more on internally developing its research, marketing, and production capabilities. By 1993 Merck was the second-largest pharmaceutical company in terms of revenues (with $10.4 billion, behind the recently merged Bristol-Myers Squibb at $11.1 billion) but the leader in profitability, averaging 23 percent of sales. Meanwhile, Pfizer's revenues reached $7.4 billion and its net income averaged only 11 percent of sales. Merck's strategy had paid off.[8]

Merck: Creating an Integrated Learning Base

Merck had its beginnings in the United States in 1887 as the American marketing branch of one of the leading German producers of fine chemicals.[9] In 1903 this subsidiary introduced the production in Rahway, New Jersey of narcotics, bismuth salts, iodine, and other fine chemicals for the American pharmaceutical industry. During World War I the company turned to the production of coal-tar-based synthetic intermediates, which it had previously received from Germany. After the United States entered the war, the U.S. government's "alien property custodian" sequestered 80 percent of the subsidiary's common stock, which was held by George Merck, president of the subsidiary and grandson of the modern German company's founder. Its rapid growth in output and income generated the funds necessary for George Merck to purchase back in 1919 the 80 percent share held by the alien property custodian and to register Merck as an American enterprise.

After the war Merck and his company maintained close personal and technical ties with its former parent company as it began to enhance its own technical and functional capabilities. Following the construction of an extensive laboratory of its own in 1933, Merck started to commercialize vitamins—B-1, at first, then B-2, followed by B-6, C, K, and culminating in 1944 with vitamin B-12, a treatment for pernicious anemia. By the end of World War II, Merck had become the largest producer of vitamins in the United States and second only to the Swiss leader, F. Hoffmann–La Roche, worldwide.

During World War II, Merck functioned as a major producer of penicillin and sulfa-based drugs used to prevent infections. After the war it cut back its penicillin output (having only 2 percent of the market by 1947) but continued to produce sulfa-based drugs until the new antibiotics replaced them. Merck joined the antibiotic revolution through its support of the research at Rutgers University being done by Dr. Selman Waksman, who would discover streptomycin. Merck agreed to manufacture and distribute the new drug, with the patents assigned to the Rutgers Research Foundation. The company also developed and commercialized cortisone, the synthetic steroid treatment for rheumatoid arthritis. Merck, however, still had no salesforce to market these products; instead, it sold them to drug companies, which marketed them under their own trade names.[10]

The pressing need for a sales organization, plus the consideration that several of the pharmaceutical industry's leaders were integrating backward to produce some of their own fine chemicals, prompted Merck to search for the best way to go about creating an integrated learning base. During the years 1947–1953, it studied the alternatives of building or buying before finally deciding to merge with Sharp & Dohme, a smaller enterprise with an excellent reputation and an experienced salesforce. A long-established producer of alkaloids and other drugs, Sharp & Dohme had acquired H. K. Mulford in 1929, thereby developing into a leader in serum antitoxins and vaccines.[11]

In the late 1950s and early 1960s Merck maintained its strength in bulk fine chemicals and expanded and enlarged its line of vitamins, vaccines, and antibiotics. Its research program produced Diuril (chlorothiazide), an important diuretic for treating high blood pressure, and later Hydrodiuril. In 1959 antibiotics accounted for 39 percent of sales, but this figure declined as the company commercialized a nonsteroid drug (Indocin) for the treatment of arthritis, two antidepressants, and another new treatment (Aldomet) for high blood pressure, as well as new drugs to prevent parasitic infections in cattle and poultry. And the 1960s saw a major move into preventive medicine, as Merck began to produce in volume effective vaccines against measles, German measles, and mumps.[12]

DEFINING THE STRATEGIC BOUNDARIES   In the 1950s Merck made substantial investments in creating subsidiaries in Latin America and Europe. Later, when the threat of price controls loomed, the company began to diversify into related products. The overseas activities proved more successful than diversification. By 1955 sales outside of the United States represented 23 percent of Merck's revenues; by 1975 the figure had almost doubled to 45 percent.

Merck's first venture into market-related new products appeared in the 1950s with the attempt to use its R&D capabilities to produce silicon for semiconductors. The lesson learned from this initial move was quick and sharp. As recalled by Henry W. Gadsen, the company's CEO at the time, "Our silicon did not sell. It was a disaster, but we learned from it." Merck closed down the operation in 1963. In the next year, it cautiously effected a more closely related entrance into over-the-counter markets with the production of Sucrets, a throat lozenge that had been developed in its laboratories.[13]

In 1968, after a careful investigation of several markets, Merck's management made the first considered move outside SIC 283 with the purchase of Calgon, the country's second-largest water treatment enterprise. The rationale, in Gadsen's words, "was that water purification is concerned with killing organisms, bacteria, and fungi, with chemicals. At Merck we have programs of long standing aimed at the same ends, seeking to produce germicidal agents."[14] Calgon had also developed some consumer products of its own, including Cling-Free, a static-free cloth softener for use in clothes dryers. These and the Sucrets business were combined into a single consumer-product division. Then, in 1972, to ensure the needed supplementary assets for Calgon's large-scale production, Merck acquired Baltimore Air Coil, a pumping company, and two additional companies, one in the United States and one in Europe, to produce chemicals from seaweed.

These latest moves represented the extent of Merck's product diversification. It pulled back slowly, evaluating the continuing returns and potential of its businesses. In 1978 it sold off its consumer-products division to Beecham, the British drug producer, for $77 million. Not until 1985, however, did Merck become more focused, divesting Baltimore Air Coil and reinforcing Calgon's business by purchasing the water treatment division of the chemical company Hercules. By 1986 Merck's specialty chemicals had dropped from 15 percent to 9 percent of its business. By 1991, specialty chemicals accounted for only 3 percent. Finally, in 1993, the last of its related water treatment line was sold to the U.K.'s English China Clays for $307.5 million.[15]

COMMERCIALIZING PRODUCTS FROM THE NEW TECHNOLOGIES
In the mid-1970s, as Merck was considering pulling back from its closely related investments in chemicals, its managers began concentrating on commercializing the new learning in microbial biochemistry and enzymology, developing new approaches to research, particularly "discovery by design." By the end of the decade Merck had created the U.S. industry's largest research establishment—4,500 persons, with expenditures of $600 million—and the industry's largest salesforce of 6,300 people. In the 1980s these new routines and substantial investments paid off. Merck produced more of the fifty best-selling drugs than any other pharmaceutical company and did so primarily through discovery-by-design techniques. It possessed the industry's most balanced medical drug line, including Vasotec for high blood pressure and Mevacor, followed by Zocor, for treating high cholesterol, Pepcid for ulcers, and Timoptic for glaucoma. In 1991 Merck was the only producer with two of the top ten pharmaceutical products worldwide, Vasotec at number two (sales of $1,745 million) and Mevacor at number eight (sales of $1,090 million).[16]

Merck not only led the way in exploiting the new learning in biochemistry and enzymology but also was among the first of the core companies to build a learning base in the fast-developing path defined by molecular biology and rDNA engineering. Its entry in the late 1970s came from its sustained search for a vaccine for deadly hepatitis B. Roy Vagelos, the head of Merck's research laboratory, sent its hepatitis team to the University of California at San Francisco, a fountainhead of the new technology, to work with

William Rutter, the head of its Department of Biochemistry and Biophysics. As a result of their cooperative efforts and those of Benjamin Hall of the University of Washington, they were able to produce the necessary protein antigen.

Consequently, Rutter licensed the basic process and then, on the basis of the contract with Merck, in 1981 formed Chiron, which quickly turned into a leading biotechnology research company (see Chapter 8). But as Louis Galambos and Jane Eliot Sewell point out in *Networks of Innovation,* the Merck team was not only involved in the discovery itself but also then conducted the research essential to develop a practical vaccine, organized the clinical trials, and designed and scaled-up the manufacturing processes. In 1986 the FDA and the West German government approved Recombivax HB, the first genetically engineered vaccine for humans, to protect against the hepatitis B virus.[17]

In this way, Merck, under the skillful guidance of Roy Vagelos from 1985 to 1994, began to acquire technical capabilities in the new molecular biology. To expand its product development as well as technical capabilities, it immediately embarked on a series of contractual agreements with new startups, including among others Biogen, Genzyme, and Repligen in 1987 and Uncogen Sciences in 1990. The scope of these agreements varied. Some were for licensing, others for clinical testing, but most were for cooperative development of new drugs that would be marketed by Merck.

As the 1980s ended, Merck was also arranging joint agreements with Du Pont and Johnson & Johnson, both of which had growing interests in pharmaceuticals. Signed in 1989, the deal with Du Pont reflected the strength of Merck's existing functional capabilities. As reviewed in Chapter 2, Du Pont had failed to create the necessary complementary capabilities in production and marketing for the drugs it had successfully developed through research. The joint marketing and research agreement called for Merck to employ its development, clinical, regulatory, and marketing skills to commercialize the fruits of Du Pont's research and development on high blood pressure and heart disease. Merck also agreed to assist Du Pont in training its recently recruited pharmaceutical salesforce through the marketing of Merck's highly successful Vasotec and its drug for Parkinson's disease. This arrangement led in 1991 to the formation of the 50–50 joint enterprise to which Du Pont consigned nearly all of its pharmaceutical business.

Merck's 50–50 joint venture with Johnson & Johnson enabled the company to reenter the OTC drug business in a grand manner. Merck provided the R&D and manufacturing capabilities, while its partner contributed the necessary capabilities in mass marketing, advertising, and distribution.[18]

In 1992 Merck acquired Medco Containment Services, the largest pharmacy benefits management company in the United States, which processed and shipped prescription drugs to 40 million Americans. Although Medco handled only 10 percent of Merck's drugs, the acquisition represented an effort to learn more about the service side of the industry—just as the Johnson & Johnson deal helped Merck to learn about the OTC business.[19]

From 1982 through 1992, Merck's return on sales steadily rose from 13.6 percent to 25.3 percent, and its earnings per share from $0.94 to $2.11. This superior financial performance, which stemmed from the years following World War II, reflects Merck's virtuous strategy of focusing on the commercialization of the products of major new technologies, while using the learning and cash generated by its earlier drugs.

Merck emerged after World War II as a leader in the prescription path by employing its base of learning opportunistically in specialty chemicals to join the therapeutic revolution. When that path leveled off, it began to redefine its boundaries by diversifying into closely related chemical products. But its primary emphasis remained on the successful commercializing of products based on the new drug technologies. Merck sustained its role as a world leader by building on the learning from past successes and reinvesting the income that resulted. Pfizer, its close rival, had embarked on the prescription path at the same time and in much the same way, but it would respond to the industry's underlying challenges in a very different manner.

Pfizer: Creating and Recreating the Strategic Boundaries

Pfizer emerged from the supporting nexus at the same time as Merck during World War II and became a first mover in the new antibiotics. Whereas Merck had remained focused, adhering to the virtuous strategy of commercializing new products based on new technologies, Pfizer caught the mood of the times and diversified widely and rapidly. It then gradually returned to its core pharmaceutical operations, while maintaining related healthcare lines. Before the early 1990s most of its new pharmaceutical products were licensed rather than commercialized internally. Thereafter, Pfizer returned to a virtuous strategy to become one of Merck's strongest competitors.

The organizational capabilities developed at Pfizer before World War II placed that company in an even better position than Merck to exploit the opportunities of the therapeutic revolution.[20] Established in 1849 in Brooklyn by Charles Pfizer and a partner, the company produced iodine preparations and boric tartaric and citric acids for pharmacists and drug companies. During the 1920s Pfizer chemists developed a new process of fermentation based on black-bread mold that enabled the company to evolve into the nation's largest producer of citric acid. With the culturing of penicillin mold involving much the same processes, the company quickly assumed the role of appointed leader in the U.S. government's World War II penicillin program. By 1945 Pfizer was producing half the world's output of penicillin.

After the war, as competitors expanded their production of penicillin, Pfizer's share dropped quickly to 23 percent by 1947. In response, the company, which had outstanding capabilities in fermentation chemistry, introduced a new "broad-spectrum antibiotic," Teramycin. Superior to penicillin, it was developed in 1950 nearly simultaneously with two other almost identical drugs, Aureomycin, commercialized by American Cyanamid's Lederle Laboratories in 1948, and Parke Davis's Chloromycetin in 1949. To market the new Pfizer drug, John McKeen, an energetic entrepreneur who had become president in 1949, started selling aggressively to doctors and hospitals. Whereas Merck waited until 1953 to acquire a marketing organization, McKeen built Pfizer's from ten detail men in 1950 to one hundred a year later. He advertised Teramycin and other drugs extensively in medical journals, a form of marketing rarely used in the industry. After its first year on the market, Teramycin accounted for one-fourth of all Pfizer's sales.[21]

During the 1950s McKeen continued to shape the company's destiny, first by adding new antibiotic drugs to its line. Pfizer's major new antibiotic, Vibramycin, turned out to be its most profitable drug. The company also used a form of Teramycin with other drugs to treat diseases in cattle, swine, and other animals. Both by acquisition and internal growth, Pfizer soon moved into the production of Salk and Sabin vaccines for polio, as well as drugs for diabetes, mental health, and other uses. At the same time it maintained its production of bulk chemicals. In the 1950s and early 1960s Pfizer also expanded abroad far more energetically than Merck by acquiring branches in Canada, Mexico, Cuba, Britain, and Belgium, and by building plants in the Britain, France, and Japan.[22]

When the output of new products declined in the early 1960s and price controls loomed over the industry, McKeen pursued a strategy of unrelated diversification with characteristic enthusiasm. Between 1961 and 1964, Pfizer acquired fourteen companies producing OTC consumer remedies, such as Ben-Gay liniment and Visine eye drops, as well as soap and toiletries. The acquisitions included Barbasol shaving soap in 1962 and Coty's full line of cosmetics and fragrances in 1963. Then, in 1968, top management strayed even beyond the boundaries of the chemical industry (SIC 28). It became a conglomerate by acquiring companies that made specialty metals and materials, including high-temperature cement and linings for steel-producing furnaces.

REDEFINING STRATEGIC BOUNDARIES   After McKeen retired in 1965, his successor focused on rationalizing the properties Pfizer had collected, selling off most of the unrelated product lines. In the early 1970s, after the next change in command, the new CEO and new president redirected their focus to healthcare. Through acquisitions they moved into the fields of medical devices and hospital-care products. The largest of these purchases were Howmedica (1972), producers of hip and knee implants, and Shirley (1979), makers of heart and lung pumps, valves, blood originators, and other high-tech devices. At the same time, Pfizer enhanced its pharmaceutical lines (including those for animal health) by spending $750 million on R&D facilities and almost $1 billion on production and marketing facilities. The company increased its relatively small research budget, concentrating research activities in a single center at Groton, Connecticut.

Nevertheless, Pfizer relied more on a comprehensive licensing program than on adding to its own technical capabilities. During the 1970s, when Merck and other competitors were beginning to exploit new learning in biochemistry and enzymology, Pfizer was still licensing, obtaining one of its most profitable products, Cefoid, an anti-infective drug, from Bayer. It also licensed another antibiotic, this time from a Japanese company. A third new drug, Procardia, a medicine for angina and hypertension, was also licensed from Bayer and succeeded in becoming a major revenue producer. Pfizer's own research capabilities, however, remained limited. Only two new drugs, Minipress, an antihypertensive, and Feldene, an anti-inflammatory, were developed internally, and Feldene did not enter the market until 1982.

During the 1980s Pfizer increasingly concentrated on enhancing its prescription drug capabilities. The ratio of R&D expenditures to sales surged from 5 percent in 1980 to 9 percent in 1988. Its number of lines broadened. Antibiotics, which had accounted for 37 percent of sales in 1980, dropped to

23 percent in 1989, while those in cardiovascular and anti-inflammatory drugs increased three and four times, respectively, during those years.[23] Nevertheless, the company continued to retain several of its older product lines.

Because Pfizer was slow in refocusing on its core capabilities and because it persisted in devoting both financial and managerial resources to broaden other product lines, it initially failed to build the necessary technical and functional capabilities based on the new learning in biochemistry and enzymology. Pfizer also failed to establish a broader network of agreements and relationships with universities and research institutions. It possessed very little in-house capability to commercialize the new molecular biology when it began in 1987 to make licensing and other arrangements with such startups as Genzyme, Moleculom, Neurogen, and Cell Tech. Consequently, it was unable to exploit rDNA opportunities in the manner of Merck and Eli Lilly.[24]

Instead, Pfizer continued to expand its hospital-product activities. It spent $115 million to acquire American Medical Systems, which eventually accounted for about a quarter of Pfizer's total healthcare sales. At the same time, Pfizer moved to prune its nonprescription healthcare lines by divesting its clinical laboratories and its diagnostic imaging and dental equipment businesses. By 1989 the company's human healthcare sales had risen from 54 percent to 64 percent of total sales. (Of these 64 percent, 26 percent was from hospital supplies.) Of the remaining 46 percent of sales, 11 percent derived from consumer products and the rest were about equally divided among animal health and specialty chemicals.[25]

Finally, in the 1990s, Pfizer under a new CEO initiated major divestitures. In 1990, it sold off its citric acid business to Archer-Daniels-Midland. Then, in 1992, there followed the spinning off of its other specialty chemicals and refractory products, followed quickly by the sale of the Coty cosmetic and fragrance divisions for $440 million and the overseas portion of its Plax mouthwash business (purchased in 1988) to Colgate-Palmolive for $105 million, and its Shirley heart-valve unit to a subsidiary of Italy's Fiat.[26]

At the same time, Pfizer's managers concentrated on enhancing the core business, primarily prescription drugs and a small hospital-products group. They had begun investing more heavily in basic research in the 1980s, generating important new drugs such as Zoloft and Norvasc that were ready for the market by the mid-1990s. In 1995 they raised the annual research budget again by 20 percent, to $1.2 billion. The most publicized of the new drugs, Viagra, indicates the proficiency of Pfizer's technical capabilities, while the fact that its Procardia XL remained a leading U.S. heart drug with sales of $1.2 billion underlines the strengthening of its functional capabilities. By 1994, 84 percent of Pfizer's sales and 95 percent of its operating income came from its healthcare products, the large majority of which were prescription drugs. Its net income rose from $722 million in 1990 to $1.3 billion four years later. Pfizer was successfully focusing on enhancing its capabilities in its long-established lines, including anti-infective and anti-inflammatory and cardiovascular products, and was beginning to develop comparable capabilities in the newer technologies.[27]

The differences in the paths followed by Pfizer and Merck after they evolved from suppliers to become core companies in the prescription drug industry suggest much about the interconnections of the strategies of growth, strategic boundaries, and the sustaining vitality of their evolving learning bases. When price regulation loomed and the wave of innovation created by the new antibiotics and closely related technologies began to level off in the early 1960s, the resulting diversifications into nonpharmaceutical products, largely through acquisition, called for the application of different production, marketing, and research capabilities. The diversion of managerial attention and of personnel and financial resources, particularly to medical instruments and devices, led to Pfizer's failure to create the technical and functional capabilities required to exploit the new developments of the industry's prescription drug base. As a result, Merck became the industry's leader and Pfizer, as a "second-level" company, had to concentrate on developing the essential know-how in the new technologies. But once Pfizer rid itself of its diversified products and concentrated on reviving its core technical and functional capabilities in prescription drugs, the company made a remarkable recovery. By the mid-1990s, it was again one of the industry's most successful competitors.

The Old-Line Pharmaceutical Companies: Eli Lilly, Abbott, SmithKline, Squibb, and Upjohn

By the middle of the twentieth century, "the old-line pharmaceutical companies," as they were termed, occupied the center of the American medical drug industry. These firms—Eli Lilly, Abbott, SmithKline French, Squibb, and Upjohn, all descended from the integrated wholesaler/manufacturers of the late-nineteenth century—increasingly producing drugs for doctors and hospitals and, in much larger quantities, for pharmacists filling doctors' pre-scriptions. They employed small staffs of detail men to handle the doctors and hospitals, and relied on large salesforces to reach the pharmacists. Some continued to manufacture and sell OTC products.

In the 1950s they greatly expanded their R&D activities, recruiting trained biologists and biochemists and strengthening their ties with university scientists. They enlarged their salesforces of detail men, usually by recruiting pharmacists. As the postwar new-product output leveled off, they evolved in somewhat the same manner. Their long-established marketing organizations facilitated their diversifying into more branded, packaged, OTC drugs than was the case for Merck, but less than for Pfizer. Nearly all of these companies diversified beyond such proprietary drugs into low-tech toiletries and cosmetics (SIC 284). More challenging were their forays into another complex high-technology industry, that of medical equipment. In the 1960s and early 1970s the firms also expanded abroad, some more energetically than others.

When new product development once again leveled off, three companies—Eli Lilly, Abbott, and Squibb—moved quickly to exploit the opportunities of the new biochemistry and enzymology, each in a distinctive way. The other two, Upjohn and SmithKline, provide, again in different ways, examples of the costs of departing from or failing to maintain the technical and functional capabilities developed in their initial integrated learning bases. At the same time, depending on the extent and nature of their initial diversification strategy, they too divested themselves of their non-healthcare products.

Eli Lilly and Company: Defining Strategic Boundaries with Care and Caution

Eli Lilly represents the most successful American producer in expanding its capabilities as new technologies enlarged existing paths of learning and created new ones.[28] The company's roots trace to 1876, when Colonel Eli Lilly, a Civil War veteran, started a manufacturing and marketing enterprise in Indianapolis, Indiana. His initial success resulted from an innovative form of gelatin capsules, which the firm still sells today. It was soon commercializing drugs based on natural and then synthetic organic sources, including analgesics and barbiturates, as well as cough drops and other OTC drugs. Its growth in the interwar years depended in large part on its successful commercialization in 1923 of insulin as a treatment for diabetes, a major medical discovery. In 1975 it still held 75 percent of that market. The company's achievement in insulin opened the way for the expansion of its research capabilities, culminating with the opening of an impressive new research complex in 1934. By the end of the 1930s Lilly's prescription drugs included liver extract for pernicious anemia, sedatives (Seconal), and drugs for heart disease.[29]

Although Lilly played only a small role in the wartime penicillin and sulfa programs, its strong technical and functional (particularly marketing) capabilities enabled it in 1952 to enter quickly into the new antibiotic markets through its commercializing of erythromycin. Fortunately for Lilly, at that moment Pfizer was just beginning to build and Merck had not yet acquired marketing capabilities. During the 1950s Lilly commercialized streptomycin and then brought out other antibiotics. It expanded its line of analgesics (morphine-related pain killers; Darvon was its major new product). By 1955 it was the major producer of the Salk vaccine for polio with a 60 percent market share. By that time, its marketing organization had become the industry's largest and acquired the reputation for being the most effective. Lilly also developed in the 1950s a line of veterinarian products and then added agricultural chemicals for much the same customers. In 1960 the two lines were consolidated into a subsidiary, Elanco.[30]

As it built along its prewar lines during the 1960s, Eli Lilly intensified its R&D efforts, increasing its production of antibiotics and becoming the dominant producer in the United States. In 1970 antibiotics accounted for over a quarter of its sales. Although the company completed an occasional acquisition, its growth at home as well as abroad was executed primarily by direct investment. By the late 1960s it had plants in Europe, Latin America, South Africa, Australia, and East Asia. Such expansion continued so that foreign sales, which had been 26 percent of total sales in 1960, represented nearly 40 percent in 1970. In the 1960s, too, it broke into the closely related fields of animal health and then into weed-killers and chemicals for agricultural markets—again, largely by direct investment.[31]

Only in the 1970s did Eli Lilly begin to follow the fashion of diversifying through acquisition, but in a different manner from that of Pfizer and closer to that of Merck. In 1971 it purchased Elizabeth Arden Cosmetics, a leader in its field, but did not make any further move into the SIC 284 path. And it entered the high-tech medical equipment field beginning in 1977 with the purchase of IVAC, a maker of thermometers and measuring equipment and IV-infusion systems. By 1989 these products accounted for 17 percent of sales.

PIONEERING IN THE NEW TECHNOLOGIES   Such carefully focused diversification did not deflect Eli Lilly from enhancing its capabilities in prescription drugs. During the late 1970s it increased its R&D expenditures (which had already reached $235 million for the year 1973) and became a leader in shaping the new-product development routines, including the use of structure-based molecular design and novel project management techniques. These efforts paid off with an increased flow of new products. The company maintained its strength in antibiotics, which still accounted for almost half of its prescription drug sales in 1979. Of these, Celcor (listed as tenth among the top ten prescription drugs in 1991), followed by Vancocin, and Mandol, followed by Moxan, were the most profitable. In the 1980s the company pioneered in the development of a new kind of drug, serotonin (a chemical secreted by the brain), developed through discovery by design. Its first new drug, Prozac, an antidepressant approved in 1987, would turn out to be Lilly's first billion-dollar product. Other new products included Dobutrex for heart failure; Nalfon, an anti-inflammatory drug; Cinobac, an antibacterial agent; and Eldstine for childhood leukemia. By 1989, eleven of its drugs enjoyed sales of over $100 million apiece.

At the same time, Eli Lilly was pioneering in the new technology. Since the insulin shortage of World War II, one of the primary goals of its research scientists had been to discover an alternative to insulin extracted from pigs and cows. So, rather like scientists at Merck who had been searching for a vaccine to cure hepatitis B, Lilly researchers went to Rutter's department at the University of California at San Francisco, arriving well before Merck's group. In 1977, Eli Lilly signed contracts with the university to fund a team to develop a new means of producing human insulin and a human growth hormone. In September 1978, the company arranged another contract with Rutter's colleague, Herbert Boyer, one of the pioneers of the molecular techniques. In anticipation of his new contract, Boyer had just recruited his first staff of five, rented his first building to develop human insulin, and then formed a new enterprise, Genentech. For the human growth hormone, the Lilly researchers had already contracted in 1977 with another team of scientists in Rutter's department. At the same time, they approached Harvard's Walter Gilbert, who then decided to commission the company he had just organized, Biogen, to develop human insulin.[32]

As was the case with Merck and Rutter's Chiron, Genentech succeeded in the discovery, but as Maureen McKelvey notes: "Lilly received [from Chiron] the initial and then upgraded the bacteria expression systems. They also developed their own competencies to grow the bacteria, purify it, modify genetic engineering techniques and biological materials, and so forth in their in-house labs. Lilly had the money to expand in-house labs quickly in relevant scientific fields."[33] Then, Lilly, as would Merck, handled the rest of the several steps involved in the development and commercializing of the drug. Lilly's human insulin was approved by the FDA in 1982, the first genetically engineered drug to be marketed worldwide. Like Merck, Eli Lilly was in place at the very beginning of a new technology that would prove equally as transformative as the Second Industrial and the Information Revolutions. With its new technical learning and its functional capabilities in place, Lilly employed its new integrated learning base to commercialize the human hormone drug for which its researchers initially contracted with the University of San Francisco. In 1987, the FDA approved that product, which was superior to Genentech's initial growth hormone.

While it was establishing its molecular biology learning base, Eli Lilly also enlarged its medical-devices business in 1984 by acquiring Advanced Cardiovascular Systems through a stock swap, and then in 1985 by purchasing Hybritech, a leading startup that produced testing and diagnostic devices based on monoclonal antibodies. By the mid-1980s, Eli Lilly's pharmaceutical business (almost entirely prescription drugs) accounted for 65 percent of its total sales, of which animal health was 10 percent. Of the company's nonpharmaceutical business (35 percent of the total), 15 percent derived from medical devices and the remaining 20 percent was divided between agricultural chemicals and cosmetics. In the 1980s, Eli Lilly had fallen behind its competitors in taking advantage of world markets. In 1991, 37 percent of its sales came from abroad, but these represented only 25 percent of income.[34]

As the new product lines came on-stream, Lilly's top management decided to sell off its non-healthcare business. Not only were the profit margins lower, but, as one senior executive stressed, they demanded a disproportionate amount of management time. In 1988 Lilly sold its Elizabeth Arden Cosmetics to Fabergé for $700 million. The following year its agricultural chemical business was turned over to a joint venture, DowElcano, in which Lilly held 40 percent of the equity and Dow Chemical the rest (see Chapter 3). By 1991 Eli Lilly had 78 percent of its sales in pharmaceuticals (9 percent of these in animal health) and 21 percent in medical devices.[35] This major diversification into a new high-technology industry almost brought Eli Lilly down, as in fact a comparable move had at SmithKline. These failures will be reviewed shortly.

Until 1991, Eli Lilly had sustained a strong financial performance for many decades. Its return on sales had fluctuated between 15.8 percent in 1935 and 23.0 percent in 1991. Over the same period, its earnings per share grew from $1.85 to $4.50. During 1992 and 1993, however, the return on sales dropped precipitously to 13.4 percent and 7.6 percent, and earnings per share to $2.81 and $1.67. In 1994, the company bounced back, reporting levels comparable to those in 1991. The troubles during 1992 and 1993 reflected the performance of the medical devices and diagnostics division.

That division had been created with the acquisition of two cardiovascular equipment companies in 1982 and 1984. Then, in 1985 and 1989, there ensued acquisitions of producers of cardiac defibrillators. At the same time, Eli Lilly purchased Hybritech, a recently established diagnostic unit, which proved unable to compete with Abbott. In the fall of 1992 Lilly recorded the first loss in its history.

The decline in income prompted the appointment in 1993 of a new CEO Randall Tobias—an outsider who had formerly been a senior executive at AT&T. Tobias quickly saw the problem and arranged to sell the medical devices and diagnostics division, which, according to one analyst, was suffering "intense competition from Abbott." The division reported sales of $1.2 billion, including Hybritech, which accounted for 18.7 percent of the division's total. Tobias accomplished the spin-off by forming a new company, Guidant Corporation, which consisted of five units in the division. Eli Lilly sold 20 percent of Guidant to the public in an initial price offering (IPO) and distributed the remaining 80 percent to its own shareholders on a tax-free basis. Tobias later sold off the remaining units in separate transactions. By 1995, as Tobias had projected, Eli Lilly was back focusing on its core pharmaceutical businesses, enhancing and expanding its learning base in prescription drugs. Like Pfizer, Eli Lilly had rediscovered the virtuous strategy.[36]

Abbott Laboratories: Redefining Strategic Boundaries in Response to Crisis

The history of Abbott's changing product lines provides an instructive variation on those of Eli Lilly in moving along new paths. Before the 1970s Abbott followed the same broad paths of learning as Eli Lilly. Serious problems, however, forced Abbott's management to concentrate on two businesses into which it had diversified. These two required different sets of technical and functional capabilities, and both sets were quite distinct from the ones developed in its prescription drug path. But Abbott's managers successfully met these challenges, and by 1990 the company had become the nation's largest producer of infant formula products and the second-largest manufacturer of hospital diagnostic and laboratory products. By 1992 it had driven Eli Lilly out of the diagnostic businesses (Johnson & Johnson was first and Baxter International the third). But Abbott paid a price; it was no longer a major developer of new prescription drugs.

Like Eli Lilly, Dr. Wallace C. Abbott began as a pill maker. In 1888 he established the Abbott Alkaloid Company in Chicago to employ a new technique for the preparation of drugs, which involved precipitating them into solid extracts and then selling them in granules. The new product gave his wholesaler/producing company a competitive edge. The cutting off of supplies of prescription drugs from Germany during World War I provided Abbott with the opportunity to become a full-scale producer of synthetic organic drugs based on coal-tar-based organic chemistry. Later, during the interwar years, Abbott's laboratories and production facilities in North Chicago produced a stream of sedatives, tranquilizers, and drugs to combat seizures, leprosy, and other diseases. During the 1930s it established branches abroad. It supplied penicillin during World War II and produced it in different forms following the war. But Abbott became a world-class producer of antibiotics only in 1952, when its researchers developed a form of erythromycin that competed with Lilly's product.[37]

In the 1950s Abbott expanded its antibiotics line and several of its prewar products, integrated backward into the manufacturing of bulk pharmaceuticals, and developed a cyclamate that turned out to be a popular sweetener. In the 1960s Abbott, like Pfizer, diversified largely through acquisition; but unlike Pfizer it took on closely related products only. In 1964 and 1966 it acquired producers of insecticides and other agricultural chemicals and manufacturers of products connected with animal health. The purchase in 1964 of the producer of Similac, a major infant foods product, strengthened its position in the nutritional field. At the end of the decade, it supplemented its earlier acquisitions in consumer products by buying makers of shampoos, condiments, and hemorrhoid medications. It also acquired Murine eyecare products. Of more significance, in 1968 it undertook a major transition into the rapidly growing field of medical and diagnostic devices and supplies.[38]

In the early 1970s, however, two diversification moves almost destroyed the company. In 1970 it had to write off its cyclamate sweetener business, which a year earlier was contributing $50 million in revenue, after the FDA banned its production as a possible cancer-causing agent. A year later Abbott was forced to recall $3.4 million worth of an improperly sealed IV solution that resulted in more than four hundred infections and forty-nine deaths.[39]

REDEFINING THE STRATEGIC BOUNDARIES   To revive the company's health, the board brought in a new management team that included Robert A. Schoellhorn, recruited from American Cyanamid's Lederle Laboratories, and two executives from Texas Instruments. Schoellhorn became CEO in 1975. This trio focused their efforts on improving the capabilities of the high-tech hospital diagnostic and service units, as well as those in the less technically complex nutritional products. At the same time, they sought to sustain Abbott's pharmaceutical capabilities. To meet these objectives, they categorized their operating divisions into two groups.

One group comprised the hospital, diagnostic, blood therapeutic, and medical electronic equipment businesses. In 1975 the company reported that this group "now accounts for 38 percent of average sales." The group's worldwide sales that year were $358 million, up 40 percent from 1974. By 1980 the group represented 52 percent of Abbott's sales, 34 percent of its profits, and 49 percent of its assets.[40]

The second group consisted mainly of pharmaceuticals and nutritional products. The nutritional line was growing faster than pharmaceuticals, and by 1980 44 percent of the group's profits derived from its nutritional division, 42 percent from pharmaceuticals, and 14 percent from agricultural, chemical, and OTC consumer products. By 1989 the nutritional percentage was up to 57 percent. Within the pharmaceutical line, antibiotics, largely erythromycin (improved in 1986), accounted for 45 percent of profits and tranquilizers for 20 percent, with cardiovascular medicines making up most of the rest. Even though the profits remained higher in pharmaceuticals, as did return on assets, Abbott's growth in its two major lines—hospital and medical equipment—was twice that of pharmaceuticals and nutritional products.[41]

A central engine to Abbott's growth was the diagnostic division within the hospital and medical equipment group headed by James Vincent, another Texas Instruments veteran, who took command of the division in 1974. The following year the division disclosed the Hybridoma technique to produce monoclonal antibodies essential to genetic engineering just as the new rDNA process was being commercialized. Vincent then recruited a team of seasoned managers from Texas Instruments, including George Rathmann, to head its R&D, and Jack Schuler for marketing.

The timing of the introduction of the product was an historical accident, as dramatic as that of the commercializing of the first antibiotics just as World War II erupted. For only two years later did Eli Lilly's team, working with Rutter's laboratory at San Francisco, take the first step to commercialize genetically engineered products. From the very start, therefore, Abbott had a leading position in this sector of the new biotechnology industry.

Next, in 1978, Vincent's division commenced work on an automatic analyzer, the Quantum, followed by the TDx analyzer for use by chemical as well as pharmaceutical companies, and then the "Vision" blood analyzer. Where Abbott led the way in the new molecular diagnostics, the major competitors in hospital and medical equipment—Johnson & Johnson and Baxter International—quickly followed. In addition to its pioneering success in new diagnostics, Vincent's unit developed the first diagnostic test for AIDS in 1985.[42]

Nevertheless, because it concentrated on building strong learning bases in its hospital and medical equipment and nutritional divisions, Abbott failed to exploit the opportunities emerging in pharmaceuticals—although it formed partnerships with universities and scientific research institutes and developed a "rennin inhibitor," which came to be a model in the use of computers in drug discovery.[43] By 1989 a *Business Week* report on Abbott listed diagnostics as accounting for profits of $330 million, hospital supplies another $200 million, nutrition $375 million, pharmaceuticals $270 million, and chemical and agricultural products only $25 million. In these lines, the company's continued growth came almost wholly from internal investment. The reshaping of the product mix might have retarded overseas growth, for foreign sales dropped from 38.2 percent of total sales in 1980 to 30.6 percent in 1989.[44]

Another reason for the falling off of foreign sales might have been Abbott's assumption of a reverse role in selling Japanese products in the United States and other markets. In 1977 Abbott formed a joint venture called TAP Pharmaceuticals with Japan's oldest and largest producer, Takeda Pharmaceutical, to commercialize and market drugs. The partners renewed their agreement in 1987, but in 1997 Takeda decided not to recommit. Instead it began to build its own sales and marketing organization in the United States, and then entered the European markets that its compatri-

Table 7.1   Financial performance of U.S. core pharmaceutical companies, 1985–1994

Company	Income as percentage of sales	Earnings per share
Merck	15%–25.9% (through 1992)	$0.42–$2.38
Eli Lilly	15.8%–22.5%	$1.85–$4.55
Schering-Plough	9.2%–19.8%	$0.80–$4.82
American Home Products	15.2%–17.0%	$2.54–$4.79
Pfizer	14.4%–15.7%	$1.72–$4.10
Abbott Laboratories	13.8%–16.6%	$0.49–$1.87
Bristol-Myers Squibb	12.0%–13.9% (premerger)	$1.93–$1.43
	17.0%–17.2% (postmerger)	$3.33–$3.62
Warner-Lambert	7.4%–10.8%	$1.53–$3.61 (1990) to $5.20 (1994)
Upjohn	6.9%–15.7%	$0.70–$2.87 (through 1991)

Source: Hoover's Handbook of American Companies, 1996 (Austin, TX: Hoover's Business Press, 1997). Data on SmithKline Beecham not available in this source.

ots in consumer electronics had completely conquered more than a decade earlier.

During the early 1990s Abbott continued to move along its existing paths. By 1994 the hospital and laboratory products still accounted for 46 percent of sales but only 37 percent of operating income. In nutrition, the performance continued to be about the same. In pharmaceuticals, however, Abbott increased its strength in terms of the number of products brought to market and the income revenue they generated. Together, they provided the other 54 percent of sales and 53 percent of income. Nevertheless, by dropping behind in pharmaceuticals, Abbott fell below Merck, Eli Lilly, and Pfizer in return on sales and earnings per share for the decade between 1985 and 1994 (see Table 7.1).[45]

From Internal Growth to Growth via Merger and Acquisition

The success of the four pharmaceutical companies whose histories have just been described rested primarily on their ability to continue to follow the virtuous strategy of growth. These companies defined their boundaries by diversifying and by acquiring and then selling smaller businesses, but they rarely merged with or acquired large enterprises.

On the other hand, large-scale acquisition and mergers proved critical to the success and failure in financial performance of the remaining six American core companies listed in Table 1.2. Because of the significance of mergers and acquisitions in the evolution of mature industries, my focus in the following sketches is on the success and failure of mergers and acquisitions and their impact on defining the boundaries of their firms. The story of SmithKline Beecham traces its changing names, from SmithKline French, to SmithKline Beckman (a resounding failure), and then to SmithKline Beecham, the first international merger of leading core companies. Squibb, on the other hand, evolved into such a successful prescription drug enterprise that it was acquired by Bristol-Myers, the leading enterprise in the OTC path. Bristol-Myers Squibb became one of the industry's successful mergers. Its evolution offers a striking contrast to that of Upjohn, a family-managed enterprise for over a century, which provides an example of a "follower," in the terms of this study, whose only alternative in the 1990s turned out to be sale or merger. The remaining three companies among the top ten in Table 1.2—American Home Products, Warner-Lambert, and Schering-Plough—are discussed in Chapter 8, which deals with the competitors initially following the OTC path.

SmithKline Beecham: Learning Strategic Boundaries at a High Cost

The history of SmithKline Beecham PLC documents dramatically the costs of the failure to follow the virtuous strategy. In 1976 the predecessor firm, SmithKline French, commercialized the antacid drug Tagamet, one of the first and most profitable products of the new "discovery-by-design" technology. But rather than reinvest these profits in its own product development, SmithKline French acquired for $1 billion Beckman, a pioneering firm in medical instruments—a related industry, but one based on a very different technology. The earnings of the company, now called SmithKline Beckman, started to evaporate. SmithKline then sold off Beckman in 1989 and merged with Beecham PLC, the least innovative of Britain's three largest pharmaceutical companies. SmithKline Beecham was unable to embark once again on the virtuous strategy to growth.

This story begins in Philadelphia in 1835 with the formation of SmithKline, a manufacturing apothecary. After a merger in 1891, the firm became known as SmithKline & French. By the end of the century it was the largest pharmaceutical wholesaler/producer in Philadelphia, the national center for that business. The firm entered the synthetic coal-tar path in 1900, reduced its offerings from five thousand to two hundred (still largely in OTC drugs), and expanded its analytical laboratories in the 1930s. In 1932 it introduced the innovative Benzedrine inhaler. With its relatively limited research background, the company played only a minor role in the World War II antibiotic crash program.[46]

In the immediate postwar years, SmithKline & French's prescription drug business relied largely on psycho-active drugs, particularly those based on Dexedrine and Benzedrine. In 1954 it introduced its highly successful anti-histamine tranquilizer, Thorazine, licensed from Rhône-Poulenc. Its first postwar OTC drug, Contac, which it put on the market in 1960, soon became the world's leading remedy for common colds. That drug was followed by other successful OTC products, such as sinus remedies and coated aspirins. But the company failed during these years to market major new prescription drugs.[47]

From 1964 to 1970, SmithKline & French diversified in a fairly systematic manner, moving into both low-tech toiletries and high-tech medical equipment. It purchased companies producing medical devices, medical electronic equipment, and sutures, as well as others operating clinical laboratories. It acquired Love, a maker of cosmetics, and Sea & Ski, producers of suntan lotions. In addition, it purchased the major food company Avocet.[48]

In the 1970s, with a change in top management, SmithKline French (by this time it had dropped the "&") began to refocus on pharmaceuticals. Possibly because of its less solid learning base in prescription drugs, its research unit pioneered in the new discovery-by-design techniques. One of its scientists, Sir James Black, seeking an anti-ulcer drug, "conceptualized a compound that blocked the acid-secreting [ulcer-creating] cells by inhibiting action of the H2 histamine receptor." Even so, "he synthesized about 700 compounds before coming up with the final molecule." That drug, Tagamet, first marketed in 1976, was a huge success. Its sales rose from $280 million in that year to $440 million in 1979. By 1980 the sales of this one product equaled the total sales of the company five years earlier.[49]

THE STRATEGIC ERROR: ENTERING RELATED MARKETS WITH DIFFERENT TECHNOLOGIES   Flush with profits, the company's top management arrived at a major strategic decision. It would leave the low-tech path, selling its OTC product lines, and continue to develop its drug research techniques. It would maintain its ties to universities and research specialists and build a $20 million research center in biology. Most important of all, SmithKline French would reduce its burgeoning cash flow by becoming a powerhouse in the medical equipment business, which it had entered modestly in 1960.

It carried out this strategy through major acquisitions. In 1978 it sold off Avocet and, in 1980, its Love Cosmetics and Sea & Ski. It then acquired Allergan Pharmaceuticals for $259 million and Humphrey Instruments at a comparable price, both manufacturers of ophthalmic devices. The move into this market was succeeded in 1984 and 1988 by the acquisition of two major producers of contact lenses. The principal step, however, occurred in 1982, when SmithKline French acquired for $1.01 billion Beckman Instruments, an innovative firm that aided in revolutionizing laboratory work in biochemistry and microbiology and was already beginning to meet these same demands in the biotechnology field. To underscore the significance of this move, SmithKline French changed its name to SmithKline Beckman.[50]

The top managers at SmithKline possessed little understanding of the technological capabilities and needs of their acquisitions. Unlike the leaders at Abbott, they were not forced to learn by saving a business in crisis. In 1984 they sensibly sold off Beckman's industrial products for $165 million in cash to General Electric. But the output, quality, and profits from Beckman's instruments and the ophthalmic devices it had acquired continued to decline. By 1988 Arnold Beckman was publicly regretting the disintegration of his former company's capabilities.

These acquisitions, in turn, deprived SmithKline's pharmaceuticals of research funds and managerial attention. Soon its initial core learning base had begun to erode. James Black and other research leaders left and were not replaced. As Alfonso Gambardella notes in *Science and Innovation,* "It did not exploit past successes to build a solid in-house scientific base and thus undermined its capabilities for enjoying cumulative advantages." By 1990 Glaxo's Zantac was capturing Tagamet's market (see Chapter 9). During the 1980s SmithKline had failed to commercialize a single important new drug. One drug that it did introduce, Selacryn, had to be withdrawn from the market because of deadly side effects. Foreign sales failed to grow, remaining steady at 25 percent of total sales. By 1987, 57 percent of Smith-Kline's sales came from prescription drugs (7 percent of these prescription drugs derived from animal health products), only 14 percent from OTC drugs, 13 percent from eye and skin care, and 16 percent from Beckman's diagnostic and analytical instruments and systems.[51]

The company's balance sheet by 1988 reflected dramatic strategic failure. Its earnings had dropped suddenly and sharply to $229 million from $510 million in 1987. Management initiated a large-scale restructuring program. Besides selling off Beckman, they planned to rationalize their ophthalmic products and other nonprescription activities by consolidating facilities and personnel. The program involved a layoff of 1,600 workers and a write-down of $400 million.[52]

But before the reconstruction plan was implemented, SmithKline merged with a leading British firm, Beecham PLC. Beecham's history parallels those of the American companies whose genesis lay in the low-tech, branded, packaged, mass-marketing branch of the industry (see Chapter 9). Like comparable American producers, it was having difficulties developing science-based prescription drug capabilities. As one commentator noted, "The merger capped a series of misadventures. SmithKline and Beecham collapsed into one another's arms like two drunks trying to hold each other up."

The merger prompted an even more sweeping corporate reconstruction of the American company than the one it had planned. The sell-off included, besides Beckman Instruments, many OTC drug products and SmithKline's eyecare and skincare divisions. Even so, SmithKline Beecham (as it became in the merger) remained in the 1990s the world's third-largest OTC drug company.[53] The postmerger history is told briefly in Chapter 9.

SmithKline's failed transition into a second high-technology product line is an impressive example of barriers to entry. Senior managers with limited experience in the instrument and diagnostic business were unable to integrate or effectively coordinate and monitor the activities of their several acquisitions. With the shift into medical equipment, the existing knowledge base in the new biochemistry and molecular genetics eroded. Thus, the costly move into a new path led to the disintegration of the company's learning bases in both paths. For SmithKline's management, the answer was to expand its lines abroad and so to profit from economies of scale, while Beecham did the same in the United States.

Squibb Corporation: Successfully Redefining Strategic Boundaries

The evolution of Squibb's successful strategy is a telling contrast to that of SmithKline's. It also serves as a unique case study of successful path defining. Squibb, established in 1858, was acquired in 1953 by the conglomerate Olin Industries (see Chapter 5). When Olin spun the division off in 1968, its manager Richard Furland became the head of the independent Squibb

Corporation. Furland's initial move was to fashion a diversified portfolio in line with the then-accepted doctrine of growth through unrelated diversification, adding several non-healthcare lines to his pharmaceutical ones. Quickly realizing the inadequacy of such a strategy, Furland refocused the company's capabilities by exploiting the new learning in microbiology and enzymology. Like SmithKline, Squibb commercialized a blockbuster drug, Capoten, used to reduce blood pressure. Then, spinning off its non-pharmaceutical lines—in contrast to SmithKline—it built a modest learning base in medical devices. By 1987 Squibb was considered to be one of the most dynamic American pharmaceutical enterprises. As such, it became a target for acquisition by Bristol-Myers, the country's largest drug producer in the low-tech, OTC sector.

Squibb had a lineage somewhat different from those of the other old-line pharmaceutical companies described above. It was established in 1858 by Dr. Edward R. Squibb to commercialize recently discovered ether, chloroform, and other drugs used in surgical procedures, and it stood in a good position to take advantage of the medical advances of the late nineteenth century. In 1905 Theodore Weiker—a German chemist financed by his father-in-law, Lowell Palmer (a wealthy American industrialist)—acquired control of the company. Weiker's experience at E. Merck's U.S. branch and his connections in Germany granted Squibb an entry into commercializing organic drugs developed through organic chemistry. By the 1930s Squibb was a well-established pharmaceutical enterprise.[54]

During World War II Squibb produced large quantities of morphine and penicillin. Later, in the early 1950s, it expanded its antibiotic lines based on bulk tetracycline provided by Pfizer.[55] Just as Squibb was beginning to explore this line of development, it was acquired in 1952 by Mathieson Chemical, which a year later merged with Olin. As one of Olin Mathieson's several divisions, Squibb maintained the production of its prewar line of drugs and continued to commercialize antibiotics, but it did not substantially expand into other pharmaceutical lines. Nor, of course, did it get involved with the acquisition and management of nondrug lines.

In 1968, when Olin Mathieson spun off Squibb to its shareholders, Squibb CEO Richard Furland, who had been an Olin lawyer, immediately acquired another of Olin Mathieson's subsidiaries, Beechnut, makers of candy, chewing gum, and other products (which in turn had recently bought Dobbs House, a food service company). The next year Furland obtained the animal health business of the Swiss drug company Ciba. In 1970 he rounded out

Squibb's portfolio by purchasing Charles of the Ritz, makers of cosmetics and perfumes, from Lanvin.[56]

Then within less than a decade, Furland transformed Squibb and placed it solidly on the prescription drug path, not by acquisition but by reinforcing internally its technical and functional capabilities. The company maintained its existing competitive strengths in antibiotics, commercialized drugs in other therapeutic areas, and in turn divested its nondrug activities. In 1972 Furland sold Beechnut's food processing and tea and coffee businesses to two British firms, Cavenham and J. Lyons, and Beechnut's bulk food business to a third company. He retained Beechnut's chewing gum, candy, and pie goods.

In 1977 and 1978 Squibb made an investment of $300 million in R&D, particularly for developing the new molecular modeling search techniques and commercializing methods. The result was the introduction of Capoten, a highly successful heart drug. As a *Wall Street Journal* reporter wrote, "Squibb's scientists designed atom by atom a compound that inhibited overproduction of angiotensin II, thereby blocking the rise of blood pressure." Capoten, approved by the FDA after some delay in 1981, proved an even greater moneymaker than SmithKline's Tagamet. It soon became the third-largest revenue-producing drug in the United States, with sales of over $1.5 billion. Its development led Squibb to commercialize other drugs: Corgard for hypertension; AZI Astreonam, an antibiotic; and Pravochol, a cardiovascular drug.[57]

Meanwhile, in 1979 and 1980, Squibb began to enter, modestly but systematically, the medical instruments and devices path through the acquisition of four small companies that produced ostomy appliances, ophthalmic and surgical instruments, and wound dressings. These were financed by the sale of Dobbs House and other food-service businesses and, in 1981, the candy and bubble gum divisions. The purchases of medical devices were carefully integrated into a single learning base. Further acquisitions of small diagnostic and other medical producers in the United States and abroad supplemented and reinforced existing lines. The restructuring process was completed with the divestiture of the animal health division (to Solvay America) and the sale of Charles of the Ritz to Yves St. Laurent for $631 million in 1986. By 1987, 85 percent of Squibb's sales were in pharmaceuticals and 15 percent in medical products. As Furland emphasized proudly to the press, "We have put our eggs in one basket."[58]

The results were impressive. The shift from diversification to a concentration on enhancing core organizational capabilities paid off. In 1988, when SmithKline's revenues were cut in half, they doubled at Squibb. The company's new heart drug, Capoten, turned into one of the world's best-selling drugs, generating revenues of a billion dollars a year, almost 40 percent of Squibb's $2.5 billion sales. The much smaller and focused medical equipment business showed a substantial profit. In addition, in 1987 Squibb launched its initial move into rDNA technology by developing a joint venture with a biotech startup, Cetus, to use that technology for the development of cardiovascular drugs. In 1988 ensued another collaboration, this time with Denmark's Nova Industri, to market human insulin. During these same years Squibb increased its sales abroad more by direct investment than acquisition, so that by 1987 foreign sales accounted for 43 percent of total sales.[59]

I turn now to Upjohn, the final company considered in this chapter. Like SmithKline it was eventually forced to merge with a European competitor to ensure its survival. This was not the result of a failed strategy, but rather of a failure to grow.

Upjohn: The Decline of a Family-Owned and -Managed Follower Company

The history of the Upjohn Company differs from that of other pharmaceutical companies listed in Table 1.2. For more than a century after its beginnings in the 1880s, the company was owned and managed by a single family, the descendants of the founder. As late as 1968 only family members sat on its board of directors. In 1993, when the great-grandson of the founder decided not to serve as CEO, the company immediately merged with Pharmacia, a Swedish enterprise. Its experience is a good example of the hazards of depending on hereditary management in the later decades of the twentieth century.

Although Upjohn had before World War II built a strong learning base in prescription drugs, comparable to those of Lilly and Abbott, its evolution more closely tracked that of Pfizer. Both had ridden the postwar wave of innovation successfully. When that wave receded, Upjohn diversified almost as extensively as Pfizer. It failed to appropriate effectively the new scientific learning but, in so doing, participated in broadening the industry's dominant path in the 1970s and 1980s. Unlike Pfizer, however, its basic capabilities in prescription drugs were not substantial enough to enable it to survive. It turned instead to merger.

Dr. William E. Upjohn established his company in 1886 in Kalamazoo, Michigan. He did so in the same way as his contemporaries Drs. Lilly and Abbott—by improving the new pill-making technology. After he had patented a new "friable pill" (one that easily dissolved in the body and thus enhanced the accuracy of a dosage), his company soon began making a variety of medicines, including antimalarial quinine pills and candy-type laxatives. But Upjohn, far more than Lilly and Abbott, sustained expansion of its line of OTC drugs. These included Cheracol, a cough syrup; Kaopectate, an antidiarrheal; and Unicap, a multivitamin pill—all products that it continued to produce throughout the twentieth century. In 1935 it followed the industry leaders by commercializing a major prescription product, the first adrenocortical hormone, extracted from beef adrenals.[60]

Upjohn's principal move in prescription drugs came in World War II with the production of penicillin and sulfanilamide. In the early 1950s, it made a major commitment to the new antibiotics by developing products based on bulk tetracycline, which Pfizer provided before building its own marketing organization. In that decade, Upjohn participated as successfully as its prescription drug competitors in the development of new products. By 1958 the company was the sixth-largest U.S. producer of antibiotics, with sales of $22.6 million. In addition to erythromycin, streptomycin, and a sulfa-based Orinase, it commercialized a range of cortisone products and new drugs such as Gelfoam (based on beef-bone gelatin), the first oral antidiabetes agent, and an injectable contraceptive, Depo-Provera.

As its output of new drugs fell off in the 1960s, Upjohn diversified more enthusiastically than Eli Lilly or Abbott, primarily through small-scale acquisitions. During the same decade it began to expand modestly abroad, again more through acquisition than direct investment. In diversifying at home, it acquired lines related to healthcare, including clinical laboratories and companies that provided healthcare services to patients in their homes. But it also shifted further afield through the purchase of a line of polymer chemicals, including in 1970 a maker of urethane foam appliances. Two years earlier it had acquired Agrow Seed, an innovator of hybrid corn seeds. Upjohn's only large-scale acquisition in the following decade, Cobb Breeding Company, a pioneer in poultry breeding, strengthened its "agricultural segment."[61]

In the 1970s senior managers concentrated on improving capabilities in commercializing new pharmaceutical products. They expanded networks with universities and research institutes, maintained a satisfactory ratio of research expenditures to sales, recorded a substantial number of patents, and instituted the new methods for discovery by design. Nevertheless, the resulting new product development was disappointingly meager, both in numbers of new drugs and overall sales, and was well behind Merck and Lilly. Although Upjohn did become a leader in licensing genetic engineering products, it was unable to commercialize the potential of the rDNA technique. Apparently too, much of the company's resources and its management's time were still required for the production and distribution of nonpharmaceutical lines. In the early 1980s, after it marketed Xanax (a tranquilizer), Halcion (a sedative), and Micronase (an antidiarrheal), its pipeline started to dry up. Pharmaceuticals remained only one of several businesses to be managed, and during the 1980s Upjohn's income as a percentage of sales fell below that of Pfizer.

In 1985 the company began to undertake major divestitures. That year, it sold its worldwide polymer chemical business to Dow and its plant health activities to NOR-AM. In 1986 it disposed of its diagnostic business and in 1990 of its home healthcare services. Its clinical laboratories had been spun off earlier in 1981. By 1991 Upjohn had evolved into a focused pharmaceutical company with what it described as "a successful agricultural segment." Its corn and vegetable seed business accounted for 8 percent of its sales and generated 19 percent of its profits. These divestitures and a mild administrative restructuring raised its income as a percentage of sales from below an average of 10 percent during the 1980s to 14 percent in the early 1990s.

Even so, as a pharmaceutical company Upjohn suffered from its failure to invest heavily in commercialized development technologies. Thus it continued to rely on its long-established drugs, particularly in the OTC sector. By the early 1990s, except for Rogaine, the first FDA-approved treatment for baldness (a drug it developed through molecular modeling), no major prescription drugs had been developed by Upjohn since the early 1980s. Nor, except in its seed business, did it successfully exploit the biotechnology, and in December 1994 sold off that business. Moreover, of all the core pharmaceutical firms, Upjohn made the least effort to expand its activities abroad. In 1991, 84 percent of its operating income still came from the United States.[62]

In 1993 the current CEO of this family-run enterprise was stricken with cancer and stepped down. He was not succeeded by its then-president, the great-grandson of Dr. W. E. Upjohn, ending a tradition that appears to have accounted for the company's lackluster performance. Four of its drugs had by then lost patent protection. The year before, earnings had dropped 30 percent to $324 million on revenues of $6.3 billion. For the new CEO, an experienced in-house executive, the only viable alternative was merger, which he soon initiated with Pharmacia, a Swedish company of exactly the same size. Each were valued at $6.3 billion. The merger opened up global markets to Upjohn and the U.S. market to Pharmacia, permitting each to benefit from the cost advantages of scale and scope, presumably the principal reason for the marriage. Upjohn probably gained more than Pharmacia from this 1995 merger, but consolidation of the activities of the two companies proved to be difficult and the resulting performance unimpressive.[63] The postmerger years are briefly recounted in Chapter 9.

Conclusion

I conclude by returning to the basic themes of the book, starting with the limits to growth. After the 1970s the evolution of the chemical and pharmaceutical industries differed widely. That difference, in turn, led to the creation of new barriers to entry, followed by major shifts in defining and redefining strategic boundaries.

By the 1970s the U.S. chemical industry had reached its limits of growth. Chemical science and engineering were no longer providing new learning needed to commercialize new technologies as they had done in the 1920s and again in the 1940s and 1950s. As a result the industry consisted of only two multisectored core chemical companies, and they, like the specialty niche companies, were focused on specialty markets.

After the 1970s the rapid growth of the pharmaceutical industry rested on the commercializing of two new sets of learning. One was based in part on new procedures, that is, discovery by design, and on new subdisciplines of biology, including microbiology and enzymology. The second set flowed from the new discipline of molecular biology, and with it the beginnings of the infrastructure of the revolutionary biotechnology.

Until the 1960s the definition of strategic barriers remained much the same as those created to commercialize the products of the polymer/petrochemical revolution in chemicals and the therapeutic revolution in pharmaceuticals. Then as growth leveled off in the 1960s, the response in both was much the same. The leading enterprises began to diversify into closely related, and then more distant, product lines and even beyond. But as the opportunities for pharmaceutical companies to commercialize new technologies appeared, the companies that were the first to redefine their strategic boundaries became the industry's leaders. Those that waited fell behind.

The differences between Merck and Pfizer in defining their strategic boundaries provide a case study on success and failure. Merck made only limited forays during the 1960s and 1970s into related products. In the 1970s it began to commercialize the new learning in microbiology and enzymology, as well as in molecular genetics and bio-engineering. Merck became the nation's leading pharmaceutical company in terms of the introduction of new drugs and the resulting financial rewards. Pfizer, on the other hand, diversified into a wide range of products in the 1960s, even becoming a conglomerate. It pulled back in the 1970s, focusing on the healthcare market and increasingly on prescription drugs. As a result, it missed out on the commercializing of the new technologies. Only in the late 1980s and 1990s—after it had spun off its related product lines including those of healthcare—did it become a strong rival to Merck.

Eli Lilly, like Merck, quickly redefined its strategic boundaries to incorporate both sets of new technologies as soon as the challenge of commercializing new products appeared. Furland and Squibb met the challenge of commercializing the new technologies in the late 1970s. So too did SmithKline French, only to lose its position in the industry because of losses from of its acquisition of Beckman and the subsequent merger with Beecham. With the resulting hiatus, little commitment to the development of new product lines meant that SmithKline Beecham only began to commercialize products from new scientific learning in the mid-1990s.

Of the remaining two companies, Upjohn, the only family-run firm, possessed neither the resources nor the management skills required to bring new product lines to market, although some of its technology was licensed. Abbott's evolutionary story is a unique one. Its strength in diagnostics resulted from what may be seen as fate. First came the events that in turn led to the discovery of diagnostic technology that permitted it to become the U.S. leader in that market. Second, it came up with monoclonal antibodies at exactly the right time to benefit from the biotechnology revolution.

CHAPTER 8

The American Companies:
The Over-the-Counter Path

In contrast to the core pharmaceutical companies considered in the Chapter 7, companies that had developed high-technology capabilities by the end of World War II, the major producers of over-the-counter (OTC) medical products listed in Table 1.2 began to focus on high-technology markets later in their corporate lives. They prospered through the 1960s primarily by selling OTC remedies and other consumer products. Following World War II, the goal of these producers had been to follow their path of learning and to grow by entering related industries in which their production and marketing capabilities appeared to provide a competitive advantage. (Of the companies listed in Table 1.2, this chapter deals primarily with Bristol-Myers, Schering-Plough, American Home Products, and Warner-Lambert.)

By the end of the 1960s, however, the OTC producers shifted their sights and sought to enter decisively the research-intensive prescription drug path. Of these companies, only Bristol-Myers tried to develop the necessary technical, functional, and managerial capabilities on its own, but it failed and so turned to merger. Two others, Plough and Warner-Lambert, each attempted to develop those capabilities by merging with a major research-intensive firm, Plough with Schering and Warner-Lambert with Parke Davis. The first succeeded in its goal; Warner-Lambert failed. Its failure led to the destruction of the capabilities of Parke Davis, one of the oldest and for many years the most innovative U.S. pharmaceutical enterprises.

The evolution of American Home Products differs from that of all the American core pharmaceutical companies listed in Table 1.2, and even from the American chemical companies listed in Table 1.1, as a consequence of its growth's being based on a strategy of acquiring and selling large enterprises. The company was established in 1926 as a merger of somewhat related companies in chemicals, food, and OTC drugs. By the mid-1990s, 91 percent of its product lines were in healthcare. Its story not only indicates the success of strategic growth through acquisition and divestiture, but also suggests the hazard of that strategy in a high-technology industry.

Bristol-Myers Squibb Company: The Challenge to Overcome Barriers to Entry

Although Bristol-Myers mounted a successful move into prescription drugs and antibiotics in the early 1950s, the decision of its managers to become a major prescription drug company came only in the 1970s. By then, the companies that had carried out the post–World War II therapeutic revolution had created powerful barriers to entry. In the late 1970s and early 1980s Bristol-Myers began an impressive effort, using the new research technologies, to develop prescription drug capabilities. But by 1988 its managers had decided that it could become competitive in the high-tech branch of the industry only through acquisition—hence the purchase of Squibb in 1989.

Established just a century earlier by William Bristol and John Myers in New York City to produce bulk pharmaceuticals, the company had quickly moved into proprietary-patented (OTC) drugs, and then into other consumer products. During the 1920s it became a master marketer that, in addition to proprietary OTC drugs, sold Ipana toothpaste, Sal Hepatica laxatives, Vitalis hair tonic, and the like through the radio shows of leading entertainers Fred Allen and Eddie Cantor.[1]

In wartime 1943, Bristol-Myers acquired Chaplin Biologicals, a small producer of acidophilus milk processed through fermentation, changed the new subsidiary's name to Bristol Laboratories, and converted it into a bulk supplier for penicillin producers. In 1954 Bristol Laboratories began making bulk tetracycline. It then reached agreement with Pfizer, the bulk producer with the strongest patent, that Bristol Laboratories would supply only Squibb and Upjohn. It next developed seven new product forms of tetracycline in order to differentiate its products from those of its competitors. In the words of its senior executive, "None of these would qualify as a major scientific advance, but they were practical and useful improvements."[2] These ventures did provide the company with its initial learning base in the industry's research-intensive branch. During the 1950s and 1960s Bristol

Laboratories continued to enlarge its stream of antibiotic products while moving into cardiovascular drugs and other lines.

While Bristol Laboratories was increasing its prescription drug business, Bristol-Myers's corporate office focused on the expansion of OTC and consumer products. Mass advertising helped its new painkillers, Bufferin and Excedrin, and its roll-on deodorant, Ban, become among the nation's best-selling OTC and consumer products. In 1959 ensued the acquisition of Clairol, the first shampoo maker to nationally advertise hair-coloring products. Clairol's founders, Bruce and Richard Gleb, joined Bristol-Myers's top management.[3]

The Glebs (Richard became Bristol-Myers's CEO in 1972) continued to grow the company through acquisitions in advertising-intensive consumer products. In 1965 came the purchases of Drackett, producers of Windex, Draino, and O'Cedar mops; in 1967, of Mead Johnson, makers of infant formulas and children's vitamins, followed by Abbott Tresses; and in 1971, of Ellen Kaye Cosmetics. Nearly all these acquisitions and smaller ones made during the 1960s were paid for by blocks of common stock.

Focusing on Prescription Drugs

During the 1970s Bristol-Myers's management began to concentrate on improving its technical and product development capabilities in its prescription lines, especially anticancer and anticholesterol drugs. The company failed, however, to commercialize a breakthrough product. In the 1970s it began to acquire small-scale enterprises, this time in related animal health products and dental and medical equipment. The move into the latter field was executed on an even more modest basis than had been the case at Squibb.

Then, in the mid-1980s, Richard Gleb and his senior managers went all out to replicate the successful strategies of Merck, Eli Lilly, and Squibb by building through internal investment a strong learning base in prescription drugs. They reorganized internal research, concentrating specifically on biochemical and enzymology learning; constructed in 1984 a multimillion-dollar research center in Wallingford, Connecticut; and signed broad research agreements with Yale and other New England universities. In 1986 the company undertook its first venture into the rDNA technology, but it did so by acquisition, not internal investment. It purchased Genetic Systems, a leading startup in the new monoclonal antibodies business, and in 1986, Omocogen, a pioneer in biogenetic anti–bone cancer therapy. These initiatives were followed by the sale of the recently acquired dental medical unit to Siemens and its animal health division to American Home Products.[4]

Despite the company's sharpened focus and impressive investments, as Gambardella points out, "Bristol-Myers's story suggests that rapid catch-up strategies are not sufficient to become a leading innovator in this industry." By the spring of 1989 Richard Gleb had reached the same conclusion. As early as 1983, Gleb, who had come to know Richard Furland personally, considered Squibb his most likely target, even though the price was high. After Bristol-Myers acquired Squibb in 1989 for $12.7 billion, the Bristol-Myers management took over. Gleb became the new CEO, with Furland staying on in a consulting position. Only four of the top thirty-six positions went to Squibb executives.[5]

The Bristol-Myers managers moved slowly and carefully as they integrated the two companies' high-tech learning bases and disposed of the non-healthcare business. By 1991 prescription drugs and medical devices accounted for 67 percent of sales (53 and 14, respectively) and 75 percent of profits. Consumer health products, including OTC drugs, amounted to 17 percent of sales and 15 percent of profits. Household goods resulted in 16 percent of sales and 10 percent of profits. Foreign sales as a percentage of total sales rose to 38 percent, in good measure a Squibb contribution.[6]

In 1992 Gleb sold off the Drackett household-goods business to S. C. Johnson & Sons for $1.5 billion. But despite predictions in the business press of Bristol-Myers Squibb's sale of its OTC drug and nutritional lines (with a combined value of $6.1 billion) and of its toiletries and beauty aids (valued at $2.5 billion), the company continued to maintain these lines. So in 1994, 75 percent of sales derived from pharmaceuticals, divided as follows: 58 from prescription drugs, and 17 from consumer health products. Of the remaining 25 percent of sales, 14 percent came from medical devices, and 11 percent from toiletries and beauty aids.

In this way, Bristol-Myers succeeded in building an effective learning base in the research-intensive path while continuing to sustain its competitive capability in its initial low-tech learning base. But it achieved this goal only through the acquisition of Squibb and, even so, had not emerged as a leader in molecular biology and genetic engineering. In the 1990s it fell behind the industry's leaders in terms of commercializing new products and financial performance.[7] As Table 7.1 indicates, its income as percent of sales and its earning per share rose significantly after the merger even though Bristol-Myers Squibb did not become a leading innovator.

Schering-Plough Corporation: The Ingredients of a Successful Merger

While the Glebs began carefully to enter the prescription drug business only in the mid-1970s, the two other mergers uniting a prescription drug and an OTC drug company occurred almost at the same moment in 1970. The successful one, Schering-Plough, united two mid-sized companies. The merger between Warner-Lambert and Parke Davis failed to bring together two major core companies.

The two learning bases that were joined to form Schering-Plough could hardly have been more different. Schering was an heir to a nineteenth-century German first mover in prescription drugs. Plough originated as the creation of a patent medicine entrepreneur, Abe Plough, who advertised his initial product as an "antiseptic healing oil the sure cure for any ill of man or beast."[8]

Schering started operations in the United States in the 1890s as the marketing unit of Germany's Schering, one of that country's leading pharmaceutical companies. During World War I it was taken over by the U.S. alien property custodian. Between the world wars, freed from U.S. government control, Schering set up plant facilities to supplement its marketing activities. But during World War II, the company again forfeited to the alien property custodian, though it continued to operate under the charge of Francis C. Brown, a government lawyer. He recruited a research team that quickly moved into full-scale commercialization of new drugs, particularly antihistamines. When the government sold the company in 1952 for $29 million to a syndicate headed by Merrill Lynch, Brown remained as its president. During the 1950s the company expanded a line of antibiotics and commercialized two new corticosteroids, Meticorten and Meticortelone, "that became the envy of the drug industry." In the 1960s, the stream of new drugs continued, including antifungals and decongestants as well as new antibiotics, the most successful being Garamycin, for the treatment of burns and urinary tract infections. During these same years, Schering also began to expand its foreign investment abroad by building plants and marketing facilities.[9]

Abe Plough had initially sold his patent medicines in Memphis, Tennessee during the first decade of the twentieth century. After World War I he enlarged his line of proprietary (patented) drugs, largely through acquisitions of small companies. Plough relied so heavily on radio advertising that by

1940 his company owned nine radio stations. The company played no role at all in the World War II antibiotic program. After that war, it continued to extend its line of OTC medicines and moved into toiletries and cosmetics. In the 1960s "an unlikely friendship" between Abe Plough and Willibald H. Cozen, a veteran Schering manager who became CEO in 1966, led to the working out of a merger.

The Schering-Plough merger, which took effect in January 1971, was realized between companies almost equal in terms of physical assets. The stockholders of Schering exchanged one share of their stock for one of the new company; shareholders of Plough received 1.3 shares. The managers of the resulting enterprise saw little need to integrate the two companies' learning bases quickly, and instead sustained operations as separate business units under their premerger names. As the company expanded abroad, the subsidiary names remained in place. However, the company's R&D was merged at the corporate headquarters at Madison, New Jersey and headed by the former dean of the University of Texas Medical School. In other words, the merger was to be managed through a variation of the multidivisional structure, with two autonomous learning bases and a corporate office of top executives and a corporate staff including R&D as well as finance, personnel, legal, and other corporate functions.[10]

During the 1970s Plough's lines remained much the same, with Maybelline cosmetics cast as the star. The Schering learning base commercialized several new prescription drugs, including an antifungal in 1975 and, in that same year, a cold remedy that developed into a nonprescription drug in 1982. However, that branch failed to participate in the new biochemistry technologies and those of "discovery by design." Indeed, by 1979, 40 percent of Schering-Plough's profits issued from one product, Garamycin, whose license was about to expire.[11]

In 1979, a new CEO, Richard J. Bennet, responded to this looming crisis. He enlarged its low-technology business by acquiring Scholl, Inc., a leading maker of footcare products, and the cosmetic firm Rimmel. For its prescription side, he hastened the commercializing of Netromycin as the successor to Garamycin.

Entering Biotechnology

Bennet's most significant move, however, was making a strong commitment to the building of an in-house learning base to commercialize biotechnology—an opportunity that was just beginning to emerge. In 1980 Schering-Plough acquired the worldwide rights to Biogen's fibraplant interferon, an anticancer protein. In the next year the company obtained two related Stanford University patents. As it initiated clinical trials, it concluded research contracts with two other universities and two research institutes. It funded further research at Biogen in 1982 by increasing its equity holdings to 13 percent. Next, the company acquired the manufacturing and marketing rights of Biogen's alpha-2 interferon for a rare cancer, hairy-cell leukemia treatment, and in 1985 reached a cross-licensing agreement with F. Hoffmann–La Roche. In 1986 the Food and Drug Administration (FDA) approved the final product, Intron A, as a treatment for chronic hepatitis. During the 1980s, Schering-Plough developed products for cancers, AIDS, and other illnesses. By 1993 Intron A had become its top-selling product; and the company had established a solid learning base in biotechnology.[12]

While Schering-Plough was completing its initial major push in rDNA, it achieved its first major high-tech acquisition in 1986 through the exchange of $835 million worth of shares in Key Pharmaceuticals, a developer of major drugs for asthma and angina with a strong salesforce of four hundred detail representatives. In 1988 it bolstered its consumer OTC business by acquiring an eyecare company.[13]

In 1987 Bennet's successor began to reduce Schering-Plough's OTC business. He sold the Scholl footcare business outside the United States and Canada for $116 million, its foreign cosmetic business to Unilever, and its domestic cosmetic business, Maybelline, to the owners of Playtex for $300 million.

Simultaneously the company continued to expand overseas so that, by 1987, 40 percent of its sales and 30 percent of its profits derived from foreign countries, a ratio that by 1994 stood at 45 and 35, respectively. The firm's success is reflected in the following financial figures. By 1991, 80 percent of its sales and 83 percent of its operating income were generated by pharmaceuticals, the rest by consumer products, mostly OTC goods. By 1994 those figures were 86 percent and 88 percent. And by then, its income/sales ratio had risen from 9.2 percent in 1985 to 19.8 percent in 1994, and earnings per share had risen from $0.80 to $4.8 in the same decade (see Table 7.1).[14]

The key to Schering-Plough's success was maintaining in its two integrated learning bases the functional capabilities in the commercializing of its existing two lines of products, then concentrating on improving its technical capabilities by making an immediate and long-term commitment to commercializing biotechnology, and finally by executing a carefully timed divestiture of most of its nonprescription drug products. In this way, the company achieved a successful and profitable transition from the advertising-intensive to the research-intensive path of the pharmaceutical industry. The contrast with Warner-Lambert's effort to implement a similar reorientation of its paths of learning is both dramatic and instructive.

Warner-Lambert and Parke Davis: A Failed, Destructive Merger

A week before the Federal Trade Commission approved the merger of Schering and Plough in the summer of 1970, it also sanctioned one between Warner-Lambert and Parke Davis. Whereas Schering-Plough represented a merger between two mid-sized firms, the other one united leaders on the industry's two paths. Warner-Lambert was one of the largest advertisers and most admired marketers in the low-tech business. Parke Davis, a smaller company, boasted a reputation since the beginning of the century as a pioneer in commercializing new drugs. Yet Warner-Lambert failed as emphatically as Schering-Plough succeeded. Warner-Lambert not only failed to make the transition into prescription drugs, but also succeeded in destroying the long-established technical capabilities of Parke Davis.

In 1856 William Warner established a new company in Philadelphia. In the 1880s, after developing proprietary sugar-coated pills and tablets, it moved, as its leading competitors had done, into the production of other OTC drugs, largely alkaloids. Then, in the early twentieth century, the Warner company evolved through acquisition (in the manner of Bristol-Myers) into a leader in OTC products and related branded and packaged consumer goods. By World War II it had acquired more than fifty companies—including Sloan's liniments, Corn Huskers toiletries, and Hudnut and DuBarry, both cosmetics—and several small enterprises in Europe.[15]

Without any research base, the Warner company played no part in the antibiotic programs of World War II. But when Elmer Bost, who had long headed the U.S. operations of F. Hoffmann–La Roche, the leading Swiss pharmaceutical company, became Warner's CEO in 1952, the firm made its initial entry into the high-tech path with the 1952 purchase of Chilicott Labs, makers of blood-vessel dilators. Chilicott, however, remained merely a side venture. Warner continued to grow as it had in the past (again in the manner of Bristol-Myers) through acquisitions, but now it took over larger companies, leaders in their specific product lines.

In 1956 it acquired Lambert Pharmaceuticals, which had built its business on the success of Listerine mouthwash. With that acquisition, the firm changed its name to Warner-Lambert. The next year witnessed the purchase of another well-known brand, Bromo Seltzer. Later acquisitions included American Chicle (1962), the second-largest chewing gum producer in the United States; American Optical (1967), maker of eyeglasses; Smith Brothers cough drops (1968); two leading candy makers that same year; and Schick (1970), the second-largest producer of razors.[16]

In 1970 Warner-Lambert moved into prescription drugs by merging with Parke Davis. Founded in 1876 in Detroit, by Henry C. Parke and George S. Davis, Parke Davis had been the most dynamic of the American wholesaler/producers, opening branch establishments before 1900 not only in the United States but in Canada, Britain, Australia, and India. In 1902 it established the first American full-scale research laboratory, which pioneered in the development of alkaloids, dye-derivative drugs, and serum antitoxins. Parke Davis also led the way in commercializing vitamins, hormones, hormone-containing materials, and new medications for syphilis, epilepsy, leprosy, and a variety of allergies. It operated as a key player in the World War II antibiotics program. Its laboratories introduced new antihistamines in 1946 and Chloromycetin in 1949, and remained a leader in antibiotics during the next two decades. Because Parke Davis was a smaller company, the merger with Warner-Lambert was executed through an exchange of shares of Warner-Lambert stock.[17]

The Warner-Lambert Executives Take Charge

After the 1970 merger Warner-Lambert's senior executives assumed management of the consolidated enterprise. Unlike the Glebs at Bristol-Myers, who had for years been transitioning into prescription drugs, the executives at Warner-Lambert continued to operate the enlarged enterprise by following their long-established routines as an advertising-intensive OTC enterprise. For example, in 1978 the company's total marketing costs were $881 million, of which $392 million reflected expenditures for advertising and promotion. In that same year, only $85 million was allocated for R&D![18]

Not until the late 1970s did top management begin to alter the company's strategy and redefine its administrative structure in hopes of making better use of its resources. The strategic goal was, as the *Wall Street Journal* reported, to "remove operations that had been a drag on the company's earnings, and free up capital both to the company's pharmaceutical research and to acquire businesses in the fast-growing medical diagnostic businesses." The second undertaking, a structural one, was to coordinate and integrate better the company's different activities. As its CEO pointed out in 1979, the personnel working for the company didn't "consider themselves Warner-Lambert people, they consider[ed] themselves Chicle people or Parke Davis people."[19]

The revised strategy called for a rejuvenation of Parke Davis's learning base and, even more, a large-scale foray into the medical equipment business through acquisition. In December 1977 ensued the purchase of Deseret Pharmaceuticals, a leading producer of hospital products, followed in 1982 by the acquisition of IMED, a manufacturer of electronic medical equipment (for $465 million), and in the next year of McBain Instruments, which made high-precision microscopic products. These additions were balanced by selling off the less-than-profitable American Optical and its clinical lines.

By then, Parke Davis and Chilicott (the Warner purchase of 1952) had been consolidated into a pharmaceutical division, and Deseret and the other acquisitions had been combined into a hospital products division. At the same time, R&D expenditures were increased, first to $100 million and then to $150 million. Capital expenditures for R&D were raised comparably in order to build plants for research on cancer and antibiotic drugs. Attempts were made to restore the older ties with universities and research institutes. But it was too late to revive Parke Davis's technical and functional capabilities; its learning base in prescription drugs had been destroyed.[20]

Moreover, the company's move into the fast-growing high-tech medical equipment industry was becoming even more disastrous than SmithKline's similar venture. By 1984 acquisitions had expanded the medical equipment line to 12 percent of sales, but only 1 percent of profits. The company's 1985 overall balance sheet showed a net *loss* (SmithKline's transition onto the same path cut its profits only by one-half). Warner-Lambert immediately wrote off $550 million in plant facilities and equipment and another $100 million in 1986. It sold Deseret to Becton Dickinson for $225 million and IMED to the Henley Group for $165 million, both for cash. Although Warner-Lambert by 1987 remained among the world's largest pharmaceutical companies in sales, only 31 percent derived from prescription drugs, 34 percent from OTC, 22 percent from chewing gum and mints, and 12 percent from "others" (razor blades and a pre–World War I product, hard gel).[21]

After 1987, senior managers emphasized the importance of improving performance of their pharmaceuticals by increasing R&D expenditures. As a result, by 1989 prescription drugs accounted for 30 percent of sales and

44 percent of operating income, nonprescription drugs for 32 percent and 29 percent, chewing gum and mints, 25 and 22 percent, with 8 percent miscellaneous. Nevertheless, growth continued to depend on the low-tech route, largely from acquisitions at home and even abroad in confectionery and toiletries (with the promotion of a new "Cool Mint Listerine," as well as the purchase of Wilkinson Sword, the third-largest producer of razors). By 1991, pharmaceuticals (the differences between prescription and OTC products are not listed) had risen to 40 percent of total sales, and income to 55 percent, while the consumer healthcare sphere accounted for 39 percent of sales, and confectionery 21 percent.

In the 1990s, however, Warner-Lambert's managers finally realized they could not compete even in low-technology pharmaceuticals. By 1994 pharmaceuticals accounted for 33 percent of sales and only 19 percent of operating income. By contrast, consumer healthcare goods provided 46 percent of sales and 53 percent of income, with confectionery accounting for 21 percent of sales and 28 percent of operating income.[22] In short, Warner-Lambert by 1994 had all but dropped out of the prescription drug market, with confectionary representing a bigger fraction of total corporate profits. Once its managers had refocused the company's strategic boundaries on its low-technology nonpharmaceutical product lines, which had proved successful throughout the twentieth century, its earning per share rose rapidly.

Obviously, Warner-Lambert's attempt between 1970 and the mid-1990s to move into the higher-value-added and more profitable prescription drug path was a resounding failure. Its income as a percentage of sales was among the lowest among the companies listed in Table 7.1, averaging below 10 percent and rarely above that mark between 1985 and 1994. Moreover, it posted the next-to-lowest average ratio of R&D expenditures to sales. The lowest was American Home Products—although that company averaged a 16 percent return on sales during the decade.

American Home Products: Evolving through Acquisitions and Divestitures

The success of American Home Products reflects a unique path of learning. The company originated with the merger of several companies in related businesses. During the seventy years following its formation in 1926, the company's senior managers at their headquarters in New York City became skilled in moving out of lower-value into higher-value paths as technologies and markets changed. Before World War II those managers became proficient in monitoring the processes of production and marketing in each of the different paths. After the war they focused on expanding their high-tech prescription drug business. They relied, however, on licensing rather than building their own in-house capabilities for drug discovery and commercialization. In the low-tech OTC sector, they consistently maintained a strong profit performance. For this reason, of the world's thirty largest pharmaceutical companies in 1984, American Home Products ranked first in sales and twenty-eighth in R&D expenditures as a percentage of sales.[23]

As the historian Williams Haynes noted, by the end of the 1930s, American Home Products had acquired firms in six major businesses: "ethical drug preparations; publicly advertised medicinal, pharmaceutical and dentifrice preparations; food products; household products; cosmetics and toilet preparations; and chemicals, organic colors and pigments, dye stuffs and intermediates." Each of these product lines was administered through a separate division integrating product development and marketing, but without significant research capability. For all but chemicals and prescription drugs, the corporate focus was on marketing, especially advertising.[24]

In prescription drugs, the company's initial learning base emerged with the purchase in 1931 of John Wyeth & Brothers, a respected mid-sized Philadelphia drug company established in 1860. The Wyeth family had made a substantial gift of its securities to Harvard University, and it was acquired from Harvard for virtually nothing.[25] By 1931 Wyeth was producing vitamins, vaccines, and serums. In addition, in 1943, American Home Products acquired Ayrest Laboratories, a maker of cod-liver oil, vitamins, and estrogen. Ayrest, as the designated producer of penicillin for Canada's armed forces, provided American Home Products with a learning base in the antibiotic revolution at its very beginning.

Early in the postwar era, American Home Products moved out of chemicals but continued to expand its other lines, both by internal investment and acquisition. In pharmaceuticals, it concentrated on enlarging its OTC business by, as before, exploiting its advertising skills. By 1979 it had developed a broader line of new prescription drugs, beginning in 1968 with Inderal, a beta-blocker drug licensed from Imperial Chemical Industries (ICI). It then licensed from others, often foreign pharmaceutical companies, Orval (an oral contraceptive); Isodril, a coronary drug; estrogens for menopausal treatment; a new antihistamine and other antibiotics; and infant nutrition formulas. By 1979 prescription drugs accounted for 39 percent of total sales and 55 percent of net income. As the company expanded its high-technology line, it divested itself of its cosmetics and toilet preparations.[26]

In 1979 the remaining 61 percent of sales from its other divisions was fairly evenly divided. Over-the-counter drugs represented 14 percent and included Anacin (second in sales to Johnson & Johnson's Tylenol); Dristan and other cold and allergy-relief medicines; and drugs for asthma, hemorrhoids, and other ills. Canned and packaged goods brought in 11 percent, including such brands as Chef Boyardee spaghetti, Mama Leone's pasta, Gulden's mustard, and others. Confectionery, including Wrigley's chewing gum and Brach's candies, provided another 11 percent. Household products, including Ecko hardware, Woolite (a cold-water wash), Black Flag insecticides, and Old English furniture polish, added 14 percent. And finally, housewares, including PAM cooking spray, accounted for 13 percent.

In the early 1980s American Home Products decided to enlarge its higher-value-added healthcare business by attaching medical equipment to its portfolio and by divesting itself of the lower-margin non-healthcare divisions. In this restructuring, it benefited from the market for corporate control that in the 1980s was facilitating the selling of operating divisions and the acquiring of those of other companies. This shift in its product portfolio started in 1982 with the purchase of Sherwood Medical Company, the leading manufacturer of medical instruments, for $425 million. This entry into medical instruments was similar to the strategy of Squibb, but took place on a much more modest scale than that of SmithKline or Warner-Lambert. The disposal of the confectionery and household goods followed. In 1984 ensued the sale of its gum business back to its former owner, William Wrigley, and two years later the sale of its candy business to the Swiss firm of Jacob Suchard. In 1986 the Ecko housewares line was divested to the Packaging Corporation of America for $388.2 million, largely in cash. In 1990 the venerable British consumer-chemical producer, Reckitt & Coleman, acquired the household goods division of American Home Products for $1.3 billion.[27]

Proceeds from these sales, supplemented by retained earnings, helped to finance the expansion of the company's healthcare businesses. In 1986 American Home Products bought Chesebrough-Pond's hospital supply products division for $260 million to reinforce its earlier acquisition of Sherwood. In 1987 came the company's purchase of Bristol-Myers's animal healthcare division for $62 million and the acquisition of VLI, producer of a contraceptive sponge, for $74 million. Most important was the company's successful bid in 1988 of $3.18 billion for A. H. Robbins, a transaction that enlarged its OTC business, making it second in sales only to Johnson & Johnson. The purchase price included $2.5 billion to cover damages resulting from litigation involving Robbins's Dalkon shield contraceptive device that had forced that company into bankruptcy. The acquisition further strengthened American Home Products's new animal health unit and its established prescription drug line. In 1987, predating the Robbins transaction and the sale of the housewares division, 75 percent of the sales and 80 percent of net income of American Home Products derived from healthcare and the remainder primarily from food and household products.[28]

By 1991, 89 percent of sales and 92 percent of profits came from its broad portfolio of healthcare products, including prescription drugs (in which it was the leader in women's health care), OTC drugs (in which its Advil and Anacin were best-sellers), nutritional products (in which its infant formula preparations ranked just behind those of Abbott and Bristol-Myers in market share), and hospital supply goods. The remaining 11 percent of sales and 8 percent of profits still derived from food.[29]

Because American Home Products was more diversified than other pharmaceutical firms, the restructuring of its product portfolio resembled more that of the chemical companies than of its pharmaceutical competitors. Its executives, like those in chemicals, acquired managerial capabilities in maintaining and upgrading product portfolios through acquisition and divestiture. Acquisitions were financed almost wholly out of retained earnings and income received from divestitures. The resulting overall financial record was impressive. In 1991 its debt of $10.5 million rendered it a debt ratio of 3.2 percent. The restructuring of its portfolio raised the profit margin from 12.2 percent to 19.4 percent between 1982 and 1990, while earnings per share rose from $1.08 to $2.38. In 1991, its return on equity was 46 percent. From 1951 through the mid-1990s, the company's earnings and dividends increased every year.

This highly successful strategy and its resulting financial performance harbored one potential flaw. Over the decades the company had built impressive capabilities in production, and, more important, marketing, as well as those activities applicable to meeting regulatory requirements. But it had yet to develop in-house capabilities in R&D. It had not established contacts with the universities and other research institutions that were so vital to building a learning base in the new sciences. Nor was the company able to make headway through licenses alone in commercializing new biotechnology. This lack of technical capabilities led to two major acquisitions late in the twentieth century.

In 1989 American Home Products acquired, for $666 million, 60 percent of the equity of the Genetics Institute. It did so less than a month after that firm had lost a significant patent suit with Amgen (see Chapter 10). The deal nonetheless provided access to one of the most successful integrated learning bases in the new technology.[30]

This same lack of technical capabilities on the part of American Home Products appears to have accounted for the larger acquisition, that of American Cyanamid in July 1994, for which the company paid $9.7 billion in cash. As described in Chapter 2, American Cyanamid was the only major American chemical company that entered the prescription drug business on a significant scale during the antibiotic revolution of the 1940s. It expanded steadily and so successfully in prescription drugs that in 1992 it spun off its remaining chemical business to its stockholders. In addition, the American Cyanamid purchase included Immunex, one of the very few biotech startups that had surpassed $100 million in revenues. In this way the acquisition of American Cyanamid provided American Home Products with a technical learning base in the innovative technologies of the 1970s and 1980s that it could hardly have built with its own internal resources.[31] (In 2002, American Home Products returned to its roots by renaming itself Wyeth Corporation, a designation that signaled its transformation from a diversified consumer products company into a pharmaceutical company.)

Conclusion

As before, I conclude this chapter by relating the evolving paths of learning of the four companies under discussion to the book's three basic themes—barriers to entry, defining strategic boundaries, and limits to growth.

Bristol-Myers provides an impressive example of the challenges to overcoming the barriers to entry created by the industry's first movers in prescription drugs. Richard Gleb defined his company's strategy to enter prescription drugs in very much the same manner as these first movers in terms of research. Nevertheless, the barriers to entry remained too high. So he acquired Squibb. Yet barriers persisted. Although the acquisition improved the company's financial record, its technological achievements remained less satisfactory than the prescription drug leaders during the 1990s. By the mid-1990s, 42 percent still came from other than prescription drugs. Unlike Pfizer, it failed to focus its research on the commercializing of new prescription drugs.

Schering-Plough, on the other hand, succeeded in overcoming the barriers created by the prescription drug companies. Its management concentrated on refocusing strategic boundaries by concentrating on expanding its high-technology business, spinning off its low-technology products, and becoming a first mover in the new biotechnology. By the mid-1990s, 88 percent of its income came from pharmaceuticals, including an ample list of successful prescription drugs.

If the evolution of Schering-Plough's path of learning permitted it to overcome the boundaries created by the first movers in commercializing prescription drugs, the other 1970s merger, that of Warner-Lambert, proved to be a disastrous failure, because it led to the destruction of the capabilities of its co-partner, Parke Davis, long one of the leading American drug companies. The senior creators of Warner-Lambert, after taking over the management of the consolidated enterprise, concentrated on maintaining its low-technology businesses by focusing on marketing and not research.

Only in the 1970s did managers enter high technology, which they did by entering into the medical equipment field only to soon learn the high cost of the barriers to entry into that market. After this lesson, they again redefined their strategic boundaries by focusing on pharmaceuticals and particularly prescription drugs. By 1989 pharmaceuticals had become their major business, with an emphasis on prescription drugs. Nevertheless, their competitors' barriers to entry remained so high that Warner-Lambert could not compete. By 1994, the remnants of its pharmaceutical business accounted for only 19 percent of its operating revenue. Redefining its strategic boundaries to the businesses in which it had been successful, it raised its earnings per share (Table 7.1).

The evolution of American Home Products (since 2002, the Wyeth Corporation) is an example of a still greater barrier to entry—that resulting from the creation of a new industry based on a new science, molecular genetics, and a new technology, rDNA. American Home Products's financial success since its beginnings in the 1920s rested on the abilities of its managers to perfect functional capabilities as they moved successfully out of old industries into new ones, beginning with chemicals, food stuffs, household products, cosmetics, healthcare, and OTC prescription drugs. After World War II, it concentrated increasingly on the pharmaceuticals, both prescription and OTC products. Here it relied almost wholly on licensing new product lines, which was the reason for a unique record. Of the top thirty U.S. pharmaceutical companies, American Home Products was first in sales and twenty-eighth in expenditures for R&D.

Licensing strategy had been successful because the company could count on the existing nexus of different industries in which they operated to provide the necessary ingredients, supplies, and services required to commercialize these products. This was not the case, however, with the coming of biotechnology. Although the fundamental new learning came in the 1960s, the basic nexus only began to appear in the 1970s and the very first new products in the 1980s. In this sense, American Home Products, the most successful company in terms of financial return, paid $10 billion in cash as an entry fee in order to become a player in a scientific revolution whose infrastructure was just being constructed.

This episode dramatizes the striking difference in the evolution of the chemicals and pharmaceutical industries since the 1970s. Without new learning from chemical science and engineering, the chemical companies have defined their strategic boundaries in a number of specialty chemicals whose basic technologies were commercialized in the 1920s and again in the 1940s and 1950s. In pharmaceuticals, new learning in biology culminating in the coming of a new science has created a medical revolution that should continue well into the twenty-first century.

CHAPTER 9

The American and European Competitors

Table 1.2 indicates that by 1993 the U.S. core pharmaceutical companies had three sets of competitors. The first group consisted of two American companies that entered from related industries—Johnson & Johnson from medical accessories and Procter & Gamble from related consumer goods. The second were the European chemical companies (described in Chapter 5) that from their beginnings operated as producers of manmade drugs. In the 1980s, they, like their counterparts in the United States, began to concentrate on the strategy of replacing their chemical businesses with prescription drugs. Here the Swiss companies moved more quickly than their German rivals.

The third set of competitors consisted of startups. Whereas new entrants emerged rarely in chemicals, the pharmaceutical startups, working with the century-old producers of medicines, were by the mid-1990s creating the infrastructure of a third basic technological revolution—that in biotechnology. They were building a revolution that would be as significant in shaping the patterns of human life as was the modern industrial economy in the last decades of the nineteenth century, or the electronic revolution that brought forth the new technologies in audio, video, and information transmission that so transformed the ways of life and work by the end of the twentieth century. Because of its significance, I leave the story of the biotechnology revolution to Chapter 10.

The Domestic Competitors

The two American domestic companies to enter pharmaceuticals successfully, Johnson & Johnson and Procter & Gamble, ranked at the time of their entry among the nation's leading marketers. Each entered SIC 283 in a distinctive way. Johnson & Johnson moved its initial nontechnical path onto both the industry's advertising-intensive and then research-intensive ones. In the third stage, Johnson worked closely with innovative biotechnology startups in much the same manner as Merck, Eli Lilly, and Abbot had in commercializing rDNA drugs. Procter & Gamble, on the other hand, entered onto the over-the-counter (OTC) drug path only in the early 1980s and did so primarily by acquisition. Its first major foray into prescription drugs came in 1982, also via acquisition. A third U.S. company, Eastman Kodak, attempted to enter in the 1980s by acquiring a major core prescription drug company; with no capabilities in the industry, however, it was quickly forced to withdraw.

Johnson & Johnson: From Bandages to OTC to Prescription Drugs

By the mid-1990s, Johnson & Johnson's more than 150 business units were classified into three categories—professional, consumer, and pharmaceuticals. Two Johnson brothers formed the company in 1886 in New Brunswick, New Jersey to make antiseptic surgical dressings. Until after World War II, its products were primarily in what the company termed the "professional" category. Produced and marketed worldwide, they included sterile bandages, sutures, Band-Aids (its first major consumer product), hospital gowns, surgical gloves, and some surgical instruments. In the 1920s, the company initiated production of related advertising-intensive consumer products, beginning with baby powders, oils and shampoos (products that soon were selling to adults), toothbrushes and pastes, mouthwashes, sunblocks and other skincare preparations, and sanitary napkins. From such a starting point, the transition onto the OTC path was easy.[1]

Robert Wood Johnson, the son of a founder, became the company's CEO in 1932 and guided its postwar expansion. He directed its first move into the prescription drug business in 1959 by acquiring McNeil Laboratories, the producer of the prescription pain reliever Tylenol. At the same time, Johnson entered the European market by purchasing a Swiss drug firm, Cilog-Chemie. Tylenol soon became a very successful OTC drug. After a massive marketing effort, it became the best-selling product in its field. To expand its OTC drugs, Johnson & Johnson in 1961 acquired Janssen, a major proprietary drug producer in Belgium, Holland, and Sweden. During the following decades, roughly half of the company's sales derived from abroad. The OTC branded lines introduced in the 1960s and 1970s included products for athlete's foot, acne and other skin maladies, antacids, and decongestants. In the 1980s the company concentrated on expanding both its pharmaceutical and its OTC lines.

In 1959 Johnson & Johnson also initiated a series of successful moves into prescription technologies. That year, it formed Ortho Pharmaceuticals, which became in 1963 one of the first producers and marketers of an oral contraceptive based on a steroid compound that it licensed from Syntex, an innovative startup and first mover in oral contraceptives (see Chapter 10). The same unit then developed and commercialized a related corticoids-based skin ointment. On the basis of acquisition and internal investment, Johnson & Johnson during the 1960s established an integrated learning base in OTC drugs and succeeded in its entry onto the prescription path. At the same time, it enlarged its professional lines by adding surgical instruments and devices.

Initial success encouraged its senior managers to advance into two other related high-technology lines—veterinary products and medical instruments and devices. But, in both cases, management soon recognized that, given their many other activities, they were unable to build the capabilities necessary to compete. In 1966, Johnson & Johnson acquired Pitman-Moore, a maker of veterinary drugs whose continuing mediocre performance occasioned its sale in 1986. Between 1978 and 1982, Johnson & Johnson acquired a major producer of diagnostic-imaging equipment, a manufacturer of CT scanners, a maker of kidney dialysis equipment, and a producer of IV treatment devices. After heavy losses, the first two of these were sold off in 1986, and the third reduced in size. The funds from these sales were diverted in part toward developing the company's technically less complex, more advertising-intensive, line of glasses, contact lenses, and other opthamalogical products. By 1989 less sophisticated surgical instruments and devices had been added to the professional lines.

Failing to overcome the existing barriers to entry, Johnson & Johnson reverted to enhancing its capabilities in both prescription and OTC drugs by pioneering in biotechnology. In 1987, its ortho diagnostics systems formed a 50–50 venture with Chiron, one of the earliest biotechnology startups, to produce and market screening tests for hepatitis C and variations of that virus. Its Ethicon division executed a similar arrangement for a treatment for burns. The Chiron tie thus provided an entry into genetic engineering (see Chapter 10). In the 1990s the company continued to build its in-house biotechnology capabilities and to maintain and expand on those in oral contraceptives, antibiotics, and the older prescription drugs.[2]

Although the top managers of Johnson & Johnson concentrated during the 1980s on its proprietary and prescription drug sectors, as the twentieth-largest advertiser in the United States in 1989 they paid close attention to the OTC consumer products by building on their success with Tylenol. In that year the company bolstered its OTC strength by forming a joint venture with Merck to translate Merck's most successful prescription drugs into OTC versions. The practice of OTC switches of prescription drugs had become more pronounced in the industry after 1984, when Upjohn and Whitehall Laboratories (subsequently a unit of American Home Products) successfully translated the painkiller ibuprofen into two popular brands, Motrin and Advil. In 1990, Johnson & Johnson's new collaborative venture acquired Mylanta, maker of a leading antacid, from ICI America.

By 1990, twenty-one years after it had entered the prescription drug industry, Johnson & Johnson had evolved into a major player in world healthcare markets. In 1989, 50 percent of its income on 40 percent of its sales derived from prescription drugs; 25 percent of its income came from consumer products on sales of 37 percent of total revenues; and its professional products accounted for 25 percent of its income on 33 percent of its sales. By then, its focus on foreign sales was also paying off, representing half of total revenues and 48 percent of its operating profits. As a result, during the 1980s Johnson & Johnson's income as a percentage of sales rose from 8.3 percent to 11.1 percent, and its earnings per share from $1.07 to $3.19.[3] The company's ability to move from medically related professional products to OTC products to prescription products is a clear example of how careful attention in defining and timing strategic moves helped to overcome barriers to entry created by the century-old core pharmaceutical companies.

Procter & Gamble: Exploiting Marketing Capabilities

When the Procter & Gamble Company entered SIC's 283 OTC path, it ranked as the nation's largest advertiser, spending over half a billion dollars a year, 80 percent of which was allocated to television advertising. In the years before World War II the company had been a leading American producer of soaps, detergents, and shortening. In the 1930s it had pioneered in the development of synthetic detergents for home use and then hair shampoos. Later, during the 1950s, under the guidance of Neil McElroy and Howard Morgens, the company transitioned rapidly into toiletries, including toothpaste (Gleem and Crest), haircare (Prell and Head & Shoulders), toilet paper (Charmin and Bounty), disposable diapers (Pampers), and on a smaller scale, into foods (Duncan Hines cake mixes, Jif peanut butter, and Folger's coffee). Several of these new lines resulted from acquisitions. By the late 1970s, 40 percent of sales remained in laundry and cleaning products, a third were in personal care, a quarter in foods, and the rest in small by-products.[4]

During the late 1970s senior managers sustained their search for high-growth businesses and were attracted to healthcare. The company had developed a few prescription products based on its knowledge of teeth, bones, and skin, but entered both the OTC and prescription drug businesses in a significant way only in 1982 by acquiring the Norwich Eaton subsidiary of Morton Norwich. Norwich Eaton's principal OTC brands were Pepto-Bismol, a stomach remedy, and Chloraseptic, a sore throat cure. Norwich Eaton also maintained a small prescription drug business built primarily around anti-infective products. Procter & Gamble complemented this foundation in 1985, the year in which transactions in the market for corporate control peaked, by buying Richardson-Vicks, makers of Clearasil, Nyquil, and other proprietary cold remedies, and the OTC business of G. D. Searle, including Dramamine for motion sickness and Metamucil, a bulk laxative.

Procter & Gamble then moved into developing OTC versions of major drugs, first jointly with Syntex for its Naprosyn, an anti-arthritic drug. Introduced in 1994 as Aleve, the product achieved first-year sales of $100 million. During the 1980s, Procter & Gamble also funded research on prescription drugs, both of its own making used in treating bone disease and those in development at its Norwich Eaton subsidiary on anti-infectives and heart disease. In 1985 Procter & Gamble obtained from the Swiss company Tillots Pharma the marketing rights in the Western Hemisphere to Asacol. A treatment for ulcerative colitis, Asacol became a blockbuster drug in the 1990s. Early on in that decade Procter & Gamble resolved to make a major commitment to prescription drugs by constructing a $300 million healthcare research center and allocating half of the center's funding to commercializing drugs for an aging population, which provided a growing market in heart, bone, and ulcer therapy.[5]

By 1994 personal care accounted for 51 percent of Procter & Gamble's operating income, laundry/cleaning 39 percent, and chemicals 10 percent. As the twentieth century ended, Procter & Gamble was only beginning to seek a path that would permit it to breach the industry's existing barriers to entry in commercializing products based on the new learning in biology and related disciplines.

Eastman Kodak: A Strategic Disaster

In 1988 a major U.S. core company with no capabilities in pharmaceuticals at all—Eastman Kodak, the nation's first mover in photographic film and equipment—acquired Sterling Drug as part of its diversification program. Sterling was the only top-thirty pharmaceuticals core company worldwide during the 1970s and 1980s not listed among the American core companies in Table 1.2. Given the existing barriers to entry, the acquisition proved disastrous for both firms.

Sterling's founder, William E. Weiss, established the firm in West Virginia in 1901 to produce painkillers and other patent medicines. At the end of World War I, Weiss scored a coup by acquiring at auction from the U.S. alien property custodian the U.S. business of the German giant Bayer. He renamed the acquisition Winthrop and in 1923 sold 50 percent of Winthrop back to Bayer, which devolved into part of I. G. Farben when the latter formed in 1925. With the advent of World War II, Sterling regained the German company's 50 percent. During the postwar years it concentrated on OTC drugs and other consumer products, developing into a major national advertiser. Sterling began introducing antibiotics and other prescription drugs in the 1970s.

When Eastman Kodak took over Sterling-Winthrop, Eastman's management announced the goal of having Sterling rank among the nation's top 10 largest—and the world's 20 largest pharmaceutical companies by the year 2000. That was the hope. The reality was that Eastman Kodak's net income plummeted from $1.394 billion in 1988 to $512 million a year later, then to $17 million in 1991. Although net income picked up again by 1993, it nonetheless remained far below the peak levels of the 1980s. In 1994, a new CEO at Eastman Kodak decided to break up Sterling Drug into parts and auction them separately. France's Sanofi acquired the prescription drug business, SmithKline Beecham took the OTC business, Johnson & Johnson the clinical laboratories, and the British company Reckitt & Coleman assumed ownership of the household products business. SmithKline Beecham then sold the U.S. OTC business to Bayer.[6]

Through these acquisitions by domestic competitors, several of the largest mid-sized American drug companies disappeared. Besides Sterling, these included Searle, Merrell, Marion, and Richardson-Vicks. Still others were lost to the U.S. core companies' foreign competitors. My point is that, after the Schering-Plough merger of 1970, no mid-sized companies were capable of catching up with the initial core companies in terms of revenues and profits. Instead they became targets for acquisition by the industry's leaders at home and abroad.

Except for Johnson & Johnson and Procter & Gamble, then, no other U.S. manufacturer of consumer products successfully entered from the broad paths defined by SIC 283, consumer chemicals. Colgate-Palmolive, which over the decades had been Procter & Gamble's foremost domestic competitor in consumer chemicals, did even not try. Nor did others like Revlon in cosmetics and toiletries, although it attempted briefly to move into hospital supplies in the late 1970s. But that venture was sold off in 1985. Nor did those in the high-tech medical equipment and devices (SIC 384 and 385), including such firms as Becton Dickinson and Baxter International, undertake concerted efforts to enter pharmaceuticals. By the 1970s barriers to entry had become almost insurmountable.[7]

The Challenges from Abroad

The evolution of the product lines of the leading European revenue producers listed in Table 1.2 that competed effectively in the American market enjoyed the advantages acquired as first movers, for they created integrated learning bases at the beginning of the commercialization of the products of medical chemistry and then of biochemistry. This was especially true of the Germans and Swiss chemical companies, as reviewed in Chapter 5. As first movers in dyes, they also became the first movers in synthetic coal-tar-based drugs. These enterprises included Hoechst, Bayer, Ciba-Geigy, and Sandoz. The only other major competitor in the U.S. market was Switzerland's F. Hoffmann–La Roche, a pharmaceutical enterprise from its beginnings in the 1890s.

The story is different for Britain and France, for until the end of World War II their prescription drug businesses were dominated by American and German core companies. Then in the late 1940s and 1950s, three companies—Glaxo, Beecham, and Imperial Chemical Industries (ICI), the first to commercialize penicillin in Britain—created Britain's first major prescription drug bases. (Beecham merged with SmithKline in 1989.) The lone French company listed, Rhône-Poulenc, continued as a successful path-follower until World War II. After the war, major government intervention was required to rebuild the French pharmaceutical industry and Rhône-Poulenc was nationalized until 1993. During these years, the company retained its earlier strength in the developments of vaccines and antitoxins.

The smaller European companies evolved by concentrating on their home markets and European ones, and the Japanese likewise focused on their home market and other East Asian ones. These European and Japanese firms often licensed products from and had alliances with U.S. core companies and startup entrepreneurial firms, just as the American competitors did with European and Japanese pharmaceutical companies. Two of the Japanese companies developed from centuries-old roots. Indeed, Takeda began in 1781, and Shionogi nearly a century later in 1871. The third, Sankyo, was formed in the late nineteenth century as Japan began to industrialize and trade with Western nations. In 1898, Parke Davis penetrated Japan, employing Sankyo as its local marketer. The fourth firm, Yamanouchi, was the youngest, established in 1923.[8]

After World War II all four Japanese companies established relationships with the American and European producers through buying and selling licenses, marketing agreements, or joint ventures to introduce new products. But until Takeda Pharmaceutical decided in 1995 not to renew its long-term agreement with Abbott Laboratories, no Japanese company created an integrated overseas subsidiary with its own development, production, and marketing units in the manner that Matsushita and Sony had done in the United States and Europe forty years earlier.

As noted in Chapter 7, Takeda initiated its first venture overseas by forming a ten-year, 50–50 joint venture with Abbott to develop and market new products in 1977 and 1987; its venture was renewed for another ten years. In 1997 TAP Pharmaceuticals became a full-fledged subsidiary of the Japanese company, responsible for the production and marketing organizations for the North American market. In 1998 a comparable subsidiary for Europe was established in Frankfurt, Germany.

Of the three German firms listed in Table 1.2, E. Merck and Schering A. G. created global enterprises in the 1890s. Their American branches would become the progenitors of the American core companies whose histories are delineated in Chapters 7 and 8. The third, Boeringer-Ingelheim, founded in 1885, was characterized in 1992 as being "too small to afford the high cost of competing in the prescription-drug market, but too large to rely solely on the industry's specialized niches." As "a secretive, and bureaucratic family-owned firm . . ., it often missed opportunities." It survived in part because, "until recently, German doctors rarely prescribed anything but German-made drugs," thanks to protective legislation. The two Swedish firms on the list are younger: Pharmacia was started in 1911 and Astra two years later.[9]

The German and Swiss Competitors:
Europe's First Movers in Pharmaceuticals

The German firms Bayer and Hoechst, it will be recalled, built strong marketing organizations in the United States before the turn into the twentieth century. By 1905 Bayer was producing drugs as well as chemicals in New York state. Hoechst remained the fountainhead of new drug development and continued to supply its worldwide organization from Europe. Although Bayer did not retrieve the trademark to its Bayer aspirin, after World War I both Bayer and Hoechst reentered the United States through I. G. Farben's 50 percent interest in Sterling-Winthrop.

The impact of World War II replicated that of World War I: the German producers lost patents and facilities, as well as positions in world markets in both pharmaceuticals and chemicals, but not their organizational capabilities. Both Bayer and Hoechst quickly returned to North America. BASF had not focused on pharmaceuticals before the war, and made minimal investments in the postwar years.

During the 1950s and 1960s these two firms rebuilt their facilities in drugs in addition to chemicals. Bayer continued to do so in the 1970s largely through acquisitions. Hoechst accomplished the same through internal investments. As described in Chapter 5, Bayer purchased Cutter Laboratories in 1977 to improve its position in the industry's research-intensive path. A year later, it acquired Miles Laboratories, a mid-sized company that had been founded in 1885. It produced Alka Seltzer and other popular OTC products. In prescription drugs, Miles enhanced its position more through direct investment than by acquisition. Hoechst benefited from the work of its French subsidiary, Roussel Uclaf, of which it had acquired controlling interest in 1974 (see Chapter 5). Both Bayer and Hoechst remained, however, relatively slow until the 1980s in incorporating the new learning in microbiology and enzymology, in part because their universities had fallen behind those in America in developing this new learning. They no longer enjoyed their dominance in biological sciences as they had before World War II.

At Hoechst U.S., by 1980, 80 percent of pharmaceutical sales derived from a single drug, the diuretic Laxic, which the company had introduced in 1964. To rectify this weakness, Hoechst made its initial move into biotechnology by signing a contract with Massachusetts General Hospital, a Harvard teaching hospital, to finance for ten years at $5 million a year the research activities of its Molecular Biology Department. Nevertheless, Hoechst made little effort to build a broader network with other institutions or to contract with biotechnology startups. As Taggart points out, Hoechst's performance in the new drug development during the 1980s was not impressive, in that it was "perceived to operate in a very staid and unspectacular manner."[10]

In 1981, Bayer, impressed by Hoechst's contract with Massachusetts General Hospital, started what it termed a "learning period" in the new science and related technologies. It expanded funding for research at its Miles Laboratories in West New Haven, Connecticut and enlarged its ties with neighboring Yale University. On the West Coast, its Cutter Laboratories negotiated contracts with Genentech. In 1984 ensued further contracts with such startups as Genetic Systems for producing monoclonal antibodies. Dome Laboratories (part of Miles) developed specialty enzymes. By 1986 Bayer's management considered the learning period completed and concluded that "even if biotechnology were not in the short run going to lead to profitable products, it had become an essential tool for drug design," and thus the enterprise should maintain capabilities in that field. Bayer did not introduce its first biotechnology drug until 1993.[11]

In the 1990s Bayer and Hoechst both enlarged their strong American positions in the more customary manner of merger and acquisitions. In 1994 Bayer bought for $1 billion (via Eastman Kodak and SmithKline Beecham) the North American OTC business of Sterling-Winthrop. In addition Bayer recovered its aspirin logo, which it had lost because of World War I; that purchase made Bayer the second-largest OTC drug producer in the United States.

The following year (as told in Chapter 3) Hoechst's management made a major commitment to pharmaceuticals and purchased for $7.5 billion Dow's subsidiary, Marion Merrell Dow. With Marion, Hoechst acquired its first producer of low-tech OTC drugs in the United States, and with Merrell, it supplemented its capabilities in prescription drugs. In 1995 Hoechst acquired for $3.5 billion the remaining 43.7 percent of its French subsidiary, Roussel Uclaf, and then consolidated it into the American acquisition, naming the new subsidiary Hoechst Marion Roussel. A massive reorganization followed, with a $763 million restructuring charge.

Hoechst then sold off its specialty chemical lines to a Swiss industrial chemical firm, Clarant, for 45 percent of Clarant's stock. Early in 1997 the company announced plans for dividing its product lines into nine independent businesses monitored by a single management board. In addition to ra-

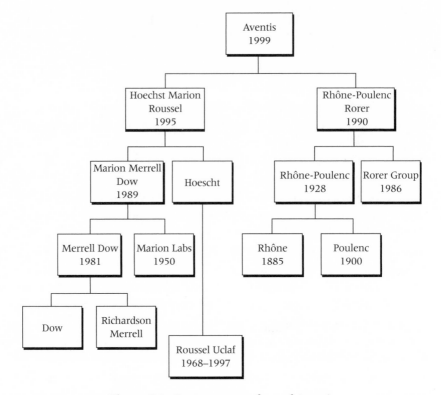

Figure 9.1 Corporate genealogy of Aventis

tionalizing activities of this huge enterprise, its chairman announced, "The company has begun a phased exit from chemical activities and is becoming a life science company."[12]

As told in Chapter 5, as the merger trend in the global pharmaceutical industry reached a culmination, Hoechst Marion Roussel merged in 1999 with Rhône-Poulenc Rorer to form Aventis, today's German giant (Figure 9.1). Since the merger, Aventis has focused on its core pharmaceutical lines in human vaccines, prescription drugs, and therapeutic proteins.[13]

Hoechst and Bayer had for over a century ranked as world leaders in both chemicals and pharmaceuticals. From the start, however, they had operated through different learning bases. In the late 1990s Hoechst appeared to be following the lead of the smaller American companies listed in Table 1.2 and their Swiss competitors by transitioning over to the pharmaceutical path, where it has always served more as the leader than either Bayer or BASF.

BASF remained a top performer in the third synthetic organic chemical path, that of film and photography—a product line that always differentiated it from the other two German rivals.

Novartis: A Swiss Giant

Although the advances in molecular biology and the resulting genetic-engineering technology were developed primarily in the United States, by 1994 the two leading Swiss enterprises—Novartis (the result of a merger between Ciba-Geigy and Sandoz) and Roche Holding played a significant role in building the infrastructure of the emerging biotechnology revolution. Roche Holding, also located in Basel, has always ranked as Europe's leading pharmaceutical company. The constituent companies of Novartis—Ciba-Geigy and Sandoz—differed from their German rivals by moving out of chemicals to focus on pharmaceuticals sooner than did Bayer and Hoechst.

The 1969 merger of Ciba and Geigy (described in Chapter 5), resulted in the consolidation of different learning bases at home and abroad and opened up an expansion of agricultural chemicals, which accounted for a major revenue source. In these same years, the smaller Sandoz (half the size of Ciba-Geigy in terms of revenues in 1982 and two-thirds in 1991) concentrated more on pharmaceuticals than did its rival. Having fallen behind in antibiotics and thus having largely missed the resulting postwar wave of innovations, Sandoz pioneered in the development of drugs for the treatment of mental diseases (including the initial development of Delsid [LSD]). The company entered largely by acquisition into nutritional goods, as well as seeds and other agricultural products. By 1991, 47 percent of Sandoz's sales were in pharmaceuticals, 18 percent in chemicals, 16 percent in agricultural products, and 11 percent in nutrition. In 1994 it enlarged its nutritional business by purchasing Gerber Products, a major American leader, for $3.7 billion.[14]

Both Ciba-Geigy and Sandoz focused more than did the Germans on the new biological advances, particularly in genetic engineering. They formed alliances and arranged contracts and investments with small biotech start-ups. Nearly all of these were in the United States. Here Ciba-Geigy led the way. Gambardella lists over twenty such agreements that Ciba-Geigy forged between 1984 and 1991. These included one with Genentech in 1984, three with Chiron in 1986, another with Biogen in that same year, and a dozen with smaller companies. Ciba-Geigy's strategy culminated in 1990 with the acquisition of 60 percent of Chiron, one of the premier American research companies in genetic engineering.[15]

In May 1996, when Ciba-Geigy and Sandoz presented their plans for a merger, they announced that the new company, to be called "Novartis," would spin off its remaining specialty chemical businesses. In the late 1990s Novartis maintained five principal lines of business: pharmaceuticals, generic drugs, consumer health (primarily OTC products), animal health, and CIBA Vision. Prescription pharmaceuticals accounted for 60 percent of sales. The company was quite profitable, with net income exceeding 20 percent of sales.[16]

Roche Holding: A World Leader

The Swiss firm Roche Holding differed from the other Swiss and German rivals in that it was the only one that did not originate as a chemical company. It was distinctive in another way. The enterprise founded as F. Hoffmann-La Roche by Fritz Hoffmann in Basel in 1894 exists today, more than a century later, fully controlled by the Hoffmann family. It also remains the only family-controlled enterprise in pharmaceuticals and chemicals among those listed in Tables 1.1 and 1.2. The company not only followed the virtuous strategy of reinvesting learning and profits into commercializing new products but also, because of the family's wealth, continued to grow by acquisitions in closely related industries. To support its rising output, it quickly built an international marketing organization and the essential research laboratories, and then integrated backward into the production of its own supplies of fine chemicals. Its American subsidiary, established in 1905 in Nutley, New Jersey, began to produce and market fine chemicals and supplies from both synthetic as well as natural sources, and then prescription drugs from these ingredients. After World War I, F. Hoffmann–La Roche (U.S.) developed techniques for the large-scale production of bulk vitamins, and captured the market from Merck and other U.S. producers of vitamins. As late as 1991, Roche Holding (corporate successor to F. Hoffmann–La Roche) possessed over 50 percent of the world's market for vitamins, another example of long-term first-mover advantages.

In the 1940s and 1950s, without the benefits of a U.S. crash program in antibiotics, the company, along with Ciba-Geigy, paved the way in benzodiazepines (tranquilizers), in which Librium, introduced in 1960, and its follow-up Valium were in 1963 the most successful. Indeed, Librium quickly became the best-selling drug in the United States, only to be surpassed by Valium, which remained the world's best-selling drug until 1981. During the previous decade the two drugs generated $2 billion in sales annually.[17]

As its postwar wave of drug introductions receded, F. Hoffmann–La Roche initiated diversification in the manner of its U.S. competitors. In 1963, starting with the purchase of a French firm, Gibaudan, it completed a series of acquisitions in the chemically related organic fragrance and flavor business. In the same year, it began acquiring clinical laboratories. After building a learning base in this new business, the American subsidiary invested internally during the 1970s, acquired in 1982 two major independent laboratories, and then merged all into a single enterprise, Roche Biomedical Laboratories, headquartered in the Research Triangle Park in North Carolina. By 1991 that subsidiary had become the second-largest medical testing laboratory in the United States.[18]

ENTERING THE NEW TECHNOLOGIES   In the 1970s, the parent company began, like Merck and Eli Lilly, to incorporate the findings of the new biological learning, setting up its Institute of Molecular Biology in Basel. In 1982 it formed a joint venture with Britain's Glaxo to use its marketing capabilities in the United States to sell Glaxo's initial product of the new drug-designed techniques, an anti-ulcer blockbuster, Zantac. Thanks to F. Hoffmann–La Roche's marketing facilities and know-how, Zantac replaced Valium (whose patent ran out in 1985) as the world's largest-selling drug. By 1992 the company's success paved the way for similar marketing arrangements with nine other foreign companies, as the United States had become not only the world's leader in drug discovery, but the largest market in the world.

Meanwhile, in the mid-1980s, with technical knowledge flowing from the new institute, and with abundant cash provided by the family owner, F. Hoffmann–La Roche launched its entry into genetic engineering through contracts and other agreements with both established and new biotechnology firms, almost all in the United States. Gambardella lists more than thirty agreements between 1984 and 1992. These include Genentech (1985), Biogen (1986), Genzyme (1987), Chiron (1988–1990), and Amgen (1988). As a result, F. Hoffmann–La Roche became a leader in genetic engineering technologies. In 1990 ensued the crowning acquisition of 60 percent of Genentech for $2.1 billion (and with Genentech came Cetus). To facilitate this expansion, the company's senior managers in 1989 reconstructed its financial and operating corporate entity into Roche Holding AG.

In 1994 Roche purchased 49.5 percent of Syntex, the pioneer in oral contraceptives based in Palo Alto, California, whose story is reviewed in Chapter 10. Roche then formed Roche Bioscience, headquartered in Palo Alto, consolidating the management of its West Coast biotechnology properties.

As Roche Holding was sustaining its status as one of the world's most powerful pharmaceutical makers, it continued to expand its OTC businesses, unlike its American competitors. It also maintained its build-up of its clinical and fragrance and flavor divisions. Its OTC business expanded through the purchase in 1991 of the OTC business of Sara Lee (an American food company). In 1996 Roche Holding bought Procter & Gamble's 50 percent interest in Procter-Syntex, a joint venture for marketing two leading proprietary drugs, Aleve and Fermstat 3. In addition, Roche Holding formed a collaboration with Bayer to co-market a number of their respective OTC drugs. In fragrance and flavors, another set of consumer products, Roche Holding spent an estimated $1 million to acquire the Cincinnati-based Tastemaker (a joint venture between Hercules and the Mallinckrodt Group). Finally, by 1995, Roche Holding became a major player in the diagnostic business by combining its clinical laboratories with those of National Health Laboratories to create the world's largest service laboratory chain. In the same year it expanded its commitment to testing laboratories by acquiring a 49.9 percent interest in the Laboratory Corporation of America.

By 1995 Roche Holding reported SF 14.7 billion in sales, 63 percent from pharmaceuticals, including both prescription, OTC drugs, and testing laboratories, 26 percent from its bulk vitamins and fine chemicals, 10 percent from fragrance and flavor business, and 6 percent from diagnostics. Between 1987 and 1993 it nearly doubled its sales from SF 7.8 billion to SF 14.3 billion. For the decade from 1986 to 1995, its income as a percentage of sales rose from 5.3 percent to 22.9 percent—an exceptional record for an enterprise operating in several related sectors.

By the mid-1990s Roche Holding had evolved into as much an American as a Swiss giant, with its massive complex of research laboratories, administrative, and other offices of Roche's Biomedical Laboratories Park in Research Triangle Park in North Carolina; the comparable headquarters in Stanford's Industrial Park, where Syntex had long been housed as its focus of molecular and genetic activities; and the even larger, much older, complex at Nutley, New Jersey. Its growth had resulted from sustained heavy internal investment, but acquisitions represented the most significant additions to the research base. Because of this vast enterprise, together with its Basel neighbor Novartis, the Swiss pharmaceutical companies, following the same set of related paths of learning, have remained for more than a century worldwide leaders in the pharmaceutical industry.

The British and French Competitors

The evolution of the British and French pharmaceutical industries differed strikingly from that of the German and the Swiss. In the nineteenth century, Britain's pharmaceutical industry consisted largely of small chemists, druggists, and makers of a small number of proprietary pills and bottled goods. The learning bases necessary for prescription drugs were established only after World War II. Nevertheless, in Britain that move into prescription drugs was far more successful than the attempts to build comparable learning bases in France.

As late as 1962 only three of the top-selling pharmaceutical companies in terms of sales in the British market listed by William Breckon were U.K. firms (see Table 9.1). Glaxo, the first mover in penicillin, was already number three; Beecham, the nation's leading OTC company, was number fourteen; and Burroughs Wellcome lagged at number eighteen. Five years later, Beecham, both by merger and by internal investment in penicillin, ranked second and Britain's major chemical company, Imperial Chemical Industries, ranked tenth; Burroughs Wellcome remained at the bottom of the list.[19]

The historian's obvious question is why were so few British companies able to operate in Britain, Europe's richest consumer market until World War II. For Britain, historically the original industrial nation, was also historically the first urban consumer society. The answer is that the Swiss and American companies listed in Table 9.1 built the capabilities that permitted them to establish powerful barriers to entry into the U.K. market before World War II. The sudden demands of World War II for antibiotics and the resulting therapeutic revolution transformed the British market, whereas neither occurred in France during the 1940s.

Table 9.1 illustrates the dominance of the American and Swiss companies in the British market as late as 1962. It also lists Burroughs Wellcome, one of the world's largest pharmaceutical companies in the late nineteenth and early twentieth centuries, which fell behind in the years before World War II

Table 9.1   Top-selling pharmaceutical companies in the United Kingdom, 1962, ranked by sales (£ millions)

Rank	Company	Sales (million £)
1	Pfizer (U.S.)	£8.4
2	Lederle (Cyanamid, U.S.)	8.3
3	Glaxo (U.K.)	7.1
4	SmithKline & French (U.S.)	4.8
5	Merck, Sharp & Dohme (U.S.)	4.2
6	Geigy (Switzerland)	4.0
7	Bayer (U.S.)	3.9
8	Parke Davis (U.S.)	3.9
9	Wyeth (U.S.)	3.9
10	May and Baker (France)	3.6
11	Ciba (Switzerland)	3.5
12	Lilly (U.S.)	3.3
13	Roche (Switzerland)	2.9
14	Beecham (U.K.)	2.8
15	Upjohn (U.S.)	2.4
16	Riker (U.S.)	2.3
17	Warner (U.S.)	2.2
18	Burroughs Wellcome (U.K.)	2.1
19	Abbott (U.S.)	1.9

Source: William Breckon, *The Drug Makers* (London: Eyre Methuen, 1972), p. 29. Breckon provides two tables for the top selling companies, in 1962 and again in 1967. The first includes Allen and Hanbury, which Glaxo acquired in 1958. In this table I've added that firm's totals to that of Glaxo. May and Baker (no. 10) had become a subsidiary of Rhône-Poulenc.

before rebounding after the war. I begin the review of the evolution of the British pharmaceutical industry with Burroughs Wellcome's story.

Burroughs Wellcome: Britain's First Mover Fades

In Britain, as Basil Achilladelis points out, "With the exception of Burroughs Wellcome, the transformation of manufacturing apothecaries into research-intensive companies was very slow. . . . Neither the manufacturing apothecaries nor the chemical companies had developed alliances with academic researchers that would allow them to participate actively in the emerging pharmaceutical industry."[20]

The founders of the one exception, Henry S. Wellcome and Silas W. Burroughs, introduced American learning in functional activities to Britain. Both were graduates of the Philadelphia School of Pharmacy and had been employed in a major American company before establishing their enterprise in London in 1880. In 1894 Burroughs set up the company's Physiological Research Laboratory, the first of its kind in Britain. Rapid overseas expansion started in 1902 with the establishment of a branch house in South Africa, followed shortly thereafter with one in Italy, in Canada and the United States in 1906, and then in China, Argentina, and India. The partners' model appears to have been Parke Davis, the first American company to build a comparable global enterprise during the 1890s.[21]

In 1924, however, Wellcome, who had become the sole partner after Burroughs's death, retired from active work and consolidated his British facilities, laboratories, and the overseas branches into the Wellcome Foundation, which, in turn, owned the Wellcome Trust and Wellcome Ltd. Having acquired the attitudes of his adopted land, Henry Wellcome then spent his time and the enterprises' income on medical research and charitable activities. At his death in 1936, his will directed five trustees to "continue the activities of the Foundation, directing all profits to charitable purposes, research in medicine, and the sciences pertaining to it, and the maintenance of museums dedicated to this research and the history of medicine." The Wellcome Foundation's operating enterprise, Wellcome Ltd., stayed alive but no longer possessed the funds to maintain a technical learning base for the commercializing of new products and processes.

After World War II, Wellcome, which had maintained its operations in the United States and Australia, began to rehabilitate its crippled learning base. Profits now were directed toward research, as well as to broad charitable projects. Its managers attempted both by acquisition and by internal investments to build a profitable line of prescription drugs at home and abroad. But progress was slow. By 1962 it ranked only eighteenth among the nineteen largest British producers in pharmaceutical revenues.

In the 1980s, however, Wellcome commenced a concentrated move into the new biological sciences and related technologies. To finance this step, in 1986 the Wellcome Trust offered 25 percent of its equity in the pharmaceutical enterprise to the public, continued to sell its shares publicly, and in 1986 sold off its animal health business for $65 million. These transactions funded research in herpes and AIDS therapy, as well as on tPA dissolvers of blood clots. Nevertheless, the Wellcome Trust recognized the fate of mid-sized companies and decided to sell off the remaining 39.5 percent of its shares in Wellcome Ltd. In an unexpected move, in 1995 Glaxo offered to acquire all of Wellcome Ltd. for $14.9 billion.

Glaxo Takes the Lead

Before Glaxo got the nod as Britain's designated leader of the government's wartime penicillin program, it was a producer of dried powdered milk, largely for babies, and vitamins. Established in New Zealand in 1880, it expanded into Britain through an effective advertising program. In the 1920s the company became the nation's favorite milk processor by adding Vitamin D to "fortify" its milk products. By the 1930s, having expanded its number of vitamins produced and by distributing its powdered milk and vitamins worldwide, it had become Britain's leading producer of nutrition products. But only with the demands of World War II did Glaxo's pharmaceutical unit become central to the development of its strategy and organizational structure.[22]

During World War II, Glaxo became Britain's primary producer of penicillin, much as Pfizer did in the United States. By 1944 Glaxo, using Pfizer's fermentation process, had built four factories that produced 7.5 billion units, or about 80 percent of total British output. After the war, it remained Britain's leader in penicillin. At the same time, the company continued to expand its vitamin lines. Its managers then exploited this learning to enter the field of hormones by developing Britain's first commercial cortisones and then a series of corticosteroids.[23]

When the introduction of new drugs fell off in Europe, Glaxo, like the American core companies, diversified into related product lines, including veterinary products and medical instruments, and it acquired a drug-distribution company. By 1981, new antibiotics and cortisone drugs had fallen off to 38 percent of sales. By the end of the 1970s, Glaxo was still smaller than the major American, Swiss, and German companies. Its initial entry into the U.S. market was a consequence of a small acquisition in 1978.

Then came Glaxo's big break. In 1982, through the application of the new biologically based drug-by-design discovery techniques, it brought out the anti-ulcer drug Zantac to challenge SmithKline's Tagamet. With its market capabilities in the United States still limited, its managers, as pointed out above, turned to F. Hoffmann–La Roche to market Zantac in the United States. Sales and profits soared. In 1984, Glaxo, in addition to expanding its European personnel and facilities, built a $40 million plant in North Carolina to manufacture the drug. By 1990 Zantac was still the world's best-selling drug, with sales close to an annual $3 billion. At that time 49 percent of Glaxo's sales derived from anti-ulcerants and 41 percent from antibiotics and respiratory drugs.

Following this resounding success, Glaxo altered its strategy, replicating that of Eli Lilly and Merck rather than SmithKline and Warner-Lambert. Between 1984 and 1987, Glaxo sold off its veterinarian and surgical products and its drug-wholesaling house, and, substantially increased its expenditures for R&D, opening the way for the introduction in 1990 and 1991 of profitable tranquilizers, antidepressants, and other serotonin drugs. Such success demonstrated Glaxo's ability to continue to exploit the opportunities of the new learning in biological sciences. Possibly because of that success, it concentrated less on molecular biology and genetic engineering. That lack might have helped to account for its quick decision to acquire Wellcome in 1995, for during the 1980s this venerable British pharmaceutical enterprise evinced strengths complementary to those of Glaxo.

Glaxo Wellcome continued to develop new drugs and in 1997 acquired Spectra Biomedical and its gene-variation technology. Three years later, following the example of others in the global pharmaceutical industry, the company consummated another huge merger with SmithKline Beecham—creating GlaxoSmithKline PLC—which made it possible to compete with Germany's Aventis and Switzerland's Novartis and Roche Holding.[24] (See Figure 9.2.)

Beecham's Group Ltd.: From OTC to Prescription Drugs

After World War II, Beecham's Group was the oldest established drug company in Britain, but the least successful of that nation's three entrants into the postwar therapeutic revolution. Beecham's, ranked fourteenth in Table 91, had by 1967 jumped to second place. Nevertheless, these sales came primarily from OTC drugs and related consumer products. It opened its first research unit only in 1947. Its first new success debuted in 1957 with the introduction of a second-generation formed penicillin nucleus, its initial prescription drug. From then on Beecham's evolution demonstrated parallels to those of the American producers in the advertising-intensive OTC path.

Philip Hill, a financier who in 1928 acquired Beecham's Pills—since 1859

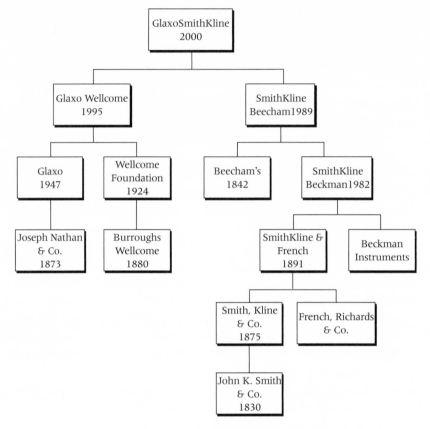

Figure 9.2 Corporate genealogy of GlaxoSmithKline

the maker of Britain's most popular laxative—fashioned Britain's largest OTC producer. He did so by acquiring over the next decade ten companies that produced patent medicines and other OTC drugs, tooth paste, shampoos and other toiletries, and health drinks. His goal, writes H. G. Lazell, Hill's successor as chairman, was to create a British challenger to "the great American international proprietary businesses," referring explicitly to Colgate-Palmolive-Peet, Procter & Gamble, American Home Products, Sterling Drug, and Bristol-Myers. Just before World War II, Hill consolidated these operating units in order to achieve the competitive advantages of scale and scope.[25]

In the 1960s Beecham's research units, working with SmithKline, developed a series of penicillin products. At the same time, Beecham licensed several successful antibiotics. As a result, the *International Directory* reports, Beecham's "lead in the antibiotics brought tremendous growth in the 1960s and 1970s." By 1969, 40 percent of Beechman's profits derived from prescription drugs. During these same years Lazell concentrated on expanding the advertising-intensive OTC and consumer products businesses, primarily through acquisitions. An effective consumer marketer, Beecham became the nation's second-largest advertiser. Nonetheless, penicillin and antibiotics remained the firm's primary profit generating products.

In the mid-1960s, according to the *International Directory*, "Beecham's products penetrated the European market." By the late 1960s its marketers had turned their attention to the United States, establishing a unit to make Brylcreem hairdressing and acquiring a feminine hygiene company.

By the late 1970s, however, Beecham's output of new prescription drugs had dropped sharply. Lazell and his successor, Ronald Halstead, adopted a strategy of paying for the rising research and development costs through profits on consumer goods. In 1978 Beecham acquired Merck's consumer division (see Chapter 7) and a perfume producer, and succeeded in the early and mid-1980s with a substantial acquisition drive in both Europe and the United States in cosmetics and fragrances, consumer products, and OTC drugs. Furthermore, in 1985, Beecham purchased Merck's Calgon. By that time consumer products accounted for 57 percent of sales, prescription drugs and animal health for 27 percent, and OTC products for 6 percent.[26]

It was clear by 1985 that this strategy was not successful. Revenue and profits were declining rapidly. Beecham had failed to develop ties with research institutes and universities and to participate in the new learning in microbiology, enzymology, and genetics by fostering bonds with the new entrepreneurial startups in rDNA technology. In the mid-1980s its prescription products still consisted primarily of penicillin and antibiotics and other technologies developed during the 1950s and 1960s. In response Beecham's board of directors removed Halstead in 1985 and, in the following year, brought in an experienced American executive, Robert Bauman, as his successor. Bauman immediately began selling off soft drinks and other non-healthcare consumer products and reconstructing Beecham's management organization.

In 1988 Bauman initiated merger talks with the senior managers of SmithKline Beckman. By then it was apparent that both companies were victims of failed strategies: Beecham's attempt to commercialize products from the new learning through profits from consumer products, and Smith-Kline's attempt at entering another high-technology industry (medical devices) with the acquisition of Beckman Instruments, which although related in marketing used a very different technology (see Chapter 7).

For Beecham, the pressure for the merger was obvious—survival. Smith-Kline's motives were more complex. The merger, accomplished through an exchange of stock, would release a much broader long-term revenue base, while the sale of Beckman Instruments would provide substantial funds for research in new areas. The company had recently launched research initiatives in microbiology and enzymology, and in biotechnology, and had formed ties to university and research institutes. In 1989 the FDA approved SmithKline's major biotechnology product for hepatitis B and a tPA clot dissolver.

Once Bauman and his associates recognized that a merger was essential for Beecham's survival, they undertook a search for "a merger of equals, in terms of financial bargaining power." SmithKline quickly became the prime target because its disastrous liaison with Beckman Instruments had resulted in a loss in capitalization of approximately $5 billion. This loss meant that Beecham could afford to merge through exchange of stock with SmithKline. The deal was consummated in 1990.

Bauman assumed the presidency of SmithKline Beecham, which would remain headquartered in London. He then brought in thirty senior managers, eleven of whom were from outside the firm, and concentrated on integrating the two companies across the Atlantic. The consolidated enterprise maintained both its high-tech and low-tech learning bases, as Bauman continued to sell off the non-healthcare products, including cosmetics, fragrances, and toiletries. By 1991 prescription drugs accounted for 66 percent of sales, consumer products for 26 percent, and animal health and clinical laboratories for 6 percent (the latter came from SmithKline). In 1994, as noted above, SmithKline Beecham acquired Sterling-Winthrop's nonprescription healthcare business for $2.9 billion, and sold that entity's nondrug business to Bayer for $1 billion. At about the same time, it invested $2.3 billion to acquire Diversified Pharmaceutical Services, a pharmacy benefit-management company that SmithKline Beecham hoped would be a captive channel for its drugs. Almost immediately thereafter, the U.S. Federal Trade Commission modified its regulations to remove the potential benefits of collaboration between drug companies and pharmacy benefits-management companies—a devastating setback for SmithKline Beecham and other major pharmaceutical companies.[27]

By 1995, after the animal health unit had been sold off, prescription drugs dropped to 60 percent of SmithKline Beecham's sales, consumer healthcare products to 29 percent, and clinical laboratories to 11 percent. Income as a percentage of sales remained lower than at Glaxo, the major U.S. core companies, and Bristol-Myers Squibb, a comparable high-technology/low-technology merger.[28]

During the 1990s SmithKline Beecham expanded its foundation in the new molecular technologies and introduced several new genetically engineered drugs. In addition, it became a global leader in rDNA research and undertook a major investment in the Human Genome Project in return for nonexclusive licensing rights.[29] As noted above, SmithKline Beecham merged with Glaxo Wellcome in 2000 to form GlaxoSmithKline PLC, creating Britain's only pharmaceutical giant. Two years before, ICI had incorporated its highly successful pharmaceutical division as Zeneca, which it then sold to the Swedish leader Pharmacia.

ICI: A Focused First Mover in Pharmaceuticals

In the mid-1990s the primarily British challenger to Glaxo was not SmithKline Beecham. Rather it was Zeneca, formerly ICI's pharmaceuticals division, which ICI had spun off as an independent company in 1993. As I pointed out in Chapter 5, ICI's entry into a new pharmaceutical technology was much more successful than earlier moves into new chemical technologies, both synthetic organic dyestuffs and petrochemicals. This success in pharmaceuticals rested on building an integrated learning base specifically to commercialize penicillin. The other reason for the pharmaceuticals division's sustained success in commercializing prescription drugs was that, as a unit of a larger multipath company, it could draw on corporate resources to cover its costs. Once established, the division remained focused on introducing new drugs whose research and development were financed by the profits from its own earlier successes.

ICI had implemented pharmaceutical research and production well before Beecham and more extensively than Glaxo. A unit within the dyestuffs department initially carried out such work. During World War II it met wartime needs by producing penicillin, sulfa drugs, and an antimalarial product. But so long as the unit operated within the dyestuffs department, it was unable to produce and market these products in an effective manner. Only in 1954 did the pharmaceuticals division receive its independence from dyestuffs, and it began to commercialize new products. As told in Chapter 5, the new division started by building its own laboratories and then its production facilities as it invested in its own national and international marketing organizations.[30]

As ICI expanded its drug line, its virtuous strategy paid off. Moreover, because it remained a division of a larger multipathed enterprise, ICI pharmaceuticals was less tempted to diversify into related products, or even into OTC drugs. Its management concentrated instead on moving into other therapeutic "areas where proven expertise exist." Its cardiovascular line that originated in 1964 introduced in the 1970s a beta-blocker, Tenormin, which in 1991 was still the fifth-largest drug in worldwide sales. It was followed by Tenoretic (a combination beta-blocker and diuretic). The same pattern was replicated for drugs used in treating cancer. Its Novadex became the world's leading breast anticancer drug in terms of sales, and was followed by Zoladex, proclaimed in 1991 as a follow-up for prostate cancer.[31]

Although ICI was only beginning to investigate biotechnology, this impressive performance provided its parent company with the funds needed to survive the difficulties resulting from its earlier less successful moves into organic chemistry and polymer/petrochemicals and to maintain its strength in its prewar learning paths. Then, in 1993, ICI spun off its pharmaceuticals division and its increasingly biologically based agricultural products as a new company, Zeneca, a maneuver that, in turn, permitted ICI to divert most of its large debt onto Zeneca's balance sheet. The principally debt-free chemical company was then able to concentrate on chemicals by acquiring in 1997 Unilever's specialty chemicals business.

It is significant that the three British core pharmaceutical companies—Glaxo, Beecham, and ICI—though from different roots, entered the prescription drug business at approximately the same time. World War II created unprecedented demand for penicillin and antibiotics, thus providing the three companies—like Pfizer and Merck in the United States—with an opportunity to become first movers in the new technology. Each of the British companies evolved in a distinctive manner. ICI was highly successful in concentrating on developing new prescription drugs whose income helped finance further drug innovations. Glaxo, after its successful blockbuster Zantac, quickly sold off its nonprescription drug activities and followed ICI's example. Beecham, unable to finance new drug developments through income provided by its consumer products business, was fortunate enough to merge with SmithKline, which unlike Beecham had commercialized products of the new learning.

% of external market (external = world minus domestic)

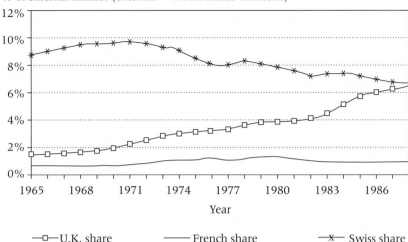

Figure 9.3 External market shares in pharmaceuticals: United Kingdom, France, and Switzerland, 1965–1988. *Source:* Lacy Glenn Thomas III, "Implicit Industrial Policy: The Triumph of Britain and the Failure of France in Global Pharmaceuticals," *Industrial and Corporate Change* 3 (1994): 454.

   The creation of the British drug prescription enterprises was initiated and financed by private corporations, not by the government. The government health policies and the national health service, of course, favored domestic companies. Although theirs was a domestic market, the funding of new facilities and the development of new capabilities were not paid for by the taxpayers. Of greater significance, as shown in Figure 9.3, the British companies made steady gains in the world market.[32] In 1965 the British had accounted for less than 2 percent of the market, well below the Swiss at about 9 percent. By the late 1980s, the British and Swiss were at parity at about 7 percent. As the chart further indicates, the share of the French industry remained flat at about 1 percent throughout this period. Where the British pharmaceutical industry succeeded in competing in international markets, France's failed.

France's Rhône-Poulenc: Failure and Government Intervention

The contrast between the British and French pharmaceutical industries is striking. France's first mover, Etablissements Poulenc Frères, merged with the nation's leading chemical company, the Société Chimique des Usines du Rhône, and the merged company remained a strong competitor until World War II. Missing out on the therapeutic revolution created by the war, the French companies failed to become competitive in commercializing innovative drugs. As a result, the French government decided to play an increasingly significant role in shaping the structure of the industry and its competitive capabilities.

Etablissements Poulenc Frères was formed in 1900 by three Poulenc brothers. They did not attempt to build a global enterprise comparable to Burroughs Wellcome, but their company did become a successful competitor to the German and Swiss first movers. It did so in good part because of its relationship with the Pasteur Institute, a leading center of medical research in Paris. During the 1920s, Poulenc continued to exploit its first-mover capabilities. After the merger with the Société Chimique des Usines du Rhône in 1928, Rhône-Poulenc introduced new drugs in biologicals, sulphmomides, antihistamines, and vitamins. During the 1930s it strengthened its position in the European markets by acquiring a leading British producer, May and Baker, of chemicals and other ingredients for drug making.

Because of the German occupation during World War II, Rhône-Poulenc was deprived of the antibiotic revolution that so benefited the American and British firms. After the war it continued to produce new vaccines and serums. But, as Achilladelis notes, "Despite its size and its strong ties with the Pasteur Institute, Rhône-Poulenc's contributions to pharmaceutical innovations during the 1960s have not matched its work of the 1930s and 1940s."[33]

In 1990 Rhône-Poulenc paid $2 billion to acquire majority control of the Rorer Group, a U.S.-based pharmaceutical and OTC company best known for its antacid product Maalox. At about the same time, the French government transferred its 35 percent stake in Roussel Uclaf to Rhône-Poulenc Rorer. The company was privatized in 1993 and began expanding into biotechnology and genetic engineering, primarily by acquisition.[34] In 1999, as noted above, it merged with Hoechst Marion Roussel to establish Aventis, one of the world's leading pharmaceutical companies.

During the period following 1970, the intervention of the French government proved decisive in shaping the French pharmaceutical industry. One reason was that after Hoechst acquired majority ownership of France's second-largest pharmaceutical enterprise, Roussel Uclaf, in 1974, foreign participation in the French industry surpassed 50 percent, and 75 percent of France's pharmaceuticals were licensed from foreign companies. And recalling Figure 9.3, only about 1 percent of French pharmaceutical products entered world markets.

Given Rhône-Poulenc's failure in commercializing pharmaceuticals, the French government in 1973 created Sanofi by merging several healthcare, cosmetic, and animal health companies into a subsidiary of the state-owned petroleum company, Elf-Aquitaine (Atochem, see Table 1.1, was Elf's comparable petrochemical subsidiary). Sanofi grew by acquisition and internal investment, but on a much smaller scale than did Rhône-Poulenc. In 1984 the government, after further acquisition, formed Sanofi Elf Bio Industries, which concentrated on the opportunities of genetic engineering, primarily in agricultural products. In 1990, Sanofi continued to grow through acquisitions, including properties from SmithKline Beecham and Eastman Kodak's Sterling-Winthrop prescription drug business.[35]

In conclusion, the French pharmaceutical industry missed out on the therapeutic revolution of the 1940s and 1950s, as well as on the new learning in biology in the 1970s and 1980s and biotechnology in the 1980s and 1990s. As a result, the French industry was not, and had little prospect of becoming, a major factor in international markets.

Conclusion: Overcoming Barriers to Entry

The evolution of the pharmaceutical industry demonstrates a major premise of this study: the first competitors to build integrated learning bases and then to use the resulting knowledge and profits to successfully commercialize the products of new technologies create powerful barriers to entry. These new technologies were based on new knowledge in chemistry and later in biology.

The American Challengers

The American competitors made three attempts to overcome the barriers to entry created by the first movers by the 1920s. After World War II, Johnson & Johnson moved carefully from healthcare supplies into OTC markets, establishing a strong position by the 1960s. Then, by defining its strategic boundaries and increasingly focusing on partnering with innovative startups in the new biological learning, it became a major competitor in world markets, with half of its income originating outside of the United States. Procter & Gamble, a mass marketer much bigger than Johnson & Johnson in total revenues, focused first on entering the OTC business and then into prescription products both through its own research and via acquisitions and joint ventures. The third attempt, that by Eastman Kodak, provides yet another example of the futility of unrelated diversification.

The European Competitors

Again the basic story involves barriers to entry. The modern science-based pharmaceutical industry had its beginnings in the Rhine Valley well over a century ago. The three major German chemical companies (Bayer, Hoechst, and BASF) and the smaller Swiss enterprises (Ciba-Geigy, Sandoz, and F. Hoffmann–La Roche, the European first mover in pharmaceuticals) at its headwaters quickly emerged to create barriers to entry that supported their strategy of dominating world markets. Thanks in good part to the British blockade of Germany during World War I, these barriers disappeared, permitting American companies to enter the high-technology branch of the industry in strength. By World War II their subsidiaries, with those of the Germans and Swiss, led in markets throughout Europe. The Germans, once again, lost their barriers during World War II. By the 1960s, for example, the Swiss and American competitors dominated the British prescription drug market.

The historical coincidence of the antibiotic revolution and the outbreak of World War II enabled three British companies (Glaxo, ICI, and Beecham) to become first movers in the new technologies. Two of these three were able to create a learning base on which to move into other therapeutic drugs, much as the German, Swiss, and U.S. leaders had done earlier. The French industry, on the other hand, with the coming of the therapeutic revolution, proved unable to create a learning base in the new technologies, and so were unable to compete in international markets during the postwar period.

German competitors including Hoechst and Bayer and the Swiss companies remained the strongest European competitors in world markets. The Swiss fared especially well because of their aggressive entry into the new biotechnology.

In the United States, the European competitors, like the domestic rivals, relied increasingly on growth strategies involving acquisition of mid-sized companies. Among the fifty largest pharmaceutical companies worldwide (in terms of revenues) in 1993, the following mid-sized competitors disappeared in the 1980s and 1990s: larger American companies gobbled up

Sterling-Winthrop, G. D. Searle, Merrell, Marion (initially), A. H. Robbins, and Richardson-Vicks, while European competitors acquired Cutter, Morton, Marion (second-hand), Rorer, and Syntex. Hence no new major pharmaceutical companies were established after the 1920s.

But the situation began to change in the 1980s. A new scientific discipline, microbiology and genetic engineering, would so transform the industry that startups for the first time in more than a century could build significant learning bases and become effective competitors. At the same time, the survivors among the century-old core pharmaceutical companies also entered the new technologies and achieved powerful first mover advantages.

Commercializing Biotechnology

The revolution created by the advent of molecular biology and genetic engineering was as significant as those triggered by the revolutions in chemistry and biology in the 1880s, in polymers and petrochemicals and in antibiotics and therapeutics in the 1940s and 1950s, and in communications and the computing revolution that began with the transistor and integrated circuits in the 1950s and 1960s.

The technology supporting the biotechnology revolution was developed in the 1970s. As Basil Achilladelis notes, "Of particular importance was the discovery of recombinant DNA processes (1975–1978). These processes insert segments of one organism's DNA—nucleic-acids that form the molecular base for heredity—into the DNA of another organism, causing the latter to produce proteins identical to those of the former. The potential for these methods for diagnosing and treating disease and for studying biological processes at a molecular level was unparalleled and would lead to the formation of the biotechnology industry."[1] The knowledge and the materials required for this technology provided the first opportunities since the 1920s for the entry of new companies that had the potential to become large integrated competitors to existing core pharmaceutical enterprises.

Luigi Orsenigo, the historian of the biotechnology industry, makes a distinction between the earlier and contemporary periods of growth: "Thus, if microbiology, biochemistry and chemical engineering had brought a fast expansion of biotechnology, both in the number of products manufactured through the techniques, and the efficiencies of the processes involved, the advent of contemporary biotechnology emerged from the impulse provided by a different scientific discipline—molecular biology—which transformed radically the knowledge base and the opportunities for innovation in biotechnology."[2]

The technological revolution beginning in the 1970s evolved from the path-breaking discovery in 1953 by James Watson and Francis Crick of the double helix structure of DNA. The following years witnessed the defining of the phenomenon, the development of genetic engineering techniques, the clarification of ingredients needed, and the discovery of new proteins, enzymes, and other building blocks. In the mid- to late-1960s, as noted in Chapter 7, major research universities began to offer courses and create departments in molecular biology.

Orsenigo pinpoints "the birth date of contemporary biotechnology" as 1973, when two scientists at Stanford and two others at the University of California at San Francisco discovered the recombinant DNA (rDNA) techniques. In 1975 scientists at Cambridge (U.K.) "employed their hybridoma technology to produce monoclonal antibodies, . . . very important tools in all the diagnostic and therapeutic processes involved in the recognition of particular molecules." Then came the discovery of the process of genetic engineering described above by Basil Achilladelis. In 1978, Genentech, the first company explicitly and solely devoted to genetic engineering, acquired its first building and its initial staff of five.

As noted in Chapter 7, a small number of core pharmaceutical companies were basic pioneers and key investors. Eli Lilly supported Genentech on research to find alternatives to insulin and to isolate human growth hormones. Merck worked with Chiron, Genentech's most successful early rival, to develop a recombinant vaccine for hepatitis B. Abbott pioneered in 1975 in commercializing and producing in volume monoclonal antibodies, a critical ingredient in the new genetic engineering. Schering-Plough invested immediately in Biogen, the developer of interferon, as well as in other startups. By 1986 these products had been approved by the Food and Drug Administration (FDA). The two Swiss giants, F. Hoffmann–La Roche and Ciba-Geigy, quickly entered the industry, licensing from and investing in new American biotechnology enterprises, resulting in close cooperation and ultimately full control of two of the most successful of these. In 1990 Roche Holding (successor to F. Hoffmann–La Roche) acquired control of Genentech, while Ciba-Geigy, which had formed a joint venture with Chiron in 1986, achieved full control of Chiron eight years later.

Creating the New Supporting Nexus

The early entrants in the new technology, Orsenigo reports, emerged from the existing nexus of the pharmaceutical industry. Entrants included instrumentation firms (New Brunswick Scientific, Dynatech, and Flow General) research companies (Cetus, Bioresponse, Biotech Research Laboratories, Native Plants, Agri Genetics), and enzyme and fermentation specialists (Novo Laboratories). They were quickly joined by new nexus startups. By the beginning of 1984 approximately one hundred firms were involved in research and development in the basic area of monoclonal antibodies. Others produced amino acids, enzymes, and other materials. The large majority of both the established companies and the newcomers remained nexus companies.[3]

A much smaller number of these nexus companies harbored larger ambitions. They sought to become integrated pharmaceutical companies that would profit from developing, manufacturing, and marketing the products their research had discovered. As Scientific Design's Ralph Landau had claimed with respect to the SEFs in the chemical industry (Chapter 4), they too believed, "That's where the money is!" Just as important was the fact that some of them, though certainly not all, realized that's where the learning is. As Orsenigo writes, "commercialization involves significant learning processes, costly irreversible and specialized investments and the means to finance them."[4]

These startups quickly discovered that the way from the nexus to the core was a rocky one. Two routes were possible: one was to build on the capabilities developed in producing monoclonal antibodies, new proteins, and the like and then to transition into more closely related, higher value-added materials and devices based on these basic products; the other was to enter into research projects with core companies, relying on the licensing of some of the resulting products for essential cash flow to finance their own product development. In either case, those that eventually became integrated companies were able to do so only by commercializing "orphan drugs"—the new therapies for relatively rare, life-threatening diseases. Under legislation passed by Congress in 1983, producers enjoyed a seven-year monopoly for such orphan drugs for markets under 200,000 potential users. The new law granted producers time to develop the functional capabilities essential to creating an integrated learning base,[5] even without strong patents.

Even so, the barriers were formidable. Indeed, as Table 10.1 indicates, by 1994, almost two decades after the commercializing of the new technology began, only seven of twenty-five leading biotechnology companies generated revenues of $100 million. An eighth, Centocor, had reached that amount briefly in the early 1990s. Of these eight only four showed a profit. And two of these, Genentech and Chiron, did so only after they were taken

Table 10.1   Financial performance of the twenty-five leading U.S. biopharmaceutical companies, 1994

Company	1994 revenues ($ millions)	1994 net income ($ millions)	Changes from 1993		Profit margin	
			Revenues	Net income	1994	1993
Amgen	$1,647.9	$436.0	20%	14%	26.5%	27.9%
Genentech	795.4	124.4	22	111	15.6	9.1
Chiron	454.0	32.0	43	74	7.0	5.8
Genzyme	310.7	32.0	17	225	9.7	3.2
Biogen	149.8	−10.6	0	NM	DEF	21.7
Immunex	144.3	−33.1	NM	NM	DEF	DEF
Genetics Institute	130.9	−18.9	28	NM	DEF	DEF
Gensia Pharma- ceuticals	71.8	−50.1	115	NM	DEF	DEF
Centocor	67.2	−63.5	−11	NM	DEF	DEF
Scios Nova	53.7	−28.0	13	NM	DEF	DEF
Curative Tech- nologies	40.6	−7.3	30	NM	DEF	DEF
Agouron Pharma- ceuticals	23.8	−7.2	86	NM	DEF	DEF
Regenereon Pharma- ceuticals	23.2	−30.7	119	NM	DEF	DEF
Vertex Pharma- ceuticals	23.1	−17.6	−21	NM	DEF	7.0
Cephalon	21.7	−36.1	28	NM	DEF	DEF
Affymax	21.4	−19.0	41	NM	DEF	DEF
MedImmune	18.9	−18.8	25	NM	DEF	DEF
Repligen	18.3	−23.4	−32	NM	DEF	DEF
Oncogene Science	16.7	−6.4	1	NM	DEF	DEF
Isis Pharma- ceuticals	15.5	−18.2	28	NM	DEF	DEF
Liposome	10.4	−33.7	−20	NM	DEF	DEF
U.S. Bioscience	8.5	−32.6	4	NM	DEF	DEF
Immune Response	7.0	−17.4	46	NM	DEF	DEF
T Cell Sciences	7.0	−11.1	−22	NM	DEF	DEF
Cytogen	2.5	−32.8	−76	NM	DEF	DEF

Source: Compiled and reorganized from Ann M. Thayer, "Biotech Companies Face Uncertain Future After Grappling with Troubles," *Chemical and Engineering News,* March 20, 1995, p. 13.

Notes: NM = not meaningful; DEF = deficit. Revenues include product sales, contract research, royalty, and interest income. Profit margin represents after-tax income as percentage of revenues.

over by F. Hoffmann–La Roche and Ciba-Geigy. Of the remaining four un-profitable firms, one came under control of American Cyanamid and the other of American Home Products (which was then acquired by American Cyanamid). The other two remained in business thanks to Eli Lilly and resources from Merck.

The following brief review of the competitive challenges from special-ized research companies examines the history of the eight such companies whose revenues reached $100 million by the early 1990s. I first consider Genentech and Chiron, the two that reached that goal by relinquishing their independence to the Swiss giants. Next I consider why Amgen and Genzyme were able to accomplish these ends on their own. Then follow the reviews of Centocor, Genetics Institute, Immunex, and Biogen—all of which had to be supported by funding from core American and Swiss pharmaceuti-cal companies.

Syntex: A Nexus Firm Succeeds in Creating an Integrated Learning Base

In this chapter I focus on the creation of a revolutionary infrastructure based on the new scientific knowledge. I start by reviewing the evolution of Syntex, a startup that commercialized a major innovation—the "pill"—an oral contraceptive in the 1960s. I do so because Syntex illustrates how suc-cessful innovators were able to commercialize a basic technology, steroids (hormones), and then produce an array of prescription drugs. Nevertheless, Syntex was unable to surmount the existing barriers to entry, and was ac-quired by the Swiss giant Roche Holding, a long-established core company.

Syntex was established in Mexico City in 1944 by two refugee scientists—a Hungarian and a German—in association with a chemist from Pennsylva-nia State University named Russell E. Marker, who had discovered a way to produce steroid hormones from the roots of a vine growing wild in Mexico. The company began selling extremely rare sex hormones in bulk to pharma-ceutical firms. At this time the major innovator in this new field of anabolic steroids (male hormones) was an old-line pharmaceutical firm, Searle.[6]

In the 1950s, under the leadership of George Rosenkranz, another Hun-garian, and Carl Djerassi, an American, embarked on the road from nexus to core. By 1956 these two innovating pioneers in the steroid field were ready to license Norethindrone, the basic compound from which the contraceptive pill would ultimately be produced. At the same time, the Ogdon Corpora-tion, a financial services firm, acquired the Mexico-based Syntex and sup-plied its initial funding.

Syntex then licensed Parke Davis to produce and market Norethindrone in the United States and Schering AG to do the same in Europe and the rest of the world. An innovative license agreement gave Syntex a percentage of the total earnings received and provided the essential cash flow needed for continuing research. Then, in 1959, Syntex signed an agreement with Eli Lilly that would pay half of certain research costs in exchange for Lilly's right to market the results of that research. The next year licenses similar to those granted earlier to Parke Davis and Schering were signed for a somewhat different product with Johnson & Johnson's subsidiary for the American market and with Ciba-Geigy abroad.

In 1960 Searle became the first to introduce an FDA-approved oral contraceptive. Early in 1962 Johnson & Johnson's subsidiary, Ortho Pharmaceuticals, debuted its Norethindrone-based pill; in 1964 Parke Davis and Syntex (with Eli Lilly) announced their FDA-approved products. Thus in the United States three of the first oral contraceptives that became available were developed by Syntex or manufactured from materials it produced.

In the meantime Syntex was establishing its own production and marketing capabilities by developing, manufacturing, and then selling in 1961 and 1962 two related corticoid drugs for small specialized markets: Andral for those chronically underweight, and Synalar, a skin anti-irritant. For the latter, a new sales force was recruited to call on the nation's three thousand dermatologists. In this way, Syntex developed the production and marketing capabilities it would need when it put forth its major birth control pill in 1964. The next year Syntex built the first of its laboratories at Stanford's industrial park in Palo Alto, soon followed by a growing complex of offices and laboratories. By 1965 Syntex had laid the foundation for an integrated core learning base in steroids and corticoids.

On this maturing learning base, Syntex developed Aarane, an antiasthma drug, and Naproxen, a new nonsteroidal anti-arthritic drug. At the same time, it entered related products for animal health and acquired a dental equipment company. By 1972 only 28 percent of its sales and 35 percent of its profits were still derived from oral contraceptives.

In 1976 Syntex introduced its follow-up anti-arthritic drug, Naprosyn, which quickly became one of the world's top-selling drugs, and Syntex's major profits source. But, despite sustained emphasis on research and the development of new compounds, Syntex was unable to bring forth another blockbuster on the scale of Naprosyn. As Gambardella points out, the company remained "really on the boundary between being a 'pure research' company and 'true manufacturer' with significant development and distribution assets." Even the joint venture with Procter & Gamble in 1988 to market Aleve, an OTC version of Naprosyn, failed to generate the financial resources required to compete in global markets. So, in 1994, Syntex accepted Roche Holding's offer of $5 billion to become the core of a subsidiary, Roche Bioscience, headquartered in Palo Alto.[7]

The revolutionary rDNA technology provided far greater opportunities for startups than did anabolic steroids. I begin the biotechnology story with Genentech and Chiron, which had developed into major biotechnology companies but, unlike Syntex, were able to complete their integrated learning bases only after they were acquired by Roche Holding and Ciba-Geigy, respectively. The learning bases of both Genentech and Chiron were formed at the University of California, San Francisco (UCSF), a major breeding ground for commercializing the new genetic and engineering technologies.

Genentech: Failure of Growth through Licensing

In 1976 Herbert Boyer, one of the discoverers of the rDNA technique and a member of the faculty at UCSF, and Robert Swanson, a venture capitalist with MIT degrees in chemistry and business, formed Genentech. As Swanson put it, in terms reminiscent of those of Landau in chemicals, "For Genentech, the strategy from the beginning was to be able to make and sell our own products. Therefore we needed not only to generate products but to manufacture them and build the marketing force to sell them."[8]

Genentech remained, however, a shell corporation until 1978, when after acquiring a small building and a staff of five, it signed in August and September its first research contracts. One was with Eli Lilly to develop a human insulin in E coli bacteria (Chapter 7). The other was with a Swedish firm, Kabi, to deliver a human growth hormone, hGH.[9]

These contracts defined the new company's basic strategic plan. The Lilly contract with 8 percent royalties would provide the cash flow from the exclusive right to manufacture and sell the resulting recombinant proteins. Through the Kabi contract, Genentech would produce and sell in the U.S. market, and Kabi would do the same in the rest of the world. The first would thus generate the cash flow required to commercialize the more complex hGH technology for a much smaller, specialized potential market than insulin.

As Genentech and its partners concentrated on the development of the human growth hormone, they continued to bring along and license new products, including interferon (alpha and beta), an anticancer drug for F. Hoffmann–La Roche, a vaccine for hoof-and-mouth disease for International Minerals and Chemicals, and a bovine growth hormone for Monsanto. Of these, the alpha interferon, which the Swiss company produced and marketed as Referon, was the most successful. By 1987 licenses for this drug and Lilly's insulin were producing annual revenues of $5 million apiece.

As the development of the human growth hormone advanced, Genentech's senior managers began manufacturing and marketing an hGH drug called Protropin that helped to prevent dwarfism in abnormal children. In 1985 the FDA approved the new drug, granting it orphan drug status. To meet the challenge of completing an integrated learning base, Genentech's board recruited G. Kirk Rabb, the experienced top manager from Abbott, to become CEO. The initial result was impressive, with sales rising from $90 million in 1985 to $401 million in 1989.

But the price of technical success remained high. In 1986 the company recorded a loss of $353 million. This figure contrasts with $11 million, the company's total income from 1978 through 1985. Moreover, in 1987 the FDA gave Eli Lilly orphan drug status for a comparable growth hormone that had been commercialized from its initial UCSF contract. Genentech sued the FDA, but without success. The FDA viewed Lilly's drug as superior and classified it as a new product.

Rabb then set his company's hopes on what he considered to be a revolutionary new drug, Activase, an aPA clot dissolver to treat heart attacks. Another orphan drug, it was to be priced at $2,200 a dose. Scheduled for introduction in 1986, the FDA held up approval for a year. Then, Wellcome instituted a patent suit, and SmithKline Beecham put forth a comparable drug at a much lower price. Meanwhile, Genentech's clinical tests had demonstrated that their product was no more effective than the lower-priced competitors. Rabb responded by increasing Genentech's advertising budget in 1989 by 360 percent. Nevertheless, the balance sheet for 1990 recorded a loss of $98 million.

By then, Rabb had decided that "nobody is going to make it alone."[10] He and his board decided to sell to F. Hoffmann-La Roche 60 percent of the company's equity for $2.1 billion, including $500 million in cash to help fund research and development on long-term products in Genentech's pipeline. The investment paid off, enabling Genentech to become a strong integrated pharmaceutical enterprise. The company produced a steady flow of protein products and accompanying profits. In 1993 came Actimrine, a specialized infection reducer, and in 1994 Prulmozyme, for cystic fibrosis. Also that year, Nutropin, a follow-up of Protropin, and others were in the clinical testing stage. By 1994 income as a percentage of sales was 15.6 percent, $124 million on $795 million sales. With the acquisition by Roche Holding, Genentech became part of one of the world's most successful pharmaceutical companies. The partnership between a startup and a core pharmaceutical enterprise set the pattern for similar relationships to follow.[11]

Chiron: Failure of Collaboration

For Chiron, establishing a relationship with a Swiss giant took longer. Chiron had emerged from the same incubator and in much the same manner as Genentech, but it devised a different strategy for growth. After Merck's researchers approached William Rutter, the head of the UCSF department, their joint work on the Merck contracts paved the way for development of a means of expressing a hepatitis B antigen in E coli bacteria. Soon thereafter, in 1981, Rutter and his colleagues founded Chiron in nearby Emeryville, California. Again, as with Genentech and Lilly, Merck carried out nearly all the postdiscovery development of Chiron's research, shepherding the product through the clinical trials and regulatory approval, and setting up the final manufacturing processes. By the time the FDA approved the first genetically engineered vaccine in 1986, Merck had acquired a substantial amount of its in-house learning base in the new biotechnology path.[12]

With the revenues from Merck and then from research contracts with Abbott and other core companies, Chiron in 1986 launched what its president, Edward Penhoet, termed the "Phase II of Chiron's life cycle." "That phase," he added, "includes a bigger role in the fruits of its research through manufacturing rights and in some cases marketing." The new "viable strategy" was defined as "collaboration." In 1986 came Biocine, a 50–50 joint venture with Ciba-Geigy, for the development, production, and marketing of rDNA vaccines. The Swiss company had already acquired a stake in Chiron at its initial public offering in 1982.

To expand its diagnostic line, Biocine undertook a joint venture with Johnson & Johnson's Ortho Diagnostics system to produce screening tests for hepatitis C and other variations of that virus. A comparable partnership followed with Johnson & Johnson's Ethicon unit, which was formed to produce an orphan drug for the treatment of burns. In the same month, Chiron established its first integrated subsidiary to use the wound-healing technology for an orphan drug employed postsurgically in corneal and other eye operations. This in-house research venture was funded through a $5.5 million R&D limited partnership. In addition to these manufacturing and marketing projects, the company held research contracts for anti-blood-clotting products with Novo Nordisk, a Danish firm, and industrial enzymes with a European food and cosmetic company.

By 1989 Chiron possessed a worldwide reputation as a research leader in the development of new genetically engineered products. The problem was that in no year since its founding had it turned a profit. That spring, in need of more operating cash, Chiron sold 8 percent of its shares to Ciba-Geigy and raised $52 million through an equity offering. Finally, in 1990, it posted its first profit of $6.8 million. The following year Chiron acquired Cetus, a major rival and neighbor in Emeryville. It did so after the FDA had refused to approve Cetus's Interleukin-2 for kidney cancer, even though the drug was being marketed in Europe. That acquisition helped to account for a loss of $425 million in 1991. Then the FDA approved Cetus's Proleukin in 1992 and Chiron's Betaseron for multiple sclerosis (licensed to Germany's Schering for the European market). As one of the most successful of the rDNA innovators in 1994, Chiron posted a net income of $32 million.

By the mid-1990s the lesson was clear: the strategy of collaboration would not work for Chiron. If the company wanted to maintain profits from its innovations, if it was to have funds critical to ensuring the flow of products in the pipelines, it could no longer remain a research company relying on collaboration with core companies to produce and sell its discoveries. So, in the fall of 1994, Ciba-Geigy, Chiron's partner in Biocine and an important shareholder, agreed to take a 49.9 percent stake in Chiron, with the option of increasing it to 55 percent after five years. As *Chemical Engineering News* reported, "The deal, completed early in 1995, should expand Chiron's access to a global regulatory, marketing, and manufacturing infrastructure as well as providing $250 million in R&D funding from Ciba-Geigy over five years."[13] This analysis proved correct. Total revenues in 1996 were $1.6 billion and net income was $55 million, making Chiron the second-largest revenue producer in the new molecular-based integrated enterprises and third in income, with Genentech as second. In both, Amgen was first and Genzyme fourth.

All three companies considered so far—Syntex, Genentech, and Chiron—

had by 1996 been absorbed into the Swiss pharmaceutical giants Roche Holding and Novartis.

Amgen and Genzyme: Making It on Their Own

Whereas Chiron and Genentech had to be saved by the Swiss leaders, Amgen and Genzyme made it on their own. They did so by following two very different routes. Even so, they succeeded only through the commercializing of high-priced orphan drugs for a select number of customers. Both succeeded by maintaining control of their licenses.

AMGEN: SUCCESS THROUGH JOINT VENTURES AND LICENSING   Amgen was established near Los Angeles in 1980 by venture capitalists and a group of biologists with connections to UCLA for an initial investment of $50,000. They selected as its CEO George B. Rathmann, who like Genentech's Rabb, had been a senior executive at Abbott. Rathmann in turn hired Gordon Binder, an executive at Ford who had been a Baker Scholar at Harvard Business School, as chief financial officer. Meanwhile, Dr. Fu-Kuen Lin, a Taiwanese scientist, had fortuitously joined the company. Amgen's beginning was precarious—at one point in 1982 it had left only six months' worth of its initial venture capital financing—but with this team at the top it would become the new industry's most successful enterprise.

By 1985 Lin and his colleagues had five genetically engineered drugs undergoing human testing. The most promising were two products: erythropoieten (EPO), and a related protein, granulocyte colony-stimulating factor (G-CSF). The first was designed to fight anemia; the second to offset the effects of radiation and chemotherapy in patients treated for cancer.[14] Amgen began clinical trials for FDA approval of EPO in 1985.

To profit from these discoveries, Rathmann and Binder implemented an impressive strategy. In 1984 Amgen formed a $12 million joint venture with a leading Japanese company, Kirin Brewery (which had attempted to enter pharmaceuticals through its capabilities in fermentation), to develop and market EPO in the United States, Europe, and Japan. Amgen then licensed Johnson & Johnson's Ortho Pharmaceutical division to market EPO (branded as Epogen) in the United States for anemia not related to dialysis, and in Europe for all its other uses. To take advantage of the small number of doctors treating dialysis patients and an orphan drug status, Amgen retained the rights to the U.S. market for the use of EPO for kidney patients whose

lives depended on kidney dialysis devices. For this market, the company began building its manufacturing facilities even before it received FDA approval in 1989. Finally, after eight years, Amgen was manufacturing and
marketing its first product. By then, Binder had succeeded Rathmann as
CEO. Called "the quintessential financial whiz," by *Business Week*, Binder
"kept researchers in funds and investors calm during the period it took to get
its first product to market."[15]

By then, however, Genetics Institute had commercialized a comparable
drug and Amgen had brought suit for patent infringement. Genetics Institute responded with a countersuit. Johnson & Johnson also instituted legal
action for what it deemed a violation of their licensing agreement. The
Johnson & Johnson case was eventually settled by an arbitrator. In the other
case, in March 1991 a federal judge ordered Amgen and Genetics Institute to
exchange royalty-free licenses. Both appealed the ruling, and the federal
district court determined that Amgen had discovered and patented the product and so received the orphan drug status. It was then that American Home
Products acquired Genetics Institute (see Chapter 8). As Binder wrote, "we
won an essential legal victory which prevented a copy-cat company from
marketing a patent-infringing knock-off of our product."[16]

In the meantime Amgen had begun to commercialize Neupogen, a G-CSF
orphan drug, which produces disease-fighting white cells to help patients
undergoing chemotherapy. Amgen retained marketing rights for Neupogen
in the United States, Canada, and Australia. Kirin Brewery held the rights to
manufacture and sell the product in Japan and then in China; arrangements
were made with F. Hoffmann–La Roche in 1988 to market (but not manufacture) the drug throughout most of Europe.

In 1992 Binder recruited Kevin Sharer, a senior executive at MCI, as president and chief operating officer to help build broader capabilities and a
stronger organization. With a fully integrated learning base, Amgen entered
a related product line in 1994 with the acquisition of Synergen, a pioneer in
the development of treatment for sepsis (blood poisoning). Synergen, like
others, had erred by building its marketing and production facilities before
the clinical tests had shown that its product, Antril, was inadequate. It was
forced to sell out at a bargain price.

By 1992 Amgen was the first biopharmaceutical firm to show sales of a
billion dollars. Its revenues in 1996 reached $2.4 billion. By then, thanks to
Binder, Amgen had definitely "made it," by becoming a financially successful integrated core pharmaceutical enterprise. It accomplished this by build-

ing an integrated learning base through the commercialization of orphan drugs, with Epogen and Neupogen accounting for nearly 90 percent of its sales. Amgen also followed plans to diversify its product line by developing Kineret, a new treatment for rheumatoid arthritis. In 2002 Amgen acquired Immunex, adding capabilities and products in oncology and anti-inflammatories; the transaction was valued at $16 billion.

GENZYME: BUILDING THE INTEGRATED LEARNING BASE FOR ORPHAN DRUGS   By the mid-1990s Genzyme had also succeeded, although its revenue and profit record was less impressive than Amgen's. It followed a very different plan for growth, one that its manager termed an "orphan drug strategy." Its initial revenues derived almost from the start from the sale of its own products rather than from licensing them to others. Established in 1981 in Boston, the company initially built its learning base only after Henri Termeer, an executive vice president at Baxter Travenol, a leading producer of medical and hospital equipment, became its CEO. In 1983, after recruiting its first salaried managers and raising the initial funds, Termeer started by producing products that were relatively easy to make and sell. Genzyme first marketed an enzyme that was an active agent in cholesterol tests. It next turned to building the testing devices themselves, then launched production in a small unit in Cambridge, Massachusetts of the hyaluronic acid used in these devices, and finally entered the production of genetically engineered hyaluronic-based drugs. At each step along the way, Genzyme manufactured and marketed its own product.[17]

In 1988 Termeer took the last step in completing Genzyme's learning base. That year, the company acquired Integrated Genetics (IG) in nearby Framingham, a producer of diagnostics and diagnostic testing products that according to one report "possessed superior technology." Termeer raised over $80 million through public offerings and innovative research partnerships, and began commercializing the most promising orphan drug of Genzyme's hyaluronic acid–based drugs, Ceredase. This drug, the first effective treatment for a hitherto incurable genetic disorder, was the most expensive drug ever marketed, averaging $150,000 a year per patient. It received FDA approval as an orphan drug in 1991.

That year, Genzyme established its factory and headquarters on the Boston side of the Charles River, near Harvard University. The next year it expanded its diagnostic business by going overseas with the acquisition of Gencor International. At home it continued with the commercializing four more orphan drugs, two for cystic fibrosis, one for cancer, and the other for severe burns, as well as bringing on-stream a follow-up to Ceredase, called Cerezym, which received FDA approval in 1994.[18]

During these same years, when the biotechnology industry was going through a full-scale shakeout, Termeer acquired several small companies at home and abroad. Some added to his existing diagnostic and testing line. Others operated in new fields such as human tissue repair and "pharming," that is, the use of genetically altered animals to produce a variety of new products. By 1995 Genzyme had developed into a full-fledged biotechnology core company, primarily by commercializing increasingly advanced products on the basis of knowledge and profits gained from previous ones.

Leading Startups Rescued by Major Core Companies

The four other companies based on molecular genetics and rDNA technology with revenues of $100 million in the earlier years of the 1990s—Genetics Institute, Centocor, Immunex, and Biogen—were either bailed out or funded by core companies as they struggled to build integrated learning bases.

Genetics Institute: Losing a Patent Suit and Its Independence

Started in 1980 in Cambridge, Massachusetts by two Harvard molecular biologists at the suggestion of Harvard's president, Derek Bok, and amply financed with $6 million from wealthy New York financiers, Genetics Institute built its initial learning base in much the same way as Amgen, developing both EPO and GM-CSF products (a competitor to Amgen's G-CSF). Like Amgen, it worked with a Japanese company, Chugai, to develop and market in Asia and then licensed its technology to Sandoz in Europe and Baxter Travenol in the United States. In 1984, again like Amgen, Genetics Institute began to process an EPO orphan drug for kidney dialysis patients. But unlike Amgen and Genzyme, its board failed to engage experienced management to continue building its essential integrated learning base.[19]

An initial public offering in 1986 generated the funds to construct a manufacturing plant. That year, Genetics Institute announced the development of Interleukin-3, a drug to speed up blood-cell production in patients undergoing cancer treatments. Meanwhile, its first product, EPO, provoked a patent suit from Amgen, the GM-CSF product prompted a suit from

Genentech, and the third product with Baxter International. In March 1989 Genentech agreed to a cross-licensing agreement but the suit continued through the courts. As noted earlier, American Home Products was apparently waiting to acquire the loser of that case, which it did. The acquisition ensured Genetics Institute the necessary funding. It quickly expanded its European and Japanese activities involving its EPO and GM-CSF products that competed with Wellcome's comparable one. After settling the Baxter suit in 1993, its Factor VIII, approved by the FDA in 1992 and licensed in several countries, became profitable.

Centocor: Saved by Eli Lilly

Centocor was formed in 1979 near Philadelphia by a group of scientists and entrepreneurs headed by Michael Wall. An MIT graduate in electrical engineering, Wall had worked for several electronics startups before founding his biomedical research company. Centocor's learning base evolved in much the same manner as Genzyme's. A pioneer in monoclonal antibodies used in test kits to detect ovarian cancer cells, Centocor soon began to create the diagnostic tests that could be processed by analyzers owned by core and other companies. Those for ovarian cancer were followed by others for gastrointestinal and other cancers, and then for heart attacks and blood clots. As the product line expanded, Centocor established several manufacturing facilities, including one in the Netherlands.[20]

By the late 1980s Centocor was poised to achieve its goal of becoming a "full-fledged pharmaceutical company" on the basis of a drug it had been perfecting since 1982, Centoxin. That drug, designed to treat sepsis, possessed an estimated market potential worldwide of from $1 billion to $1.5 billion. In 1990, Centocor raised "a hundred million dollars through stock offerings and selling investment interests . . . to begin building a large-scale sales network and manufacturing facilities." Then, in April 1992, came the decision "that Centocor's data for Centoxin didn't demonstrate the drug's effectiveness." Eli Lilly stepped in to provide $50 million in return for 5 percent of the stock and the marketing rights to Centoxin (with Centocor receiving half the profits) and the marketing rights to another product, Reo Pro, if Centoxin was not approved. Eli Lilly's intervention "came just in time to save Centocor from collapse." Since then, it has relied on Lilly's marketing and distribution (Reo Pro's sales were $254 million in 1997) as a producer of diagnostic products and tests, and has become a research specialist in peptide products.

Immunex: Supported by American Cyanamid, Then by American Home Products

Immunex differs from the other biotechnology companies just reviewed in that it was started by a hard-driving entrepreneur with little experience in the drug or medical care business. Steve Duzan formed Immunex in Seattle in 1981, after recruiting an experienced immunologist and a Ph.D. in biotechnology. The company focused increasingly on the potential of G-CSF and succeeded in developing an orphan drug, Leukine, for a market similar to Amgen's Neupogen. Only after receiving FDA approval of Leukine in 1991 did Immunex begin to form a sales force. As Duzan told the press, "In this business you've got to become a marketing organization. Because it is the only way you can get enough cash flow to sustain your research."[21]

But it was too late, since Amgen was already there, and Leukine's limited efficacy was no match for Neupogen. For the distribution of its product, Duzan led a sales force of only fifty. By 1993 Amgen's Neupogen showed sales of $290 million and Immunex's Leukine of $23 million. In June 1993 American Cyanamid acquired the controlling share (53.5 percent) of Immunex, merging it with its Lederle oncology unit. With this backing, Immunex became a viable competitor. In 1994, after American Home Products acquired American Cyanamid, Immunex benefited from access to new sales channels. In 1998 Immunex introduced ENBREL, an arthritis remedy, which became a bestseller.[22]

Biogen: Failure Followed by Success

The Biogen story is one of high hopes dashed by crushing reality followed by realistic responses. The company was established in 1978 by Harvard's Walter Gilbert, winner of the Nobel prize in 1980 for his exploratory work in the rDNA field. Biogen survived in its early years on the basis of royalty income from licensing its work on immune-system proteins called "interferons." Merck and SmithKline licensed the technology to commercialize hepatitis B vaccines, Abbott for developing hepatitis B diagnostics, and Eli Lilly for human insulin. In addition, Schering-Plough's investment of $8 million enabled Biogen its initial entry into molecular genetic engineering and permitted it to become a leader in alpha interferon products. In Biogen's promising early years, Gilbert enthusiastically expanded its research facilities in Cambridge and set up laboratories and offices in Switzerland, Belgium, and Germany. But quickly cash flow shortages set in, becoming an overpowering reality by 1985. By then, Gilbert, to remain solvent, had sold 90 percent of Biogen's patents.[23]

Later that year a distressed board replaced Gilbert with James L. Vincent, the seasoned executive from Abbott, who had built that firm's initial learning base in rDNA diagnostics. Vincent quickly sold its Swiss facilities to Glaxo, those in Belgium to Roche, and shut down the Zurich laboratory and other activities in Germany. He then spent the latter half of 1986 and all of 1987 renegotiating Gilbert's patent agreements. New royalties soon began to provide revenue flows rising from $1.7 million in 1986 to $150 million in 1996. "In the first half of 1988, I could finally see we were going to survive financially," Vincent noted. "That's when I started to build the management team to have an operating company."[24]

The completed manufacturing and marketing organization permitted Vincent to achieve the goal of commercializing two promising drugs—Hirulog, for the prevention of blood clotting in heart patients, with potential of sales of $1 billion, and a beta interferon molecule for treating hepatitis. However, when in 1994 the clinical trials demonstrated that Hirulog was no more effective than the drug it was to replace, Vincent and his handpicked successor James Tobin, formerly president and chief operating officer of Baxter International, sold that product off and turned to beta interferon, which Biogen's scientists had discovered possessed greater potential as an orphan drug used to treat multiple sclerosis. Introduced as Avonex, the drug competed with Betaseron, the beta interferon product that Chiron had acquired with the acquisition of Cetus and then licensed to Germany's Schering AG. Schering immediately sued the FDA for violation of the orphan drug status it had obtained for Betaseron. Nevertheless, in May 1996 the FDA approved Avonex on the grounds that it was a superior product. By then Biogen had built a $60 million production plant and hired a senior executive from Britain's Zeneca to assemble a sales force. By the end of 1997 Biogen's Avonex reached twenty-five thousand patients and its rival Betaseron twenty thousand, even though the drug cost the patient $8,500 per year.

After nearly two decades, Biogen finally achieved its goal of becoming a profitable integrated enterprise. But, as its senior managers realized, its cash flow was still insufficient to fund new-product development. So in late 1997 the company arranged with Merck to develop an anti-asthma drug. Biogen retained the marketing rights for products with orphan drug status, such as those treating inflammatory bowel disease and renal failure. Merck provided $145 million (an amount close to Biogen's total revenues in 1994) in return for the rights to commercialize and market the anti-asthma and other potential products for larger markets. As Vincent pointed out, its strategy now called for "six 50- to 75-person field forces aimed at six big dollar, small-target populations."[25]

The New Nexus

Biogen's segmentation of the market defined the competitive relationships between the integrated biotechnology startups and the long-established core companies at the close of the twentieth century. The new companies would commercialize drugs for high-priced, small-population markets, while the established ones produced drugs for the major markets. By the late 1990s the most successful of the new startups were beginning to move beyond orphan drugs. Genentech, Chiron, Amgen, Genzyme, Immunex, and Biogen had all established viable integrated learning bases, with Immunex and Genetics Institute on their way. But, in so doing, four of these companies (Genentech, Chiron, Immunex, and Genetics Institute) had ceded their independence. By 1994 the major core companies of Eli Lilly, Merck, Schering-Plough, Johnson & Johnson, SmithKline Beecham, F. Hoffmann–La Roche, and Ciba-Geigy had developed functional learning bases in the new biotechnology path that enabled them to obtain the FDA approval required for the U.S. market.[26] In addition to acquiring some biotech startups, the core companies also licensed technology and/or formed joint ventures with other startups.

In this manner, the infrastructure of the coming twenty-first century medical revolution was beginning to take shape in the new startups and the century-old core companies. The startups concentrated strategically on the initial stages of commercializing the products of new technologies by focusing on high-priced drugs for highly specialized markets and on so-called platform technologies. The core companies, meanwhile, focused on drugs for the mass markets, while also collaborating with the startups to carry the specialized drugs from development (including FDA approval) through production and marketing (including advertising).

Physical location also helped the successful startups to attain their goals. Close ties to leading research universities enhanced the startups' technical capabilities. Of the eight largest revenue-producing biopharmaceutical companies in 1994, three—Genentech, Chiron, and to a lesser extent, Amgen—were created with and continued to be nurtured by ties with the University of California. So too, the technical capabilities of three others—Biogen, Genetics Institute, and Genzyme—were nourished in the Harvard–MIT environment. The other two, based in Seattle and Philadelphia, respectively, failed in their attempts to move out of the nexus, in part because local universities had not played pioneering roles in commercializing the new technologies.

An awareness of the difficulties that specialized research firms faced in their efforts to move out of the nexus and commercialize the new technology helps to clarify the role of the nexus in knowledge-based industries. Molecular genetics and the rDNA techniques called for new personnel, materials, and new knowledge in a way similar to biochemistry and enzymology in the 1970s and the new polymer/petrochemical techniques in chemicals a generation earlier. In the earlier cases, the existing companies primarily met the new needs by adding new personnel and laboratories. Thus research companies like Sigma-Aldrich, one of the earliest (established in 1945), and Cetus, one of the latest (formed in 1971), and the specialized engineering firms in chemicals could meet the necessary demands. In chemicals, in much the same manner, the broader network sustained the petroleum companies as they became participants in the polymer/petrochemical revolution.

The new rDNA technology required another new set of scientists, materials, and services that the existing nexus firms could not supply. The core companies had to look elsewhere—to the startups. As Orsenigo reports, in 1985, 80 percent of the publicly held new startups were supplying materials for the new biotechnology industry.[27] The coming of the rDNA technology, unlike that of the earlier technological discontinuities, opened with a burst of new companies. That burst ensured a new level of competition among the enterprises in the supporting network, competition that would bring lower prices, limited profits, and shorter corporate lives for the producers of the essential supplies and services. Their revenues from royalties were rarely enough to generate the cash flow necessary to create an integrated learning base—hence the importance of the orphan drug legislation.

Conclusion: Strategic Success and Failure in Commercializing the New Technology

This chapter provides a case study of the creation of a new path of learning based on the coming of a new scientific discipline—molecular genetics. It also provides a unique example of building a high-technology industry before the competitive barriers to entry were created, strategic boundaries were defined, and the process of growth began. That is, a new nexus had to be created to provide new products, equipment, and research techniques and services, as well as newly trained research scientists and their assistants. At the outset, only the century-old core pharmaceutical companies possessed the product development, production, and marketing capabilities necessary to commercialize products on a global scale. Thus Merck and Eli Lilly sponsored research at the University of California and at Harvard that yielded the first commercial biotechnology products. Researchers at those universities then launched their own startups, with Genentech, Chiron, and Biogen the first of these.

As the nexus expanded, the strategic goal of the new startups, as a Genentech founder proclaimed, was to manufacture and sell the products the company invented—that is, to create an integrated learning base in proteins. In pursuing this goal, the startups defined strategies to generate the income necessary to fund the building of the company's manufacturing and marketing facilities. One strategy was to license their successful innovative products, much as Syntex had done in the 1950s and 1960s. Here Chiron's "collaborative" strategy is a good example. The other approach was to start with a new nexus product and build on the income and learning in that process to commercialize an increasingly complex line of products, a strategy that Genzyme perfected during the 1980s and early 1990s.

Genzyme's success emphasizes the significance of the Orphan Drug Act (1983), which provided a seven-year monopoly to makers of new life-saving drugs for a market under two hundred thousand users. Those seven years provided the critical time needed for a startup to create its integrated learning base so essential if their products were to reach national and international markets.

The legislation, in turn, was a major factor that led to the U.S. dominance in the creation of the infrastructure of the biotechnology revolution. By the mid-1990s the American companies, including those acquired by the Swiss companies, were in some cases beginning to create barriers to entry to ensure their continuing competitive strength as the biotechnology revolution continues and commercialization of genomics research begins.

PART IV

Paths of Learning

CHAPTER 11

The Three Revolutions: Industrial, Information, and Biotechnology

This volume and its companion, *Inventing the Electronic Century: The Epic Story of the Consumer Electronics and Computer Industries,* focus on three revolutions that have transformed life and work on this planet during the past century and a half: the Industrial, the Information, and the Biotechnology Revolutions. *Inventing the Electronic Century* deals with the second of these revolutions; the present volume reviews the first and the beginning of the third. In this chapter, I compare and contrast the histories of all three revolutions and offer some summary observations and conclusions.

Common Characteristics of the Three Revolutions

What then are the common underlying characteristics involved in creating the infrastructure of the three revolutions?

The first common characteristic is that the products of the new learning, based on the new science, were commercialized—brought into public use—by private, profit-seeking enterprises. Private and public universities and research institutions played critical roles in creating the broader technical knowledge, but they did not transform it into new products for everyday use. Such products only came into being after for-profit enterprises had built the learning bases that integrated their technical knowledge with their product development, production, marketing, and distribution capabilities. These enterprises clearly benefited from maintaining close ties to sources of learning. They also benefited from government crash programs during international crises and certain public policies—for example, the Orphan Drug Act—in quieter times.

The second common characteristic is that these for-profit enterprises were geographically concentrated in the United States, northwestern Europe, and Japan. These areas clearly provided the most fertile environment for commercializing the new products because they were close to sources of raw material and energy, as well as to rich sources of learning in universities and research institutes. Then, even within these regions, the activities of the pro-profit enterprises clustered in a very few specific areas, a tiny sample of possible global industrial locations.

The most successful of Europe's chemical and pharmaceutical industries are still concentrated in the Rhine Valley. In the United States, the early headquarters of the core chemical companies resided in a broader region from the Atlantic Ocean to the Mississippi River, north of the Mason-Dixon Line and south of the Erie Canal, and then expanded to include California and Texas and neighboring states after the oil companies began to commercialize petrochemicals. The smaller specialty chemical companies have been more highly concentrated within what the historians term the "old Northwest"—the area bounded by the Ohio River on the south, the Mississippi River on the west, and the Great Lakes on the north. The American pharmaceutical industry today is largely situated in the Northeast—that is, New York City and eastern New Jersey and Pennsylvania (only three of the companies listed in Table 1.2—Abbott, Eli Lilly, and Upjohn—were located in the old Northwest), while the emergence of the new biotechnology infrastructure has occurred primarily in California and Massachusetts. Similar geographic clustering marked the creation of the infrastructure of the Information Revolution, occurring in New York, Boston's Route 128, Silicon Valley, Houston, and Seattle in the United States, and in the Tokyo-Osaka industrial region in Japan.

The third characteristic common to the three revolutions is that the for-profit enterprises that succeeded over the long term in commercializing products from the underlying technologies followed definite paths of learning. These paths were initially defined as the first movers and their close followers created barriers to entry by building their integrated learning bases—the set of coordinated technical, functional, and managerial capabilities—that enabled them to develop, produce, distribute, and sell first in national and soon after in world markets.

These enterprises then reinvested and grew by expanding their original integrated learning bases and by diversifying into related technologies and markets. A supporting nexus of suppliers of critical products and services emerged to assist them and thus formed the infrastructures of the respective high-technology industries. By the end of the 1920s the infrastructures of both the chemical and pharmaceutical industries were essentially complete. By contrast, the infrastructures of the audio, video, and information technology industries were primarily shaped during the second half of the twentieth century. The infrastructure of the biotechnology industry began to emerge in the 1970s and is still taking shape today.

Once the infrastructures were completed, new entrants have been extremely rare. Only two of the top fifty chemical companies and none of the top thirty pharmaceutical companies listed in Tables 1.1 and 1.2 were established after the 1920s. The two chemical companies that entered thereafter—Dow Corning and Air Products, both in the 1940s—were truly exceptions, formed to exploit new technologies amid the extraordinary conditions of World War II.

Strategy and Structure, Economies of Scale and Scope

The critical first step in the unfolding paths of learning worldwide was the formation of powerful barriers to entry. The core companies in the respective high-tech industries achieved this by devising a business strategy and a supporting management structure that enabled them to commercialize new products based on the new learning in science and engineering. The virtuous strategy entailed investing the earnings and learning from one successful product commercialization to the commercialization of another related product or by making acquisitions to accomplish the same thing. Together with the multidivisional structure, the virtuous strategy permitted the maximum exploitation of economies of scale and scope, and hence the establishment of formidable barriers to entry.

A critical aspect of the virtuous strategy is the continuing commercialization of related products through internal development and acquisitions—as distinct from attempting growth through unrelated diversification. Richard Whittington and Michael Mayer in *The European Corporation: Strategy, Structure and Social Science* provide useful definitions of these strategies. A company pursuing related diversification operates multiple businesses, with "no business as large as 70 percent of turnover [sales], but market and technological relations between the different businesses." A multibusiness company with a strategy of unrelated diversification, in contrast, operates with no business accounting for more than 70 percent of turnover but with no linking or market and technological relationship between them.[1] By the 1960s enterprises using this strategy of growth were known as "conglomerates."

The multidivisional structure adopted to support related diversification enabled governance of multiple integrated learning bases. The division managers were responsible for the financial and operational performance, and for their units' overall success and failure. Corporate headquarters consisted of the senior executives who evaluated performance of the individual divisions and planned and readjusted the overall broad strategy of their companies on the basis of these evaluations. In addition, headquarters included a corporate staff that provided a broad range of services, including basic research and product development, for the divisions and the company as a whole.

The companies using the virtuous strategy and multidivisional structure created powerful barriers to entry by lowering unit costs and benefiting from economies of scale and scope. As noted in Chapter 1, economies of scale reflect the speed and volume of a product's commercialization through an integrated learning base. Economies of scale were particularly important in process industries such as chemicals. There, for example, the accepted standard rule was that unit costs dropped by a ratio of 40–60 percent until the plant capacity reached a minimum efficient scale. Moreover, in this process industry involving constant mixing of a variety of chemicals at different speeds and temperatures and under different pressures, the ability to control the flow of throughput in the plant (a process that was greatly enhanced with the coming of computers) also lowered unit costs.

Again, as noted in Chapter 1, economies of scope or joint cost result from the use of the same materials, equipment, personnel, and knowledge as are employed in research and development, production, marketing, and distribution of products for more than one market. And again, these economies proved extremely significant in the chemical industry. The huge expense of production facilities meant that producers capable of using them to make more than one product line would enjoy important cost advantages.

Both increasing scale and scope, then, constitute powerful competitive weapons. In addition, an increase in throughput also further maximizes the cost advantages of scope. As Paul Nightingale has pointed out, these unit cost advantages resulted not only from the "static economies of scale and scope in production" but also "the dynamic economies of scale and scope in knowledge." In high-technology industries, these dynamic economies based on new learning in chemicals and pharmaceuticals again were particularly significant.[2]

As the basic infrastructure of the two industries was being completed in the 1920s, the core chemical and pharmaceutical companies benefited more from the dynamic economies of scale and scope in knowledge than the static ones of production. This remained true again in the 1940s and 1950s during the contemporaneous polymer/petrochemical and therapeutic revolutions, and again with the coming of the new learning in biotechnology during and after the 1970s. Moreover, even when the commercializing of new learning receded in importance, the economies of scale and scope became reasons for lowering costs through merger by consolidating facilities and achieving administrative efficiencies.

These same concepts explain the failure of conglomerate organizations, including some of the leading chemical and pharmaceutical companies that pursued strategies of unrelated diversification in the second half of the twentieth century. The conglomerates were unable to benefit from economies of scope and to some extent the related economies of scale. They also failed to benefit from dynamic economies of scale and scope in learning. Indeed, the headquarters of a conglomerate did not require a large corporate staff to assist in the integrating of the joint costs and to capture and transfer learning. Such headquarters consisted of a small number of senior executives and a financial and legal staff. As a result, a form of governance employed in conglomerates became known as "management by the numbers."

As Whittington and Mayer point out, conglomerate building worked only in the short term, "as a potentially rapid way to riches. There are good prospects of milking profits for a decade or so. After that, however, the conglomerates tend to hit a brick wall, entering a period of either decline, takeover, or break-up."[3] Certainly, one of the basic lessons of history in American business during the past half century is that unrelated diversification in the form of conglomerates failed in commercializing new products and, except in the short term, failed financially. I examine a most striking example of the destructive nature of the conglomerate in *Inventing the Electronic Century,* the companion volume to the present work, where the decisions of the senior executives at the Radio Corporation of America (RCA) to adopt a strategy of unrelated diversification not only destroyed their company but also the consumer electronics industry of the United States.

Chapter 2 presented a straightforward chronological account of the evolution of the fifty largest chemical and the thirty largest pharmaceutical companies as they competed in national and world markets. In this concluding chapter, I analyze their evolving paths of learning as they were shaped by the basic themes of this book: first, the creation of barriers to entry, given the interrelatedness of technologies and markets; second, the ways they defined and redefined their strategic boundaries; and third, how they responded to limits to growth. To understand the nature of the last, recall my definition of high-technology industries in Chapter 1: in these industries growth is based on the commercializing of new learning in science and engineering—in this book, in chemistry, biology, and related sciences. This new learning provided the basis for commercializing a number of related products for different markets.

Chapters 3–6 reviewed the evolution of the chemical industries, and Chapters 7–10 those in pharmaceuticals. The evolution of the chemical and pharmaceutical industries is remarkable for two reasons. First, the industries initially appeared after the 1880s when the coming of the railroad, the steamship, the telephone, and the telegraph made possible mass production and mass distribution to national and international markets (historians terms the post–1880s period the Second Industrial Revolution). A small number of large enterprises quickly dominated world markets. Second, the evolution of the chemical and pharmaceutical industries shifted after the 1960s when chemistry no longer provided the basis for new learnings to be commercialized into new products, whereas biology did so in spades, reshaping existing disciplines, adding new ones, and in the 1980s ushering in a whole new science—molecular biology and genetic engineering.

Evolving Paths of Learning in the Chemical Industry

Building Barriers to Entry

The European chemical producers established during the last two decades of the nineteenth century quickly created powerful barriers to entry in national and international markets by commercializing a broad set of new technologies based on organic, and to a lesser extent, inorganic chemistry. The first movers—Bayer, Hoechst, and BASF in Germany and their Swiss rivals—dominated European and international markets in both the new chemical and pharmaceutical industries well before the coming of World War I.

The withdrawal of these barriers to entry during the decade after 1914 ensured the initial growth of the modern chemical industry in the United

States. During the 1920s, five of the six American core chemical companies created integrated learning bases through direct investment, primarily resting on German technologies developed in organic and inorganic chemistry. The exception was Allied Chemical, which established its integrated learning base by acquisitions and mergers. A supplier of existing basic chemicals, Allied did not invest in R&D.

By the end of the 1920s, the five had successfully commercialized products in five to seven of the SIC industrial chemical categories. During the same decade of the 1920s, most of the smaller focused (specialty) companies had been established. They not only provided essential chemicals to the major American companies but also for customers in a wide variety of other industries. By the end of the 1920s, the infrastructure of the U.S. chemical industry had been completed.

Defining Strategic Boundaries

In defining their strategic boundaries, both core and niche companies operated within the industry's competitive arena, focusing on their initial product lines until the second major period of the chemical industry's growth—the polymer/petrochemical revolution of the 1940s and 1950s. This resulted from the unanticipated massive demand created by World War II for high-octane aviation gasoline, supplemented by a smaller but nevertheless sizable call for synthetic rubber. In 1935 Du Pont launched the initial commercializing of polymer-based end-products—nylon and neoprene. That same year Shell Oil, Jersey Standard (Exxon), and Phillips, the pioneers during the 1920s in commercializing petrochemicals, began experimenting in polymerizing petroleum feed stocks and intermediates to produce high-octane gasoline. The commercializing of that process began shortly before the Japanese attack on Pearl Harbor.

After the war the oil companies followed the example of their industry's leading enterprise, Jersey Standard, and began to redefine their strategic boundaries to include fabrics, specialized plastics, fertilizers, and other businesses. By the 1970s these petrochemical enterprises realized that the barriers to entry created by the long-established chemical companies were too high to overcome. So they retreated and instead concentrated on feedstocks, intermediates, and commodity polymers. The oil companies that successfully redefined their boundaries received a quarter of their revenues from petrochemicals.

By the 1960s and into the 1970s Du Pont's profit margin was twice that of its competitors. At the same time Dow, by redefining its strategic boundaries to expand into petrochemicals, was conquering the world market in intermediates and basic polymers. Monsanto and American Cyanamid had successfully defined their strategic boundaries, based in both polymers and petrochemicals, but operated on a smaller scale. Union Carbide, on the other hand, as it fell behind Du Pont and Dow, dramatically redefined its strategic boundaries by pursuing unrelated diversification. It quickly paid the price of moving into markets in which its learned capabilities provided almost no competitive advantages.

Encountering Limits to Growth

During the 1970s the major chemical companies abruptly began to redefine their strategic boundaries again. The shift reflected recognition that the chemical industry had reached its limits to growth. Chemical science and engineering were no longer generating new learning needed to commercialize a continuing stream of new products. As a result, with Du Pont leading the way, development superseded research—D over R. New products continued to be introduced, but they were developed from the basic technologies of the 1920s and the 1950s and 1960s. After the second oil crisis and a double-dip recession in the early 1980s, the major American chemical companies began redrawing their strategic boundaries to strengthen their existing integrated learning bases. As a result, the American industry shifted during the 1980s into producing specialty chemicals, the domain of the focused companies from their start in the 1920s.

At the same time, the surviving chemical majors began to explore the biological sciences as a source of new learning and continuing growth. But none succeeded. Dow and Du Pont invested in pharmaceuticals but eventually retreated. American Cyanimid and Monsanto achieved their goal of shifting to pharmaceuticals only to be acquired by major pharmaceutical companies, American Home Products and Pharmacia, respectively.

As the American companies focused on specialty chemicals, their European counterparts—primarily the Rhine Valley companies—continued to serve multiple major markets. Following World War I, the German Big Three quickly returned to world markets under the leadership of I. G. Farben, as did the Swiss with their comparable Basel AG. Neither the British nor the French responses of the 1920s—the formation of Imperial Chemical Industries (ICI) and the merger of Rhône and Poulenc—proved able to surmount the quickly restructured barriers.

The pattern of World War I held again during the decade of the 1940s and 1950s, but in a way more challenging for the Europeans because during the World War II years the American companies had fashioned the polymer/petrochemical revolution. By the 1960s and 1970s, however, all of the Rhine Valley companies had returned to the American market. Of these, Hoechst and Bayer proved most successful in reclaiming their positions in fibers and industrial chemicals, while Bayer focused on pharmaceuticals and photographic equipment. In the late 1980s the leaders of Hoechst recognized limits to growth in chemicals and thus began to transform the company into a pharmaceutical enterprise. The eventual result was the formation of Aventis in 1999.

The Swiss, by forming Basel AG, continued to compete with the Germans in high-end chemical products during the interwar years. After World War II, Basel AG was disassembled, although Ciba and Geigy later merged. Facing limits to growth in the 1980s, Ciba-Geigy focused on commercializing pharmaceuticals, particularly in the new molecular biology, fashioning alliances and then purchasing new rDNA startups. Finally, in 1995, this redefinition of strategic boundaries led, in turn, to the merger of Ciba-Geigy and Sandoz to form Novartis, followed by the spinning off of its chemical businesses. By the end of the century, Novartis and Roche Holding, the world's pharmaceutical leader, rendered the Swiss second only to the Americans in commercializing products of the emerging biotechnology infrastructure. Of the other two European leaders, Britain's ICI was able to participate in the polymer/petrochemical revolution and thus became an effective competitor in international markets. Later ICI decided to focus on chemicals and sold its pharmaceutical business. Meanwhile, France's Rhône-Poulenc failed in both chemicals and pharmaceuticals.

Paths of Learning in the Pharmaceutical Industry

Building Barriers to Entry

The pharmaceutical industry differed from the chemical industry in that the American and European industries evolved from very different beginnings. The leading American companies came into being beginning in the 1880s by mass producing over-the-counter (OTC), nonprescription drugs based on natural sources. The European first movers, on the other hand, started by commercializing new learning in chemistry to produce manmade drugs as well as a variety of manmade materials.

The first movers included Germany's Big Three and their Swiss challengers, as well as F. Hoffman–La Roche, the global leader in the drug industry for well over a century. As in chemicals, barriers to entry in pharmaceuticals, created before World War I, were eliminated during the decade after 1914. Again as in chemicals, leading American companies during the 1920s, including Eli Lilly, Abbott, and SmithKline, used the opportunity to stage their entry and began to commercialize new prescription drugs.

Defining Strategic Boundaries

World War II's demands for antibiotics created a therapeutic revolution that transformed the pharmaceutical industry worldwide, even more profoundly than the polymer/petrochemical revolution had in the chemical industry. During the war the OTC companies became producers of prescription drugs, as did the chemical company American Cyanamid. Of more significance, two companies in the supporting nexus of the pharmaceutical industry, Merck and Pfizer, developed into major core companies in the 1950s as soon as they acquired the marketing and distribution capabilities essential to completing their integrated learning bases.

Again, following the evolutionary pattern in polymer/petrochemicals during the 1960s, growth in terms of the number of new drugs commercialized sharply dropped off. The OTC companies returned to defining their strategic boundaries by focusing on nonprescription drugs and then entered consumer chemicals and even food and household goods. So too, did the prescription drugmakers, particularly Pfizer, but also Abbott and Upjohn.

Escaping Limits to Growth

In the 1970s and early 1980s, as the chemical industry was evolving toward specialty chemicals in the face of declining growth, the pharmaceutical industry entered a new era based on new learning in biochemistry, microbiology, enzymology, and the new scientific discipline of molecular genetics. This resulted in another major redefinition of strategic boundaries.

The companies that focused on commercializing the new learning, assisted by the new computer-based techniques of "discovery by design"—Merck, Eli Lily, Squibb, and SmithKline French—became the industry's leaders. Abbott also succeeded when, more by chance than careful strategic planning, it became a first mover in the new biotechnology revolution.

Pfizer and Upjohn, on the other hand, missed out on the initial opportunities for exploiting growth. Pfizer, the industry's leading diversifier in the 1950s and 1960s, began only in the 1980s to narrow its strategic boundaries by focusing on healthcare, and only in the 1990s when it concentrated on commercializing prescription drugs did it become a major competitor. At Upjohn, the failure to meet the challenges of the new learning reflected a weakness of a family-managed enterprise in a high-technology industry. By the 1990s its only strategic choice was to merge, which it did in 1995 with Sweden's Pharmacia (subsequently part of Pfizer).

In the meantime, SmithKline French had learned a major lesson about the role played by the barriers to entry in defining strategic boundaries, as is suggested by its changing corporate names. With its profits from its successful blockbuster, Tagamet, it acquired Beckman, a first mover in electronic medical equipment, and became SmithKline Beckman. Quickly learning that the underlying technology was not related, it spun off Beckman and then merged with what had become Britain's leading pharmaceutical company as SmithKline Beecham. In 1989 the company was absorbed by Britain's leading drug company to become GlaxoSmithKline. In the early 1980s, Warner-Lambert had made a similar disastrous move in unrelated diversification. In the 1990s Eli Lilly would also commit much the same mistake in betting on technologically complex medical devices and soon had to withdraw.

During the 1970s, as prescription drug companies were meeting the challenges of the new learning in biology, the goal of the remaining four OTC enterprises listed in Table 1.2 was to become full-fledged makers of prescription drugs. But by that time the barriers to entry were already too high; the only way to enter was through merger. So, Bristol-Meyers acquired Squibb in 1989. The mergers of Schering and Plough and of Warner-Lambert and Parke Davis provide an excellent contrast of successful and failed mergers. At Schering-Plough, the integrated learning bases of both companies were kept intact. As the prescription drug lines were steadily increased, the OTC products were constantly decreased. At Warner-Lambert, on the other hand, the Warner-Lambert OTC managers took charge. Unskilled in the commercializing of prescription drugs, their strategic decisions quickly destroyed Parke Davis's capabilities. As a result, by the mid-1990s, Warner-Lambert was no longer a significant producer of prescription drugs, and eventually fell prey to takeover by Pfizer.

The story of American Home Products (Wyeth) offers another important historical lesson about the price of entry into the emerging biotechnology industry. After its formation in the 1920s it became a specialist in defining its strategic boundaries in related industries. It undertook little research, instead relying on licensing, as it became expert in creating integrated learning bases for its related businesses. As a result, by 1984, American Home Products ranked first in sales and twenty-eighth in R&D expenditures among the top thirty American pharmaceutical companies. The company had relied on the industry's existing nexus to provide the necessary ingredients and services. But since these did not yet exist in quantity in molecular biology, leaders of American Home Products were willing in 1989 to pay $666 million to acquire Genetics Institute and, in 1994, $9.7 billion in cash for American Cyanamid. Thus American Home Products paid $10.4 billion to participate in the biotechnology revolution.

The European competitors in pharmaceuticals remained the German Big Three and the two Swiss first movers in chemically based pharmaceuticals. By the 1970s Hoechst, Bayer, and the recently merged Ciba-Geigy had restored their interwar positions in the American prescription drug markets. What differentiated the Swiss from the Germans was their commitment to commercializing the products of the new learning, particularly that of biotechnology. Hoechst and Bayer made only minor acquisitions, whereas the Swiss moved quickly into a number of alliances with American biotech startups in the 1980s and into the 1990s. In 1989, Roche acquired Genentech and in 1994 Ciba-Geigy took control of Chiron. Ciba-Geigy's transformation was completed the following year with the formation of Novartis, a pure pharmaceutical company after the spin-off of its chemical businesses.

For the British and French drug industries, the coincidence of the outbreak of World War II and the initial introduction of antibiotics had a dramatic impact. In 1960 Britain's prescription drug market was still supplied almost wholly by Swiss and American companies. The huge demand for antibiotics permitted Glaxo, ICI, and to a lesser extent Beecham to become major competitors in international markets. During the war, occupied France missed out on the antibiotic revolution and the subsequent therapeutic revolution. As a result the postwar period proved very challenging. During the 1980s the French produced less than 1 percent of pharmaceuticals sold in world markets. Moreover, the first Japanese producers to enter the international markets was the joint venture of the Takeda Pharmaceutical Company and Abbott; only in the 1990s did it become an independent enterprise.

Finally, Chapter 10 provided a foretaste of the future by describing the beginnings of the infrastructure of the Biotechnology Revolution. In the 1960s concerted large-scale research efforts in molecular biology began at major universities and research institutes. Then, in the 1970s, a new supporting nexus of companies began providing new materials and skills essential to commercializing drugs based on the new learning. With the establishment of this nexus, the 1980s saw the commercializing of new biotechnology products by both the century-old pharmaceutical enterprises and the new startups. By the 1990s a division of labor had been established, with the core pharmaceutical companies concentrating on mass markets and the startups on specialties. Now under way for decades, with the human genome finally mapped, the potential of the biotechnology industry remains enormous, comparable to that of the information industries in the 1960s.

A concluding historical lesson of the shaping of the Second Industrial Revolution in chemicals and pharmaceuticals is that, while the number of producers increased in pharmaceuticals, the number of mid-sized and even major producers was significantly reduced by merger and acquisition. In comparison, only a handful of enterprises created the Information Revolution.

Evolving Paths of Learning in the Information Revolution

Whereas the histories of the modern chemical and pharmaceutical industries provide a remarkable story in terms of their very different evolutions, that of the industries that created the Information Revolution based on audio, video, and information technologies was truly an epic story. A single U.S. company, the Radio Corporation of America, created the audio and video industry worldwide between the 1920s and the 1960s. Then within a decade it destroyed itself and with it the U.S. industry. RCA did so first by attempting to produce a mainframe computer and then by becoming a conglomerate, producing in several different markets. Its failed strategy permitted a very small number of Japanese firms—Sony, Matsushita, Sanyo, and Sharp—to capture markets worldwide.

There are, of course, other differences in the evolution of the two sets of high technology industries. For example, there is the difference in timing of the creation of the respective infrastructures, with that for chemicals and pharmaceuticals forming between the 1880s and the 1920s, and that for the information industries primarily between the 1950s and the 1990s. This difference emphasizes that the Information Revolution was a second-generation phenomenon, descended from the other major high-technology industry of the Second Industrial Revolution—that of electrical and telecommunications machines and equipment based on the then-new electrical science.

In the United States the first mover in consumer electronics was RCA, a joint venture of General Electric, Westinghouse, and AT&T. In Europe it was Telefunken, a joint venture of Siemens and AEG (Allgemeine Elektricitats-Gessellschaft). So too, the electronic computer was primarily crafted by International Business Machines (IBM), the builder of the first major information processing enterprise using electrically driven punched-card tabulators.

As I pointed out in Chapter 1, the products of the new electronics industries did not compete with the existing products of the Second Industrial Revolution. Of more importance, the number of technologies commercialized in the electronics industries was tiny in comparison to those based on chemical and biological science. Essentially they consisted of hardware devices—the vacuum tube, transistor, integrated circuit, memory chip, and microprocessor—to transmit and to receive messages, as well as software to process the information resident in and flowing among these devices. Except for the vacuum tube, these electronic technologies blossomed after World War II, but German electronic pioneers were slow to recover. On the other hand, Japan's national infrastructure was rebuilt quickly by the major electrical companies that had built the nation's initial electrical equipment infrastructure in the first decades of the twentieth century based on Western technology. Again using technology developed in the United States during the late 1940s and 1950s, the Japanese were able in the 1960s and 1970s to capture not only Asian markets but also much of the European market.

Paths of Learning in the Audio and Video Technology Industries

The electronics industries began with RCA, established in 1920 as a patent pool that also included General Electric (GE), Westinghouse, and AT&T. The U.S. Navy had urged the formation of such a pool to ensure that the commercializing of wireless spark technology for ship-to-shore transmissions be under U.S. control. But at that same moment a new technology—the continuous wave voice transmission, based on the electronic vacuum tube, and the resulting voice and broadcasting equipment—was being perfected largely in the research laboratories of GE, Westinghouse, and AT&T. By 1922, twenty-six radio stations had been licensed. By the end of 1923, the number was 556. Sales of radio receiving sets had reached $5 million and by 1926 soared to over $200 million.

During the 1920s RCA's first CEO, young David S. Sarnoff, transformed the RCA patent pool into a fully integrated learning base. RCA became essentially a marketing organization for the products GE and Westinghouse manufactured. Meanwhile, AT&T was legally separated from RCA to concentrate on telecommunications, and Sarnoff established two broadcasting systems, NBC and ABC (the latter was spun off in World War II). This move in turn prompted William Paley to form CBS.

In 1930 Sarnoff completed his mission in two steps. First, he convinced GE and Westinghouse to allow RCA to acquire Victor Talking Machine, the world's largest producer of phonographs, with foreign subsidiaries. Second, he arranged for GE and Westinghouse to exchange their marketing and some research facilities for RCA stock. RCA now had a fully regaled learning base

In the 1930s RCA dominated the industry in terms of scale in the production of radios, tubes, components, and networks. Sarnoff then turned the laboratories that he had acquired from Westinghouse to commercializing black-and-white television. In this effort, RCA was challenged by Philco, its most successful competitor, by Paley's CBS, and then by Zenith Radio. In July 1940 RCA introduced the first telecast with proper fanfare. With the attack on Pearl Harbor in December, further research on television was postponed until the end of World War II. When the war ended, RCA returned to perfecting its black-and-white television and expanded its still tiny number of broadcasting programs.

In 1947, Sarnoff, now as chairman, and Frank Folsom as CEO redefined RCA's strategic boundaries. It would license its new product to all comers while maintaining its own product focus on the production of tubes and components, where it had only one major competitor Sylvania. Black-and-white television sales boomed. In 1958 RCA enjoyed 70 percent of the market for tubes and components. RCA's revenues from manufacturers soared from $271 million in 1948 to $476 million in 1950, with the major share coming from the sale of tubes. As a result, during the 1950s half its income came from licensing and sales in consumer electronics manufacturing.

During that decade RCA concentrated its income and enhanced capabilities to commercialize color television. Philco, Paley's CBS, Zenith, and two smaller companies followed suit. By 1956, however, they all had given up, but RCA persevered. By 1959 came the first profit from color television. By 1965 its revenues doubled as its sales passed the $2 billion mark, making it the twenty-sixth largest industrial enterprise in the United States.

In this way, then, RCA, by following the virtuous strategy of reinvesting its learning and profits from radio, commercialized the first black-and-white television, and in turn, with color television dominated world markets. Then RCA adopted a strategy of unrelated diversification. In so doing, it destroyed itself, and with it the American consumer electronics industry.

THE DESTRUCTION OF RCA AND THE U.S. AUDIO AND VIDEO INDUSTRIES   RCA embarked on a new strategy in 1964. Although it had very limited capabilities in information processing, it sought to commercialize a mainframe computer to challenge IBM's soon-to-be-completed System 360. As the project fell behind schedule, Robert Sarnoff, who became CEO in 1968, fashioned an alternative strategy—one that would transform the company into a massive conglomerate through acquisitions. In the late 1960s and early 1970s came the purchase, among others, of a publishing house, then a sporting goods company, followed by Hertz Rent-A-Car, a real estate developer, frozen food producers, a leading carpet manufacturer, and several financial services units.

In 1975 the failure of this strategy prompted RCA's directors to take strong actions. They replaced Sarnoff, but it was not until another new CEO, Thornton Bradshaw, arrived in 1981 that the company began seriously to divested its unrelated businesses. By this time, however, it was too late. RCA continued to struggle, and in 1986 was acquired by GE. Also by then, Philco and Sylvania were no longer independent companies and Paley's CBS had given up the production of consumer electronics. Zenith, the lone remaining American producer, held on until 1995, when a Korean industrial group acquired it.

THE JAPANESE INDUSTRY CONQUERS WORLD MARKETS   As RCA self-destructed, three Japanese companies—Matsushita, Sanyo, and Sony—and one European—Philips—redefined the industry's paths of learning in consumer electronics worldwide. Of the Japanese companies, Matsushita was the oldest, having been established in 1918. It produced electrical appliances and, licensing from RCA, radios in the 1930s. Sanyo, originally part of Matsushita, never pioneered significant innovative products. Sony, formed in 1946, was the first to commercialize new electronic products. In Europe Philips Incandescent Lamp Works, founded in 1891 in Holland and a first mover in the production of light bulbs, entered the production of radio receiving and broadcasting equipment in the 1920s, using licenses from the German company Telefunken.

After Japan's crushing defeat in 1945, Konosuke Matsushita reestablished his enterprise in the 1950s. First, in 1950, the Allied Occupation authorities required that he spin off part of his enterprise as Sanyo Electric Industrial. Two years later, he acquired technical capabilities by negotiating a joint venture with Philips to form Matsushita Electronics, of which Philips held 35 percent. His next step in 1955 was to acquire control of the Japan Victor Company (JVC). RCA had sold JVC to a Japanese company under pressure from Japan's government in 1937. This move provided Matsushita with an integrated learning base in electronic equipment.

With Philips and JVC providing technical capabilities and thus product development, Konosuke Matsushita focused on marketing, not only of radios and black-and-white televisions, but also of his broader line of household appliances and personal care products such as hair dryers, creating the most powerful marketing organization in Japan. In 1959 he built a similarly impressive marketing organization in the United States, focusing on electronic products. He did the same the following year in Europe. By the 1970s Matsushita's Panasonic was close to becoming a household word in the United States and Europe. In 1979, Matsushita enhanced its global position by acquiring Motorola's Quasar.

The proof of Matsushita's marketing capabilities came earlier in the 1970s with the successful marketing strategy in commercializing the video cassette, which enabled Matsushita's VHS to drive Sony's technically superior Betamax out of the market. This victory was achieved not only by having its own (Panasonic) marketing organization, as well as that of its JVC, sell the product. Its managers also arranged for Sanyo and Sharp, as well as two computer companies, Hitachi and Mitsubishi Electric, to produce and market VHS worldwide. The resulting economies of scale and scope were so impressive that by 1984 VHS was outselling the Sony Betamax by four to one. Despite the higher quality of Betamax, the low cost and versatility of VHS prevailed.

It was Sony's technical and product development capabilities, however, not Matsushita's marketing ones, that were primarily responsible for Japan's epic conquest of world markets. Sony created the barriers to entry that drove all the U.S. competitors and, in time, the one European competitor, Philips, out of the audio and video industry. Akio Morita and an associate formed in 1946 a partnership that became known as Sony; its first major successful product, introduced in 1955, was a transistor-based miniature radio. In the early 1960s Morita built, following Matsushita's example, a marketing organization in the United States and then in Europe. Its success in the United States led to the establishment in 1970 of a color television plant in California, with production of 450,000 units. Before that, in the late 1960s, Sony's color Trinitron tube, superior to RCA's tube, was capturing the market from RCA's most profitable television business. In 1970 Sony designed the basic format for the video cassette recorder, on which both Matsushita VHS and its own Betamax were produced. In 1978 followed the Walkman, the ultimate in the advantages of scope and miniaturization.

In the early 1980s Sony's major achievement was in commercializing a basic new technology—the digitization of sound, one of the principal technological triumphs of the twentieth century. In 1982 the company, in partnership with Philips, produced the compact disk (CD). Philips developed the laser-scanning disk and Sony the digital sound (music) technology, based on pulse-controlled modulation. In the next year came the CD-ROM, which, at the very same time that IBM was beginning to mass produce and mass market its personal computer, became a vehicle for handling digital graphics (including color) and so greatly expanded the horizons of the unfolding Information Revolution. The resulting knowledge base and profits enabled Sony, again working with Philips, to commercialize the digital video disk (DVD), and then in the mid-1990s the DVD-ROM.

Throughout the 1990s Sony followed its fundamental virtuous strategy of defining its strategic boundaries by using its learning and income from commercializing one product to commercialize another. In 1993 the firm entered the electronic game market with Play Station. Its sales soon shot ahead of the existing leaders Nintendo and Sega. Strength in digital technology also led to its success in becoming the leading producer of digital cameras. Only in one area did Sony seem to falter, which involved the distantly related product it acquired with its purchase of Columbia Pictures in 1989. The barriers to entry into the motion picture industry were so high that that venture alone accounted for a loss of $3.3 billion in 1993. Nevertheless, Sony could afford to persevere; by the end of the century, its motion picture business was becoming profitable.

As for Sony's major competitors, Matsushita made little attempt after its victory in the VCR battle to introduce new audio and video products. It focused instead on the commercialization of industrial electronic products, including computer peripherals. Philips, meanwhile, played a curious role in the evolution of the audio and video industry. From 1952 on, after it acquired a 35 percent stake in Matsushita's new subsidiary, Matsushita Electronics, Philips provided Matsushita with its technical capabilities, and certainly played a key role in its product development. Dating from the 1970s, it was the essential collaborator with Sony in commercializing the CD, the CD-ROM, and later the DVD and DVD-ROM. In the late 1980s Philips attempted to commercialize a CD-Interactive (CDI) for television. The project failed, creating losses of $2.7 billion in 1990 and $500 million in 1993.

Nevertheless, Philips's major financial losses in audio and video products, particularly in Europe, resulted from the competition of its two allies, first from Matsushita and then from Sony. As a result, after 1992, when Philips sold back its securities in Matsushita Electronics to Matsushita, the Dutch company began to move away from the audio and video business—a withdrawal that was well on its way by the end of the century. A study of Philips's role in creating that industry provides a fascinating research opportunity for historians of business and technology.

Paths of Learning in the Information Processing Industry Defined by IBM

The epic story of IBM is comparable to that of Sony. Each dominated their industries in commercializing new technologies; each played the commanding role in shaping the paths of learning during the creation of the infrastructures of the respective parts of the information revolution during the second half of the twentieth century. One difference was that IBM had established its fully integrated worldwide learning base in the 1920s, whereas Sony began to build its learning base leading to dominance only in the 1960s.

From the start in 1914, when Thomas Watson Sr. became sales manager of the Computer Tabulating Company, which had been formed in 1911 (renamed International Business Machines in 1924), IBM dominated the world's information processing industry, first in punched-card tabulators and then in computers. By following the same virtuous strategy as did Sony, it created barriers to entry that shaped the industry's paths of learning in information technology.

During the 1920s IBM enhanced its strong European base by expanding a marketing organization and then building a factory in Germany. By 1930 its economies of scale were such that it enjoyed 85 percent, and Remington-Rand 15 percent, of total revenues from electrically powered punched-card tabulators. During the 1930s appeared several improved products. Then, in

1946, IBM introduced the 603, the "Electronic Multiplier," the first tabulator to be powered by electronic tubes, followed by the 605, which became, in Thomas Watson Jr.'s words, "the Model T of the computing industry." Next, in 1960, came the transistor-powered 1401, an overwhelming success.

In 1963 IBM's computer revenues stood at $1.2 billion, with Sperry Rand in a distant second place with revenues of $145 million. IBM's revenues were more than twice those of the rest of the U.S. industry combined. IBM's dominance rested, of course, on its three decades of perfecting its product development, production, marketing, and distribution learning base.

Two years earlier, in 1961, planning commenced for the System 360, which would dominate the large-scale computing market for the rest of the century, a complex and costly commercializing of a family of computers consisting of five, then six, new processors spanning a two-hundred-fold range in performance and priced accordingly, and thus achieving the maximum economies of both scale and scope. Such success required half a decade of development work at a cost of more than $6 billion. The System 360 began to reach the market in 1967. Its successor, System 370, announced in the early 1970s, added a number of improvements.

The System 370 was, in turn, followed by the commercializing of the next new product, Future Systems, with a formal announcement in 1970 that it would appear in 1974. That project failed. The technical challenges were simply too complex. By the mid-1970s IBM's mainframe technology had reached its limits of growth, in terms of commercializing new products.

As IBM was completing its System 360, four other American computer companies attempted to commercialize competitive products. RCA and General Electric, the two major electronic companies that had the technical capabilities comparable to IBM, would prove to lack the necessary integrated learning bases that IBM had enjoyed since its beginning. Consequently, RCA sold its computer business to Sperry Rand and GE did so to Honeywell, a producer of control and instrument products. On the other hand, two business machinery companies—Burroughs Adding Machine and National Cash Register—did succeed in creating a profitable product. They did so by focusing their mainframes on the markets in which they had created barriers to entry since the early 1880s, as the Second Industrial Revolution began.

NEW PATHS OF LEARNING   In the 1960s two entrepreneurial enterprises built their integrated learning bases on each side of the barriers to entry created by IBM's Systems 360 and 370. On the high-end side, William Norris commercialized his supercomputer for complex scientific and engineering work in 1964. At the low end, Kenneth Olsen's Digital Equipment Corporation (DEC) introduced its PPD-8 in 1965, the first minicomputer produced in volume. Norris's Control Data Corporation (CDC) dominated its market until 1972 when his chief designer, Seymour Cray, established a competing product.

The minicomputer path flourished after 1965. Olsen's PPD-8, selling at a remarkably low price of $18,000, was used for a wide variety of computing tasks with the customers often providing their own software. Olsen immediately created a marketing organization of twenty-six sales offices in six countries. His initial major rival, Scientific Data Systems, on the other hand, concentrated on government orders and failed to create an extended marketing organization. Despite its impressive growth after incurring a loss of $1.3 million in 1975, Scientific Data was no longer a significant competitor.

Other entrepreneurs quickly followed DEC, as the barriers to entry had not yet been established. In 1968 Edson de Castro, a designer of the PPD-8, formed Data General. In 1971 came Prime Computer and in the next year Hewlett-Packard, the most successful of Digital's followers that produced computers for broader, more general purposes. Then came minicomputers for specialized tasks. An Wang began in 1976 to market his data processing computer. At the same time two fault-tolerant systems came on the market of which Tandem was the most profitable. Nevertheless, the most successful of DEC's followers was not surprisingly IBM. By 1982 IBM's minicomputer revenues were just under $2 billion, DEC's $1.9 billion, and Hewlett Packard $600 million, followed closely by Data General, Wang, Prime, and Tandem.

At this juncture three young men with close ties to Stanford University commercialized the one major new technology since the mainframe, whose product—the workstation—within less than a decade replaced the minicomputer. In 1982 they formed Sun Microsystems with Scott McNealy as CEO. Using a new RISC chip (Reduced Instruction Set Computing) and a new UNIX operating system created at the Bell Laboratories, they launched the server. Because of an earlier antitrust decision, AT&T licensed its chip free of charge. As the first mover, Sun was able to build its integrated learning base before its rivals. The most successful competitors were long-established computer companies—Hewlett-Packard, IBM, and DEC.

By 1987, after Sun had created its national and then international marketing organization, its managers immediately licensed Fujitsu, the leading

Japanese company, and Philips in Europe. Hewlett-Packard's highly success-ful Spectrum quickly created its worldwide marketing network, and the company licensed its product to Hitachi. IBM's initial attempt to produce workstations failed. Then in 1991 it marketed a successful RS600. On the other hand, DEC, still committed to the minicomputer and its VAX technol-ogy, fell behind. Indeed in 1990 Olsen attempted to produce a mainframe. In the meantime, the two other major Japanese computer companies, NEC and Toshiba, had acquired the workstation technology from Stanford's MIPS Computer Systems.

During the decade of the 1980s IBM once again transformed information technology in mass producing and mass marketing the personal computer that had been commercialized by young hobbyists. Before reviewing the im-pact of the IBM PC clone, I review the impact of the barriers to entry created by the coming of the Systems 360 and 370 on the evolution of the computer industry worldwide.

THE EUROPEAN FAILURE TO OVERCOME THE IBM SYSTEMS 360 AND 370 BARRIERS TO ENTRY   In Britain, France, Germany, and Italy, entrepreneurs supported extensively by their governments, except for Italy, attempted to surmount the barriers to entry created by the commercializing of IBM Systems 360 and 370. All tried and all failed. With these failures their managers turned to Japan to provide them with mainframes on an OEM ba-sis—that is, putting their labels on Japanese-made computers.

In Britain, the industry had its beginnings in 1959 with the formation of International Computers and Tabulators. Then with the initial announce-ments of IBM's System 360, the British government converted that enter-prise into its champion, giving it the name International Computers Ltd. (ICL). It then merged several smaller companies into this enterprise. But during the 1970s, large-scale government intervention failed to make its national champion profitable. Finally, in 1981, ICL gave up. Its managers turned to Fujitsu to provide mainframes on an OEM basis.

France's response was much the same as Britain's. In 1963 the De Gaulle government fashioned its "Plan Calcul" to be carried out by the Compagnie International de l'Informatique (CII). By 1973 the French government real-ized that its reliance on Plan Calcul was a failure. The French company joined with Siemens, Europe's major producer of electronic equipment, and the Dutch firm Philips to produce a European challenger, UNIDA. That proj-ect quickly collapsed, sending Siemens in 1975 to Fujitsu to obtain one of the early Amdahl-based Japanese products on an OEM basis (as reviewed shortly). The French government, however, continued to pour funds into computers during the 1980s and into the 1990s with neither technological nor financial success.

The Italian story differs in that C. Olivetti, it's leading computer manufacturer and one of Europe's major producer of typewriters and electrical and electronic-based office machinery, failed to produce a competitive information technologies (IT) product. When the Benedetti brothers acquired the company from the bankrupt Olivetti family, they immediately went to Hitachi to acquire OEM large-scale computers.

Having reviewed the failure of the European industry and, at the request of the European competitors, the sourcing of technology from Japan, I return to IBM's second restructuring of information technology through mass production and mass marketing of personal computers initially commercialized by young hobbyists.

THE IBM PC CLONE TRANSFORMS DATA PROCESSING   In the 1980s IBM's personal computer (PC) once again transformed the computer industry. That technology was developed by young hobbyists. By 1977 three pioneers had created their learning bases for producing and marketing microcomputers—Apple, Commodore, and Tandy. In 1980, IBM sent a team to Boca Raton with instruction to mass produce and mass market its personal computer. In 1981 IBM's revenues were $500,000, behind Apple's $600,000. In 1984 they were $5 million. IBM thus created almost overnight a multibillion dollar business, with almost no barriers to entry. Because of an earlier antitrust ruling, IBM had to license its products to all comers. As a result, in 1985, *Business Week* reported more than two hundred producers of clones were in business. All had to use an Intel 8000 microprocessor and a Microsoft DOS operating system.

Because the personal computer was used by individuals, not by institutions as were the existing mainframe and minicomputers, two new sectors of the data procession industry quickly emerged. In software, the new industry was volume-produced packaged software applications for use by individuals. In hardware came the large-scale production of networking devices to connect individual computers within an establishment, then those in nearby local areas (LANS), and later, wider geographical areas (WANS). The first movers in this new networking technology during the 1980s were Cisco, the commercializer of the router, and Novell, that of networking software. They prospered in the late 1980s and early 1990s, as did the pioneers of the new industry of packaged software for individual customers. Here the first movers included Oracle, Lotus, WordPerfect, Adobe, and others.

IBM gained little from the mass marketing of its PC, except that as the clones poured out of the assembly plants, the transformation all but eliminated the existing U.S. mainframe competitors. Only IBM could afford the loss of revenues resulting from the shift from institutional to individual users. (Those losses at IBM amounted to $15 billion between 1991 and 1993).

The beneficiaries of the PC revolution were, of course, Intel and Microsoft. Their stories provide some of the best examples in industrial history of the power of economies of scale and scope, not only to create barriers to entry but also to drive existing enterprises out of a new industry.

Intel in 1971 was the first to commercialize microprocessors, primarily used in dedicated control systems, automobiles, automated product lines, and the like. By 1977, even before the coming of the PC, the price had plummeted from $110 to $20. As the power of its microprocessors sharply increased, Intel's microprocessor was selling between $5 and $8. By the 1980s Intel was accounting for 80 percent or more of the world's production of microprocessors.

Whereas Intel's strength consisted in the industrial economies of scale and scope in production, Microsoft's rested as much on the dynamic economies of scale and scope in knowledge. The development of its three Windows operating systems during the 1980s required two or three years of intensive development work. The resulting barriers to entry gained were almost insuperable.

Nevertheless, the extraordinary advantage of Bill Gates's Microsoft lay in the consideration that another new industry was created with the IBM PC— that is, packaged software. His increasing hold over the new industry began with the DOS operating system used by a multitude of PC clones. At the same time, Microsoft developed its own Windows operating system. Windows 1 came onto the market in 1985. It was not a success. Windows 2, introduced in 1988, included the graphical user interface similar to the one that Apple had commercialized, and was much more successful. By the advent of Windows 3, Microsoft had also brought along popular spreadsheet and word-processing systems that closed down Lotus, WordPerfect, and Borland International as independent companies. Then, in 1993, Windows NT was unveiled, and Microsoft quickly replaced Novell as the leading producer of networking software.

Next came Gates's move into Internet technology. In 1993 Jim Clark and Mark Andreesen had introduced the first browser, greatly facilitating use of the World Wide Web. Meanwhile, Cisco Systems had already commercialized the router. Gates then immediately packaged a comparable browser acquired from another pioneering company, Spy Glass, and bundled it into Windows 95 as the Microsoft Internet Explorer. Microsoft had thereby created probably the most powerful monopoly in U.S. industrial history.

With such advantages, Intel and Microsoft quickly drove the pioneers with their proprietary systems out of business. By the 1990s Apple remained the one successful personal computer company still using its own proprietary operating system. The competing IBM clones disappeared even more quickly. The leading four—Dell, Gateway, Packard Bell, and AST Research—had entered the industry through marketing and production, not technological innovation.

THE JAPANESE CHALLENGE   During the decade of the 1970s, when the microprocessor-based PC was transforming the world's computer industry, four Japanese companies—Fujitsu, Hitachi, Nippon Electric Company (NEC) and Toshiba—were beginning to seriously challenge IBM and the U.S. mainframe industry using technologies acquired from the United States. In this same era, unlike the Japanese consumer electronics manufacturers that were conquering world markets based on their own research, the Japanese computer companies competed at home and abroad with U.S. technology in mainframes in the 1970s and in workstations in the late 1980s.

In mainframes, the acquisition of IBM's Systems 360 and 370 technology was unplanned. In 1970, with the announcement of System 370, Japan's ministry of international trade and industry (MITI) inaugurated a "New Series Project," a cooperative undertaking by the Japanese companies to produce a line of comparable computers. Fujitsu and Hitachi were assigned to concentrate on the high end of the IBM product line and NEC and Toshiba on the middle range. The other two, Mitsubishi Electric and Oki, played supporting roles.

In that same year, Gene Amdahl, the designer of IBM Systems 360 and 370, left IBM to start his own company. Unsuccessful in raising $44 million in the United States, he turned to Fujitsu, which by providing the funds became the dominant stockholder in Amdahl's company. Its first product was made in Japan. Beginning in 1975, Fujitsu and then Hitachi were producing in Japan their version of Amdahl's System 370. Once IBM's technology be-

came a relatively open book in Japan, Toshiba and NEC were soon manufacturing middle-level products. Success in adopting the U.S. mainframe technology meant that the Europeans came to Japan for their mainframes.

One underlying reason for the Japanese success was its impressive commercializing of a new memory chip, the DRAM (Dynamic Random Access
Memory), initially introduced by Intel in 1971. As its New Series Project was
being fulfilled, MITI formed a new project, the Very Large-Scale Integrated
(VLSI) circuit, which would coordinate the activities of the four major computer companies in commercializing the DRAM memory chip.

The immediate success of the MITI-sponsored Japanese cooperative effort
in capturing the world's market for memory chips provides an impressive
example of scale economies creating barriers to entry. In 1972, when Intel
introduced the first mass-produced DRAM, the Japanese had 5 percent of
the world's memory-chip market. With the second-generation 4-K-bit chip,
Japan's share rose to 17 percent. In 1979, after introducing the 16-K-bit, Japan's share reached 71 percent. The advent of the 265-K-bit in 1982 quickly
destroyed the U.S. production of memory chips. Intel and the other U.S.
makers had by 1985 exited from the industry, as the Japanese accounted for
92 percent of the production of DRAMS.

At the same time, the coming of the PC revolution saved the American
semiconductor industry. No Japanese competitor had any hope of entering
the production of microprocessors and operating systems, which was protected by Intel's and Microsoft's economies of scale and scope. So, as the five
American leaders were shutting down their memory plants, they were simultaneously building even larger microprocessor plants.

Nevertheless, the Japanese challenge remained. Although Japan's companies had missed the PC revolution (except for Toshiba, which licensed an
IBM clone), IBM and the four Japanese leaders continued to dominate the
European markets in mainframes and other related large systems. Equally
significant, the same four, as just pointed out, became first movers in workstations.

In the 1990s the demand for computer power soared with the coming of
the LANS (Local Area Networking Systems) and the WANS (Wide Area Networking Systems) increased the demand for computing power, and with it
the markets for both large-scale systems and servers. The Japanese companies successfully competed with the American leaders in meeting this demand, as evidenced by industry rankings in 1997 (see Table 7.2 in *Inventing
the Electronic Century*, pp. 223–224, for complete listings for the ten largest IT
companies in 1997).

In large-scale systems IBM and Fujitsu led the way with revenues each of $5 billion, followed by NEC with $4 billion, and Hitachi with $2 billion. In servers IBM again was first with $7.5 billion, followed by Hewlett-Packard and Compaq, each with $4 billion. Then came NEC and Toshiba at $2.5 billion, with Hitachi and Fujitsu at $1 billion.

In desktops and software the Japanese Big Four were also challenging the U.S. companies. In desktops, IBM had revenues of $13 billion, followed by Compaq with $11 billion, then came Fujitsu with $10 billion, Toshiba with $8 billion, and NEC (which had acquired Packard Bell) with $7.5 billion. Next came Dell also with $7.5 billion. Apple and Hewlett-Packard had $6.5 billion and Gateway $5 billion.

IBM again led the way in software with $13 billion, well ahead of Microsoft with $10 billion. Then came Hitachi with $5.5 billion and Fujitsu $4.7 billion. The American leaders included Computer Associates with $3 billion, Oracle with $2 billion, and Novell with $1 billion. At the end of the twentieth century, the U.S. leaders and the Japanese challengers were sharing international markets. The European companies had all disappeared more than a decade earlier.

Lessons from the Three Revolutions

At the conclusion of this second of my two volumes on the high-technology industries, four principal lessons emerge from the histories of the three revolutions.

The first lesson is that the long-term leaders of each revolution succeeded by following virtuous strategies—that is, they used the profits and learning from each generation of new products to commercialize the next generation, and they defined their strategic boundaries around the capabilities in their integrated learning bases. They did not—or not for long—pursue unrelated diversification. In the epic story of audio and video electronics, the contrasting fates of RCA and Sony dramatically illustrate this point. RCA essentially created the industry and came to dominate world markets, but it pushed a step too far by attempting to enter mainframe computers and then compounded its misfortune by becoming a conglomerate through unrelated acquisitions. These missteps so weakened the company that it was eventually forced onto the auction block and broken apart. Sony, on the other hand, continued to commercialize new technologies in closely related areas, including audio and video equipment, and remains at the dawn of the twenty-first century the industry leader by far. In information technology

IBM's virtuous strategy has ensured its continued dominance in worldwide markets that is unparalleled in industrial history.

In chemicals and pharmaceuticals, virtuous strategies also separated winners from losers. Among major chemical companies, Bayer, Hoechst, BASF, ICI, Du Pont, and Dow, and most of the focused companies prospered over many decades by commercializing new products from their integrated learning bases. Their experiences differed sharply from those of Union Carbide, Allied Chemical, and Witco, to cite a few examples, which diversified into unrelated areas and ultimately lost their independence. In pharmaceuticals, Roche Holding, Merck, and Eli Lilly exemplify continuously successful companies with virtuous strategies, in contrast to Warner-Lambert, SmithKline, or Rhône-Poulenc, which failed to innovate continuously and therefore struggled continuously.

A second lesson from the histories of the three revolutions concerns the length of time necessary to complete the infrastructure for the respective industries. In the high-technology industries surveyed here, completion of the infrastructures required about fifty years. During that time the leading competitors emerged along with the supporting nexus of suppliers of specialized products and services. Once an infrastructure was in place, however, successful new entrants became extremely rare.

A very small number of companies built the basic infrastructure—four in consumer electronics and about a dozen in information processing. With the privatizing of the Internet in the mid-1990s and other contributions from the evolution of the telecommunications industry—the other major high technology industry of the Information Revolution—the infrastructure was in place for the creation of a new economy. As Roger Alcaly noted in 2002, "The new economy is just emerging, but even at this relatively early stage, its productivity improvements compare favorably with those in both the first and the second industrial revolution."[4] In audio and video, only Sony remains an innovative high-technology company, and after commercializing the new video digital technologies from the 1970s through the 1990s, it now concentrates on its music and motion picture businesses.

Other signs of the completion of the infrastructure include the strategies of the major information processing companies. IBM, for example, has been moving aggressively into services and software. By 1996, 47 percent of its revenues derived from services (30 percent) and software (17 percent). In other major segments, a few leading companies are dominant—Intel in microprocessors, Cisco in routers, and Microsoft in operating systems. Still another sign is industry consolidation. In 2002 Hewlett-Packard merged with Compaq, which had bought DEC a few years earlier. The number of competitors to serve as continuing sources of innovation has thus dwindled. The Japanese competitors, meanwhile, have rarely generated major technical innovations, but they have been highly successful followers.

The third lesson from the histories of high-technology industries involves the relationship between learning and growth. The science and technology essential to the continuing growth of high-technology companies can peter out. They may no longer serve as major sources of opportunities for commercialization. The most vivid example is the chemical industry, which experienced two periods of growth, first between the 1880s and the 1920s, and again during the 1940s and 1950s. Since the 1950s, however, chemical science and engineering have ceased to generate major new product opportunities. As a result industry leaders have succeeded by focusing on product and process development rather than on fundamental research. The companies have become, in effect, manufacturers of specialty chemicals. At the same time, the limits to learning in chemistry and chemical engineering partly stimulated the efforts, ultimately ill fated, of some producers to diversify into unrelated areas.

In the same period—the 1960s and 1970s—some pharmaceutical companies also perceived limits to learning and began to diversify. However, biology and related disciplines—microbiology, enzymology, and the beginnings of molecular biology—simultaneously were starting to account for significant new learning that could be commercialized. The resulting commercialization of new drugs, in turn, redefined the strategic boundaries of long-established makers of prescription drugs.

Then, in the 1980s, the advent of molecular genetics, an entirely new scientific discipline, led to the building of a new nexus in terms of new medical supplies, services, and training that in turn served as the beginning of the creation of an infrastructure for the Biotechnology Revolution. This nexus then provided a source of new startup business enterprises that played a major role in that creation. Beginning in the 1980s the infrastructure grew, including both the new startups and long-established pharmaceutical companies that commercialized the products of the new molecular science and engineering. The dual relationship was firmly established by the mid-1990s, with substantial numbers of competing enterprises of both types. Meanwhile, the progress of the Human Genome Project plus the potential of a new technology, nanotechnology, suggests the continuing broad potential of the Biotechnology Revolution. Infrastructure development is well on its way and will probably continue for several more decades.

Thus, early in the twenty-first century, one of the two technology pioneers of the Second Industrial Revolution, the chemical industry, is no longer a high-tech industry. Pharmaceuticals, however, remains a dynamic high-tech industry as biotechnology is contributing to revolutionary changes on a scale comparable to those of the Second Industrial and Information Revolutions.

The fourth and final lesson of this review of the evolution of high-technology industries applies to leaders and practitioners in these and comparable industries. The long view reveals clear patterns of success and failure based on real experience. Embedded in these patterns are the key concepts of barriers to entry, strategic boundaries, and limits to growth.

NOTES

INDEX

Notes

2. Evolving Paths of Learning

1. The Standard Industrial Classification (SIC) was developed by the U.S. government to facilitate tracking of national economic performance. In this study, I use the categories contained in the *Standard Industrial Classification Manual,* published in 1987 by the Executive Office of the President, Office of Management and Budget. The manual lists as two-digit classifications each major industrial activity. For chemical and allied products, that classification is SIC 28. Within SIC 28 are listed three-digit subclassifications (see Table 1.1) covering the industry's major sectors. Within each three-digit subclassification are additional four-digit subclassifications or sectors; each sector includes a range of similar products, as the example indicates.

3. The Major American Companies

1. See Ashish Arora and Alfonso Gambardella, "Evolution of Industry Structure in the Chemical Industry," in Ashish Arora, Ralph Landau, and Nathan Rosenberg, eds., *Chemicals and Long-Term Economic Growth: Insights from the Chemical Industry* (New York: Wiley/Interscience, 1998), pp. 379–414.
2. Information on Du Pont before World War II comes from Alfred D. Chandler Jr. and Stephen Salisbury, *Pierre S. du Pont and the Making of the Modern Corporation* (New York: Harper & Row, 1971). Du Pont is also reviewed in three Chandler works: *Strategy and Structure: Chapters in the History of American Industrial Enterprise* (Cambridge, MA: MIT Press, 1962); *The Visible Hand: The Managerial Revolution in American Business* (Cambridge, MA: Harvard University Press, 1977); and *Scale and Scope: The Dynamics of Industrial Capitalism* (Cambridge, MA: Harvard University Press, 1990).

   See also William S. Dutton, *Du Pont: 140 Years* (New York: Charles Scribner's Sons, 1949); David A. Hounshell and John K. Smith Jr., *Science and Corporate Strategy: Du Pont R&D, 1902–1980* (New York: Cambridge University Press, 1988); and Graham D. Taylor and Patricia E. Sudnick, *Du Pont and the International Chemical Industry* (Boston: Twayne Publishers, 1984).

The goal of the initial merger was to acquire 60 percent of the production facilities, not 100 percent. As Arthur J. Moxam, one of the planners of the merger, noted, "the essence of manufacture is steady and full product. The demand of the country for powder is variable. If we owned all therefore when slack times came we would have to curtail product to the extent of diminished demands." Chandler, *Visible Hand,* p. 442.

For Nobel's commercializing of the initial innovation, see William J. Reader, *Imperial Chemical Industries,* vol. 1: *The Forerunners, 1870–1926* (Oxford: Oxford University Press, 1970), ch. 2.

3. Du Pont's World War I experience, its subsequent diversification, and the resulting new structure are summarized, with specific sources cited, in Chandler, *Strategy and Structure,* ch. 2.

4. For the interwar years, in addition to the above, see Williams Haynes, *American Chemical Industry,* vol. 6: *The Chemical Companies* (New York: D. Van Nostrand, 1949), pp. 133–137. For ammonia, see Chandler, *Scale and Scope,* pp. 175–177, 184–190, and, for great detail, Hounshell and Smith, *Science and Corporate Strategy,* pp. 183–188, ch. 12 for Stine's research program, and ch. 13 for neoprene and nylon.

5. For wartime developments and postwar plans, see Hounshell and Smith, *Science and Corporate Strategy,* ch. 16. This and the next quotation are from ibid., pp. 337 and 364. For polyethylene, see pp. 480–482. By 1945 Du Pont was producing a limited 750 tons per year. Haynes, *Chemical Companies,* summarizes the wartime applications of Du Pont's technologies, pp. 134–137.

6. See Hounshell and Smith, *Science and Corporate Strategy,* for Dacron, pp. 407–420; for Orlon, see pp. 394–407.

7. Ibid., for Teflon and Mylar, pp. 482–491; for elastomers, pp. 499–500; for fabrics and finishes, p. 536.

8. Ibid., for agricultural chemicals, pp. 446–447, 451–464; for percentage of herbicide market, see p. 458. By the early 1990s Du Pont was the second-largest and most profitable producer of herbicides in the world (*Chemical Week,* Sept. 8, 1993).

9. Hounshell and Smith, *Science and Corporate Strategy,* pp. 480–482, 491–499; the quotation is from p. 482.

10. Ibid., p. 533; Taylor and Sudnick, *Du Pont,* pp. 187–194.

11. Hounshell and Smith, *Science and Corporate Strategy,* ch. 22. See Robert A. Burgelman and Leonard R. Sayles, *Inside Corporate Innovation: Strategy, Structure and Managerial Skills* (New York: Free Press, 1986), esp. chs. 1, 8, 9; see also Norman Fast, *The Rise and Fall of New Venture Divisions* (Ann Arbor, MI: UMI Research Press, 1979).

12. Hounshell and Smith, *Science and Corporate Strategy,* pp. 424–439, 480, 488, 499, 548, 582.

13. Ibid., pp. 405, 582–583, 587. For photographic films including x-rays, see pp. 543, 554; for biochemicals, see ch. 20. The quotation is from p. 331.

14. Taylor and Sudnick, *Du Pont,* pp. 205–206, *Chemical Week,* Feb. 20, 1980 and

Sept. 2, 1981; Ralph Landau's interview with Edward Jefferson, Mar. 22, 1995, pp. 11–13 (copy in author's personal files).

15. These transactions are reported in the leading business journals and can be followed by examining the Du Pont entry in *Predicast* for these years.

16. *Chemical Week*, May 9, 1990, p. 32, Mar. 4, 1992, pp. 16–18, and Dec. 23–30, p. 28.

17. The information in this and the next paragraph is from Hounshell and Smith, *Science and Corporate Strategy*, pp. 446–451, 589–590; *Chemical Week*, May 9, 1990, p. 32; *Business Week*, Oct. 28, 1989.

18. *Chemical Week*, Oct. 21, 1992, pp. 38–39, quotation from p. 38; see also *Financial Times*, Jan. 16, 1990, p. 3.

19. See *Chemical Week*, May 9, 1990, p. 32, for a recap of Du Pont's strategy as of 1990.

20. For the Conoco spin-off, see *Forbes*, Oct. 18, 1999, pp. 88–89; *Hoover's Online*, Oct. 2001. For the end of Du Pont's pharmaceutical ventures, see ibid.

21. This brief review of more than a century comes from Thomas Derdak, ed., *International Directory of Company Histories*, vol. 8 (Chicago: St. James Press, 1994), pp. 147–150; Haynes, *Chemical Companies*, pp. 123–133; Don Whitehead, *The Dow Story: The History of Dow Chemical Company* (New York: McGraw-Hill, 1968); and a recent impressive company history of over six hundred pages: E. N. Brandt, *Growth Company: Dow Chemical's First Century* (East Lansing, MI: Michigan State University Press, 1997). For product commercialization through World War I, see ibid., chs. 1, 3, and 4; and more succinctly in Haynes, *Chemical Companies*, pp. 113–119.

22. For magnesium, see Brandt, *Growth Company*, pp. 71–72, 101–104, 107, and 110, supplemented by Haynes, *Chemical Companies*, pp. 116–117; Whitehead, *The Dow Story*, pp. 85–86, 136–137.

23. For Dowell and Ethyl Dow, see Brandt, *Growth Company*, pp. 155–157, 235–239, supplemented by Whitehead, *The Dow Story*, pp. 127–129, 131, and 134–135.

24. For styrene, vinylidene chloride, and Saran Wrap, see Brandt, *Growth Company*, pp. 230–232 and 235; Haynes, *Chemical Companies*, pp. 121–122; quotation from p. 121. For Etocal and Methocel, see Brandt, *Growth Company*, pp. 228–229.

25. For the impact of World War II, see Whitehead, *The Dow Story*, ch. 12. Brandt, *Growth Company*, pp. 177–185, provides essential details, including Dow's participation in the synthetic rubber program, a move that led to the creation of the Canadian subsidiary. Ibid., pp. 192, 194, and 198.

26. For the Baton Rouge plant, see Whitehead, *The Dow Story*, pp. 232–234; Brandt, *Growth Company*, pp. 285–287.

27. Joseph L. Bower, *When Markets Quake: The Managerial Challenge of Restructuring Industry* (Boston: Harvard Business School Press, 1986), p. 105. In Ralph Landau's interview with Frank D. Popoff, Sept. 28, 1995, Popoff recalled that "our financing has been a shameless address to debt financing for as long back as we can remember," p. 1. For Popoff's comments on the commitment to vertical integration, see ibid., pp. 4–5 (copy in author's personal files).

28. Brandt, *Growth Company*, pp. 296–297 (Asahi); quotation from p. 296; p. 287 (BASF); pp. 374–375 (Distiller's and Pechiney); for Schlumberger, see Whitehead, *The Dow Story*, pp. 250–251. Brandt describes Dow's international expansion in fascinating detail in chs. 14, "Dow in Europe," 15, "Dow and Latin America," and 16, "Dow in Asia."

29. Brandt, *Growth Company*, p. 295. For Dow's products in the 1960s and 1970s, including pharmaceuticals, see ibid., pp. 340–344.

30. See ibid., pp. 531–532, for the meeting and the new strategy; for structure, see Bower, *When Markets Quake*, pp. 107–108.

31. The acquisitions and divestitures described in this and the next two paragraphs of text are summarized in *Hoover's Handbook of American Business* (Austin, TX: Reference Press, 1993), p. 245; Derdak, ed., *International Directory*, vol. 8 (1994), pp. 147–150; John M. Stopford, *Directory of Multinationals*, 3d ed. (New York: Stockton Press, 1989), pp. 394–397. See also useful articles in *Chemical Week*, July 23, 1988, pp. 22–25, Sept. 9, 1988, Nov. 23, 1988, pp. 22–25, and April 5, 1989, pp. 25–27; *Business Week*, Aug. 7, 1989, pp. 62–64. Also valuable is Sarah Lane, "Corporate Restructuring in the Chemical Industry," in Margaret Blair, ed., *Takeovers, LBOs and Changing Corporate Forms* (Washington, D.C.: Brookings Institution, 1992), pp. 24, 27.

32. Stopford, *Directory of Multinationals* (1989), p. 395.

33. For this and the next paragraph of text, see *Hoover's Handbook* (1996), pp. 312–313; *Moody's Industrial Manual* (1990), pp. 1120–1121; *MIT Working Papers*, "Chemicals," p. 79; *Chemical Week*, July 23, 1988, pp. 22–25, Apr. 5, 1989, pp. 25–27, July 29, 1989, p. 14, and Sept. 18, 1991, p. 15; *Business Week*, Aug. 7, 1989, pp. 62–64. The remaining 3 percent of sales came from hydrocarbons and an unsuccessful energy project.

34. Derdak, ed. *International Directory*, vol. 1 (1988), pp. 365–367; *Hoover's Handbook* (1993), p. 410; Brandt, *Growth Company*, pp. 533–534.

35. In the words of a senior executive who advocated the purchase, "Marion Laboratories had the premier sales organization in the United States." But, he added, "It had no research worth the name, and fairly mediocre manufacturing facilities." Reality struck quickly. By 1993, earnings per share dropped sharply. Senior managers had become fully aware of the basic weaknesses due to the expiration of patents in its major businesses. Brandt, *Growth Company*, pp. 555–557, 560–564, provides an excellent review of the weaknesses of Marion Merrell Dow that led to its sale to Hoechst. See also Derdak, ed., *International Directory*, vol. 9 (1994), pp. 328–329; *Hoover's Handbook* (1996), p. 313.

36. Nitin Nohria, Davis Dyer, and Frederick Dalzell, *Changing Fortunes: Remaking the Industrial Corporation* (New York: Wiley, 2002), p. 61.

37. For Monsanto's history to the early 1970s, see Dan J. Forrestal, *Faith, Hope, and $5,000: The Story of Monsanto* (New York: Simon & Schuster, 1977); see also Milton Moskowitz, Michael Katz, and Robert Levering, *Everybody's Business: An Almanac* (New York: Harper & Row, 1980), pp. 610–614; Derdak, ed., *International Directory*, vol. 1 (1988), pp. 365–367, and vol. 9 (1994), pp. 355–357. For the years up to World War II, see Haynes, *Chemical Companies*, pp. 282–287.

38. Spitz, *Petrochemicals*, pp. 245, 256, 355–356, 400; *Moody's Industrial Manual* (1988), pp. 4115–4122.

39. For Chemstrand, see Forrestal, *Faith, Hope, and $5,000*, ch. 8; Spitz, *Petrochemicals*, pp. 289–290; Taylor and Sudnick, *Du Pont*, pp. 179–180; for consumer products and All, see Forrestal, *Faith, Hope, and $5,000*, ch. 9.

40. For the new-enterprise division, see Forrestal, *Faith, Hope, and $5,000*, pp. 210–211; quotation from p. 210. For Fisher, see pp. 213–214. Britain's General Electric Company initially held a one-third interest in Fisher, which Monsanto soon acquired.

41. Forrestal, *Faith, Hope, and $5,000*, pp. 238–246. For biotechnology, see *Chemical Engineering*, Feb. 23, 1981, p. 20; *Journal of Commerce*, Oct. 29, 1981, p. 7A. Monsanto's initial entry into molecular biology and Schneiderman's role is reviewed in Nohria, Dyer, and Dalzell, *Changing Fortunes*, pp. 86–87. See also *Chemical & Engineering News*, Feb. 23, 1981; *Journal of Commerce*, Oct. 29, 1981.

42. The transactions listed in this and the following paragraphs of text can be followed in *Predicast* for these years. See also *Chemical Week*, Sept. 28, 1988, pp. 6–8, Aug. 21, 1989, pp. 66–67, Dec. 6, 1989, pp. 30–31, Aug. 1, 1990, Sept. 2, 1991, and Jan. 27, 1992; *Hoover's Handbook* (1994), p. 615. For the 1996 transition to biotech in the next paragraph, see *New York Times*, May 5, 1998.

43. See Nohria, Dyer, and Dalzell, *Changing Fortunes*, pp. 88–93, for the complete story of Monsanto's failure; quotation from p. 93.

44. American Cyanamid's story before 1947 is succinctly reviewed in Haynes, *Chemical Companies*, pp. 21–25. Haynes lists the acquisition and the products manufactured. Further information is supplied by Moskowitz et al., *Everybody's Business*, pp. 599–601; *Fortune* 22 (September 1940): 102–104; Derdak, ed., *International Directory*, vol. 7, pp. 24–26; Spitz, *Petrochemicals*, p. 244; L. F. Haber, *The Chemical Industry, 1900–1930* (Oxford: Clarendon Press, 1971), pp. 88–90.

45. For aureomycin, see Peter Temin, *Taking Your Medicine: Drug Regulation in the United States*, (Cambridge, MA: Harvard University Press, 1980), pp. 69–75; Michael Pearson, *The Million Dollar Bugs* (New York: G. P. Putnam's Sons, 1969), chs. 1 and 2.

46. For Jefferson Chemical, see Spitz, *Petrochemicals*, pp. 310, 319.

47. The information for this and the following paragraph in the text is from Derdak, ed., *International Directory*, vol. 8 (1993), pp. 25–26; Moskowitz et al., *Everybody's Business*, p. 601.

48. *Hoover's Handbook* (1991), p. 72. By 1989, American Cyanamid was the third-largest producer of vaccines worldwide. See Louis Galambos with Jane Eliot Sewell, *Networks of Innovation: Vaccine Development at Merck, Sharp & Dohme, and Mulford, 1895–1995* (New York: Cambridge University Press, 1995), p. 213.

49. For Union Carbide's history to the 1930s, see Haynes, *Chemical Companies*, pp. 429–438; to 1975, see Chandler, *Scale and Scope*, pp. 173–174, 180–181.

50. Spitz, *Petrochemicals*, pp. 251–252; Derdak, ed., *International Directory*, vol. 9 (1994), p. 517.

51. Bower, *When Markets Quake*, pp. 101–102.

52. For Carbide's conglomerate acquisitions in the 1960s, see Derdak, ed., *International Directory*, vol. 9 (1994), pp. 517–518.

53. Ibid., p. 518; on the BCG model of portfolio planning, see Nohria, Dyer, and Dalzell, *Changing Fortunes*, p. 65.

54. For asset sales in the 1970s, see Bower, *When Markets Quake*, pp. 103–104; *Moody's Industrial Manual* (1988), p. 4373; Stopford, *Directory of Multinationals*, p. 1328.
    Nohria, Dyer, and Dalzell, *Changing Fortunes*, pp. 72–73 reviews these strategic shifts; quotation from p. 72.

55. Spitz, *Petrochemicals*, pp. 507–511; Bower, *When Markets Quake*, pp. 102–104; see also *Chemical Week*, Nov. 25, 1987, pp. 99–101.

56. The course of events can be followed in the *Wall Street Journal*, esp. in 1985, Jan. 21, p. 2, Aug. 15, p. 3, Sept. 3, p. 1, Dec. 9, p. 3; and in 1996, Jan. 1 and 10, p. 1, and almost daily until mid-1986.

57. The chronology of the transactions and the amounts involved in the fire sale can be followed in *Predicast*'s list of articles on Union Carbide, supplemented by those in the index of the *Wall Street Journal*. Union Carbide's $2.5 billion recapitalization was so significant that it changed the practice of investment banking houses in the financing of mergers and acquisitions from "the dominant bank model" to the "core group model," the details of which form the introductory chapter to Robert G. Eccles and Dwight B. Crane, *Doing Deals: Investment Bankers at Work* (Boston: Harvard Business School Press, 1988); also valuable is ch. 4 of that book, "How Customers Manage Banks."

58. *Chemical Week*, Nov. 25, 1987, pp. 99–101; June 8, 1988, pp. 29–30; Oct. 29, 1990, pp. 70–72; Jan. 23, 1991, pp. 53–54; Feb. 19, 1992, pp. 24–25; May 13, 1992, p. 56. See also *New York Times*, Dec. 22, 1991, p. 20; *Hoover's Handbook* (1996), pp. 868–869; and *Moody's Industrial Manual* (1991), p. 4308.

59. *Hoover's Handbook* (1996), pp. 868–869.

60. *Hoover's Online*, October 2001.

61. For Allied Chemical's early years, see Haynes, *Chemical Companies*, pp. 9–10, and the sketches of the five different premerger companies. Their activities were so different from each other that Haynes reviews them separately. Also essential are Derdak, ed., *International Directory*, vol. 1 (1988), pp. 414–416; Edward L. Hennessey Jr., *Allied Corporation: Strength through Diversification* (Princeton, NJ: Newcomen Society, 1984).

62. For Eugene Weber's legacy, see Alfred D. Chandler, "Development, Diversification, and Decentralization," in Philip E. Freeman, ed., *Postwar Economic Trends in the United States* (New York: Harper & Bros., 1960), pp. 275–277. See also Derdak, ed., *International Directory*, vol. 1 (1988), pp. 414–416; quotation from p. 414.

63. For the corporate transactions in this and the following paragraph of text, see Moskowitz et al., *Everybody's Business*, pp. 571–574; Jeff Madrick, *Taking America* (Toronto: Bantam Books, 1987), pp. 230–233.

64. For the Henley Group, see *Hoover's Handbook* (1991), p. 285; *Wall Street Journal*,

May 31, 1990, A4. For Allied Signal's revenue by product segments, see *Hoover's Handbook* (1991), p. 64

4. The Focused American Companies

1. William Haynes, *American Chemical Industry,* vol. 6: *The Chemical Companies* (New York: D. Van Norstrand, 1949), pp. 203–207, summarizes the Hercules story through the end of World War II. The company's history is told in detail in Davis Dyer and David B. Sicilia, *Labors of a Modern Hercules: The Evolution of a Chemical Company* (Boston: Harvard Business School Press, 1990), chs. 2–6. The brief review presented here relies almost wholly on this well-researched and ably presented corporate history. Chapter 4 covers the World War I years, Chapters 5 and 6 the immediate postwar years and the 1920s. The percentage of sales in the 1920s is given on p. 181. The book also provides a detailed case study of how organizational capabilities evolve. It was on Hercules's experience that Edith Penrose based much of her seminal study *The Theory of the Growth of the Firm* (Oxford: Oxford University Press, 1959).
2. Dyer and Sicilia, *Labors of a Modern Hercules,* chs. 7 and 8.
3. The postwar expansion of the two existing sets of product-specific capabilities and the creation of the new polymer/petrochemical set (next paragraph of text) are described in Dyer and Sicilia, *Labors of a Modern Hercules,* chs. 9 and 10.
4. For dimethylterephthalate (DMT) and polypropylene and downstream products, see ibid., pp. 283–306.
5. Ibid., pp. 354–355.
6. In ibid., ch. 11, the authors cover the growth of the company between 1962 and 1973. The table on p. 344 shows profits by departments for 1965–1970 and so indicates the success of the operating units. Overseas profitability is discussed on p. 352.
7. See ibid., pp. 363–373, for a review of the ventures of Hercules's new-enterprise department.
8. The information for this and the two following paragraphs of text are from ibid., ch. 12; for Hecrofina, see p. 393; for quotations, see pp. 386, 389, 403.
9. For Himont, see ibid., pp. 415–418, 424–425; for Hollingsworth's quotation in following paragraph of text, see p. 424.
10. For product portfolio changes after 1987, see ibid., pp. 418–423; *Chemical Week,* Apr. 17, 1991, p. 17–19, and Nov. 11, 1992, p. 61. For percent of sales and profits, see Thomas Derdak, ed., *International Directory of Company Histories,* vol. 22 (Chicago: St. James Press, 1998), pp. 262–263; see also *Hoover's Handbook of American Companies* (Austin, TX: Reference Press, 1995), pp. 442–443.
11. *Hoover's Online,* May 2002. See also corporate news releases from 1998–2002 on the company's Web site at www.herc.com.
12. For a summary of Rohm and Haas through World War II, see Haynes, *Chemical Companies,* pp. 356–358. The information for this company's history comes primarily from Sheldon Hochheiser, *Rohm and Haas: History of a Chemical Company*

(Philadelphia: University of Pennsylvania Press, 1986). Chapters 3–5 take the story to 1933. For the synthetic intermediate for leather, Oropan, see pp. 6–24; for dyes and other textile products, Ambersol and Paraplex, pp. 44–49; and for the insecticide, Lethane, pp. 100–102. The company's recent history is covered in Derdak, ed., *International Directory*, vol. 26 (1999), pp. 422–426.

13. Hochheiser, *Rohm and Haas*, ch. 5, gives the Plexiglas story.

14. See ibid., ch. 7, for post–World War II growth of its product lines, ch. 8 for expansion abroad, ch. 10 for developments from 1960 to 1975, ch. 11 for diversification; see also David A. Hounshell and John Kenly Smith Jr., *Science and Corporate Strategy: Du Pont R&D, 1902–1980* (New York: Cambridge University Press, 1988), p. 480.

15. Hochheiser, *Rohm and Haas*, pp. 162–165, 199–201.

16. Ibid., pp. 200–203. The figures on profits and foreign sales are in John M. Stopford, *Directory of Multinationals*, 4th ed. (New York: Stockton Press, 1989), pp. 1101–1102. See also Derdak, ed., *International Directory*, vol. 26 (1999), p. 424.

17. For Rohm and Haas in the 1990s, see Derdak, ed., *International Directory*, vol. 26 (1999), p. 425; *Hoover's Online*, May 2002.

18. This and the following two paragraphs on Air Products and Chemicals summarize information in Stopford, ed., *Directory of Multinationals*, vol. 1 (1989), pp. 18–20; Derdak, ed., *International Directory*, vol. 1 (1988), pp. 297–299. The full story is told in Andrew J. Butrica, *Out of Thin Air: A History of Air Products and Chemicals, Inc., 1940–1990* (New York: Praeger, 1990), especially ch. 8.

19. Butrica, *Out of Thin Air*, p. 229.

20. *Chemical Week*, Mar. 2, 1988, pp. 20–22; the quotation is from p. 29. For percentage of sales by geographic regions, see Stopford, ed., *Directory of Multinationals*, p. 20.

21. *Chemical Week*, Mar. 14, 1990, p. 17.

22. *Chemical Week*, Feb. 27, 1991, pp. 29–30; see also *Chemical Week*, Apr. 7, 1993, pp. 21–22.

23. For Great Lakes Chemical Corporation, see Derdak, ed., *International Directory*, vol. 14 (1996), pp. 216–218; *Moody's Industrial Manual* (1997), p. 3495. Emerson Kampen, *Great Lakes Chemical Corp.: A History of Innovation and Success* (New York: Newcomen Society, 1989), provides data to the late 1980s.

24. Derdak, ed., *International Directory*, vol. 14 (1996), p. 217.

25. For Nalco, see Derdak, ed., *International Directory*, vol. 12 (1996), pp. 346–348; *Moody's Industrial Manual* (1997), pp. 6116–6117; *Hoover's Online*, May 2002.

26. For the discover of silicones and the formation of Dow Corning, see Margaret B. W. Graham and Alec T. Shuldiner, *Corning and the Craft of Innovation* (New York: Oxford University Press, 2001), pp. 129–130, 157–159; for building the postwar product line, see ibid., pp. 161–162. See also *Business Week*, Mar. 2, 1991, pp. 37–38; *Chemical Week*, Jan. 20, 1993, p. 33; *Hoover's Online*, May 2002.

27. For Lubrizol, see Derdak, ed., *International Directory*, vol. 1 (1988), pp. 360–362; quotation from p. 360; *Moody's Industrial Manual* (1990), pp. 5885–5886, (1997), pp. 5952–5983; *Hoover's Online*, May 2002.

28. For International Flavors and Fragrances, see Derdak, ed., *International Directory,* vol. 9 (1994), pp. 290–292.

29. For Cabot Corporation, see Derdak, ed., *International Directory,* vol. 8 (1994), pp. 77–79; *Moody's Industrial Manual* (1997), p. 2868; Thomas D. Cabot, "A Short History of Cabot Corporation," in Elkan Blout, ed., *The Power of Boldness: The Master Builders of American Industry Tell Their Success Stories* (Washington, D.C.: Joseph Henry Press, 1996), esp. pp. 156–157; supplemented by *Boston Globe,* February 20, 2000, G1–2.

30. For Witco Corporation, see Derdak, ed., *International Directory,* vol. 16 (1997), pp. 540–543; William Wishnik, *The Witco Story* (New York: Newcomen Society, 1976), carries the story to 1975. See also *Moody's Industrial Manual* (1991), pp. 6540–6541, and (1997), pp. 7042–7043; *Hoover's Online,* May 2002.

31. Nathan Rosenberg, "Technological Change in Chemicals: The Role of University-Industry Relations," in Ashish Arora, Ralph Landau, and Nathan Rosenberg, *Chemicals and Long-Term Economic Growth: Insights from the Chemical Industry* (New York: Wiley, 1998), pp. 193–201; quotation from Little, p. 201; "six-tenths rule" (in next paragraph of text), p. 197.

32. For the specialized engineering firms, see Ashish Arora and Nathan Rosenberg, "Chemicals: A U.S. Success Story," pp. 96–97, and Ashish Arora and Alfonso Gambardella, "Evolution of Industry Structure in the Chemical Industry," pp. 392–397, in Arora et al., *Chemicals and Long-Term Economic Growth;* quotation from p. 395.

33. Peter Spitz, *Petrochemicals: The Rise of an Industry* (New York: Wiley, 1988), p. 303, lists these companies. For Badger, see p. 393; for UOC, see pp. 164–171, 184–194 (quotation from p. 185); for Scientific Design, see pp. 318–331.

34. For this and the next two paragraphs of text on Scientific Design, see Ralph Landau, "Entrepreneurs, Managers, and The Importance of Finance," in Blout, *Power of Boldness,* pp. 45–54; quotations from pp. 42, 43; see also p. 3.

5. The European Competitors

1. The history of the three German companies is reviewed in Alfred D. Chandler, Jr., Takashi Hikino, and David Mowery, "The Evolution of Corporate Capabilities and Corporate Strategy and Structure within the World's Largest Chemical Firms: The Twentieth Century in Perspective," in Ashish Arora, Ralph Landau, and Nathan Rosenberg, eds., *Chemicals and Long-Term Economic Growth: Insights from the Chemical Industry* (New York: Wiley, 1998), ch. 13, pp. 415–457. In the same volume, see also Jonathan Peter Murmann and Ralph Landau, "On the Making of Competitive Advantage: The Development of the Chemical Industries of Britain and Germany Since 1850," ch. 2, pp. 27–70; Ashish Arora and Alfonso Gambardella, "Evolution of Industry Structure in the Chemical Industry," ch. 12, pp. 379–413. See also Alfred D. Chandler, Jr., *Scale and Scope: The Dynamics of Industrial Capitalism* (Cambridge, MA: Harvard University Press, 1990), pp. 474–481 for the story through World War I. See also L. F. Haber, *The Chemical Industry during the Nineteenth Century* (Oxford: Oxford University Press, 1958),

pp. 170–179, and Haber, *The Chemical Industry, 1900–1930* (Oxford: Oxford University Press, 1971), pp. 90–107.

2. These data are from Haber, *The Chemical Industry, 1900–1930,* pp. 121, 145.

3. For the early history of I. G. Farben, see Chandler, *Scale and Scope,* pp. 565–584.

4. For rationalization, the operating communities, and the laboratories, see ibid., pp. 568–573. The quotation is from p. 568 (Duisberg's italics), from the text of the merger agreement of Oct. 2, 1925, in the Bayer archives.

5. E. K. Bolton, director of the chemical department (Du Pont's central research department) to Jasper Crane, vice president, June 11, 1936, in Du Pont company files at Hagley Museum and Library, Greenville, Delaware.

6. W. J. Reader, *Imperial Chemical Industries: A History,* vol. 1: *The Forerunners, 1870–1926* (London: Oxford University Press, 1970), p. 185.

7. The detailed basic story of the breakup of I. G. Farben into its constituent companies during the Allied occupation is reviewed in Raymond G. Stockes, *Divide and Prosper: The Heirs of I. G. Farben under Allied Authority, 1945–1951* (Berkeley, CA: University of California Press, 1988). Also for Hoechst, see Karl Winnaker, *Challenging Years: My Life in Chemistry* (London: Sidgwick & Jackson, 1972), ch. 6, esp. pp. 171–175, 185.

8. Raymond G. Stokes, *Opting for Oil: The Political Economy of Technological Change in the West German Chemical Industry, 1945–1961* (New York: Cambridge University Press, 1994), provides details on how the Big Three shifted to oil and the new product lines. For BASF's entry into synthetic fibers, see E. N. Brandt, *Growth Company: Dow Chemical's First Century* (East Lansing, MI: Michigan State University Press, 1997), p. 295. For additional information on the Big Three, see Thomas Derdak, ed., *International Directory of Company Histories,* vol. 1 (Chicago: St. James Press, 1988), pp. 306–307, and vol. 13 (1996), pp. 76–77.

9. For Hoechst, see Winnaker, *Challenging Years,* ch. 6, esp. pp. 171–175, 185. This impressive autobiography is one of the best studies of the German leaders after World War II. See also Stokes, *Opting for Oil;* Chandler, Hikino, and Mowery, "Evolution of Corporate Capabilities," pp. 438–439. See Davis Dyer and David B. Sicilia, *Labors of a Modern Hercules: The Evolution of a Chemical Company* (Boston: Harvard Business School Press, 1990), pp. 296–300, for the U.S. side, and Winnaker, *Challenging Years,* pp. 206–210, for Hoechst's side.

10. Dyer and Sicilia, *Labors of a Modern Hercules,* pp. 354–355; Winnaker, *Challenging Years,* pp. 192, 370–372. Hoechst had commercialized a high-grade polyester fiber, Trevira, based on ICI patents that expired in 1968. For the purchase of the Celanese film division, see Benjamin Gomes-Casseres and Krisla McQuade, "Hoechst and the German Chemical Industry," Harvard Business School Case Study N9–390–146 (rev. Feb. 28, 1990), p. 10.

11. For BASF, see Derdak, ed., *International Directory,* vol. 1 (1988), p. 307; *Hoover's Handbook of World Business* (Austin, TX: Reference Press, 1993), p. 138. For sale of 50 percent to Phillips, see *Moody's International Edition* (New York: Moody's Investor Services, 1986), p. 1520.

12. For Bayer, see Derdak, ed., *International Directory,* vol. 1 (1988), pp. 310–311.

13. Derdak, ed., *International Directory,* vol. 13 (1996), pp. 76–77, 653; *Hoover's Global 250: The Stories behind the Most Powerful Companies on the Planet* (Austin, TX: Hoover's Business Press, 1997), pp. 104–105.

14. For Ciba, Geigy, and Sandoz, see Haber, *Chemical Industry during the Nineteenth Century,* pp. 115–121; Haber, *Chemical Industry, 1900–1930,* pp. 159–162, 164, 173; for Ciba-Geigy, see Derdak, ed., *International Directory,* vol. 8 (1994), pp. 108–110; for Sandoz, see Derdak, ed., *International Directory,* vol. 1 (1988), pp. 671–673. See also John M. Stopford, *Directory of Multinationals* (New York: Stockton Press, 1989), pp. 275–276 for Ciba-Geigy and pp. 1125–1127 for Sandoz.

15. Haber, *Chemical Industry during the Nineteenth Century,* pp. 307–309; W. J. Reader, *Imperial Chemical Industries: A History,* vol. 2: *The First Quarter Century, 1926–1952* (London: Oxford University Press, 1975), pp. 190–191; William Haynes, *American Chemical Industry,* vol. 6: *The Chemical Companies* (New York: D. Van Nostrand, 1949), pp. 80–81; Derdak, ed., *International Directory,* vol. 8 (1994), p. 109.

16. For the merger and its post–World War II background, see Paul Erni, *The Basel Marriage: History of the Ciba-Geigy Merger* (Zurich: Publications Department, Neue Zurcher Zeitung, 1979), chs. 2–4; quotation from p. 35.

17. Derdak, ed., *International Directory,* vol. 8 (1994), pp. 110–111; *Hoover's Handbook of World Business,* pp. 188–189; *Chemical Week,* Sept. 12, 1990, p. 12.

18. ICI's story to 1956 is told in impressive detail by Reader in his two volumes constituting *Imperial Chemical Industries: A History.* The company's story is summarized in Chandler, Hikino, and Mowery, "Evolution of Corporate Capabilities," pp. 441–446, covering the period to 1945.

19. For ICI's profit record, see Reader, *ICI,* vol. 1, p. 413.

20. Quotation from ibid., p. 357.

21. Reader, *ICI,* vol. 2, p. 187; see Chandler, *Scale and Scope,* p. 364. Quotation from Reader, *ICI,* vol. 1, p. 359.

22. Reader, *ICI,* vol. 2, ch. 19 for plastics, and ch. 20 for fibers.

23. Reader, *ICI,* vol. 2, p. 461.

24. This and the following paragraph of text come from Andrew M. Pettigrew, *The Awakening Giant: Continuity and Change in Imperial Chemical Industries* (Oxford: Basil Blackwell, 1985). Pettigrew carefully reviews in detail the operations and their interactions through 1982 by focusing on four divisions: agricultural, petrochemical, plastics, and general chemicals and alkalis. Chapters 5 and 6 of *The Awakening Giant* on the agricultural division provide an excellent example of Pettigrew's approach.

25. Ibid., pp. 76–77, for statistics.

26. For this and especially the following paragraph on ICI's restructuring, see Derdak, ed., *International Directory,* vol. 4 (1992), pp. 667–669; *Hoover's Handbook of World Business* (1993), pp. 270–271; *Hoover's Global 250* (1995), pp. 258–259; Joseph Bower, *When Markets Quake: The Management Challenge of Restructuring*

Business (Boston: Harvard Business School Press, 1986), ch. 7 for the ICI–BP swap.

27. Reader, *ICI,* vol. 2, pp. 286, 460–461. Reader points out that ICI policy from the start was to invent their own pharmaceuticals, not to license them. See James Taggart, *The World Pharmaceutical Industry* (London: Rutledge, 1993), p. 268; William Breckon, *The Drug Makers* (London: Eyre, Methuen, 1977), pp. 39–41 for ICI, pp. 33–35 for Beecham, and pp. 37–38 for Glaxo. Ibid., p. 29, gives us the changes in rankings from 1962 to 1967. See also chapter 9 of this book.

28. Taggart, *World Pharmaceutical Industry,* pp. 267–287, p. 271 for sales by therapeutic categories.

29. Geoffrey Owen and Trevor Harrison, "Why ICI Chose to Demerge," *Harvard Business Review* (March-April 1995), pp. 133–142, provides a useful overview.

30. *Moody's International Manual* (1995), pp. 63–66, has details on ICI's assets and current product lines. *The Economist,* May 10, 1997, p. 63, reviews the bid for Unilever's specialty chemical division. Additional details can be found at *Hoover's Online,* May 2002.

31. For Henkel before World War II, see Chandler, *Scale and Scope,* pp. 378–379, 431–432, 516–517; see also Derdak, ed., *International Directory,* vol. 3 (1991), pp. 32–33.

32. As Crosfields's historian wrote, "The deal with Henkel was ultimately to prove the most profitable stroke of business Crosfields ever made." Chandler, *Scale and Scope,* pp. 432.

33. For Henkel after World War II, see *Hoover's Handbook of World Business* (1993), pp. 252–253; *Hoover's Global 250,* pp. 236–237.

34. *Hoover's Online,* June 2003.

35. For Solvay before World War II, see Haber, *Chemical Industry, 1900–1930,* pp. 137–138, and scattered references to its U.S. and European holdings; see also Derdak, ed., *International Directory,* vol. 1 (1988), pp. 394–395.

36. For Solvay after World War II, see Derdak, ed., *International Directory,* vol. 1 (1988), p. 395; *Moody's International Manual* (1995), pp. 4763–4764, lists the product lines for each of Solvay's business sectors. See Bower, *When Markets Quake,* pp. 128, 148 for the move into PVC.

37. *Hoover's Online,* June 2003; Solvay, Annual Report for 2002.

38. For VGF, see Chandler, *Scale and Scope,* pp. 307–309, 443, 513, and 583–584. For Akzo, see Derdak, ed., *International Directory,* vol. 13 (1996), pp. 21–23; *Chemical Week,* Jan. 20, 1993, p. 19.

39. For Rhône-Poulenc's early history, see Haber, *Chemical Industry, 1900–1930,* pp. 160–161, 166, 303–306; Patrick Fridenson, "France: The Relatively Slow Development of Big Business in the Twentieth Century," in Alfred D. Chandler Jr., Franco Amatori, and Takashi Hikino, *Big Business and the Wealth of Nations* (New York: Cambridge University Press, 1997), ch. 7; quotation from p. 234; Derdak, ed., *International Directory,* vol. 10 (1995), pp. 470–471.

40. After Rhône-Poulenc exited dyes, Kuhlmann Establishments, which had reentered the dye industry during World War I, remained the only French producer.

For Kuhlmann and France's position in the interwar dye industry, see Reader, *ICI*, vol. 2, pp. 191–195.

41. For Rhône-Poulenc between World War I and 1982, see Derdak, ed., *International Directory*, vol. 10 (1995), pp. 471–472; Fridenson, "France," pp. 233–235; quotation from p. 234.

42. For Rhône-Poulenc's restructuring after 1982, see Derdak, ed., *International Directory*, vol. 10 (1995), pp. 471–472; Bower, *When Markets Quake*, p. 142, for government spending in 1983; for later portfolio changes, see *Hoover's Global 250*, pp. 426–427. Also for Rhône-Poulenc Rorer's acquisition and Rorer's product line, see *New York Times*, Mar. 13, 1990; *Moody's International Manual* (1996), pp. 6372–6373.

43. Chandler, *Scale and Scope*, p. 707.

6. The American Competitors

1. Williams Haynes, *American Chemical Industry*, vol. 5: *Decade of New Products* (New York: D. Van Nostrand, 1944), p. 211.

2. For Shell, see Peter H. Spitz, *Petrochemicals: The Rise of an Industry* (New York: Wiley, 1988), pp. 82–89, 521, 530, 538–554; Kendall Beaton, *Enterprise in Oil: A History of Shell in the United States* (New York: Appleton-Century-Crofts, 1957), pp. 502, 507, 521, 530, 546.

3. For Standard of California, see Haynes, *American Chemical* Industry, vol. 6: *The Chemical Companies* (New York: D. Van Nostrand, 1949), pp. 316–319; *Moody's Manual of Investments* (New York: Moody's Investors Services, 1946), p. 2289.

4. George S. Gibb and Evelyn Noland, *History of Standard Oil Company (New Jersey)*, vol. 2: *The Resurgent Years, 1911–1927* (New York: Harper & Brothers, 1956), pp. 544–546.

5. The section in Beaton, *Enterprise in Oil*, entitled "Development of 100 Octanes," pp. 560–574, provides an excellent detailed review of the introduction of the polymerization process and resulting catalytic cracking techniques, including references to the roles of Jersey Standard and Phillips. Useful, too, is Spitz, *Petrochemicals*, pp. 82–89.

6. Henrietta M. Larson and Kenneth Wiggins Porter, *History of Humble Oil & Refining Company: A Study in Industrial Growth* (New York: Harper & Brothers, 1959), pp. 556–565.

7. Beaton, *Enterprise in Oil*, p. 575. The synthetic rubber Buna program based on butadiene was much smaller than the 100-octane project. See ibid., pp. 592–598; Larson and Porter, *History of Humble Oil*, pp. 597–600. Again, Shell, Jersey Standard, and Phillips were the leading players.

8. Joseph L. Bower, *When Markets Quake: The Management Challenge of Restructuring Industry* (Boston: Harvard Business School Press, 1986), pp. 16–17.

9. Spitz, *Petrochemicals*, p. 340.

10. The information on the postwar period of Jersey's petrochemical business comes largely from Bennett H. Wall et al., *Growth in a Changing Environment: A History of*

Standard Oil Company (New Jersey), Exxon Corporation, 1950–1975 (New York: McGraw-Hill, 1988), ch. 5. For Howard's and Rathbone's recommendations, see pp. 175–184, 189–200, and 225–227.

11. Ibid., pp. 197–200.

12. Ibid., pp. 192–197; quotation from p. 215.

13. Ibid., pp. 197–212, 225–226; quotation from p. 204.

14. Ibid., pp. 215–229.

15. Ibid., p. 229–238;, quotation from p. 230; profit figures, p. 237.

16. Bower, *When Markets Quake,* pp. 112–117; Wall, *Growth in a Changing Environment,* p. 237.

17. *Hoover's Handbook* (Austin, TX: Reference Press, 1993), p. 106; *Hoover's Handbook* (1995), p. 351.

18. For Shell, see Bower, *When Markets Quake,* pp. 113–115, 175–180, quotations on pp. 175–176; see also Thomas Derdak, ed., *International Directory of Company Histories,* vol. 14 (1996), pp. 439–440. For Shell's percentage of product revenues worldwide, see *Hoover's Global 250: The Stories behind the Most Powerful Companies on the Planet* (Austin, TX: Hoover's Business Press, 1997), p. 250.

19. For Phillips, see Derdak, ed., *International Directory,* vol. 4 (1991), pp. 521–523; quotations from pp. 522, 523; see also Spitz, *Petrochemicals,* pp. 264, 295, 336, 340, 540; Beaton, *Enterprise in Oil,* p. 522; *Hoover's Handbook* (1996), p. 697. Phillips's recovery was held up in October 1989 by an explosion at the plastics plant in Texas that caused $500 million in damage.

20. For Standard of California (Chevron), see Derdak, ed., *International Directory,* vol. 4 (1991), his letter on the company's chemicals. See also *Hoover's Handbook* (1991), p. 163; (1996), pp. 213–214. See *Moody's Industrial Manual* (New York: Moody's Investors Services, 1996), p. 2894, for the sale of Ortho to Monsanto.

21. For Standard of Indiana (Amoco) and Landau's contribution, see Derdak, ed., *International Directory,* vol. 14 (1996), pp. 23–24; *Hoover's Handbook* (1991), p. 120; Ralph Landau, "Entrepreneurs, Managers, and the Importance of Finance," in Elkan Blout, ed., *The Power of Boldness* (Washington, D.C.: Joseph Henry Press, 1996); quotations in this and preceding paragraphs in text from ibid., p. 46; see also Spitz, *Petrochemicals,* pp. 327–328.

22. For Arco and Landau's contribution, see Derdak, ed., *International Directory,* vol. 10 (1995), pp. 110–111; Landau, "Entrepreneurs, Managers, and the Importance of Finance," pp. 46–53. For the spin-off of Arco Chemicals and Lyondell, see Derdak, ed., *International Directory,* vol. 4 (1991), pp. 456–457; quotation from p. 457; *Hoover's Online,* June 2003.

23. For Standard Oil of Ohio (Sohio, BP America), see Derdak, ed., *International Directory,* vol. 7 (1993), pp. 57–58; Spitz, *Petrochemicals,* pp. 297, 380, 545; quotation from p. 297.

24. For Ashland Oil, see Derdak, ed., *International Directory,* vol. 4 (1991), p. 374; quotation from p. 374; *Hoover's Handbook* (1995), p. 113.

25. For Socony-Mobil (Mobil), see Derdak, ed., *International Directory,* vol. 7 (1993), p. 353; Spitz, *Petrochemicals,* p. 549; see also Beaton, *Enterprise in Oil,* pp. 575–580.

26. For Texaco, see Derdak, ed., *International Directory*, vol. 14 (1996), p. 442; Spitz, *Petrochemicals*, p. 319; *Hoover's Handbook* (1991), p. 529; (1993), p. 531; (1996), p. 529.

27. For Occidental, see Derdak, ed., *International Directory*, vol. 4 (1991), pp. 480–482; *Hoover's Handbook* (1989), p. 415; (1991), p. 433; (1994), p. 650; *Moody's Industrial Manual* (1996), pp. 4683–4684.

28. For Elf-Acquitaine, see Derdak, ed., *International Directory*, vol. 7 (1993), p. 484; *Hoover's Global 250* (1997), p. 190. See also Patrick Fridenson, "France: The Relatively Slow Development of Big Business in the Twentieth Century," in Alfred D. Chandler, Jr., Franco Amatori, and Takashi Hikino, eds., *Big Business and the Wealth of Nations* (New York: Cambridge University Press, 1997, p. 234.

29. The history of diversification in these companies is well summarized in Michael Ollinger, "The Limits of Growth of the Multidivisional Firm: A Case Study of the U.S. Oil Industry from 1930–1990," *Strategic Management Journal*, 15 (Sept. 1994): pp. 503–520. For percentage of revenues, see company entries in *Hoover's Handbook* (1993); percentages for coal are not listed for either Exxon or Mobil.

30. For General Electric, see Kendall Burr, *Pioneering in Industrial Research: The Story of General Electric Research Laboratory* (Washington, D.C.: Public Affairs Press, 1957), pp. 61–63, 114–117, and 134–139; quotation from p. 137.

31. Ibid., pp. 154–155, 179; Robert Slater, *The New GE: How Jack Welch Revived an American Institution* (Homewood, IL: Business One Irwin, 1993), pp. 32–39; General Electric Co., Annual Report for 1991, p. 11; for 1993, p. 15; *Hoover's Online*, June 2003.

32. For PPG, see Alfred D. Chandler, Jr., *Scale and Scope: The Dynamics of Industrial Capitalism* (Cambridge, MA: Harvard University Press, 1990), p. 114; Derdak, ed., *International Directory*, vol. 3 (1991), pp. 731–733.

33. For Eastman Chemical, see Derdak, ed., *International Directory*, vol. 14 (1996), pp. 174–175; quotation from p. 175; Spitz, *Petrochemicals*, pp. 245, 289, 294; *Hoover's Handbook* (1995), pp. 324–325. In 1991 chemicals accounted for 18 percent of sales and 23 percent of operating income.

34. *Hoover's Online*, June 2003.

35. W. R. Grace's experience as a conglomerate to the end of the 1980s is summarized in Derdak, ed., *International Directory*, vol. 1 (1988), pp. 547–549, supplemented by Milton Moskowitz, Robert Levering, and Michael Katz, *Everybody's Business: A Field Guide to the 400 Leading Companies in America* (New York: Doubleday Currency, 1990), pp. 529–530.

36. For Davison Chemicals and Dewey & Almy, see Haynes, *American Chemical Industry*, vol. 6, pp. 94–96, 99–101.

37. The quotation is from *York Times*, Nov. 5, 1991, D1, D5; see also *Hoover's Handbook* (1993), p. 303; John M. Stopford, *Directory of Multinationals*, 4th ed. (New York: Stockton Press, 1992), p. 304. Since 1991 Grace has continued to sell off most of its remaining other businesses. See *Chemical and Engineering News*, May 29, 1994, pp. 26–27; *Moody's Industrial Manual* (1996), p. 3397.

38. *Hoover's Online*, June 2003.

39. Derdak, ed., *International Directory*, vol. 13 (1996), pp. 379–381, provides a more

detailed review of Olin's conglomerate experience before 1990 and its more focused growth, largely through internal investment after that date; see also *Forbes,* Dec. 7, 1992, pp. 122–123.

40. *Hoover's Online,* June 2003.

41. For Ethyl Corporation, see Derdak, ed., *International Directory,* vol. 10 (1995), pp. 289–291; Stopford, *Directory of Multinationals* (1989), pp. 465–467. For a much more complete account up to circa 1980, see Joseph C. Robert, *Ethyl: A History of the Corporation and the People Who Made It* (Charlottesville, VA: University of Virginia Press, 1983).

42. *Moody's Industrial Manual* (1997), p. 3278; Ethyl Corporation Web site, June 2003.

43. For the FMC Corporation, see Derdak, ed., *International Directory,* vol. 11 (1995), pp. 133–135, which provides a more detailed account.

44. *Hoover's Online,* June 2003. Quotation is preceding paragraph in text from Derdak, ed., *International Directory,* vol. 11 (1995), p. 135.

45. For Morton International, see Derdak, ed., *International Directory,* vol. 9 (1994), pp. 358–359; *Hoover's Handbook* (1996), pp. 620–621; *Business Week,* July 8, 1991, p. 82. See also *New York Times,* June 6, 1997, F5, which provides an interesting comparison of Morton's salt and air bag businesses.

46. For Lyondell and Equistar, see *Hoover's Online,* June 2003.

47. For Huntsman Chemical, see Sarah J. Lane, "Corporate Restructuring in the Chemical Industry," in Margaret Blair, ed., *Takeovers, LBOs, and Changing Corporate Forms* (Washington, D.C.: Brookings Institution, 1992), pp. 28–32; Derdak, ed., *International Directory,* vol. 8 (1994), pp. 261–263; *Hoover's Online,* June 2003; Huntsman Corporation Web site, June 2003.

7. The American Companies: The Prescription Path

1. Jonathan Liebenau, *Medical Science and Medical Industry: The Formation of the American Pharmaceutical Industry* (Baltimore: Johns Hopkins, 1987), chs. 1–2, pp. 30–37, 49–51; quotation from p. 34.

2. Ibid., pp. 109–112; Heinz Redwood, *The Pharmaceutical Industry: Trends, Problems, and Achievements* (Felixstowe, England: Oldwicks Press, 1987), pp. 26–30, for the new technologies. Redwood's dates for the extractive chemical wave are 1917–1932. See also Peter Temin, *Taking Your Medicine: Drug Regulation in the United States* (Cambridge, MA: Harvard University Press, 1980), pp. 4, 59, 63–64, 227.

3. Redwood, *The Pharmaceutical Industry,* p. 43. For the therapeutic revolution, see Temin, *Taking Your Medicine,* ch. 4. Particularly useful is Temin's review of the discovery of antibiotics, including penicillin (pp. 64–75), that occurred after sulfa drugs were discovered in 1935. The consumer expenditures on drugs is given on p. 4. Also valuable is Basil Achilladelis, "Innovation in the Pharmaceutical Industry," in Ralph Landau, Basil Achilladelis, and Alexander Scriabine, eds., *Pharmaceutical Innovation: Revolutionizing Human Health* (Philadelphia: Chemical Heritage Press, 1999), pp. 162–168.

4. Temin, *Taking Your Medicine*, p. 4.

5. Margaret Sharp and Ilaria Galimberti, "Coherence and Diversity: Europe's Chemical Giants and the Assimilation of Biotechnology," University of Sussex, ESRC Centre on Science, Technology, Energy, and Environmental Policy, July 1993, p. 14.

6. Alfonso Gambardella, *Science and Innovation: The U.S. Pharmaceutical Industry during the 1980s* (New York: Cambridge University Press, 1995), pp. 23–24.

7. The story of the critical creation of the new scientific discipline is well told in Victor K. McElkeny, *Watson and D.N.A.: Making a Scientific Revolution* (Cambridge, MA: Perseus Publishing Group, 2003), esp. chs. 6–8 and pp. 201–205 for Watson's role at Harvard.

8. Capsule histories of Merck and Pfizer, with financial information, are found in *Hoover's Handbook of American Companies: Profiles of Major U.S. Companies* (Austin, TX: Reference Press, 1995), pp. 600–601, 690–691.

9. For an overview of Merck, see Thomas Derdak, ed., *International Directory of Company Histories*, vol. 1 (Chicago: St. James Press, 1988), pp. 650–652. Much more detail is provided in two papers by Louis Galambos and Jeffrey L. Sturchio, "Transnational Investment: The Merck Experience, 1891–1925," in Hans Pohl, *Transnational Investment from the 19th Century to the Present* (Stuttgart: Verlag, 1994), pp. 227–243, and "The Origins of an Innovative Organization: Merck & Co., Inc. 1891–1960" (typescript, 1992). For a review of the commercialization of vitamins, see idem at pp. 19–28. I am grateful to Professor Galambos for providing me with a copy of this paper.

10. Temin, *Taking Your Medicine*, pp. 66–70.

11. Galambos and Sturchio, "The Origins of an Innovative Organization," pp. 29–30; Louis Galambos with Jane Eliot Sewell, *Networks of Innovation: Vaccine Development at Merck, Sharp & Dohme, and Mulford, 1895–1995* (New York: Cambridge University Press, 1995), chs. 1–3. Professor Galambos also provided me with a copy of a relevant document from the Merck corporate archive: "Memorandum for the files from Orville H. Schell, Nov. 17, 1947. Re: Applicability of Federal Antitrust Laws to Possible Entry of Merck & Co., Inc., into the Pharmaceutical Business." This document provides an excellent review of Merck's situation as to possible acquisition of Sharp & Dohme, as well as its own position in the industry.

12. Louis Galambos and Jeffrey L. Sturchio, "Sustaining Innovation: Critical Transaction at Merck & Co., Inc." (unpublished manuscript, May 1997), p. 23. For the measles, rubella, and mumps vaccines, see Galambos with Sewell, *Networks of Innovation*, pp. 97–122.

13. "Merck in the Golden Years: Growth of a Leader in Health Care," pp. 18–20, in the company's monthly journal in the Merck corporate archive. For a brief overview of Merck's program of diversification, see Louis Galambos, "The Authority and Responsibility of the Chief Executive Officer: Shifting Patterns in Large U.S. Enterprises in the Twentieth Century," *Industrial and Corporate Change* 4, no. 1 (1995): 196–197.

14. "Ready, Aim," an interview with Henry W. Gadsen on the company's diversi-
    fication in the company's magazine, 1970; "Memorandum on the company's
    withdrawal from research management and marketing operations in
    electrochemicals, Dec. 12, 1963"; and "Selected events in the development of
    Merck's consumer product business as documented from Merck annual reports,
    1962–1977," all in Merck corporate archive.

15. For the sale to English China Clays, see *New York Times,* June 12, 1993;
    Galambos, "Authority and Responsibility," 197–198.

16. James Taggart, *World Pharmaceutical Industry* (London: Routledge, 1993),
    pp. 163–164, 166–169, 174, 179–182. A useful review of Merck's product port-
    folio is in *New York Times,* Feb. 16, 1992. Louis Galambos and Jeffrey L. Sturchio,
    "Pharmaceutical Firms and the Transition to Biotechnology: A Study in Strategic
    Innovation," *Business History Review* 72 (Summer 1998): 255–256, provides a
    brief review of Merck's response to the new learning. See also Gambardella, *Sci-
    ence and Innovation,* p. 23 for Mevacor as an example of discovery by design, and
    p. 24 for the top ten pharmaceutical products in 1991.

17. Galambos with Sewell, *Networks of Innovation,* pp. 197–205, for the development
    of an rDNA hepatitis B vaccine. For contracts with rDNA startups, see
    Gambardella, *Science and Innovation,* pp. 70–72.

18. Taggart, *World Pharmaceutical Industry,* pp. 164–165; *Business Week,* Oct. 23, 1989;
    "Memorandum on Entry into the Over-the-Counter Healthcare Market, Mar.
    28, 1989 (copy in Merck corporate archive); "Du Pont and Merck to Begin a Re-
    search and Marketing Collaboration," Merck press release, Sept. 28, 1989. In
    1990, Johnson & Johnson and Merck Consumer Pharmaceuticals acquired Im-
    perial Chemical Industries's U.S. OTC division for $450 million, and in the fol-
    lowing year purchased Rhône–Poulenc's European OTC business. See *New York
    Times,* May 23, 1991.

19. *New York Times,* Aug. 5, 1993; *Hoover's Handbook* (1995), pp. 600–601.

20. For an overview of Pfizer's history, see Derdak, ed., *International Directory,* vol. 9
    (1994), pp. 402–405. Edmund T. Pratt, Jr., *Pfizer, Bringing Science to Life* (Prince-
    ton, NJ: Newcomen Society/Princeton University Press, 1985), (pp. 7–11), is
    particularly useful for its review of the development of penicillin.

21. Pratt, *Pfizer,* pp. 11–14; Temin, *Taking Your Medicine,* pp. 66, 69–74. McKeen's ag-
    gressive strategy is well defined in Milton Moskowitz, Michael Katz, and Robert
    Levering, *Everybody's Business: An Almanac* (San Francisco: Harper & Row, 1980);
    Derdak, ed., *International Directory,* vol. 9, p. 403.

22. This and the following paragraph are based on Derdak, ed., *International Direc-
    tory,* vol. 9, pp. 402–405; John M. Stopford, *Directory of Multinationals* (New York:
    Stockton Press, 1989), pp. 998–1000; *Moody's Industrial Manual* (New York:
    Moody's Investors Services, 1988), pp. 3305–3308.

23. Pfizer's performance in the 1970s and 1980s is reviewed in detail in Taggart,
    World Pharmaceutical Industry, pp. 206–230. Especially useful are tables featuring
    Pfizer's financial performance, revenues by product segment, and country mar-
    kets, as well as R&D expenditures.

24. Gambardella, *Science and Innovation,* pp. 54, 74–77; table 3.5 lists Pfizer's set of agreements with other drug companies.

25. Taggart, *World Pharmaceutical Industry,* pp. 214–217; see also *Hoover's Handbook* (1991), p. 432. The percentage of specialty chemicals reflects the company's pre–World War II business.

26. *Business Week,* July 1, 1991, pp. 86–87; *New York Times,* Dec. 12, 1991, Mar. 17, 1992, and Aug. 18, 1992. See also *Moody's Industrial Manual* (1991), pp. 3297–3299. Pfizer sold its Shirley heart-valve unit in 1992 after a defective product forced the company to set aside $300 million to meet claims from resulting lawsuits. This accounts for the company's decline in revenues noted in Table 1.2.

27. See *Hoover's Handbook* (1996), pp. 690–691. In addition, animal health accounted for 7 percent of sales and 2 percent of income, with consumer products accounting for 5 percent and 2 percent, respectively. For Pfizer's network of agreements in the new molecular technology and its rDNA startups, see Gambardella, *Science and Innovation,* pp. 73–75.

28. For an overview of Eli Lilly, see Derdak, ed., *International Directory,* vol. 11 (1995), pp. 89–91. James A. Madison, *Eli Lilly: A Life, 1885–1977* (Indianapolis, IN: Indiana Historical Society, 1989), chs. 4–5, provides information on the interwar years.

29. Temin, *Taking Your Medicine,* pp. 79–80.

30. The information in this and the following paragraph comes from Derdak, ed., *International Directory,* vol. 11 (1995), pp. 89–90; *Hoover's Handbook* (1989), p. 223; Stopford, *Directory of Multinationals,* pp. 448–450; Thomas Malnight, "Eli Lilly and Company (A): Globalization," Harvard Business School Case Study No. 391–032 (1990) (rev. Mar. 18, 1993, and his Harvard Business School doctoral dissertation, Managing the Globalization Process: An Exploratory Process (1992). See also the detailed article in *Business Week,* Oct. 29, 1979, pp. 135–145. Diversification in the 1970s reduced expansion abroad, so that foreign sales as a percentage of total sales dropped off.

31. For Lilly's investment in the new learning and discovery by design techniques, see Gambardella, *Science and Innovation,* pp. 24 (for top ten), 31–32, 87–90; see also Malnight dissertation, pp. 2, 3, 21; *Business Week,* Nov. 23, 1992, pp. 70–75.

32. The beginnings of Genentech and its relationship with Eli Lilly are told in an impressive and well-documented manner in Maureen D. McKelvey, *Evolutionary Innovations: The Business of Biotechnology* (New York: Oxford University Press, 1996), chs. 6–8; pp. 130–133 are particularly relevant for Gilbert's activities. See also the references in my endnotes to chapter 11. For Eli Lilly's search for substitutes for existing sources of insulin, see Madison, *Eli Lilly,* pp. 106–107.

33. Derdak, ed., *International Directory,* vol. 11 (1995), p. 91; *Hoover's Handbook* (1993), p. 258.

34. *Business Week,* Nov. 23, 1982.

35. Derdak, ed., *International Directory,* vol. 11 (1995), p. 758; *Hoover's Handbook* (1993), p. 258.

36. *Hoover's Handbook* (1996), pp. 336–337; Derdak, ed., *International Directory*, vol. 11 (1995), p. 89.

37. For an overview of Abbott, see Derdak, ed., *International Directory*, vol. 11 (1995), pp. 7–9; Taggart, *World Pharmaceutical Industry*, pp. 185–186; Stopford, *Directory of Multinationals*. For erythromycin, see Temin, *Taking Your Medicine*, pp. 77–78.

38. *Moody's Industrial Manual* (1986), p. 1; Derdak, ed., *International Directory*, vol. 11 (1995), pp. 7–8; Stopford, *Directory of Multinationals*, p. 481.

39. The crisis and response are described in *Business Week*, Apr. 26, 1976; Robert Teitelman, *Gene Dreams: Wall Street, Academia, and the Rise of Biotechnology* (New York: Basic Books, 1989), ch. 12.

40. Quoted in Taggart, *World Pharmaceutical Industry*, p. 191, from the company's 1975 "Review of Operations."

41. For this and the next paragraph of text, see ibid., pp. 189–194.

42. For this paragraph of text and the next, see Teitelman, *Gene Dreams*, pp. 115–121, which reviews Abbott's swift rise to dominance and its impact on the new rDNA startups, including among others Genetic Systems, Hybritech, Oncogen, and Syva.

43. Gambardella, *Science and Innovation*, p. 38.

44. For this and the following paragraph of text, see *Business Week*, Oct. 30, 1989, pp. 136–137. These estimated figures for 1989 are the only ones that list pharmaceuticals and nutrition separately. The combined figures of the two in *Moody's Industrial Manual* (1991), p. 6, are somewhat higher. For Abbott's deal with Takeda, see *Business Week*, May 20, 1982; *Chemical Week*, Apr. 17, 1985, p. 10; Derdak, ed., *International Directory*, vol. 40 (2001), p. 11.

45. *Hoover's Handbook* (1996), pp. 44–45.

46. For an overview of SmithKline before the merger with Beecham, see Derdak, ed., *International Directory*, vol. 1 (1988), pp. 692–694.

47. For Thorazine, see Temin, *Taking Your Medicine*, pp. 79–80.

48. *Moody's Industrial Manual* (1988), pp. 6289; Stopford, *Directory of Multinationals* (1989), pp. 1178–1182; Moskowitz et al., *Everybody's Business*, pp. 243–244.

49. Gambardella, *Science and Innovation*, pp. 24–25.

50. Information in this and the next paragraph of text is based on *Wall Street Journal*, Nov. 6, 1981; *Moody's Industrial Manual* (1988), p. 6289; Milton Moskowitz, Robert Levering, and Michael Katz, *Everybody's Business: A Field Guide to the 400 Leading Companies in America* (New York: Doubleday, 1990), pp. 168–170. The last reference includes Beckman's comment in the following paragraph.

51. Gambardella, *Science and Innovation*, pp. 95–96; quotation from p. 96. See also *New York Times*, Sept. 30, 1988; *Chemical Week*, Oct. 5, 1988; Stopford, *International Directory* (1989), pp. 1178–1182.

52. *Wall Street Journal*, Apr. 12, 1989.

53. Taggart, *World Pharmaceutical Industry*, pp. 441–442, has a useful evaluation of strengths and weaknesses of the merger. For postmerger performance, see Stopford, *Directory of Multinationals* (1992), p. 1242; *Hoover's Global 250* (1997), pp. 486–487.

54. For an overview of Squibb, see Derdak, ed., *International Directory,* vol. 1 (1988), pp. 695–697; Temin, *Taking Your Medicine,* pp. 31, 66.

55. Temin, *Taking Your Medicine,* pp. 66, 67, 69, 72, 153.

56. *New York Times,* Jan. 28, 1968; *Wall Street Journal,* Mar. 5, 1969, Mar. 5, 1971, Oct. 27, 1971, and Dec. 6, 1971.

57. Derdak, ed., *International Directory,* vol. 1, 1988, p. 697; Gambardella, *Science and Innovation,* pp. 93–95; *Wall Street Journal,* May 28, 1987, featuring the quotation.

58. *Wall Street Journal,* Nov. 9, 1986; see also *Business Week,* Oct. 10, 1988, pp. 68, 76; Gambardella, *Science and Innovation,* pp. 94–95. In 1985 Squibb also sold off an electronic medical company that did not fit in with the other purchases.

59. *Business Week,* Aug. 14, 1988, and Dec. 3, 1990.

60. For Upjohn, see Derdak, ed., *International Directory,* vol. 8 (1994), pp. 547–548; for antibiotics and sulfa-based drugs, see Temin, *Taking Your Medicine,* pp. 72, 80.

61. For this and the next paragraph of text, see Derdak, ed., *International Directory,* vol. 8 (1994), p. 548; *Moody's Industrial Manual* (1988), pp. 4001–4002. The quotation is from p. 4002.

62. *Wall Street Journal,* Feb. 2, 1990; *Business Week,* June 4, 1990, p. 100; Gambardella, *Science and Innovation,* pp. 53–54, 81; *Hoover's Handbook* (1993), pp. 558–559. Although Upjohn was a leader in genetic engineering patents, its name does not appear on Orsenigo's list of research contracts by established companies. See Luigi Orsenigo, *The Emergence of Biotechnology: Institutions and Markets in Industrial Innovation* (New York: St. Martin's Press, 1989), pp. 117, 119, 124, 131.

63. *Business Week,* May 3, 1993, p. 36, an article entitled "At Upjohn a Grim Changing of the Guard."

8. The American Companies: The Over-the-Counter Path

1. For an overview of Bristol-Myers, see Thomas Derdak, ed., *International Directory of Company Histories* (Chicago: St. James Press, 1988), vol. 1, pp. 710–712; see also vol. 9 (1994), pp. 88–91.

2. Peter Temin, *Taking Your Medicine: Drug Regulation in the United States* (Cambridge, MA: Harvard University Press, 1980), pp. 70, 72, 75; quotation from p. 75.

3. For this and the following paragraph of text, see John M. Stopford, ed., *Directory of Multinationals* 3rd ed. (New York: Stockton Press, 1989), pp. 204–206; *Moody's Industrial Manual* (New York: Moody's Investor Services, 1969), p. 1453, and (1988), pp. 126–133. The 1988 *Moody's* includes a long letter from Richard L. Gleb, chairman of the board, that appeared in the company's 1987 annual report.

4. For this and the following paragraph of text, see Alfonso Gambardella, *Science and Innovation: The U.S. Pharmaceutical Industry during the 1980s* (New York: Cambridge University Press, 1995), pp. 31, 49, 87, 92–95, 131; quotation in the next paragraph of text from p. 92; see also Robert Teitelman, *Gene Dreams: Wall Street,*

Academia and the Rise of Biotechnology (New York: Basic Books, 1989), pp. 143–145, 153–154, 180–185; *Moody's Industrial Manual* (1988), p. 126 (for animal health but not dental sales.)

5. *Business Week,* Aug. 14, 1989, pp. 80–81, Dec. 3, 1990, pp. 138–139.

6. For this and the following paragraph of text, see *Business Week,* Aug. 10, 1992, pp. 90–91; *New York Times,* Feb. 16, 1993; *Hoover's Handbook of American Business* (Austin, TX: Reference Press, 1993), p. 167, and (1996), pp. 178–179.

7. Bristol-Myers sold off Genetic Systems in 1991 and Omocogen in 1992, with its high-priced Taxol for ovarian cancer. *Business Week,* Aug. 10, 1992, Feb. 1, 1993, and Feb. 22, 1993; *Moody's Industrial Manual* (1993), pp. 121–125, which includes Gleb's letter to stockholders in the 1992 annual report; *Hoover's Handbook* (1996), pp. 778–779. The complex story of Bristol-Myers Squibb's relatively unsuccessful performance after the mid-1990s is best reviewed in the article "Will Pain Ever Let Up at Bristol Myers?" in *New York Times,* May 18, 2003, sec. 3, pp. 1, 12.

8. For an overview of Schering-Plough, see Derdak, ed., *International Directory,* vol. 1 (1988), pp. 683–685. The Abe Plough quotation is from Milton Moskowitz, Michael Katz, and Robert Levering, *Everybody's Business: The Irreverent Guide to Corporate America* (San Francisco: Harper & Row, 1980), p. 241.

9. For the merger, see *Wall Street Journal,* June 24 and Oct. 1, 1970, and Oct. 2, 1973; Derdak, ed., *International Directory,* vol. 1 (1988), p. 683.

10. *Wall Street Journal,* April 30, 1982; *Hoover's Handbook* (1991), p. 485; Stopford, ed., *Directory of Multinationals* (1989), pp. 1140–1142; *Moody's Industrial Manual* (1988), p. 6001. According to *Moody's,* foreign subsidiaries had one of the two names but overseas operating units did not.

11. Derdak, ed., *International Directory,* vol. 1 (1988), pp. 684–685. See the same source for Bennet's activities referred to in the following paragraph of text.

12. For the Biogen connection, see *Wall Street Journal,* Oct. 23, 1980. For the approval of Intron A, see *Business Week,* June 16, 1986. For F. Hoffmann–La Roche, see *New York Times,* July 24, 1985; *Hoover's Handbook* (1993), p. 493. In 1982 came the purchase of Driax, a Swiss-owned company based in Palo Alto, California; *Wall Street Journal,* Apr. 30, 1982; see also Gambardella, *Science and Innovation,* pp. 49, 52, and 68.

13. For Key Pharmaceuticals, see *Wall Street Journal,* Mar. 20, 1986, and Apr. 4, 1990. For sales listed in the following paragraph of text, see *Hoover's Handbook* (1993), p. 493; *Wall Street Journal,* Apr. 4, 1990.

14. Stopford, ed., *Directory of Multinationals* (1989), p. 1142; *Hoover's Handbook* (1993), p. 485, and (1996), pp. 760–761.

15. For an overview of Warner-Lambert, see Derdak, ed., *International Directory,* vol. 1 (1988), pp. 710–712, and vol. 10 (1995), pp. 549–551.

16. Stopford, ed., *Directory of Multinationals* (1989), pp. 1399–1400; *Moody's Industrial Manual* (1988), pp. 4420–4425.

17. For Parke Davis before World War II, see Williams Haynes, *The American Chemical Industry,* vol. 6: *The Chemical Companies* (New York: D. Van Nostrand, 1942),

pp. 320–324. See also Alfred D. Chandler Jr., *Scale and Scope: The Dynamics of In-dustrial Capitalism* (Cambridge, MA: Harvard University Press, 1990), pp. 155 and 164; Temin, *Taking Your Medicine*, p. 69. For the merger terms, see *Moody's In-dustrial Manual* (1988), p. 4420. With the merger, the company's name was changed from Warner-Lambert Pharmaceuticals to Warner-Lambert Company.

18. Moskowitz et al., *Everybody's Business*, p. 251.

19. The first quotation is from *Wall Street Journal*, Apr. 16, 1981; the second, that of the company's CEO, from Moskowitz et al., *Everybody's Business*, p. 251.

20. *Wall Street Journal*, Nov. 27, 1985, and March 7, 1986; Stopford, ed., *Directory of Multinationals* (1989), p. 1400.

21. *Business Week*, Sept. 24, 1990; *Hoover's Handbook* (1993), p. 573, and (1996), p. 913.

22. *Hoover's Handbook* (1993), p. 573, and (1996), p. 913.

23. James Taggart, *World Pharmaceutical Industry* (London: Routledge, 1993), p. 35; see also Gambardella, *Science and Innovation*, p. 84.

24. For an overview of American Home Products, see Haynes, *American Chemical In-dustry*, vol. 6, pp. 28–30; quotation from p. 28. Haynes noted that the company's products were "nationally advertised and distributed proprietary remedies, some of them having been on the market for 30 years bearing well-known brand names." See also Derdak, ed., *International Directory*, vol. 10 (1995), pp. 68–70, for a discussion of the company's acquisitions before the end of World War II that stresses its "marketing genius."

25. Moskowitz et al., *Everybody's Business*, also notes that Stuart Wyeth at his death in 1929 willed his controlling securities to Harvard. By 1931, the price of these had plummeted.

26. Moskowitz et al., ibid., pp. 213–215, lists product lines and percentages of total sales represented by each in 1979. The 1989 breakdowns of sales by line of busi-ness appear in Stopford, ed., *Directory of Multinationals*, 4th ed. (1992), p. 87.

27. For the new strategy, see *Fortune*, July 25, 1983, p. 59. For Sherwood, see *Busi-ness Week*, Feb. 17, 1982, p. 92. For Wrigley, see *Wall Street Journal*, April 17, 1984. For Suchard, see *Wall Street Journal*, Nov. 26, 1986.

28. For information in this and the next paragraph of text, see Gambardella, *Science and Innovation*, pp. 101–102. For Chesebrough-Ponds hospital supply, see *Wall Street Journal*, Sept. 18, 1986. For Bristol-Myers animal health, see *Wall Street Journal*, Oct. 2, 1987. For A. H. Robbins, see *Wall Street Journal*, Feb. 17, 1987, and Jan. 26, 1988. For percentages, see Stopford, ed., *Directory of Multinationals* (1988), p. 72. The figures are undated but end with the year 1987.

29. For the financial information in this and the following paragraph of text, see *Hoover's Handbook* (1993), p. 110, and (1996), pp. 78–79; Derdak, ed., *Interna-tional Directory* (1995), p. 70.

30. For the Genetics Institute, see *New York Times*, Sept. 20, 1991, and references in Chapter 10.

31. *Business Week*, Sept. 15, 1994, p. 29; *Chemical Week*, Aug. 24, 1994 (unpaginated reprint); *Hoover's Handbook* (1997), pp. 78–79.

9. The American and European Competitors

1. For this and the next three paragraphs of text on Johnson & Johnson to the mid-1980s, see Thomas Derdak, ed., *International Directory of Company Histories*, vol. 8 (Chicago: St. James Press, 1994), pp. 281–283; *Moody's Industrial Manual* (New York: Moody's Investor Services, 1988), pp. 4001–4003; John M. Stopford, ed., *Directory of Multinationals* (New York: Stockton Press, 1988), pp. 689–691; *Hoover's Handbook of 500 Major American Companies*, (Austin, TX: Reference Press, 1991), pp. 317.

2. For the partnership with Chiron, see Chapter 10, endnote 12. For that with Merck, see *Chemical Week*, Apr. 5, 1989; *Wall Street Journal*, Mar. 29, 1980, p. 84; and *Business Week*, Apr. 10, 1989, pp. 64, 67, and May 28, 1990, pp. 86–89.

3. *Hoover's Handbook* (1996), pp. 498–499.

4. For Procter & Gamble through the mergers of the 1980s, see Derdak, ed., *International Directory*, vol. 8, 1994, pp. 431–434; Stopford, ed., *Directory of Multinationals*, 4th ed. (1992), pp. 1072–1075; *Business Week*, Oct. 21, 1985, pp. 111–112; *Chemical Week*, Mar. 31, 1982, p. 13, and Nov. 13, 1985, p. 12.

5. For Procter & Gamble's deal with Syntex, see Alfonso Gambardella, *Science and Innovation: The U.S. Pharmaceutical Industry during the 1980s* (New York: Cambridge University Press, 1995), p. 99. For the company's commitment to pharmaceuticals, see *New York Times*, Nov. 4, 1997, D1, D4; Davis Dyer, Frederick Dalzell, and Rowena Olegario, *Rising Tide: Lessons from 165 Years of Brand Building at Procter & Gamble* (Boston: Harvard Business School Press, 2004), ch. 18.

6. For the Eastman venture into pharmaceuticals, see Derdak, ed., *International Directory*, vol. 9 (1993), pp. 163–164; *Hoover's Handbook* (1996), pp. 326–327; *Business Week*, May 16, 1994, p. 32; *New York Times*, June 24, 1994, D10, and Oct. 15, 1994, D4. For Sterling's history before the acquisition, see Derdak, ed., *International Directory*, vol. 1 (1988), pp. 698–700.

7. Baxter, a leading provider of hospital supplies and a producer of medical devices, was by the 1980s producing IV solutions and equipment, and devices for kidney dialysis and blood therapy. In the mid-1990s, after forming a partnership with Genentech, it became a major player in rDNA diagnostics and collaborated with Genetics Institute to develop Factor VII. See Derdak, ed., *International Directory*, vol. 10 (1995), p. 142. For Revlon, see *Hoover's Handbook* (1991), p. 344; Jeff Madrick, *Taking America* (New York: Bantam Books, 1987), pp. 267–269. Revlon sold its medical business to the Rorer Group in 1985 for $690 million.

8. In addition to Chapter 7, for Takeda Chemical Industry, see Derdak, ed., *International Directory*, vol. 1 (1988), pp. 704–706, 754. See also James Taggart, *The World Pharmaceutical Industry* (London: Routledge, 1993), pp. 376–390, esp. pp. 386–387. For Shinogi, see Derdak, ed., *International Directory*, vol. 1 (1988), pp. 435–437. For Sankyo, see ibid., pp. 364–365. For Yamanouchi, see Taggart, *World Pharmaceutical Industry*, pp. 406–421.

9. For Merck and Schering AG, see Alfred D. Chandler, Jr., *Scale and Scope: The Dynamics of Industrial Capitalism* (Cambridge, MA: Harvard University Press, 1990),

pp. 481–482. Another German competitor, J. D. Riedel, also built an international business, opening its New York branch in 1908. Ibid., p. 482. For Boeringer-Ingelheim, including the quotation, see *Economist*, May 2, 1995, pp. 82–85. For the Swedish companies, see Derdak, ed., *International Directory,* vol. 1 (1988), pp. 664–665, 625–626.

10. For Hoechst's sales of Laxic, see Derdak, ed., *International Directory,* vol. 1 (1988), pp. 670–676; see also Derdak, ed., *International Directory,* vol. 18 (1997), pp. 234–237. The diuretic Laxic was a follow-up of the early sulfa drugs. The quotation from Taggart is from *World Pharmaceutical Industry,* p. 360, and see p. 365. See also Margaret Sharp and Ilaria Galimberti, "Coherence and Diversity: Europe's Chemical Giants and the Assimilation of Biotechnology," July 1993, STEEP Discussion Paper No. 5, ESRC (Economic and Social Research Council), p. 20. The hospital contract gave Hoechst the first option on rights to a range of products and the training of Hoechst's U.S. staff. Much of that work went into plant genetic engineering. For the acquisition of Roussel Uclaf, see Derdak, ed., *International Directory,* vol. 1 (1988), p. 670.

11. For Bayer, see Sharp and Galimberti, "Coherence and Diversity," pp. 20–23; quotation from p. 24; *Business Week,* Jan. 23, 1995, pp. 70–71; also, in addition to Chapter 10, see Derdak, ed., *International Directory,* vol. 13 (1996), pp. 76–77.

12. For Hoechst, see *Hoover's Global 250: The Stories behind the Most Powerful Companies on the Planet* (Austin, TX: Hoover's Business Press, 1997), p. 250; Derdak, ed., *International Directory,* vol. 18 (1997), pp. 236–237; quotation from *Chemical Insights* no. 597 (Jan. 1, 1997): 1–2. See also *Wall Street Journal,* Feb. 18, 1997, p. 1.

13. "Aventis," in *Hoover's Online,* May 2002.

14. In addition to this chapter for Ciba-Geigy, see Chapter 5, esp. endnote 14. For Sandoz, see Derdak, ed., *International Directory,* vol. 1 (1988), pp. 671–673; *Hoover's Handbook of World Business* (Austin, TX: Reference Press, 1993), pp. 188–189, 426–427; *New York Times,* May 26, 1994, Dl, D64, for the Gerber acquisition. In 1991 Sandoz acquired two holdings in biotechnology startups—60 percent of Systemix in 1991 and 6 percent of Genetic Therapy—for a total of $295 million. See Louis Galambos and Jeffrey Sturchio, "The Pharmaceutical Firms and the Transition to Biotechnology: A Study in Strategic Innovation," *Business History Review* 72 (Summer 1998): 268.

15. For the merger, see *New York Times,* Mar. 6, 1996, D1, D4. *Moody's International Manual* (New York: Moody's Investor Services, 1996), pp. 9588, 9660; see also *Hoover's Handbook of World Business* (1993), pp. 189 and 427, for each company's revenues before the merger.

16. "Novartis," *Hoover's Online,* May 2002.

17. For F. Hoffmann–La Roche to the 1960s, see Derdak, ed., *International Directory,* vol. 1 (1988), pp. 642–644, and vol. 14 (1996), pp. 403–406.

18. Gambardella, *Science and Innovation,* pp. 66–69; Maureen D. McKelvey, *Evolutionary Innovations: The Business of Biotechnology* (New York: Oxford University Press, 1996), p. 196; *Hoover's Handbook of World Industry* (1993), pp. 404–405; *Hoover's*

Global 250, pp. 432–433; Derdak, ed., *International Directory,* vol. 1 (1995), pp. 424–426, for Roche Biochemical Laboratories. See Derdak, ed., *International Directory,* vol. 14 (1996), pp. 403–406, for Roche Bioscience.

19. William Breckon, *The Drug Makers* (London: Eyre Methuen, 1972), p. 29. Of the top companies, Riker Laboratories, ranked sixteenth in 1962, is the only one not covered in the previous chapters. It was a subsidiary of Rexall Drug, a major U.S. retail drug chain and successor to Drugs, Inc., which produced some of its own products. It later became part of the conglomerate Dart Industries. See Chandler, *Scale and Scope,* pp. 164, 755; *Moody's Industrial Manual* (1955), p. 246, and (1969), pp. 2152–2153.

20. Basil Achilladelis, "Innovation in the Pharmaceutical Industry," in Ralph Landau, Basil Achilladelis, and Alexander Scriabine, eds., *Pharmaceutical Innovation: Revolutionizing Human Health* (Philadelphia: Chemical Heritage Press, 1999), pp. 45–47; quotation from p. 46.

21. For an overview of Burroughs Wellcome, see Derdak, ed., *International Directory,* vol. 1 (1988), pp. 713–714; Chandler, *Scale and Scope,* pp. 368–369, 372. For post–World War II developments, see Derdak, ed., *International Directory,* vol. 1 (1988), pp. 714–715; Taggart, *World Pharmaceutical Industry,* pp. 287–315. For the later merger with Glaxo, see *Hoover's Global 250* (1997), pp. 224–225; *Moody's International* (1996), pp. 1036; *New York Times,* Jan. 27, 1995, D1.

22. The Glaxo story can be followed in Derdak, ed., *International Directory,* vol. 1 (1988), pp. 639–641; Breckon, *The Drug Makers,* pp. 37–38. For recent years, see Taggart, *World Pharmaceutical Industry,* pp. 240–249. Glaxo's move into corticosteroids was based on the license from Schering USA; Derdak, ed., *International Directory,* vol. 1 (1988), p. 640.

23. For Glaxo's role in wartime penicillin production, see Achilladelis, "Innovation in the Pharmaceutical Industry," pp. 86, 164. For the development and use of corticosteroids, see ibid., pp. 243–245.

24. *Hoover's Online,* 2002.

25. For an overview of Beecham through the 1960s, see Derdak, ed., *International Directory,* vol. 3 (1991), pp. 65–67; Breckon, *The Drug Makers,* pp. 29, 33–35; Taggart, *World Pharmaceutical Industry,* p. 237; Chandler, *Scale and Scope,* p. 370. Of particular value on Beecham's move into prescription drugs is H. G. Lazell, *From Pills to Penicillin: The Beecham Story, A Personal Account* (London: Heinemann, 1975), quotation on p. 30.

26. For Beecham's global acquisitions in the 1970s and early 1980s, see Derdak, ed., *International Directory,* vol. 32 (2000), pp. 429–434, quotation on p. 430. For the merger with SmithKline, see Taggart, *World Pharmaceutical Industry,* pp. 441–442; *New York Times,* July 27, 1989; *Wall Street Journal,* July 27, 1989. The story of the setting for the merger, the initial negotiations of the merger itself, and the integration of the two companies is described in detail by the participants in Robert P. Bauman, Peter Jackson, and Joanne T. Lawrence, *From Promise to Performance: A Journey of Transformation at SmithKline Beecham* (Boston: Harvard Business School Press, 1997), esp. pp. 24–29, 65–66, 82–87, and ch. 3 in its entirety. For

postmerger activities, see Derdak, ed., *International Directory*, vol. 32 (2000), pp. 432–433; *Hoover's Global 250* (1997), pp. 486–487; Bauman, Jackson, and Lawrence, *From Promise to Performance*, chs. 6–10.

27. *Business Week*, Oct. 30, 1995, p. 124.

28. *Hoover's Global 250* (1997), pp. 486–487.

29. *Business Week*, Mar. 4, 1996, p. 80; *New York Times*, Mar. 4, 1996.

30. These paragraphs on ICI build on my review in Chapter 5. For the beginning of its initial learning base in penicillin, see W. J. Reader, *Imperial Chemical Industry: A History: The First Quarter Century* (London: Oxford University Press, 1975), pp. 286, 459–461.

31. See Taggart, *World Pharmaceutical Industry*, pp. 272–274 for new drug development, and pp. 267–287 for a broader analysis of ICI's recent performance in pharmaceuticals; see also Gambardella, *Science and Innovation*, pp. 24, 71, 85, 88; *Hoover's Handbook of World Business* (1993), pp. 270–271. For the sale of Zeneca, see endnotes 28 and 29 in Chapter 5.

32. Lacy Glenn Thomas III, "Implicit Industrial Policy: The Triumph of Britain and the Failure of France in Global Pharmaceuticals," *Industrial and Corporate Change* 3 (1994): 451–489, chart on p. 454.

33. For Rhône-Poulenc, in addition to this chapter, see *Moody's International Manual* (1996), pp. 3697–3699; Derdak, ed., *International Directory*, vol. 1 (1988), pp. 666–670. The quotation is from Achilladelis, "Innovation in the Pharmaceutical Industry," p. 87.

34. *Hoover's Global 250* (1997), p. 426.

35. For Sanofi, see Derdak, ed., *International Directory*, vol. 1 (1988), pp. 676–677. For recent developments, see *Pharmaceutical Executive* 17, no. 3 (March 1997): 42–52. For a broader analysis of British and French differences, see Thomas, "Implicit Industrial Policy," pp. 451–489.

10. Commercializing Biotechnology

1. Basil Achilladelis, "Innovation in the Pharmaceutical Industry," in Ralph Landau, Basil Achilladelis, and Alexander Scriabine, eds., *Pharmaceutical Innovation: Revolutionizing Human Health* (Philadelphia: Chemical Heritage Press, 1999), pp. 93–94.

2. Luigi Orsenigo, *The Emergence of Biotechnology: Institutions and Markets in Industrial Innovation* (New York: St. Martin's Press, 1989), pp. 36–37 for this quotation, p. 39 for the next, p. 125 for the one following, p. 129 for the next, and finally p. 128. Orsenigo considers "contemporary biotechnology" to be the commercializing of the new discipline in molecular biology. As he explains, "The rDNA technique consists essentially in the production of hybrid gene material by joining pieces of DNA from different organisms together in vitro and then inserting this hybrid material into a host cell. . . . This recombinant cell becomes the unit producing the desired proteins." Orsenigo considers genetic engineering to be a "new technological paradigm," [using Giovanni Dosi's terms] "in that it has cre-

ated a new body of knowledge characterized by particular rules, heuristics, directions of research product and process." See pp. 38–39.

3. Ibid., pp. 125–128.

4. Ibid., p. 128.

5. Among the useful general articles providing information on the emergence of "contemporary biotechnology" involving the pharmaceutical industry that includes references to these companies are *New York Times,* Nov. 3, 1991, pp. D3, 12; *Chemical and Engineering News,* Apr. 27, 1992, pp. 30–32, Mar. 20, 1995, pp. 12–14; *Business Week,* Sept. 26, 1994, pp. 86–92. Louis Galambos and Jeffrey Sturchio, "Pharmaceutical Firms and the Transition to Biotechnology: A Study in Strategic Innovation," *Business History Review* 72 (1998): 250–278, provides the best brief overview of these developments and includes an excellent bibliography. Valuable also is Alexander Scriabine, "The Role of Biotechnology in Drug Development," in Landau, Achilladelis, and Scriabine, eds., *Pharmaceutical Innovation,* esp. pp. 279–298, which includes a brief review of the eight companies considered here. Excellent for the broader environment in which this chapter is set is Sheldon Krimsky, *Biotechnics and Society: The Rise of Industrial Genetics* (New York: Praeger, 1991), ch. 2, "The Emergence of the New Biotechnology Industry," and ch. 4, "Science and Wall Street: Academic Entrepreneurship in Biology."

6. For the Syntex story, see the sponsored publication *A Corporation and a Molecule: The Story of Research at Syntex Corporation* (Palo Alto, CA, 1966); Alfonso Gambardella, *Science and Innovation: The U.S. Pharmaceutical Industry during the 1980s* (New York: Cambridge University Press, 1995), pp. 99–101. For Roche Biomedical Laboratories and Roche Bioscience, see Thomas Derdak, ed., *International Directory of Company Histories,* vol. 11 (Chicago: St. James Press, 1993), pp. 424–426, and vol. 14 (1996), pp. 701–703. For Searle and the development of steroid technology, see Achilladelis, "Innovation in the Pharmaceutical Industry," p. 243.

7. Gambardella, *Science and Innovation,* pp. 99–101; quotation from p. 101.

8. To achieve credibility before acquiring personnel and facilities, "Boyer intentionally selected an easily replicated cell with a simple composition, sometostain," Derdak, ed., *International Directory,* vol. 8 (1994), p. 209. Pages 209–211 provide a useful overview of Genentech's evolution; see also Robert Teitelman, *Gene Dreams: Wall Street, Academia, and the Rise of Biotechnology* (New York: Basic Books, 1989), pp. 11–14, 24–26, 193–194.

9. Maureen D. McKelvey, *Evolutionary Innovations: The Business of Biotechnology* (New York: Oxford University Press, 1996), chs. 6–8, has a detailed, well-documented, and fascinating account of the formation of Genentech and its commercialization of the new rDNA technology. For the Lilly and Kabi contracts, see ibid., pp. 134–135, 142, for other contracts, p. 137, for Protopin, pp. 249–252. See also Teitelman, *Gene Dreams,* pp. 11–14, 24–26, 193–194.

10. *Business Week,* Sept. 26, 1994, p. 85.

11. *Hoover's Handbook of American Companies* (Austin, TX: Reference Press, 1997),

pp. 628–629, *New York Times,* May 8, 1998. For Genentech's products in 1997, see Scriabine, "Biotechnology in Drug Development," p. 284.

12. For overview of Chiron, see Derdak, ed., *International Directory,* vol. 10 (1995), pp. 213–214. For its earlier years see *Bio/technology* 5 (Feb. 1987): 121–126; *Pharmaceutical Executive* 14, no. 10 (Oct. 1994): 40–42. See also *New York Times,* Nov. 4, 1993, and Nov. 22, 1994; Louis Galambos with Jane Eliot Sewell, *Networks of Innovation: Vaccine Development at Merck, Sharp & Dohme, and Mulford, 1895–1995* (New York: Cambridge University Press, 1995), pp. 198–200; Galambos and Sturchio, "Pharmaceutical Firms in Transition to Biotechnology," p. 262. For quotation in the following paragraph of text, see Arthur Klausne, "Chiron: Looking Good," *Biotechnology* 5 (Feb. 1997): 122.

13. *Chemical and Engineering News,* Mar. 20, 1995, p. 13; see also Scriabine, "Biotechnology in Drug Development," pp. 278–279.

14. For Amgen, see Gordon M. Binder, *Amgen* (New York: Newcomen Society, 1998); Derdak, ed., *International Directory,* vol. 10 (1995), pp. 78–81; *Hoover's Handbook* (1997), pp. 154–155. For Synergen, see *Business Week,* Sept. 26, 1994; *New York Times,* Mar. 30, 1993.

15. *Business Week,* Industrial Technology Issue, Apr. 30, 1992, p. 69.

16. Binder, *Amgen,* p. 12.

17. For Genzyme, see Derdak, ed., *International Directory,* vol. 13 (1996), pp. 239–242; quotation from p. 239. For the acquisition of Integrated Genetics and the development of its diagnostics business Genzyme Genetics, see Harvard Business School Case Study N9–797–073, Mar. 6, 1997.

18. "Henri Termeer's Orphan Drug Strategy," *Forbes,* May 21, 1991, pp. 202–205. *New York Times,* Jan. 24, 1993, and Mar. 7, 1991, quotation from the latter citation. After the acquisition, Genetics Institute sold off its share of a partnership it had with Wellcome to build and operate a plant in Rhode Island. See Derdak, ed., *International Directory,* vol. 8 (1994), p. 217.

19. For Genetics Institute, see Derdak, ed., *International Directory,* vol. 8 (1994), pp. 215–218; *New York Times,* Mar. 7, 1991. See also Scriabine, "Biotechnology in Drug Development," pp. 285–286, and for Centocor, pp. 280–282; Immunex, pp. 287–288; and Biogen, p. 280.

20. For Centocor, see Derdak, ed., *International Directory,* vol. 14 (1996), pp. 98–100, including the quotation in the following paragraph of text. See also Teitelman, *Gene Dreams,* pp. 110, 114. Centocor hired its marketing managers from Abbott, ibid., pp. 175, 184–185.

21. For Immunex, see Derdak, ed., *International Directory,* vol. 14 (1996), pp. 254–256; quotation is from p. 255.

22. Seriabine, "Biotechnology in Drug Developments," p. 288.

23. For Biogen, see Derdak, ed., *International Directory,* vol. 14 (1996), pp. 58–60; Lawrence M. Fisher, "The Rocky Road from Startup to Big Time Player: Biogen's Triumph against Odds," *Strategy & Business* 8 (1997): 55–63. McKelvey, *Evolutionary Innovation,* p. 132, tells of Eli Lilly's contact with Gilbert.

24. *Boston Globe,* Dec. 7, 1997, F5, F7; quotation from F7.

25. Ibid.

26. Henry Grabowski and John Vernon, "Innovation and Structural Change in Pharmaceuticals and Biotechnology," *Industrial and Corporate Change* 3 (1994): 435–448.

27. Orsenigo, *Emergence of Biotechnology,* p. 130.

11. The Three Revolutions

1. Richard Whittington and Michael Mayer, *The European Corporation: Strategy, Structure, and Social Science* (London: Oxford University Press, 2000), p. 124.

2. Paul Nightingale, "The Economies of Scale in Experimentation: The Knowledge and the Technologies in Pharmaceutical R&D," *Industrial and Corporate Change* 9, no. 2 (June 2000): 317–359, provides an outstanding analysis of the complementarity of the economies of scale and scope in commercializing products in the high-technology industries; quotation from p. 327.

3. Whittington and Mayer, *The European Corporation,* pp. 216–217.

4. Roger Alcaly, *The New Economy: What It Is, How It Happened, and Why It Is Likely to Last* (New York: Farrar Strous and Giroux, 2003), p. 49. Alcaly's comparisons of long-term productivity of the new economy to those of the Second Industrial Revolution are impressive. For the evolution and contributions of the global telecommunications industry in the second half of the twentieth century, see Martin Fransman, *Telecoms in the Internet Age: From Boom to Bust to ?* (Oxford: Oxford University Press, 2002).

Index

Aarane, 265

Abbott, Wallace C., 198, 209

Abbott Alkaloid Co., 198

Abbott Laboratories, 15, 33, 182–183, 192–
193, 197–201, 204, 208–209, 226, 231,
237, 246, 261, 267–268, 275–276, 284,
292, 294

Abbott Tresses, 215

ABC, 297

Absorbents, 91

Accumulatatoren Fabri. *See* AGFA

Acetates, 50, 64, 87, 118, 134, 162–163

Acetylene, 42, 71–72, 118–119

Achilladelis, Basil, 246, 256, 260–261

Acne drugs, 232, 234

Acquisitions, 26, 28, 30, 285, 289–290,
293–294, 298–299, 305, 307, 309;
American core chemical companies, 42,
45, 51, 54, 58–60, 63–67, 71, 73–75, 77,
79, 81–82; American focused chemical
companies, 91, 93–94, 98–100, 102–103,
106, 108; European chemical competitors, 120, 123–124, 126, 130–131, 133,
135, 138–139, 143; American chemical
competitors, 144, 150, 154, 158–159,
164–168, 171–172, 174; American prescription drug companies, 183–185, 188,
190–192, 194, 196–197, 202, 204–207,
209, 212; American OTC drug companies, 214–227; American/European drug
competitors, 231–232, 234–236, 238–
239, 241–243, 245, 247–248, 251–252,

254, 256–259; in biotechnology, 261–
262, 264, 268–269, 271–272, 274–275

Acrylics, 51, 65–67, 70, 73, 83–84, 92–94,
131, 155, 157

Acrylonitrile, 70, 155, 157

Additives, fuel, 56, 74, 84, 86, 98–99, 102–
103, 108, 150, 167–168, 174

Adhesives, 61, 101, 106, 133, 135, 170

Adobe, 306

Adrenocortical hormones, 209

Advanced Cardiovascular Systems, 196

Advil, 226, 233

Agee, William, 79–80

AGFA (Accumulatatoren Fabri), 116–120,
123, 141

AGFA-Anesco, 119

Agricultural products, 26–28, 30; and
chemical industry, 45, 47, 51, 53–55, 60–
69, 71, 73, 75–76, 82, 87, 90, 93–94, 97,
103, 118, 121–122, 126, 128, 130–132,
146, 150–153, 165, 168–169, 172–173;
and pharmaceutical industry, 194, 198,
209–210, 241, 257

Agrigenetics, 103, 262

Agrow Seed, 209

A. H. Robbins, 225–226, 259

AIDS testing/drugs, 200, 219, 247

Air bags, 170

Air Liquide, 95–96

Air Products and Chemicals, 13, 83–84, 86,
91, 94–96, 111, 285

Air Reduction Co., 95–96

Airwick Industries, 126

Akzo, 13, 21–22, 66, 115, 133, 137–138, 143

Akzo Nobel, 138

Albemarle, 168

Alcaly, Roger, 310

Aleve, 234, 244, 266

Algemene Kunstzijde-Unie, 137–138

Alkalis, 127, 130, 158, 167

Alkaloids, 178, 184, 198, 220–221

Alka-Seltzer, 123, 238

Alkyd resins, 161

Alkylation, 147

Allegheny Ludlum, 122

Allen and Hanbury, 246

Allergan Pharmaceuticals, 204

Allergy drugs, 221, 225

Allgemeine Elektricitats Gessellschaft, 296

Allied Chemical, 20–21, 28–29, 41–42, 44, 71, 77–82, 112, 123, 136, 289, 310

Allied Corp., 79–80

Allied Laboratories, 58–59, 61

Allied Signal, 13, 29, 41, 71, 80–82

Alloys, 42, 72–73, 75, 106–107

Aluminate Sales Corp., 99

Aluminum, 75, 118, 133, 139, 166–168

Amdahl, Gene, 305, 307

Amerada Hess, 66

American Chicle, 221–222

American Cyanamid, 13–14, 20, 28, 30, 34, 157, 171, 189, 199, 227, 246, 264, 275, 290, 292, 294, 319n48; as American core chemical company, 41, 59, 69–71, 81–82

American Home Products, 15, 30, 33–34, 71, 82, 201–202, 233, 250, 264, 271, 274–275, 290, 293–294; as American OTC drug company, 213, 216, 223–229

American Medical Systems, 191

American Optical, 221

American Viscose, 64, 138, 168–169

Amgen, 226, 243, 263–264, 269–273, 275, 277

Ammonia, 42, 44–45, 47, 78, 99, 116, 118, 128, 130, 136, 146, 157

Ammunition, 42, 166–167

Amoco Chemicals, 154

Amoco Oil Co., 13, 23, 76, 111, 145, 153–154, 159–160, 168, 172–173. *See also* Standard Oil of Indiana

Amoco Production, 154

Anacin, 225–226

Andreesen, Mark, 307

Anemia drugs, 184, 194, 270

Angina drugs, 190, 219

Antacids, 202–204, 232–233, 256

Antibiotics, 18, 70–71, 82, 131, 140, 142, 181, 183, 185, 190, 192, 195, 199, 206, 215, 217, 222, 227, 232, 236, 241–242, 245, 249–251, 260; development of, 30, 32–34, 179, 184, 188–189, 194, 198, 200, 203, 206, 214, 218, 220–221, 224, 235, 248, 253–254, 256, 292, 294

Anticoagulants, 51

Antidepressants, 185, 195, 249

Antidiarrheal drugs, 209–210

Antifungal drugs, 217–218

Antihistamines, 59, 140, 179, 203, 221, 224, 256

Anti-inflammatory drugs, 190–192, 195, 272, 276

Antitoxins, 184, 236

Antiviral drugs, 51, 187

Apache Petroleum, 60

Apple Computer, 305–307, 309

Archer-Daniels-Midland, 155, 191

Arco (Atlantic Refining Co.; Atlantic Richfield), 13–14, 23, 111–112, 145, 153–155, 159–160, 171–173

Arco Chemical Co., 77, 154–155, 171

Argentina, 150, 247

Aromatics, 47, 57, 110, 121, 148–149, 160, 171

Arora, Ashish, 41

Arthritis drugs, 67–68, 184–185, 234, 265, 272, 275

Aruba, 150

Asahi-Dow Chemical, 58, 60

Asbestos, 166

Ashland Oil Co., 13, 23, 90, 145, 148, 153–156, 159, 173

Asphalt, 78

Aspirin, 63, 66, 117, 178, 203, 238–239

Associated Octal, 98

Asthma drugs, 219, 225, 265, 276–277
Astra, 15, 237
Astra Zeneca, 37
Astreonam, 207
AST Research, 307
Astro Turf, 65–66
Atlantic Refining Co. *See* Arco
Atlantic Richfield. *See* Arco
Atlas Powder Co., 43, 86, 130
Atropine, 178
AT&T, 296–297, 303
Aureomycin, 70, 189
Australia, 66, 99, 102, 105, 133, 221, 247, 271
Austria, 136
Aventis, 31, 37, 116, 124, 140, 143, 240, 249, 256, 291
Avocet, 203–204
Avonex, 276
Ayrest Laboratories, 224

Baby powder, 231
Badger Co., 110, 155
Bakelite, 22, 161
Bakelite Co., 72
Baldness drugs, 210
Baltimore Air Coil, 185–186
Band-Aids, 231
Barbasol, 190
Barbiturates, 178, 193
Barrett, 78
Barriers to entry, 5–6, 8–11, 17–18, 284–286, 288–289, 291–293, 299, 301–306, 308, 312; American core chemical companies, 54, 68, 80–82; American focused chemical companies, 104, 112; European chemical competitors, 133, 140–141; American chemical competitors, 151, 172; American prescription drug companies, 205; American OTC drug companies, 214, 227–228; American/ European drug competitors, 233, 235, 245, 257–259; in biotechnology, 262, 264, 279
Basel AG, 125–126, 141, 290–291
BASF, 13, 20, 26, 58, 238, 240–241, 258, 290; as European chemical competitor, 114–118, 120–122, 124–125, 128, 137–138, 141–143
Batteries, 71–72, 75–76
Bauman, Robert, 251–252
Baxter International, 200, 236, 274, 276, 338n7
Baxter Travenol, 272–273
Bayer, 13, 15, 20, 22, 26–27, 63, 67, 178, 190, 288, 290–291, 294, 310; as European chemical competitor, 114–118, 120–125, 137, 141–143; as European drug competitor, 235–236, 238–241, 246, 258
Beam, John, 168
Beckman, Arnold, 204
Beckman Instruments, 202, 204–205, 212, 252, 293
Becton Dickinson, 222, 236
Beecham, 15, 34, 36, 132, 186, 202, 205, 212, 293–294; as European drug competitor, 236, 245–246, 249–252, 254, 258. *See also* SmithKline Beecham
Beechnut chewing gum, 166, 206–207
Behring, Emil von, 117, 178
Behring Werke, 120
Belgium, 16, 21, 55, 64, 78, 90, 107–108, 133, 135–137, 189, 231, 275–276
Bell Laboratories, 303
Bemberg, J. P., 137
Bendix, 79–80
Ben-Gay liniment, 190
Bennet, Richard J., 218–219
Benzedrine, 203
Benzene, 56, 156–157
Benzodiazepines, 242–243
Beta-blockers, 224, 254
Betaseron, 269, 276
BetzDearborn, 91
Bhopal disaster, 29, 76
Billingham, 128
Binder, Gordon, 270–271
Biochemistry, 20, 35, 51, 61, 67, 180–181, 186, 190–191, 193, 204–205, 215, 218, 236, 260, 278, 292
Biocine, 268–269
Biogen, 65, 187, 195, 219, 241, 243, 261, 263–264, 273, 275–279

Biotechnology, 5, 18, 36, 60, 62, 65–68, 71, 82, 103, 123, 126, 142, 165, 283–285, 287, 291–295, 311–312, 341n2; and American prescription drug companies, 181, 200, 204, 208, 210–212; and American OTC drug companies, 218–220, 226–229; and American/European drug competitors, 230, 232, 238–239, 241, 243–244, 252, 254, 256–258; revolution in, 260–279

Biotech Research Laboratories, 262

Bismuth, 183

Black, James, 203–204

Bleaches, 42, 55, 127–128, 141, 167

Blood clot drugs, 51, 267–268, 274, 276

Blood pressure drugs, 52, 185–187, 190, 206–207

Bobengen, 120

BOC, 95

Bodman, Samuel, 106–107

Boeringer-Ingelheim, 15, 237

Boesky, Ivan, 153

Bok, Derek, 273

Bombay Dye and Manufacturing Co., 90

Bone disease drugs, 234

Boots, 90, 93

Borden Chemical & Plastics, 66, 158

Borland International, 306

Bosch, Carl, 117, 128

Bost, Elmer, 220

Boston Consulting Group, 74, 106

Bower, Joseph, 58, 147, 152

Boyer, Herbert, 182, 195, 266, 342n8

BP (British Petroleum), 67, 121, 131, 153, 160, 173

BP America, 13, 23, 145, 153, 160, 173. *See also* Standard Oil of Ohio

BP Amoco, 160

Bradshaw, Thornton, 298

Brandt, E. N., 58

Brazil, 58, 68, 100, 104, 126

Breckon, William, 245–246

Breck shampoo, 70

Bristol, William, 214

Bristol Laboratories, 214–215

Bristol-Myers Co., 33, 202, 206, 250, 293; as American OTC drug company, 213–216, 220–221, 225–227

Bristol-Myers Squibb, 15, 30, 54, 183, 201–202, 216, 253, 293

Britain, 15–16, 19, 21–22, 31–32, 34, 36, 290–291, 294, 304, 319n40; chemical industry in, 42, 58, 61, 68, 86, 88, 90, 93, 95, 97–100, 102, 105, 107–108, 110, 114–116, 119–122, 125–134, 136–139, 141–143, 157; pharmaceutical industry in, 186, 189, 202, 205, 221, 225, 235–236, 245–255, 258, 276

British Dyestuffs Corp., 127, 129

British Dynamite, 42

British Petroleum. *See* BP

Broken Hill Properties, 66

Bromide Products, 60

Bromine/bromide products, 22, 55–56, 60, 84, 86, 97–98, 168, 170

Bromo Seltzer, 221

Bronfman family, 50

Brown, Francis C., 217

Brunner, Mond, 127–128, 136

BSM, 66

Bufferin, 215

Burma Oil, 130

Burn drugs, 269, 273

Burroughs, Silas W., 247

Burroughs Adding Machine, 302

Burroughs Wellcome, 245–248, 256

Butadiene, 65, 72, 146, 152, 327n7

Cabot, Godfrey, 105

Cabot, Samuel, 105

Cabot Corp., 14, 85–86, 104–107, 112–113

Caffeine, 41, 63, 178

Cain, Gordon M., 50, 158

Cain Chemical, 50, 158

Calcium chloride, 42, 55, 71–72, 75

Calcium cyanamide, 69

Calcium phosphate, 70

Calco Chemicals, 69

Calgon, 185–186, 251

California Spray Chemical Corp., 146

Canada, 57, 60, 66, 69, 73, 97, 102, 105,

108, 123, 150, 189, 219, 221, 224, 247, 271, 317n25

Cancer drugs, 132, 179, 215, 219, 222, 254, 267, 269–270, 272–275

Capoten, 207–208

Carbide and Carbon Chemical Co., 72

Carbon black, 85, 105–107, 152

Carbon electrodes, 71–72, 77

Carbon tetrachloride, 55

Carboxymethylcellulose, 87

Cardizan, 62

Carnegie, Andrew, 43

Caro, N., 69

"Cash cows," 74, 106

Cassella, 116–117, 120, 141

Catalysts, 147, 152, 156, 164–166

Catalytic Construction Co., 95

Caustic soda, 55, 63, 136

Cavenham, 207

CBS, 297–298

Celanese Corp., 123–124

Celebrex, 67–68

Cellophane, 44, 120, 122, 166–167

Cell Tech, 191

Celluloid, 22, 44

Cellulose products, 22, 56–57, 64, 84, 87, 89, 91, 120, 139, 163

Cement, 162, 166

Centocor, 262–264, 273–274

Ceredase, 272–273

Cerezym, 273

Cetus, 208, 243, 262, 269, 276, 278

Chaplin Biologicals, 214

Charles of the Ritz, 207

Chemical engineering, 109, 142, 211, 260

Chemical industry, 284–291, 295, 311–312; American core companies, 41–82; American focused companies, 83–113; European competitors, 114–143; American competitors, 144–174

Chemstrand, 64

Cheracol, 209

Chesebrough-Pond, 225

Chevron Corp., 13, 23, 67, 145, 148, 153, 160. *See also* Standard Oil of California

Chevron-Texaco, 153, 160

Chewing gum, 166, 206–207, 221–223, 225

Chicago Chemical Co., 99

Chile, 43

Chilicott Labs, 220, 222

China, 247, 271

Chiron, 126, 182, 187, 196, 232, 241–243, 261–264, 266, 268–270, 276–277, 279, 294

Chloraseptic, 234

Chlorine/chloride products, 41, 55–57, 61, 63, 81, 102, 130, 136, 147, 158, 162, 167

Chloroform, 41, 55, 206

Chloromycetin, 189, 221

Chlorothiazide, 185

Cholera vaccine, 178

Cholesterol drugs, 186, 215, 272

Chromium, 76

Chugai, 273

Ciba, 20, 27, 125–126, 141, 178, 206, 241, 246, 291

Ciba-Geigy, 13, 15, 27, 31, 37, 51, 68, 90, 182, 291, 294; as European chemical competitor, 126, 131, 142–143; as European drug competitor, 236, 241–242, 258; and biotechnology, 261, 264–266, 268–269, 277

Cilog-Chemie, 231

Cincinnati Chemical Co., 125

Cincohonine, 178

Cinobac, 195

Cisco Systems, 305, 307, 310

Cities Service Co., 157

Citric acid, 189, 191

Clairol, 215

Clarant, 239

Clark, Jim, 307

Clean Air Act, 168

Cleaners, household, 57, 60, 62, 70, 134–135, 215

Clorox Co., 51, 70, 135

Coal, 120, 144, 159, 168, 172

Coal-tar products, 78, 116, 125, 178, 183, 198, 203

Coatings, 56, 138, 162, 170

Cobalt, 106

Cobb Breeding Co., 209
Codeine, 178
Cod-liver oil, 224
Cognis, 135
Coke, 78
Cold drugs, 203, 218, 225, 234
Colgate-Palmolive, 104, 191, 236
Colgate-Palmolive-Peet, 250
Colitis drugs, 234
Colombia, 150
Commodore, 305
Compagnie Internationale de
    l'Informatique, 304
Compaq, 309, 311
Computer Associates, 309
Computer industry, 301–311
Computer Tabulating Co., 301
Conglomerates, 79, 144, 163–170, 172–
    174, 190, 205, 212, 286–287
Conoco, 50, 52–53, 159–160
ConocoPhillips, 160
Contac, 203
Contact lenses, 204, 232
Container Corporation of America, 156,
    159
Contraceptives, 209, 224–226, 232, 244,
    264–265
Control Data, 303
Coolants, 76, 99
Copiers, 48
Copper, 167
Core companies, 8–10, 18, 20–21, 26, 28–
    29, 31–32, 36, 277, 284, 286–287, 289,
    292; chemical industry, 41, 55, 80–81,
    83, 89, 113, 137, 143–144, 151; pharma-
    ceutical industry, 177, 201–202, 213,
    230, 235–237, 248, 259, 262, 264, 271
Corn Huskers products, 220
Corning Glass Works, 56, 100–101
Corporate raiders, 29, 71, 76–77, 80–81,
    91, 153
Corticosteroids, 217, 248, 265
Cortisone, 184, 209, 248, 252
Cosden, 164
Cosmetics, 179–180, 190–191, 193–194,
    196, 203, 207, 215, 218–220, 224, 236,
    251

Costa Rica, 150
Coty, 190–191
Cough drops/syrup, 185, 193, 209, 221,
    234
Courtaulds, 22, 137–138
Cozen, Willibald H., 218
Cray, Seymour, 303
Crest toothpaste, 233
Crick, Francis, 182, 261
Crompton Corp., 109
Crompton & Knowles, 109
Cronar, 49, 53
Crosfields, 133, 326n32
Cuba, 189
Cutter Laboratories, 122, 238–239, 259
Cyanamides, 69, 81
Cyanide, 41
Cyclamates, 198–199
Cystic fibrosis drugs, 268, 273
Cytec, 14, 71, 171

Dacron, 46
Dart Industries, 340n9
Data General, 303
Davis, George S., 221
Davison Chemicals, 164, 166
DDT, 27, 126
De Castro, Edson, 303
Decongestants, 203, 217, 225, 232
Defibrillators, cardiac, 197
DEGUSSA, 45, 134
Dell, 307, 309
Denmark, 208, 269
Deodorants, 215
Deralin, 47
Deseret Pharmaceuticals, 222
Detergents, 57, 60, 64, 102, 108, 129, 134–
    135, 138, 233
Development capabilities, 6, 26, 36, 46,
    51–52, 111, 128, 182, 187, 215, 283, 299
Dewey & Almy, 164
Dexedrine, 203
Diabetes drugs, 179, 189, 194, 209
Dial Corp., 70
Diamond Shamrock, 158
Diapers, disposable, 233
Digital Equipment Corp., 303–304, 311

Dimethylterephthalate, 88–90, 122, 124

Dingman, Michael, 80

Diphtheria vaccine, 69, 178

Distillers Co., 58, 88

Diuretics, 185, 238, 254

Diuril, 185

Diversification, 11, 17, 19, 21, 28, 35, 180, 285–287, 290, 293, 298, 309, 311; American core chemical companies, 44, 49, 51, 69, 74, 77, 79, 81; American focused chemical companies, 106–108; European chemical competitors, 125, 127, 132; American chemical competitors, 144–145, 148, 150, 159, 163–164, 166, 169, 172; American prescription drug companies, 183, 185–186, 188, 190, 192–193, 195, 197–199, 202–203, 206–209, 211–212; American/European drug competitors, 243, 259

Diversified Pharmaceutical Services, 252

Divestitures: American core chemical companies, 51, 54, 60, 66–67, 70, 75, 77; American focused chemical companies, 106–107; European chemical competitors, 131, 133, 135, 137–138, 143; American chemical competitors, 151, 157, 164, 167, 171–174; American prescription drug companies, 186, 190–191, 193, 196, 202, 204–207, 210; American OTC drug companies, 214, 220, 222, 225–226; American/European drug competitors, 232, 236, 239, 248

Djerassi, Carl, 264

DNA, 35, 103, 181–182, 186, 191, 200, 208, 210, 215, 219, 228, 231, 251, 253, 260–261, 266, 268–269, 273, 276, 278, 291, 341n2

Dobbs House, 206–207

"Dogs," 74

Dome Laboratories, 239

Dome Petroleum, 60

Dompak, 60

Dow, Herbert, 55

Dow AgroSciences, 63

Dow Banking Corp., 58

Dow Chemical Co., 13, 16, 20, 22, 26, 28–31, 196, 210, 290, 310, 317n25; as

American core chemical company, 48, 54–64, 66–67, 69, 71, 73, 75, 77, 81–82; and American focused chemical companies, 88–91, 94, 97, 100–102, 105, 112–113; and European/American chemical competitors, 121–122, 124, 136, 148–149, 168, 174

Dow Corning, 13, 56, 85–86, 94, 96, 100–101, 111, 285

DowElanco, 61–62, 196

Dowell Division, 56, 58, 60

Drackett, 215–216

Draino, 215

Dramamine, 234

Dristan, 225

Drugs, Inc., 340n19

DuBarry, 220

Duco enamel paint, 44

Duisberg, Carl, 118

Du Pont (company), 13, 16, 20–22, 27–28, 30–31, 187, 289–290, 310, 316n2; as American core chemical company, 41–55, 57, 59–60, 63–67, 69, 71–74, 77, 81–82; and American focused chemical companies, 86, 88–89, 92–93, 97, 112–113; and European/American chemical competitors, 119, 121–122, 124, 127, 129–131, 133, 138, 151, 158, 160, 162, 166, 174

Du Pont, Alfred, 43

Du Pont, Coleman, 43

Du Pont, Eugene, 42

Du Pont, Lammont, 42

Du Pont, Pierre, 43

Du Pont de Nemours, E. I., 42

Dure, Bradley, 164

Duzan, Steve, 275

Dyes, 20, 22, 27, 32, 44–45, 69–70, 78, 92, 97, 115–121, 125, 127–129, 131, 139, 141, 170, 178, 221, 253, 326n40

Dynal, 73

Dynamite, 42, 87, 127

Dynatech, 261

Eastern Dynamite Co., 42

Eastman, George, 162

Eastman Chemical, 162–163

Eastman Kodak Co., 14, 17, 22, 123, 231, 235, 239, 257–258; as American chemical competitor, 144, 160, 162–163, 173
Ecko housewares, 225
Economies of scale/scope, 10–11, 17, 20–21, 44, 107, 109–112, 115, 131, 134, 143, 162, 205, 285–288, 299, 306, 308
Edison Electric, 161
Ehrlich, Paul, 117, 178
Elanco, 194, 196
Elastomers, 45, 47, 53, 151, 153
Eldstine, 195
Electrolytic process, 41–42, 55, 69, 71–72, 78, 99, 116, 136, 139
Electro-Metallurgical Co., 72
Electronics industry, 295–311
Elf-Aquitaine, 145, 158, 257
Elf-Atochem, 13–14, 145, 148, 157–158, 173, 257
Eli Lilly & Co., 15, 33, 61–63, 215, 231, 243, 246, 249, 284, 292–293, 310; as American prescription drug company, 177, 182–183, 191–198, 200–201, 208–210, 212; and biotechnology, 261, 264–268, 274, 277, 279
Elizabeth Arden cosmetics, 194, 196
Ellen Kaye cosmetics, 215
El Salvador, 150
E. Merck, 15, 178, 206, 237
Emerson Electric Co., 67
Emory, 135
English China Clays, 186
Enjay Co., 150–151
Envirodyne, 76
Enzyme Technology Corp., 98
Enzymology, 18, 35, 180–181, 186, 190, 193, 206, 211–212, 215, 238, 251–252, 278, 292, 311
Epilepsy drugs, 221
Epogen, 272
Epoxy, 96
Equistar Chemicals, 171
Erythromycin, 194, 198–199, 209
Erythropoieten, 270, 273–274
Essex Chemical, 61
Esso Chemical Co., 150–151

Estrogen, 224
Ether, 206
Ethical drugs, 32, 34, 122, 178
Ethicon Division, 232, 268
Ethyl Corp., 14, 56, 164, 167–168, 174
Ethylene, 50, 53, 57, 72, 75, 77, 119, 147, 151–152, 158, 171
Etocal, 56–57
Ever Ready batteries, 71–72, 76
Excedrin, 215
Expansion, 19; American core chemical companies, 64; American focused chemical companies, 92, 96, 100; European chemical competitors, 132, 134; American chemical competitors, 152–153; American prescription drug companies, 194; American OTC drug companies, 219, 225
Explosives, 20, 41–43, 55, 63, 66, 84, 86–87, 90, 117, 127–128, 166
Exxon Chemical, 61, 100, 151
Exxon Corp., 13, 23, 26, 51, 90, 145, 148, 150–153, 159–160, 289. *See also* Standard Oil of New Jersey
ExxonMobil, 153, 156, 160
Eye drops, 190, 198
Eye drugs, 186, 269

Fabergé, 196
Faberloid, 64
Fabricoid, 44
Farben. *See* I. G. Farben
Federal Trade Commission, 220, 252
Feldene, 190
Fermstat, 244
Fertilizers, 64, 66, 69, 117–118, 128, 130, 136, 141, 146, 150–151, 153, 164–165, 167, 173
Fever depressants, 116
F. Hoffmann–La Roche, 32, 122, 126, 178, 182, 184, 219–220, 292; as European drug competitor, 236, 242–243, 248, 258; and biotechnology, 261, 264, 267, 271, 277. *See also* Roche Holding
Fiat, 191
Fibers/fabrics, synthetic, 22, 26–27, 44–46,

49, 51–53, 64–68, 70, 72–74, 79, 88, 91, 93, 120–121, 123–124, 129–130, 133, 137–139, 148, 150–151, 154–155, 157, 163, 173

Films, 20, 26, 44, 51, 88, 106, 120–122, 130, 148, 167; photographic, 32, 47, 49, 53, 116, 118–119, 123, 139, 162–163, 241; packaging, 56, 60, 73, 75–76, 150

Film Tec, 60

Finland, 100

First Boston, 76

First Colony Insurance Co., 168

First movers, 7–9, 17, 30, 284, 291, 294, 296, 308; American core chemical companies, 42, 45–46, 55–56, 69, 80; American focused chemical companies, 112; European chemical competitors, 114, 127, 133–134, 141; American chemical competitors, 145–146, 148, 152–153, 168, 173–174; American prescription drug companies, 188; American OTC drug companies, 217, 227; American/European drug competitors, 236, 254, 256, 258–259

Fisher Controls, 67

Fisher Governor Co., 65

Fisher International, 65, 319n40

Flame retardants, 97–98, 166

Fluorides, 79

Fluoropolymers, 47, 53

FMC Corp., 14, 164, 168–169, 174

FMC Technologies, 169

Focused companies, 21–22, 83–86, 112–114, 173, 284, 289

Folsom, Frank, 297

Food and Drug Administration, 51, 101, 182, 187, 196, 199, 207, 210, 219, 261, 265, 267–277

Food/flavors, synthetic, 20, 41, 63, 66–67, 85, 89, 91, 103–104, 122, 132–133, 198–199, 203, 206–207, 243–244

Food & Machinery Co., 168

Food Machinery Corp., 168

Foot-care products, 218–219

Ford Motor Co., 51, 95

Ford Parker Chemicals, 135

Formica, 69–70

Foster-Wheeler, 110

Fragrances, synthetic, 70, 85, 89, 91, 103–104, 122, 132–133, 139, 190–191, 207, 243–244, 251–252

France, 14–15, 22, 31–32, 34, 36–37, 290–291, 294, 304–305, 326n40; chemical industry in, 44, 58, 60, 64, 66–67, 95–98, 100, 102, 104, 108, 110, 115–117, 120, 122, 125, 134, 136, 138–143, 145, 158, 173; pharmaceutical industry in, 189, 235–236, 238–239, 243, 245–246, 255–258

Frank, A., 69

Friedenson, Patrick, 139–140, 158

Fujitsu, 77, 303–304, 307, 309

Fumed silica, 105–106

Funai Pharmaceuticals, 59

Functional capabilities, 6–9, 32, 36, 44, 49, 51, 59–60, 72, 74, 77, 94, 101, 104, 127, 129, 177, 179, 181, 184, 187, 191–194, 196, 198, 207, 222, 228, 284

Fungicides, 45, 93, 130, 168

Funk, Edward J., 131

Funk Seeds, 126

Furland, Richard, 205–207, 212, 216

Gadsen, Henry W., 185

GAF (General Aniline and Film), 76, 119

Galambos, Louis, 187

Gambardella, Alfonso, 41, 204, 241, 243, 265–266

Garamycin, 218

Gas: industrial, 73, 75, 77, 83–84, 95–96, 99, 171; natural, 57, 72, 99, 105–107

Gasoline. *See* Petroleum companies

Gates, Bill, 306–307

Gateway, 307

G. D. Searle, 66–67, 234, 259, 264

GE (General Electric), 14, 91, 106, 144, 160–162, 173, 204, 296–297, 302, 319n40

Geigy, 20, 27, 125–126, 141, 178, 241, 246, 291. *See also* Ciba-Geigy

Gelatin, 193, 209

Gelfoam, 209

Gencor International, 272
Geneen, Harold, 79
Genentech, 65, 195–196, 239, 241, 243, 261–264, 266–270, 274, 277, 279, 294, 338n7
General Aniline and Film (GAF), 76, 119
General Chemicals, 78
General Electric. *See* GE
General Mills, 135
General Mining Union, 76
General Motors Corp., 56, 167
Genetic engineering, 18, 35–36, 54, 61–62, 66–68, 71, 103, 124, 126, 288, 339n10, 341n2; by prescription drug companies, 181–182, 186–187, 196, 200, 210–212; by OTC drug companies, 215–216; by drug competitors, 232, 241–243, 249, 256–257, 259; and biotechnology, 260–261, 266, 268–269, 272
Genetics Institute, 226, 263–264, 271, 273–274, 277–278, 294, 338n7, 343n18
Genetic Systems, 215, 239
Genomics, 18, 279, 295, 311
Genzyme, 187, 191, 243, 263–264, 269–270, 272–274, 277–279
Georgia Pacific, 77
Gerber Products Co., 241
German measles vaccine, 185
Germany, 4–5, 15–17, 19–22, 26–27, 30–34, 37, 284, 288–291, 294, 298, 301, 304; chemical industry in, 41, 45, 55, 58, 60, 62–63, 66, 69, 72, 78, 80, 88, 91–92, 95–96, 98–99, 108, 110, 114–130, 133–137, 141–142, 144; pharmaceutical industry in, 178, 183–184, 187, 198, 206, 217, 230, 235–242, 245, 248–249, 256, 258, 275–276
Getty Oil Co., 157
Giacco, Alexander F., 90
Gilbert, Walter, 195, 275–276
Glad Wrap, 73
Glass, 42, 56, 100–101, 139, 161–162
Glaucoma drugs, 186
Glaxo, 15, 34, 132, 204, 276, 294; as European drug competitor, 236, 243, 245–246, 248–249, 253–254, 258

GlaxoSmithKline, 37, 249, 253, 293
Glaxo Wellcome, 15, 37, 249, 253
Gleb, Bruce, 215, 217, 221
Gleb, Richard, 215–217, 221, 227
Gleem toothpaste, 233
Glidden, 131
Grace. *See* W. R. Grace & Co.
Grace, J. Peter, 164–165
Gramamycine, 217
Graphite Oil Products Co., 102
Grasselli Chemical Co., 45
Great Depression, 45–46, 81, 87, 105, 119, 125, 163
Great Lakes Chemical Corp., 14, 84, 86, 96–98, 101, 113, 171
Greece, 58, 136, 150
Greenewalt, Crawford, 46
Griesheim-Elektron, 95–96, 116–118, 141
Growth strategies, 10–12, 17, 21–22, 58–59, 74, 98, 142, 159, 192, 202, 258, 285–288
Guidant Corp., 197
Gulf Oil Co., 147–148, 153

Haas, Otto, 92
Haber, Fritz, 117, 128
Haeger and Kaesner, 60
Halcion, 210
Halcon, 111
Hale, Charles, 97
Hall, Benjamin, 187
Halstead, Ronald, 251
Hammer, Armand, 157–158
Handiwrap, 62
Hanson, 132
Harvey-Jones, John, 131
Hatco Chemicals, 164
Haynes, William, 145, 224
Head & Shoulders shampoo, 233
Heart disease drugs, 52, 62, 132, 179, 187, 190–192, 194–195, 199, 207–208, 215, 224, 254, 267, 274
Heart pumps, 190–191, 333n26
Hemorrhoid drugs, 198, 225
Henkel, 13, 21, 91, 115, 133–135, 141–143, 326n32

Henkel, Fritz, 134
Henley Group, 80, 222
Hennessey, Edward L., 79–80
Hepatitis testing/drugs, 186–187, 195, 219, 232, 252, 261, 268, 275–276
Herbicides, 45, 47, 64–65, 71, 93, 97, 194, 316n8
Hercofina, 90
Hercules, 13, 26, 28, 51, 122, 129, 142, 186, 244; as American focused chemical company, 83–84, 86–93, 95–96, 112
Hercules Powder Co., 43, 51, 86, 121
Hewlett-Packard, 303–304, 309, 311
Heyman, Samuel, 29, 76–77, 91
Hill, Philip, 249–250
Himont, 90–91
Hitachi, 299, 304–305, 307, 309
H. K. Mulford, 177, 184
Hoechst, 15, 20, 26–27, 30–31, 62, 88, 151, 171, 178, 288, 290–291, 294, 324n10, 339n10; as European chemical competitor, 114–118, 120–125, 129–130, 137, 141–143; as European drug competitor, 236, 238–241, 258
Hoechst Celanese, 13, 124, 140
Hoechst Marion Roussel, 37, 124, 239–240, 256
Hoffmann, Fritz, 242
Hoffmann–La Roche. See F. Hoffmann–La Roche
Hollingsworth, David, 90–91
Hong Kong, 107
Hoof-and-mouth disease drugs, 267
Houdry Chemicals, 95
Howard, Frank, 149
Howmedica, 190
Human Genome Project, 253, 311
Human growth hormone, 71, 195–196, 221, 261, 266–267
Humble Oil and Refining Co., 147, 150–151
Humphrey Instruments, 204
Huntsman Corp., 14, 157, 171–172
Hybritech, 196–197
Hyde, J. Franklin, 100
Hydrogen, 84, 95–96, 99

Hypertension drugs, 190, 207
Hystron Fibers, 88, 122, 124

IBM (International Business Machines), 296, 298, 300–310
Icahn, Carl, 153, 157
ICI (Imperial Chemical Industries), 21–22, 31, 34, 37, 51, 54, 86, 88, 99, 224, 236, 245, 253–254, 258, 290–291, 294, 324n10, 326n27; as European chemical competitor, 114, 121–122, 125–133, 136, 139–140, 142–143
ICI America, 13, 233. See also Standard Oil of Ohio
ICI Zeneca, 15, 31, 132, 163, 253–254
I. G. Farben, 22, 26, 76, 118–120, 125–129, 137, 139, 141–142, 146, 235, 238, 290
IMED, 222
Immunex, 227, 263–264, 272–273, 275, 277
Immunology, 33, 178
Imperial Chemical Industries. See ICI
Implants, silicone, 100–101
Inderal, 224
India, 29, 76, 90, 221, 247
Industrial gases, 73, 75, 77, 83–84, 95–96, 99, 171
Industrial Revolution, 5, 19–20, 41, 124, 162, 177, 196, 283–285, 288, 295–296, 302, 312
Infant formulas, 198, 215, 224, 226
Information processing industry, 301–311
Information Revolution, 5, 181, 196, 283–285, 295–296, 300, 310, 312
Inks, 107
Innopack, 66
Insecticides, 27, 47, 51, 55, 73, 76, 87, 90, 92–93, 118, 121, 126, 129–130, 146, 153, 168, 198, 225
Insulators, 47, 101, 161
Insulin, 179, 182, 194–196, 208, 261, 267
Intel, 306–308, 310
Interferons, 261, 267, 275–276
Interleukin, 269, 273
International Business Machines. See IBM
International Chemical Corp., 122

International Flavors and Fragrances, 14, 85–86, 101, 103–104
International Minerals and Chemicals, 267
Internet, 307, 310
Intron, 219
Iodine, 183, 189
Iowa Beef, 157, 159
Ipana toothpaste, 214
Iran, 29, 50, 130
Italy, 58, 60, 90, 99–100, 107, 110, 136, 191, 247, 304
IVAC, 194–195
Ivory soap, 134

James River Corp., 66
Japan, 5, 7, 12, 14–15, 23, 284, 294–296, 298–301, 304–305, 307–309, 311; chemical industry in, 51, 58–62, 102, 110, 126, 163; pharmaceutical industry in, 189–190, 200, 237, 270–271, 273–274
Japan Victor Co., 299
J. D. Riedel, 339n9
Jefferson, Edward, 51
Jefferson Chemical Co., 70, 157
J. Lyons, 207
Johnson, Robert Wood, 231
Johnson Controls, 67
Johnson & Johnson, 15, 225; as American prescription drug company, 182, 187–188, 198, 200; as American drug competitor, 230–233, 235–236, 257; and biotechnology, 265, 268, 270–271, 277
John Wyeth & Brothers, 177, 224. *See also* American Home Products
Joint ventures, 294, 296, 299; American core chemical companies, 52, 56, 58–60, 62, 64, 70–71, 77; American focused chemical companies, 90–91, 94, 99–100, 103; European chemical competitors, 121–122, 125–126, 130, 137; American chemical competitors, 151, 157, 169; American prescription drug companies, 187–188, 196, 200, 208; American/European drug competitors, 232–233, 237, 243–244, 258; in biotechnology, 261, 268–270, 277

Joyce, William, 91
Junk bonds, 76–77

Kabi, 266
Kalle, 116–117, 120
Kami Paint, 51
Kampen, Emerson, 98
Kaopectate, 209
Kelco Division, 67
Key Pharmaceuticals, 219
Kidney dialysis, 165, 232, 270–271, 273, 338n7
Kirin Brewery, 270–271
Koch, Robert, 178
Koninklijke Zout Organon, 138
Kuhlmann, 125, 158, 326n40

Laboratory Corporation of America, 244
Laflin & Rand Powder Co., 42–43
Lambert Pharmaceuticals, 221
Landau, Ralph, 110–112, 154, 262, 266
Lasso, 65, 67
Laxatives, 209, 214, 234, 250
Laxic, 238, 339n10
Lazell, H. G., 250–251
Learning bases, 8–10, 17–18, 21, 27, 29, 32, 36, 180, 283–286, 289, 292–293, 297, 299, 301–302, 309–310; American core chemical companies, 48–49, 54–55, 60–61, 63, 65, 69–70, 72, 77–78, 80–81; American focused chemical companies, 88, 93–94, 97, 100, 102–103, 107, 111; European chemical competitors, 118, 126, 129, 131, 134–135, 137, 139; American chemical competitors, 144–145, 160, 162, 164, 170; American prescription drug companies, 183–184, 186, 192–193, 196–197, 200, 203–205, 207–208; American OTC drug companies, 219, 222, 224, 226–227; American/European drug competitors, 232, 243, 245, 247, 252–253, 259; in biotechnology, 262, 265–268, 271–273, 277–279
Leather, synthetic, 44, 92
Lebanon, 150
Lederle Laboratories, 69–70, 189, 199, 246, 275

Le Floch-Prigent, Löik, 140
Leprosy drugs, 198, 221
Leukemia drugs, 195, 219
Lever Brothers, 64, 134
Lexan, 161
Libenau, Jonathan, 177
Librium, 242–243
Libya, 157, 164
Lilly. *See* Eli Lilly & Company
Lilly, Eli, 193, 209
Lime, 130
Limits to growth, 10–11, 80, 112, 141, 211, 288, 290–295, 302, 312
Lin, Fu-Kuen, 270
Linde Air Products, 72
Link Belt Corp., 168–169
Lion Oil Co., 64
Liquefied natural gas, 106–107
Listerine mouthwash, 221, 223
Little, Arthur D., 109
Little, Royal, 79
Lotus, 306
Love cosmetics, 203–204
Lubricants, 22, 93–94, 101–103, 108, 157, 168
Lubrizol, 14; as American focused drug company, 84–86, 101–103, 113
Lummus Co., 110
Lycra, 149, 153
Lyondell Petrochemical Corp., 14, 155, 158, 171

Magnesium, 55–57, 118, 120
Magnesium chloride, 55
Mahoney, Richard J., 66
Malaria drugs, 131, 178, 209, 253
Malaysia, 100
Mallinckrodt Group, 244
Managerial capabilities, 6–9, 44, 49, 179, 192, 226, 284
Manhattan Project, 46
Marion Laboratories, 30, 61–62, 318n35
Marion Merrell Dow, 61–62, 124, 235, 239, 259
Marker, Russell E., 264
Marketing/distribution capabilities, 7, 26, 33, 36, 52, 60, 111, 138, 179, 183, 187–

188, 192, 194, 213, 226, 265, 283, 292, 299
Martin Marietta, 79–80
Mathieson Chemical Corp., 166, 206
Matsushita, Konosuke, 299
Matsushita Electric Corp., 295, 298–301
May and Baker, 246, 256
Maybelline cosmetics, 218–219
Mayer, Michael, 285, 287
McBain Instruments, 222
McBee, Earl T., 97–98
McElroy, Neil, 233
McKeen, John, 189–190
McKelvey, Maureen, 196
McLanahan Oil Co., 97
McNealy, Scott, 303
McNeil Laboratories, 231
Mead Johnson, 215
Measles vaccine, 185
Medco Containment Services, 188
Mental disease drugs, 241
Merck, 15, 30, 32–34, 52–54, 67, 82, 215, 292, 310; as American prescription drug company, 177, 182–196, 201, 210, 212; as American drug competitor, 231, 233, 243, 246, 249, 251, 254; and biotechnology, 261, 264, 268, 275–277, 279. *See also* E. Merck
Merck, George, 184
Mergers, 36–37, 287, 289, 293, 311; American core chemical companies, 42, 58, 71–72; American focused chemical companies, 95–96, 103; European chemical competitors, 124–125, 127, 137–140, 143; American chemical competitors, 153, 160, 162, 168; American prescription drug companies, 183–184, 202, 205, 208, 211–212; American OTC drug companies, 214, 218, 220–221, 228; American/European drug competitors, 239–241, 243, 245, 249, 252–252, 255–257
Merrell-Dow Pharmaceuticals, 59–62, 235, 239, 259
Merrill Lynch, 217
Metallocene, 152
Metamucil, 234
Methanol, 90, 130, 156

Methocel, 57
Methyl, 47
Methyl acrylate, 92
Meticortelone, 217
Meticorten, 217
Mevacor, 186
Mexico, 189, 264
Microbiology, 18, 20, 35, 178, 180–181,
    186, 204, 206, 211–212, 238, 251–252,
    259, 292, 311
Microsoft Corp., 305–310
Miles Laboratories, 13, 123, 238–239
Milk, powdered, 248
Millennium Chemicals, 171
Missile propellants, 87, 91
Mitsubishi, 77
Mitsubishi Chemicals, 50
Mitsubishi Electric, 299, 307
Mitsui Petrochemicals, 151
Mobay, 121–122
Mobil Corp., 13, 145, 148, 153, 156, 159–
    160, 173. *See also* Standard Oil of New
    York
Modular housing, 27, 48–49, 89
Molecular biology, 30, 35, 124, 181–182,
    186–187, 191, 195–196, 200, 211, 216,
    241, 244, 249, 260–261, 273, 278, 288,
    291, 294–295, 311, 341n2
Molecular genetics, 20, 82, 205, 212, 228
Moleculom, 191
Monomers, 92–94
Monsanto, 13, 20, 26, 28, 30, 37, 89, 93,
    121–122, 151, 153, 267, 290, 319n40; as
    American core chemical company, 41,
    59, 63–69, 71, 74, 77, 81–82
Monsanto Oil Co., 66
Montedison, 90–91
Montgomery Ward, 156, 159
Morana, 103–104
Morgens, Howard, 233
Morita, Akio, 299
Morphine, 178, 194, 206
Morton International, 14, 94, 164, 169–
    170
Morton Norwich, 234, 259
Morton Salt, 169–170, 174

Morton Thiokol, 60, 66, 170
Motorola, 299
Motrin, 233
Mouthwash, 191, 221, 223, 231
Moxam, Arthur J., 316n2
Multiple sclerosis drugs, 269, 276
Mumps vaccine, 185
Murine eye drops, 198
M. W. Kellogg, 110
Myers, John, 214
Mylar, 47, 49, 53

Nalco Chemical, 14, 85–86, 96, 98–101,
    113
Naphthalene, 155
Naphthalic acid, 146
Naprosyn, 234, 265–266
Narcotics, 178, 183, 194, 206
National Aluminate Co., 99
National Aniline and Chemical, 78
National Carbon, 72
National Cash Register, 302
National Health Laboratories, 244
National Starch, 133
Natural gas, 57, 72, 99, 105–107
NBC, 297
Nederlandse Kunstzijdefabriek, 137
Neoprene, 45, 47, 53, 289
Netherlands, 58, 66, 100, 103–105, 111,
    117, 133, 137–138, 150, 231, 274, 298,
    301, 304
Neupogen, 271–272, 275
Niagara Spray and Chemical Co., 168
Nicotine, 178
Nightingale, Paul, 286
Nintendo, 300
Nippon Copper, 168
Nippon Electric Co., 304, 307–309
Nitrates, 43–45, 64, 117–118, 128, 168
Nitrocellulose, 20, 41–44, 54, 81, 84, 86–
    87, 92, 127
Nitrogen, 84, 95–96
Nitroglycerin, 41–43
Nobel, Alfred, 41–42, 127, 138
Nobel Industries, 127–128, 138
Norethindrone, 264–265

Norris, William, 303

Norwich Eaton, 234

Norwich Pharmaceuticals, 170

Nova Industri, 208

Novartis, 31, 37, 68, 126, 142–143, 241–242, 245, 249, 270, 291, 294

Novell, 305–306, 309

Novocain, 117, 178

Novo Nordisk, 262, 269

NutraSweet, 67

Nutrients, 122, 198–199, 225–226, 224, 226, 248

Nylon, 45–47, 51, 53, 64–65, 79, 93, 129, 131, 150, 289

Occidental Oil Co., 13, 145, 148, 156–159, 173

O'Connor, John T., 79

Octal Associates, 98

Ogdon Corp., 264

Oil/oil companies. *See* Petroleum companies

Oils, multiviscosity, 93–94

Olefins, 47, 51, 57, 77, 121, 148–149, 152, 160, 168, 171

Oleo chemicals, 133, 135

Olin Corp., 14, 163, 166–167, 205–206

Olin Mathieson Chemical Corp., 166, 173, 206

Olivetti, 305

Olsen, Kenneth, 303–304

Ophthalmic products, 204–205, 207, 232

Oracle, 306, 309

Organizational capabilities, 6–11, 26, 52–53, 71, 73, 137, 148, 189, 208, 238

Organization of Petroleum Exporting Countries (OPEC), 28, 50, 159

Orlon, 46–47

Orphan Drug Act, 279, 284

Orphan drugs, 36, 262, 267, 269–276, 278–279

Orsenigo, Luigi, 260–261, 278, 341n2

Ortho Pharmaceuticals, 232, 265, 268, 270–271

Otsuka Pharmaceutical, 59

Over-the-counter (OTC) drugs, 32, 34, 36,

123, 266, 291–293; and prescription drug companies, 178–180, 185, 188, 190, 193, 199, 202–206, 209–210; companies producing, 213–229; and prescription drug competitors, 231–235, 238–239, 242, 244–245, 249–251, 254, 256–258

Oxirame Corp., 111

Oxygen, 42, 72, 84, 95

Packaging Corporation of America, 225

Packard Bell, 307, 309

Pain killers, 116–117, 178, 193–194, 215, 225–226, 231, 233–235

Paints/finishes, 44–45, 47, 51, 53–54, 69, 92, 117, 122–123, 127, 131–132, 138, 161–162

Paley, William, 297–298

Palmer, Lowell, 206

Panasonic, 299

Paper/paper chemicals, 66, 87, 89, 91, 99, 166–167, 174

Paper Makers Chemical Corp., 87

Parke, Henry C., 221

Parke Davis, 33, 177, 189, 217, 220–222, 228, 237, 246, 265, 293

Parkinson's disease drugs, 187

Pasteur, Louis, 178

Patent medicines, 178, 217, 235, 250

Pechiney Ugine Kuhlmann, 58, 97, 139

Penhoet, Edward, 268

Penicillin, 33, 70, 131, 139, 183–184, 189, 194, 198, 206, 209, 214, 224, 236, 245, 248–251, 253–254

Pennwalt, 158

Pennzoil, 157

Pepto-Bismol, 234

Performance Chemicals, 166

Petrochemicals. *See* Polymers

Petrofina, 90, 164

Petroleum companies, 23, 26–29, 31, 33, 284, 289–290; and American core chemical companies, 45, 48, 50, 52, 56–60, 65–66, 72–73, 79–80; and American focused chemical companies, 89–90, 93, 97–99, 102–104, 108, 111–112; as

Petroleum companies *(continued)*
European chemical competitors, 120–
122, 128, 130–131, 136, 140; as American chemical competitors, 144–160,
164–165, 167, 172–173. *See also specific
petroleum companies*
Pettigrew, Andrew, 130–131, 325n24
Pfizer, 15, 32, 34, 37, 68, 214, 227, 246,
248, 254, 292–293, 333n26; as American prescription drug company, 183,
188–194, 197, 201, 208–210, 212
Pharmaceutical industry, 284–285, 291–
295, 311–312; American prescription
drug companies, 177–212; American
OTC drug companies, 213–229; Ameri-
can/European competitors, 230–259;
and biotechnology, 260–279
Pharmacia, 15, 30, 68, 82, 208, 211, 237,
253, 290, 293
Pharmacia & Upjohn, 68
Phenol, 55, 63, 66, 72, 88
Philco, 297–298
Philips Incandescent Lamp Works, 298–
301, 304
Phillips Petroleum, 13, 23, 26, 121–122,
145–147, 149, 152–153, 159–160, 172,
289
Phosphates, 64, 69–70, 164, 168
Photographic films, 32, 47, 49, 53, 116,
118–119, 123, 139, 162–163, 241
Pickens, T. Boone, 153
Pierre Cardin fragrances, 70
Pioneer Hy-Bred International, 54
Pittsburgh Plate Glass, 14, 144, 160–162,
173
Plasticizers, 92, 108, 151
Plastics, 27; produced by core chemical
companies, 46–48, 50, 53, 56–61, 64–67,
70, 72–73, 75, 79, 81; produced by fo-
cused chemical companies, 92, 106–108;
produced by chemical competitors, 121,
127, 148, 150–151, 161–164, 173
Plexiglas, 92
Plough, Inc., 33, 213, 217–218, 220, 293.
See also Schering-Plough Corp.
Plough, Abe, 217–218

Poland, 125
Polio vaccine, 58, 189, 194
Polyester, 46–47, 49, 53–54, 66, 88–89,
121–124, 129–131, 142, 154, 324n10
Polyethylene, 23, 26, 46–48, 50, 53, 59,
66, 72–73, 75, 88, 121, 129–131, 136,
147–148, 151–155, 158, 167, 171
Polymers, 16, 20, 22–29, 209–211, 253–
254, 260, 278, 284, 287, 289–291; produced by core chemical companies, 41,
45–48, 50, 52–53, 55–59, 64–66, 68, 70,
72–73, 75–77, 79–81; produced by focused chemical companies, 83–84, 87–
94, 96, 98–99, 106, 110–113; produced
by chemical competitors, 120–122, 126,
129–131, 133, 136–139, 142, 144–158,
160, 164, 166, 171–173
Polyolefins, 77, 152
Polypropylene, 23, 48, 57, 64, 75, 88–90,
121, 130, 147–152, 154–155, 171
Polystyrene, 23, 57, 64, 66, 72, 75, 148,
171
Polyurethane, 60, 84, 96, 122, 154, 171
Polyvinyl chloride, 23, 50, 64, 72, 75, 96,
129–131, 136, 147, 151, 158, 161, 167
Pool, Leonard, 95
Popoff, Frank D., 317n27
Poulenc Frères, 139, 142, 255–256, 290
Praxair, 14, 77, 96, 171
Prescription drugs, 20, 32–36, 51, 70, 82,
123, 132, 264, 292–293, 311; companies
producing, 177–212; and OTC drug com-
panies, 213–218, 220–221, 223–224,
226–228; and drug competitors, 230–
240, 244–245, 247, 249, 251–254, 258
Prest-O-Lite, 72
Prestone antifreeze, 76
Prime Computer, 303
Procardia, 190, 192
Procter & Gamble, 15, 70, 104, 134–135,
170, 266; as American drug competitor,
230–231, 233–234, 236, 244, 250, 257–
258
Production capabilities, 6–7, 52, 138, 182–
183, 187, 192, 213, 216, 265, 283
Propane, 72, 147, 153

Propellants, 43, 86–87, 89, 91, 170

Proprietary drugs, 32, 123, 178–179, 193, 214, 220, 233, 244

Propylene, 77, 93, 111, 147, 154, 171

Prozac, 195

Pyroxylin, 22, 44

Quasar, 299

Queeney, John F., 63

Quest, 133

"Question marks," 74

Quinine, 178, 209

Rabb, G. Kirk, 267

Radio, 296–299

Radio Corporation of America. *See* RCA

Ralston Purina, 76

Rathbone, Monroe, 149–150

Rathmann, George, 200, 270–271

Rayon, 22, 44, 46, 64, 120, 127, 133, 137–139, 141, 143, 168

Razors, 221, 223

RCA (Radio Corporation of America), 287, 295–300, 302, 309

R&D. *See* Research and development

Reader, William, 119, 128–130

Reckitt & Coleman, 225, 235

Redwood, Heinz, 179

Refrigerants, 79, 97, 146

Reliance Electric, 159

Remington Arms Co., 166

Remington-Rand, 301

Repauno Chemical Co., 42

Research and development (R&D), 6, 11, 21, 32–33, 35, 284, 286, 289–290, 294–296, 307, 318n35; in American core chemical companies, 43–46, 49, 51–52, 54, 61–62, 65, 78–82; in American focused chemical companies, 111–112; in European/American chemical competitors, 115–120, 126, 131–132, 151, 161; in American prescription drug companies, 179–181, 183, 185–188, 190–196, 200, 203–204, 207, 209; in American OTC drug companies, 213–216, 218–223, 226, 228; in European/American

drug competitors, 238–239, 242, 245–247, 249, 251–252, 256, 258; in biotechnology, 261–262, 265, 267–269, 275, 277–279

Resins, 45, 50, 53–54, 69, 77, 87–89, 91–94, 101, 119, 126, 129, 151, 161–162

Restructuring, 19–20, 28–29, 35, 290, 305; American core chemical companies, 68; American focused chemical companies, 91; European chemical competitors, 131–132, 136–138, 140; American chemical competitors, 144; American prescription drug companies, 205, 207, 210; American OTC drug companies, 226

Revlon, 104, 236

Rheinische Olefin Werks, 120–121

Rhône-Poulenc, 13, 15, 21–22, 32, 66–67, 76, 158, 203, 290–291, 310, 326n40; as European chemical competitor, 115, 134, 137–140, 142–143; as European drug competitor, 236, 246, 255–257

Rhône-Poulenc Rorer, 31, 37, 124, 140, 240, 256

Richardson-Vicks, 59, 234–235, 259

Riker Laboratories, 246, 340n19

Roche Biomedical Laboratories, 243–244

Roche Bioscience, 244, 266

Roche Holding, 15, 17, 32, 142, 291, 294, 310; as European drug competitor, 241–242, 244, 246, 249; and biotechnology, 261, 264, 266, 268, 270, 276

Rockefeller, John D., 43, 145

Rocket motors, 91, 170

Roessler & Haaslacher, 45

Röhm, Otto, 92

Rohm and Haas, 13, 28, 63, 65, 164, 170, 174; as American focused chemical company, 83–84, 86, 91–96

Rorer, 140, 256

Rosenkranz, George, 264

Roundup (herbicide), 65, 67

Roussel Uclaf, 31, 122, 124, 140, 238–239, 256

Royal Dutch Shell, 121, 145–146, 152, 160

Rubber, synthetic, 23, 27, 33, 289, 317n25, 327n7; produced by core chemical companies, 45, 47, 50–51, 57, 63–64, 67, 69; produced by focused chemical companies, 87, 97, 105; produced by chemical competitors, 118, 120, 123, 129, 147, 149–151, 153, 159, 164
Russia, 125, 136, 157
Rutter, William, 182, 187, 195–196, 200, 268

Sabin polio vaccine, 189
Saccharin, 41, 63, 81
Salk polio vaccine, 58, 189, 194
Salvarsan, 117, 178
Salt, 41, 55, 94, 130, 169–170
Sandoz, 15, 27, 31, 37, 68, 178, 273, 291; as European chemical competitor, 125–126, 141–143; as European drug competitor, 236, 241–242, 258
Sankyo, 15, 237
Sanofi, 235, 257
Sanyo, 295, 298–299
Sara Lee baked goods, 244
Saran Wrap, 56, 60, 62
Sarnoff, David S., 297
Sarnoff, Robert, 298
Saudi Arabia, 60, 157
Scale, economies of, 10–11, 17, 20, 44, 107, 109–112, 115, 131, 134, 143, 162, 205, 285–288, 299, 306, 308
Schering AG, 33, 108, 178, 213, 217–218, 220, 237, 265, 276, 293
Schering-Plough Corp., 15, 235, 261, 275, 277, 293; and American prescription drug companies, 182, 201–202; as American OTC drug company, 213, 217–220, 227–228
Schick razors, 221
Schlumberger, 58, 60
Schoellhorn, Robert A., 199
Scholl, 218–219
Schuler, Jack, 200
Scientific Data System, 303
Scientific Design, 83, 110–111, 154, 262
S. C. Johnson & Sons, 216

Scope, economies of, 10–11, 17, 21, 44, 109–112, 115, 143, 285–288, 299, 306, 308
Seagrams, 50, 53
Sealants, 61, 101, 106, 164–166
Searle. *See* G. D. Searle
Sears Roebuck, 156
Sea & Ski, 203–204
Sectors, 21
Sedatives, 116–117, 179, 194, 198, 210
Sepsis drugs, 271, 274
Serotonin, 195, 249
Serums, 70, 93, 116, 178, 184, 221, 224, 256
Shampoo, 62, 70, 179, 198, 215, 231, 233, 250
Sharer, Kevin, 271
Sharp Corp., 295, 299
Sharp & Dohme, 177, 184, 246
Shell Chemical, 75
Shell Oil Co., 13, 23, 51, 145–147, 149, 152, 158, 160, 171–172, 289
Shell U.K., 98
Shinogi, 15, 237
Shirley, 190–191, 333n26
Siemens, 216, 296, 304
Siemens Nixdorf, 77
SightSavers, 101
Sigma-Aldrich, 278
Signal Co., 80
Silicon/silicone products, 55–56, 77, 85–86, 100–101, 104–105, 120, 133, 140, 161, 185
Simonize car wax, 73, 170
Sinclair Oil Co., 154
Sinus drugs, 203
Skin-care products, 231–232
Skin irritant drugs, 265
SmithKline, 33, 36, 222, 225, 236, 248–250, 254, 275, 292, 310; as prescription drug company, 177, 183, 193, 197, 204–208
SmithKline Beckman, 15, 202, 204, 212, 251–252, 293
SmithKline Beecham, 15, 36–37, 267, 277, 293; as prescription drug company, 201–

202, 205, 212; as European drug competitor, 235–236, 239, 249, 251–253, 257
SmithKline French, 192, 202–204, 212, 246, 292–293
Sneath, William, 75
Soap, 132, 134–135, 141, 179, 190, 233
Socal. *See* Standard Oil of California
Société Chimique des Usines du Rhône, 139, 256
Socony Vacuum, 147, 156
Soda ash, 42, 78, 127–128, 130, 136, 141, 162
Sodium chloride, 41, 55, 130, 169–170
Sohio. *See* Standard Oil of Ohio
Solvay (Belgium), 21, 55, 78; as European chemical competitor, 127, 135–137, 141, 142, 143
Solvay America, 13, 78, 136
Solvay process, 42, 55, 78, 116, 127, 135–136
Solvents, 61, 150
Sonneborn Chemical and Refining Co., 108
Sony Corp., 295, 298–301, 309–310
South Africa, 102, 247
South Korea, 58, 60, 298
Spain, 64, 99, 102, 150
Specialization, 21–23, 26, 30
Specialized engineering firms (SEFs), 21, 23, 26, 83, 86, 109–113, 154–155
Sperry Rand, 302
Spin-offs, 43, 77, 124, 130, 133, 138, 144–145, 168–172, 242, 253, 294
Spitz, Peter H., 110, 148, 155
Squibb Corp., 33, 166, 214–216, 225, 227, 292–293; as American prescription drug company, 183, 192–193, 202, 205–208, 212
Standard Industrial Classification, 21, 41, 44, 315n1
Standard Oil of California, 23, 145–146, 149, 152–153, 156. *See also* Chevron Corp.
Standard Oil of Indiana, 23, 72, 111, 145, 147, 153, 172. *See also* Amoco Oil Co.
Standard Oil of New Jersey, 23, 56, 121, 145–152, 167, 172–173, 289. *See also* Exxon Corp.

Standard Oil of New York, 145. *See also* Mobil Corp.
Standard Oil of Ohio, 23, 145, 147, 153, 155, 159. *See also* BP America
"Stars," 74
Stauffer Chemical Co., 131, 140
Stearates, 108
Stellite Division, 106
Sterling Drug, 163, 235, 250
Sterling-Winthrop, 123, 235, 238–239, 252, 257, 259
Sterns, 177
Steroids, 179, 184, 232, 264–266
Stine, Charles M. A., 45
Stone & Webster, 110
Storck, William J., 14
Strategic boundaries, 9–11, 26, 28, 30, 288–290, 292–294, 297, 309, 311–312; American core chemical companies, 49, 61, 66, 68, 74–75, 80–82; American focused chemical companies, 83, 92, 94–95, 107, 112–113; European chemical competitors, 136, 141–142; American chemical competitors, 144, 148, 154–155, 158–159, 173; American prescription drug companies, 185–186, 188, 190, 192, 199, 202, 211–212; American OTC drug companies, 227–229; American/European drug competitors, 257; in biotechnology, 279
Streptomycin, 184, 194, 209
Styrene, 56–57, 64–65, 72, 75, 119, 147, 152, 171
Styrofoam, 56
Styron, 56
Suchard, Jacob, 225
Suez Lyonnaise des Eaux, 100
Sulfa drugs, 70, 139, 179, 184, 194, 209, 253
Sumitomo, 61
Sun Microsystems, 303
Sun Oil Co., 154
Supporting nexus, 8–9, 18, 21, 35, 181–183, 261–264, 277–279, 285, 294–295, 310–311
Swanson, Robert, 266

Sweden, 15, 30, 37, 68, 82, 100, 138, 208, 211, 231, 237, 253, 266, 293

Switzerland, 5, 15–17, 20, 22, 26–27, 30–34, 37, 288, 290–291, 294; chemical industry in, 51, 58, 68, 90, 104, 114–116, 119, 122, 124–127, 141–142; pharmaceutical industry in, 178, 184, 206, 220, 225, 230–231, 234, 236, 239–242, 244–246, 248–249, 255–256, 258, 261, 264, 267–268, 270, 275–276, 279

Sylvania, 297–298

Syntex, 232, 234, 244, 264–266, 269, 279

Syphilis drugs, 117, 178, 221

Tagamet, 202–204, 207, 248, 293

Taggart, James, 239

Takeda Pharmaceutical Co., 15, 200, 237, 294

Tandem, 303

Tandy, 305

Tantalum, 106–107

TAP Pharmaceuticals, 200, 237

Tar, 108

Tastemaker, 244

Technical capabilities, 6, 9, 32, 36, 283–284, 299, 301; in chemical industry, 44, 46, 49, 51, 60, 72, 74, 77, 94, 99, 106, 109, 127–129, 138, 146, 156; in pharmaceutical industry, 177, 179, 181–182, 184, 187, 190–194, 198, 204, 207, 215, 219–220, 222, 227, 277–278

Teflon, 47, 53

Telefunken, 296, 298

Television, 297–301

Temin, Peter, 179

Terize Division, 60

Termeer, Henri, 272–273

Tetanus vaccine, 69, 178

Tetracycline, 206, 209, 214

Texaco Oil Co., 13–14, 70, 90, 102, 145, 148, 153, 156–157, 160, 168, 171, 173

Texas Gulf, 164

Texas Instruments, 199–200

Thermoplastics, 61, 65, 67, 69, 106, 151, 161

Thiokol, 170

Thomson Houston, 161

Throughput, 11

Titanium dioxide, 44–45, 53–54, 70, 106, 133, 162, 171–172

Tobias, Randall, 197

Tobin, James, 276

Toothpaste, 179, 214, 231, 233, 250

Toshiba, 304, 307–309

Tranquilizers, 179, 198–199, 203, 210, 242–243, 249

Tredeghar Industries, 168

Trevira, 121–122, 129, 324n10

Tungsten, 75

Turpentine, 87

Tylenol, 225, 231, 233

Typhoid vaccine, 69

Tyvek, 49

Ulcer drugs, 62, 179, 186, 203, 234, 243, 248–249

Unilever, 13, 21, 31, 54, 132–135, 219, 254

Union Carbide and Carbon Corp., 73

Union Carbide Corp., 13–14, 20, 22, 28–29, 91, 95–96, 106, 129, 140, 151, 157, 167, 171, 290, 310, 320n57; as American core chemical company, 41–42, 48, 63, 71–78, 81–82

Union Texas Natural Gas Co., 79

Unipol, 75–76, 151

Uniroyal, 51

United Agriseeds, 60

United Alkali, 127, 129

United Technologies, 79–80

Universal Oil Products, 154–155

Upjohn, William E., 208–210

Upjohn Co., 15, 33, 37, 60, 214, 233, 246, 284, 292–293; as American prescription drug company, 177, 183, 192–193, 201–202, 208–212

Uranium, 73, 75, 159

Urethane, 50, 77, 96, 108, 154, 209

U.S. Steel Corp., 95

Vaccines, 58, 69–71, 93, 116–117, 126, 224, 319n48; development of, 178–179,

182, 184–187, 189, 194, 236, 256; and
biotechnology, 261, 267–268
Vagelos, Roy, 186–187
Valium, 242–243
Van Ameringen, Arnold Lewis, 103–104
Vanilla, 63, 67
Vasotec, 186–187
Venezuela, 99, 102
Vereinigte Glanzstoff Fabriken, 21–22, 133,
137, 141, 143
Vernal, 178
Veterinary drugs: developed by prescrip-
tion drug companies, 189–191, 194,
196–198, 206–207; developed by OTC
drug companies, 215–216, 226; devel-
oped by drug competitors, 232, 242,
248–249, 252; and biotechnology, 265,
267
Vincent, James, 199–200, 276–277
Vinyl acetate, 50
Vinyl chloride, 50, 61, 72, 158
Vinylidene chloride, 56–57
Virginia Cellulose Co., 87
Virtuous strategies, 17, 47, 89, 102, 188,
197, 201–202, 242, 254, 285–286, 297–
298, 300–301, 309–310
Vista Chemical Co., 50
Vitamins, 123, 179–180, 184–185, 209,
215, 221, 224, 242, 244, 248, 256
Volcker, Paul, 111
Von Hyden, 178

Waksman, Selman, 184
Wall, Bennett, 150
Wall, Michael, 274
Walter, Henry, 104
Wang, An, 303
Warner, William, 220
Warner-Lambert Co., 15, 33, 201–202,
246, 249, 293, 310; as American OTC
drug company, 213, 217, 220–223, 225,
228
Washburn, Frank, 69
Water treatment chemicals, 22, 60, 85–86,
91, 98–100, 165, 185–186

Watson, James, 182, 261
Watson, Thomas, 301–302
Weber, Eugene, 78, 80–81
Weiker, Theodore, 206
Weiler-ter-Mer, 116
Weiss, William E., 235
Welch, Jack, 106, 161
Wellcome, 15, 247–248, 267, 274,
343n18
Wellcome Foundation, 247
Westinghouse Corp., 296–297
Whitaker Corp., 51, 170
Whitehall Laboratories, 233
"White knights," 80
Whittington, Richard, 285, 287
Winchester Firearms Co., 166–167
Windex, 215
Wishnik, Robert, 107
Witco, 14, 66, 143, 310; as American fo-
cused chemical company, 85–86, 105,
107–109, 112–113
Woolite, 225
World War I, 16, 19, 21, 32–33, 43–44, 55,
63, 66, 78, 80–81, 86, 92, 114, 117, 119,
123, 125, 127, 134, 136, 141–142, 144,
162, 179, 183–184, 198, 217, 235, 238–
239, 258, 288, 291–292, 326n40
World War II, 16–17, 20, 23, 28–30, 32–34,
44–47, 57, 64, 69–70, 72, 81, 83, 87–88,
92, 94–95, 99, 101, 103, 105, 107, 113–
114, 120, 126, 128–129, 131, 133, 135,
137, 139, 142, 144–145, 147, 153–156,
160, 162, 164, 168–169, 172, 179, 184,
188–189, 194–195, 198, 200, 203, 206,
209, 213–214, 218, 220–221, 224, 235–
236, 238, 248, 253–254, 256, 258, 285,
289, 291–292, 294, 296, 299
W. R. Grace & Co., 14, 163–167, 173–
174
Wrigley, William, 225
Wrigley's chewing gum, 225
Wyeth Corp., 30, 71, 227–228, 246, 293.
See also American Home Products

Xanax, 210

Yamanouchi Pharmaceutical, 15, 237
Yugoslavia, 58, 60
Yves St. Laurent, 207

Zantac, 204, 243, 248–249, 254

Zeneca, 31, 126, 132, 163, 253–254, 276.
    See also ICI (Imperial Chemical Indus-
    tries); ICI Zeneca
Zenith Corp., 297–298
Ziegler, Karl, 88, 121, 152